POLICE INTERROGATION
AND AMERICAN JUSTICE

Richard A. Leo

Police Interrogation
and American Justice

HARVARD UNIVERSITY PRESS

Cambridge, Massachusetts, and London, England   2008

In memory of Welsh S. White (1940–2005)

Copyright © 2008 by Richard A. Leo
All rights reserved
Printed in the United States of America

Library of Congress Cataloging-in-Publication Data

Leo, Richard A., 1963–
Police interrogation and American justice / Richard A. Leo.
   p. cm.
Includes bibliographical references and index.
ISBN-13: 978-0-674-02648-3 (alk. paper)
ISBN-10: 0-674-02648-9 (alk. paper)
1. Police questioning—United States. 2. Interviewing in law enforcement—United States.
3. Criminal investigation—United States. I. Title.
HV8073.3.L46 2008
363.25'40973—dc22   2007018771

Contents

Acknowledgments

My first debt of gratitude is to Richard Ofshe for suggesting that I study police interrogation during our "plastics" conversation on Shattuck Avenue in Berkeley some time ago. I am also grateful to Richard for his friendship and generosity over the years. I thank Jerry Skolnick for serving as my dissertation mentor in graduate school, and for nurturing my early interest in police investigation and interrogation. I thank Frank Zimring for helping me conceive the structure of this book and for pressing me—more than anyone else—to write it. Frank provided brilliant comments on every chapter draft I gave him and met with me regularly during the 2003–2004 academic year to discuss it. His altruistic efforts and critical insights were rivaled only by those of David T. Johnson, who closely read many early chapter drafts and made numerous detailed and thoughtful suggestions for improvement. A dear friend, David is the most astute critic I know.

I thank Gary Marx, Mark Cooney, and Fred Pampel for providing intelligent and insightful feedback on a much earlier version of the manuscript. I also thank a number of friends and colleagues who have more recently read and commented on parts of this manuscript: Simon Cole, Valerie Jenness, Elizabeth Loftus, John Pray, Carol Tavris, George Thomas III, Peter Tiersma, the late Welsh White, and Marvin Zalman. I am especially grateful to Valerie Jenness for her helpful comments on several chapter drafts, as well as for her help with so many other things in the past decade. And to George Thomas, who has been a gracious friend, collaborator, and fellow traveler for many years. I also thank Chris Slobogin and the other (still anonymous) reviewer for Harvard University Press for reading the entire manuscript and making detailed suggestions for improvement.

Over the years, I have enlisted the research assistance of a number of students at the University of Colorado, Boulder, and the University of California,

Irvine. I thank all of them, especially Ryan Bashor, Avita Jaswal, Paul Kaplan, Elizabeth Kim, Michelle King, Tory Marinello, Portia McCullough, Natasha Nichols, Jennifer Owen, Anika Padhiar, Jennifer Sellinger, Greg Ungar, Erin Varnado, Christine Washburn, and Brandon Zborowski. For superb help with library materials and research, I thank Jane Thompson of the University of Colorado, Boulder, Law School and Amy Wright of the University of San Francisco Law School.

I thank several individuals who, many years ago, helped me gain access to some of the historical materials that I rely on in Chapters 2 and 3 of this book. Herman Goldstein kindly guided me through the American Bar Foundation Study documents located at the Criminal Justice Library at the University of Wisconsin, Madison. Robert Fogelson, Mark Haller, and Kevin Mullen made primary historical materials available to me. Chris Thale helped me locate many biographies of detectives, police chiefs, and well-known criminals in the late nineteenth and early twentieth centuries. Robert Fogelson, Mark Haller, Dan Martin, Phil McArdle, the late Eric Monkonnen, David R. Johnson, David Tanenhaus, and Samuel Walker made helpful suggestions about historical sources relevant to this project. I also thank the research and support staffs at the Federal Research Center in Suitland, Maryland, and the National Archives in Washington, DC, for their assistance.

I am also grateful to many individuals who, at one time or another in the past decade, provided me with more contemporary interrogation and confession-related materials: Dick Burr, Paul Cassell, Alex Christie, Donald Connery, John Conroy, Mark Dames, Marie Deans, Steve Drizin, Kate Germond, Gigi Gordon, Eric Gordy, Suzanne Johnson, Yale Kamisar, Saul Kassin, Kevin Lafky, Norm Lapera, Anne Leahey, Randy Leavitt, Pat Ledford, Larry Marshall, Gary Marx, Paul Mones, Peter Neufeld and Barry Scheck, Richard Ofshe, Robert Perske, Joan Petersilia, Becky Peterson, Barry Pollack, Darcy Purvis, Michael Radelet, Alison Redlich, David Rudovsky, Peter Sarna, Mark Sauer, Laurie Shertz, Cheryl Stepnioski, Cindy Stine, Howard Swindle, Tom Sullivan, Sherri Sweers, Jack Trimarco, Deja Vishny, Chuck Weisselberg, the late Welsh White, John Wilkens, Andrew Wistrich, Steven Wisotsky, and Alex Wood. Many others—criminal defense attorneys, prosecutors, and civil attorneys—provided me with interrogation and confession-related materials in connection with ongoing litigation but are too numerous to name individually.

I am grateful to the many police detectives and interrogators I have studied, interviewed, or taught over the years (also too numerous to name) and to the following organizations: the Alameda County District Attorney's Office, the Broward County Sheriff's Office, the California State Attorney General's Office, the Federal Law Enforcement Training Center, the Hayward Police Department, the Long Beach Police Department, the Miami Beach Police Department, the Oakland Police Department, and the Vallejo Police Department.

I thank Rosann Greenspan for arranging my visit to the Center for the Study of Law and Society at U.C. Berkeley in the 2003–2004 academic year, during which a substantial portion of the first draft of this manuscript was completed. I also thank several law faculties to whom I presented portions of this book in the 2005–2006 academic year and from whom I received helpful comments: Loyola Law School of Los Angeles, Seattle University Law School, Washington University Law School, and the University of San Francisco Law School. My new colleague Peter Honigsberg merits a special note of appreciation for his advice about the manuscript. I also thank Jeffrey Brand, Dean of the University of San Francisco Law School.

I wrote much of this book while I was a professor of criminology and professor of psychology at the University of California, Irvine. I remain grateful to my former colleagues in both departments and at the Center for Psychology and Law for creating a supportive and engaging multidisciplinary research environment. Special thanks to Elizabeth Loftus, Bill Thompson, Simon Cole, Jodi Quas, Jennifer Skeem, Elizabeth Cauffman, and Pete Ditto. I continue to miss all of you.

I thank Elizabeth Knoll, my editor at Harvard University Press, for encouraging me, editing me, and pushing me—always with characteristic wit and intelligence—to move this project forward. This book never would have taken its present shape without her valuable efforts and insights. I am especially grateful to Tom Wells for providing superb editorial assistance with the first full draft of the manuscript, to Terry Kornak for her subsequent editorial suggestions, and to Martin Tulic for preparing the index.

Welsh White, a professor of law at the University of Pittsburgh and a leading criminal procedure scholar, encouraged me for many years to write this book and regularly inquired about it. Welsh graciously read everything I sent him and provided almost instantaneous substantive and editorial feedback. Sadly and unexpectedly, he was diagnosed with lung cancer in the summer of 2005 and died several months later. Welsh was an irreplaceable friend and close colleague, a proud booster but candid critic, a generous and thoughtful collaborator. He was always available to bounce ideas around, trade interesting stories, and promptly read and comment on any paper or chapter I sent him, even as he was dying of cancer. Perhaps more than any other friend or colleague, he would have been gratified to see this book published. With sadness, I dedicate this book to his memory.

Finally, I thank my wife, Kimberly Richman, for tolerating my obsessive diversions and long leaves of absence during the writing and rewriting of this book. Her love, companionship, and support carried me through the most trying moments of this process. My gratitude to her is beyond words.

Introduction

Police interrogation is an important and inherently fascinating subject for social scientists and legal scholars. The process of modern interrogation—as well as the confessions it often produces, the crimes it sometimes solves, and the competing interests and ideologies it implicates—raises a multitude of important issues: How do police elicit confessions from reluctant suspects? How should they be permitted to interrogate in a democratic society that needs both crime control and due process to maintain public confidence in its institutions of criminal justice? How should law and public policy regulate police interrogation to accommodate the competing interests and values at stake while promoting fair procedures and achieving just results?

As a practical matter, interrogation involves some of the most important governmental functions in any society: the investigation of crime, the apprehension of offenders, the restoration of order, and the deterrence of future crime. As a symbolic matter, police interrogation is a microcosm for some of our most fundamental conflicts about the appropriate relationship between the state and the individual and about the norms that should guide state conduct, particularly manipulative, deceptive, and coercive conduct in the modern era. In short, police interrogation and confession-taking go to the heart of our conceptions of procedural fairness and substantive justice and raise questions about the kind of criminal justice system and society we wish to have.

Interrogation and confession-taking is of interest to a wide audience. To political scientists and sociologists, police interrogation offers a paradigm case of the constitutional exercise and control of state power in a democratic society. To psychologists, police interrogation offers a natural laboratory for the study of how social influence affects perception formation,

1

decision-making, and behavior in a closed, high-pressure environment in which the stakes may be high for both parties. Social psychologists are especially interested in understanding the counterintuitive processes that lead suspects—especially innocent ones—to confess, as well as how judges and juries evaluate confession evidence. To criminologists, interrogation is a microcosm of police organization, culture, and behavior; it offers a window into the logic and inherent contradictions of modern police work in America and is central to understanding what will occur at later stages in the criminal process, from prosecution and plea bargaining to trial and sentencing. To legal scholars, interrogation and confession raise fundamental philosophical and policy questions about the nature and role of law, agency, notification, voluntariness, compulsion, coercion, proper police procedure, due process, and how the balance of advantage should be struck between the state and the accused. Sociolegal scholars are interested in how the law on the books differs from police interrogation in practice, the impact of law on police behavior and ideology, and the multiple meanings, constructions, and uses of law in the interrogation process.

Interrogation and confession-taking is also of interest to many others. The American public is fascinated by police interrogation, which is often the subject of many of our most popular television shows. Interrogation and confession scenes also recur in American theater and cinema. This is because virtually every criminal investigation is a richly textured narrative and morality play involving innocence and guilt, good and evil, and justice and injustice. In American cinema, police interrogation and confessions often become the high point of these narratives. The drama and power struggle of interrogation hold our rapt attention as they feed our vicarious desire for justice, catharsis, and, ultimately, resolution and restoration.

Police interrogation and confession-taking is enormously important for society. It is, of course, often necessary in investigating and solving crime, especially felony crime. Some crimes, such as conspiracy and extortion, or even rape and child abuse, frequently can be conclusively solved only by a confession since there may be no other evidence of guilt. Other serious crimes, such as murder, are more commonly solved by confessions than by any other type of evidence (Gross, 1996). Done properly, police interrogation can thus be an unmitigated social benefit. It can allow authorities to capture, prosecute, and convict wrongdoers and deter crime. These are enormously important outcomes. Done improperly, however, police interrogation can be an unmitigated social disaster. Coercive interrogation can lead to police-induced false confessions, which, in turn, can lead to the wrongful prosecution, conviction, and incarceration of the innocent (Leo and Ofshe, 1998a). Improper interrogation can also lead to loss of public confidence in the accuracy and integrity of the criminal justice system, skeptical juries that refuse to convict, and even social protest.

Police interrogation and confession-taking is also important to criminal justice officials, whose decisions can significantly affect the fate of individuals caught up in the system. Police interviews and interrogation are fundamentally about information acquisition and control. As a Rand Corporation study concluded in 1975, the quality of information that police obtain is the single most important factor in whether police will be able to solve a crime (Greenwood and Petersilia, 1975). Prosecutors make significant charging decisions, plea bargaining moves, arguments to juries, and sometimes even sentencing recommendations based on confession evidence alone. Confessions are the bane of defense attorneys, who often strenuously attack their legitimacy, voluntariness, or reliability. Judges are obligated to make numerous evidentiary decisions in pretrial hearings and criminal trials based on confession evidence. And juries often rely on confessions—indeed, they usually give them more weight than any other type of evidence—in making their judgments of innocence and guilt (Leo and Ofshe, 1998a).

Despite the importance of police interrogation to scholars, policymakers, the public, and criminal justice officials, in many ways we know very little about it. And no wonder: it is often intentionally hidden from view. Although technological advances have made it both easy and inexpensive to memorialize custodial police–citizen encounters, interrogation remains for the most part shrouded in secrecy. Most interrogation occurs in the bowels of a police station, off tape, unscrutinized by the public, the media, or the criminal justice system.

Because it is hidden from public view, interrogation remains a mystery to most people and even to most criminal justice officials. What actually occurs inside American interrogation rooms is sometimes counterintuitive. Most people are not aware, for example, that police detectives receive highly specialized training in manipulative and deceptive interrogation methods and strategies. Most people cannot identify the specific interrogation techniques police use. Most people—even many police and criminal justice officials—therefore do not understand how interrogation can distort a suspect's perceptions and lead him to make incriminating statements against his self-interest.

Partly because it has been a secret police activity, interrogation has recurrently sparked legal and political controversy in recent American history. As the journalist William Hart has noted (1981:7), "No law enforcement function has been more visited by controversy, confusion and court decisions than that of the interrogation of criminal suspects." In the first third of the twentieth century, there were numerous popular controversies over the alleged use of the third degree—physical force or psychological duress—to extract confessions. They culminated in the famous Wickersham Commission Report in 1931 that extensively documented and condemned the widespread use of third-degree tactics. This watershed report was followed five years later by the landmark United States Supreme Court decision *Brown v. Mississippi* (1936), which held that police use of physical force during interrogation violated the Fourteenth Amendment and thus invalidated any physically coerced confession.

In the middle third of the century, interrogation controversies tended to focus on how best to circumscribe and check police discretion through the rules of constitutional criminal procedure. The controversies culminated in the 1966 U.S. Supreme Court decision *Miranda v. Arizona*, which required police to inform suspects of their constitutional rights to silence and legal counsel and to elicit knowing and voluntary waivers from them before commencing interrogation. It generated a firestorm of controversy that continues to this day (Schulhofer, 2006).

With the advent of DNA technology and the release of several hundred innocent men and women from prisons across the country in the 1990s and the early twenty-first century (Gross, Jacoby, Matheson, Montgomery, and Patil, 2005), the most recent source of controversy has been the problem of police-induced false confessions and wrongful convictions. The numerous exonerations of the innocent in recent years have changed the landscape of interrogation and confession in America and will likely result in their own set of reforms as well. All of these controversies, however, share at least one common feature: the paucity of direct knowledge about what occurs during many interrogations.

To be sure, there is a well-developed theoretical and applied psychological literature on interrogation and confession-taking. It includes literally hundreds of studies dating back to Hugo Munsterberg's 1908 classic, *On the Witness Stand* (see Ofshe and Leo, 1997b; Gudjonsson, 2003; Kassin and Gudjonsson, 2004; Davis and O'Donahue, 2003). Yet there are comparatively few direct or observational studies of interrogation by psychologists, who for ethical reasons cannot easily replicate inside university laboratories the inherently stressful and potentially coercive conditions of modern interrogation. And though interrogation is central to the study of policing, the criminal investigation process, and modern detective work (see, e.g., Skolnick, 1966; Sanders, 1977; Ericson, 1981), criminologists and sociologists have largely ignored it. Outside of the social sciences, the academic study of police interrogation has been left almost entirely to the legal academy. Lawyers, law students, and law professors have created a formidable law review literature, but, with rare exceptions, it focuses almost entirely on the doctrinal and ethical aspects of interrogation case law rather than on the routine activities of police interrogators and criminal justice officials.

This book is a comprehensive study of police interrogation in America. It aims to shed light on one of the earliest and most influential stages of the legal process and arguably still one of the darkest corners of the American criminal justice system. The book is based largely on the type of data most other scholars do not have access to: direct observations of hundreds of police interrogations. A little more than a decade ago, I contemporaneously observed more than one hundred interrogations inside the Criminal Investigation Division of the Oakland Police Department, as well as sixty videotaped interrogations by the Hayward and Vallejo Police Departments, in northern California (see Leo, 1996a). Since then, I have analyzed several hundred more electronically recorded interrogations by American police departments across the United States.

This book is also based on several other sources of original data. I have attended numerous introductory and advanced police interrogation training courses and seminars; analyzed police interrogation training manuals and unpublished training materials from 1940 to the present; interviewed many police interrogators, criminal justice officials (e.g., police managers, prosecutors, and judges), and criminal suspects; and analyzed archival and historical materials (e.g., government commission reports, newspaper stories, and court cases) as well as contemporary case documents (e.g., police interrogation tapes and transcripts, police reports, and pretrial and trial transcripts). In the past decade, I have studied more than 2,000 felony cases involving interrogations and confessions.

I argue that American police interrogation is strategically manipulative and deceptive because it occurs in the context of a fundamental contradiction. On the one hand, police need incriminating statements and admissions to solve many crimes, especially serious ones; on the other hand, there is almost never a good reason for suspects to provide them. Police are under tremendous organizational and social pressure to obtain admissions and confessions. But it is rarely in a suspect's rational self-interest to say something that will likely lead to his prosecution and conviction. American police in the modern era have succeeded in eliciting confessions by developing interrogation methods that rely on fraud, persuasion, and impression management. Their goal is to elicit incriminating statements from suspects in order to build the strongest possible case against them and thereby assist the prosecution in securing conviction and incarceration.

The fundamental contradiction of American police interrogation is related to many other contradictions. To mention a few: interrogation remains largely secret even though America is arguably the world's leading democracy and most open society; police have created "scientific" interrogation methods, yet they are in reality pseudo-scientific; interrogation is designed to persuade suspects that they have no choice but to confess, but the law requires that all confessions be voluntary; police proclaim truth as the goal of interrogation, yet interrogators regularly rely on deception and sophisticated forms of trickery; while confessions are presented as reliable indicators of a suspect's culpability, interrogation is a social process through which culpability is orchestrated and constructed (not always accurately); and although juries view confession evidence as the most damning indicator of a suspect's guilt, it is sometimes among the most unreliable forms of evidence.

The key to understanding the larger institution of police interrogation in America (as opposed merely to a specific instance of interrogation and confession-taking) is to identify its systemic contradictions and then explain their logic and consequences. Those contradictions are political, psychological, legal, and criminological. They reflect the idiosyncratic historical development of interrogation practices in America, the conflicting goals of criminal investigation, the contradictions of modern police work, the conflicting imperatives of the American adversarial system of criminal justice, and the multifaceted nature of confession evidence. Short of fundamentally changing the American adversarial system so that it no longer needs confession evidence to solve many crimes or so that it actually becomes in a suspect's rational self-interest to give police a truthful confession, the systemic contradictions of American interrogation ultimately cannot be resolved. They can only be managed, more or less effectively, depending on the values, interests, and goals we wish to pursue. However, once we understand these tensions and contradictions we are in a better position to evaluate how courts and legislatures should regulate police interrogation practices, the policy reforms we should promote, and ultimately what social value we should place on confession evidence.

Police detectives rely on deceptive and fraudulent interrogation techniques because of the structure of the American criminal justice system and the expectations of society: we demand that police solve crimes at high rates in order to apprehend and incarcerate "the bad guys," and American law permits, if not authorizes, police to use many of the manipulative and deceptive interrogation techniques that I describe. The dilemmas are therefore systemic, not individual. I cast an unflinching eye on the practices of American police interrogators not because I wish to condemn them but because I seek to accurately describe, analyze, and understand what interrogators do and its consequences for the pursuit of justice.

This is a book about police interrogation in America, not American military interrogation in the world. The two differ in significant ways. The purpose of domestic police interrogation is to gather incriminating evidence from a suspect that can be used to secure a criminal conviction, while the purpose of military interrogation is to gather intelligence that will, presumably, save lives. The techniques, and their perceived legitimacy by government officials, also differ: While domestic police use sophisticated psychological interrogation methods that have been developed as an alternative to the third degree, military interrogators appear to use highly coercive techniques that include both physical and psychological torture (Rose, 2004; Marguiles, 2006; McCoy, 2006). The two kinds of interrogation are also regulated differently: the former by the United States Constitution, the latter— in theory—by the laws of war and the Geneva Convention. Nevertheless, domestic and military interrogation raise similar concerns about the limits of governmental power, the morality of means and potential abuse of rights, and the reliability of interrogation-induced statements and admissions. Because military interrogations are not electronically recorded and rarely leave a publicly accessible paper trail, they are difficult to study empirically. Despite the revelations in recent years about American interrogation practices in Afghanistan, Iraq, Guantanamo Bay, and elsewhere (Hersch, 2004; Begg, 2006; Harbury, 2006), we know even less about it than we do about domestic police interrogation.

Finally, a word about my own values, commitments, and beliefs. When I began studying the problems of police interrogation and confession-taking in America more than a decade ago, my interest was purely academic: I wanted to learn how police routinely interrogated custodial suspects, the social psychology of interrogation and confession, and the impact of law on police behavior and case outcomes. Several years later, as I began to concentrate more of my energy on the problems of psychological coercion, police-induced false confessions, and wrongful convictions, my work became more applied. I have since consulted or served as an expert witness for many attorneys—including state and federal prosecutors and civil attorneys, but primarily criminal defense attorneys—in cases that typically involve disputed interrogations or confessions. Some of these cases are well known and highly controversial.

I believe that police interrogation is a necessary and valuable police activity in a democratic society, so long as it is conducted fairly and legally. What is considered fair and legal will inevitably change over time (Marx, 1992), but this does not render contemporary norms arbitrary or absolve us from making important distinctions in policy debates. Contrary to the suggestions of two leading American police interrogation training manuals (Inbau, Reid, Buckley, and Jayne, 2001; Zulawski and Wicklander, 2002), I am not an "opponent" of police interrogation. In fact, I have lectured to American police on numerous occasions; trained police interrogators in Louisiana, Texas, Florida, and the Republic of Cyprus; and even served on an advisory committee to one large police department (Long Beach, California). I have also lectured to, worked with, and testified on behalf of American prosecutors. One of my goals has always been to educate others—undergraduates, graduate and law students, judges and juries, the media, and police themselves—to improve the quality of police interrogation in America and increase the likelihood that police will elicit confessions from the guilty while decreasing the chance that they will elicit them from the innocent.

CHAPTER 1

Police Interrogation and the American Adversary System

An interrogation is much like a trial in that two adversaries use persuasion and propaganda to further their cause.

—Brian Jayne and Joseph Buckley (1993)

By definition . . . interrogation is a guilt-presumptive process, a theory-driven social interaction led by an authority figure who holds a strong a priori belief about the target and who measures success by his or her ability to extract a confession.

—Saul Kassin (2005)

No other class of evidence is so profoundly prejudicial . . . Triers of fact accord confessions such heavy weight in their determinations that the introduction of a confession makes the other aspects of trial in court superfluous, and the real trial, for all practical purposes, occurs when the confession is obtained.

—Supreme Court Justice William Brennan in
Colorado v. Connelly (1986)

America is known for its adversary system of criminal justice. Comparative legal scholars tell us that we have the most adversarial criminal justice system in the world (Pizzi, 1999; Kagan, 2001). At the same time, Americans repeatedly tell themselves—in the print media, on television shows, and even in scholarly publications—that we have the best criminal justice system of any country (see, e.g., Dershowitz, 1982). Yet both popular and academic discussions often fail to examine the underlying structure of our adversary system; criminologists, in particular, frequently fail to recognize how our adversarial institutions both enable and constrain the quest for just procedures and accurate outcomes. Rather than thinking deeply about the adversary structure of American criminal justice and its influence on everyday procedures and outcomes, much popular and academic writing in criminology and law is descriptive with a normative edge: once we learn the facts of a case or the practices of a particular criminal justice actor or institution, we are implicitly (if not explicitly) invited to make or support moral arguments about the way the case should have ended or how a particular practice or institution should be changed.

This book takes a different, more systemic, approach. I argue that to understand the multifaceted institution of American police interrogation we must first see it as an intrinsic part of our adversary system and procedures. In other words, we must study police interrogation as it is embedded in a particular set of adversarial values, rules, and practices—what we might call the American *process* of criminal justice. This approach will help explain the evolution, structure, and practice of American police interrogation. It will also help us understand better the ongoing dilemmas and contradictions underlying legal and policy analyses that seek to regulate police interrogation and confession evidence.

That police interrogation must be seen as part of the larger adversarial process is hardly obvious. Most social science scholarship about police interrogation does not make this connection in any meaningful way. Psychologists, for example, typically fail to delve very far below the surface of police techniques or to understand the underlying structure or complexity of interrogation. Instead, they tend mostly to take for granted the adversarial process. Sociologists and criminologists have taken a broader view of policing, but they have largely ignored the study of criminal investigation and rarely situated any aspect of it within a substantive analysis of the adversarial process and system of American justice (for an exception, see Skolnick, 1966, 1982). Although legal scholarship has been more generally attuned to the adversary structure of our legal system, lawyers, law professors, and legal scholars studying police interrogation and confession evidence have tended to focus their analyses narrowly on the facts of particular cases or the rhetoric of legal doctrines, eschewing any sustained analysis of the structure of American police interrogation for more doctrinal and policy-focused approaches.

There is another reason why scholars and others often fail to see police interrogation as a fundamental part of the larger adversarial system. The criminal investigation process (of which interrogation is a prominent part) occurs *before* the moment we tend to think of as the start of the adversarial process, which is when the prosecutor has filed criminal charges. The phrase "adversary system" is typically used to describe the pretrial and trial processes that commence *after* police interrogation and confession-taking have occurred. Indeed, the popular image of the adversary system is that of a lawyer-conducted trial with all of its one-sided presentations, challenges, and arguments, not of the investigative stage of police work that precedes the prosecutor's evaluation and charging decision. The criminal investigation stage is typically characterized as a "fact-finding" process rather than an adversarial one. It is the lawyers who are supposed to be partisan-advocates, not the police investigators (McCoy, 1996).

But empirical study of police detectives reveals that they are anything but neutral or impartial in their collection and construction of case evidence against criminal suspects during the interrogation process (McConville, Sanders, and Leng, 1991; Williams, 1998). Rather, as we will see, American police interrogators are highly partisan, strategic, and goal directed. The entire process of interrogation is structured to advance the penal interests of the state and secure a conviction. Yet, unlike courtroom lawyers, police interrogators do not represent themselves as the suspect's adversary. Instead, in what must be one of the deepest ironies of American criminal justice, they portray themselves as the suspect's advocate. To advance the state's interests, American interrogation is designed to create a number of illusions: that the suspect has no meaningful option other than to comply with the interrogator's wishes and demands; that the interrogator's motivation is really to help the suspect; and that the suspect is better off by admitting some version of guilt than by denying culpability or terminating the interrogation. To persuade a suspect of these illusions, American police regularly rely on psychological interrogation techniques that involve deception, trickery, and manipulation.

The structure, culture, and practice of American police interrogation are orchestrated to maximize the state's ability to prosecute the suspect and to undermine his ability to present a successful defense later in the trial process. The history of American police interrogation represents a movement away from a nakedly inquisitorial model of interrogation (the era of the third degree) toward an adversarial model of interrogation (the era of science and psychology). But the adversarial model often can succeed only if police keep their agenda hidden, not only from suspects, but also from courts, the media, and the public. I argue here that the adversarial model of American police interrogation is thus steeped in two fundamentally different types of fraud, one internal to the process and the other external to it. In the first, detectives engage in trickery or role deception (e.g., pretending to be the suspect's advocate) and deceit (e.g., inventing or falsifying case evidence against him) in the interrogation room to create the illusion that it is in the suspect's best interest to confess. In the second, police engage in impression management for outside audiences by representing the interrogation process as little more than a noncustodial interview whose benign but noble purpose is merely to advance the public's interest in truth-finding; they attempt to shift the focus away from their interrogation strategies and toward the suspect's incriminating statements, which are usually unrecorded.

The Adversary Process of American Justice: An Introduction

The term "adversary system" refers both to a specific method of dispute resolution and more broadly to a type of legal system. As a method of dispute resolution, the adversary system contains distinctive procedures and embodies a particular style of decision-making. It is premised on the idea that the best outcomes in criminal matters are most likely to emerge through the partisan clash of opposing viewpoints in which each side pursues its narrow self-interest. As a type of legal system, the adversary system is firmly rooted in Anglo-American legal historical developments (see Langbein, 2003). It is based on a legal ideology that contains assumptions about the proper relationship between the state and the accused, and about the proper allocation of rights and obligations necessary to achieve this relationship. Because of its distinctive features, the adversary system is often associated with the United States and England and contrasted with inquisitorial systems found in continental Europe.

The adversary system of criminal justice, however, is different from the adversary system of civil justice. In the United States (as well as Britain) there is not one but two adversary systems. The civil adversary system exists to arbitrate disputes between private parties. In it, the government is neutral and attempts to facilitate disputes in a way that minimizes total error. By contrast, in the criminal justice adversary system, the government is always the moving party, and the procedures, presumptions, and burden of proof are much different than in the civil adversary system. My analysis in this book focuses on the criminal justice adversary system.

The proper roles of the parties, their representatives, and criminal justice officials in the adversary system are sharply defined. The system adjudicates legal disputes by pitting the two parties against each other and assigning to them the responsibility of gathering evidence, presenting their cases, and challenging their opponents. The disputants are represented by attorneys who act as their agents and whose obligation is to zealously advocate the client's interest. This entails presenting the client's position in the best possible light and challenging the other side's assertions and evidence as vigorously as possible. In the adversary system, the principal function of the judge (who is presumed to be neutral) is to oversee the advocate's adherence to the rules of criminal procedure. Acting as a referee, the judge is supposed to reach decisions—for example, on matters such as the admissibility of evidence and the purposes for which it is to be used—by applying the appropriate legal principles. Like the judge, the jury is cast in a passive and impartial role: it is supposed to apply the law to the case facts and base its ultimate verdict on the strength of the evidence and arguments presented by the opposing parties.

Two Visions of the Adversary System

The adversary system is premised on multiple, inconsistent, and sometimes conflicting goals: to resolve disputes in a procedurally fair manner; to control unchecked state power; to protect a suspect's legal rights; and to promote truth-finding. Embodied within these multiple objectives are two competing visions of the primary purpose of the system. I call these the "truth" and "government control" models of adversary justice.

The Truth Model

In theory, the adversary system promotes truth-finding through the adversaries' partisan pursuit of their clients' self-interest. The attorney's obligation, however, is not to pursue truth itself but to zealously advocate the client's interest, which means portraying him in the most favorable light and presenting facts in a way that is most consistent with his position, within the existing rules of law and procedure. In practice this means that the attorney may prevent the introduction of highly probative evidence (by, e.g., preventing his client from testifying), prevent the introduction or attack the veracity of unfavorable evidence, attack the credibility and testimony of opposing witnesses, minimize the importance of unfavorable facts, and try to construe inferences from ambiguous evidence in the client's favor.

By emphasizing the pursuit of self-interest and delegating to the parties the control of gathering and presenting evidence, the adversary system is supposed to stimulate the most diligent search for truth. Apart from motivating the parties to assiduously discover the facts, the adversary clash of partisan perspectives is supposed to leave the finder of fact in the most informed position to adjudicate between disputed claims.

The pursuit of truth is better achieved in the civil adversary system, where the moving party's burden of proof is based on a "preponderance of evidence" standard, than it is in the criminal justice adversary system, where the state's burden of proof is based on a "beyond a reasonable doubt" standard. This means that in the civil adversary system the moving party ultimately prevails if the jury finds its assertions "more likely than not" to be true (i.e., at least 51 percent likely to be true). Although no simple percentage can be assigned to the "beyond a reasonable doubt" standard in the criminal justice system, some observers have suggested that it is likely 95 to 99 percent (Givelber, 1997). The civil system has additional truth-seeking advantages: unlike the criminal justice system, there is no presumption of innocence and no constitutional rights or safeguards to interfere with either party's discovery of case facts. Further, in the civil adversary system the moving party must persuade only two-thirds of the jury members of its claims in order to prevail, whereas in the criminal justice system the state must persuade all (typically twelve) jurors of its assertions to convict the defendant.[1]

The Government Control Model

The government control model subordinates truth-seeking to placing limits on concentrated or unchecked governmental power. It draws on the adversary system's historic distrust of state power. The government control model reflects the classic liberal idea that the greatest danger to an enlightened citizenry is the state itself because of the possibility that concentrated state power may become unaccountable and persecute the innocent. Because it seeks to protect individuals against the arbitrary exercise of government authority, the adversary system, according to this view, intentionally structures the procedural balance of advantage in favor of the defendant and against the prosecution. It does so by formally endowing the accused with a number of procedural rights, presumptions, and privileges while saddling the prosecution with procedural burdens and holding it to different standards.

The accused enjoys, for example, a presumption of innocence, the right to confront adverse witnesses, the right to have compulsory process for obtaining witnesses, the right to silence, and the right to counsel, among other things, while the prosecution has a unilateral obligation to reveal facts unfavorable to its case and carries the burden of proving the accused's guilt beyond a reasonable doubt.

The philosophy underlying this approach is captured in Blackstone's famous aphorism that it is better to let ten guilty individuals go free than wrongfully convict one innocent man or woman (Packer, 1968; but see Volokh, 1997). For many, this error-preference rule stands for the proposition that there can be no worse error in an adversarial system of criminal justice than the wrongful conviction of an innocent person. But there is more to this idea than merely designating one type of error worse than another: it reflects the philosophy that state power must be checked in the adversary system in order to prevent the kind of unjust or corrupt *structure* coming into place that would *regularly* risk the wrongful conviction of the innocent. The philosophy and procedures underlying the error-preference rule—which are instantiated by the presumptions, privileges, and rights enjoyed by the criminal defendant and the corresponding obligations and burdens imposed on the prosecution—are intended to hold state agents accountable at each stage of the criminal process, from arrest through prosecution and sentencing.

The government control model is in tension with the truth model because the former necessarily places limits on the state's pursuit of truth. If a society wishes to maximize the ability of its criminal justice system to find facts and discover truth, then it will allow the state an unfettered capacity to search, seize, surveil, investigate, and interrogate criminal suspects. As Alan Dershowitz (1996: 42) has written :

> If the only goal of the adversary system were to find "the truth" in every case, then it would be relatively simple to achieve. Suspects would be tortured, their families threatened, homes randomly searched, and lie detector tests routinely administered. Indeed, in order to facilitate this search for truth, we could all be subjected to a regimen of random blood and urine tests, and every public building and workplace could be outfitted with surveillance cameras. If these methods—common in totalitarian countries— are objected to on the ground that torture and threats sometimes produce false accusations, that objection could be overcome by requiring that all

confessions induced by torture or threats must be independently corroborated. We would never tolerate such a single-minded search for truth, nor would our constitution, because we believe that the ends—even an end as noble as truth—do not justify every possible means.

Such a government would, of course, run directly opposite to the government control model's vision of adversarial justice.

Even if we reject such intrusions for reasons of civil liberties, we might still imagine a government system that attempts to maximize its ability to discover case facts and pursue truth by lowering the burden of proof—perhaps to one based on a balance of probabilities, as in the civil justice system—in criminal cases. Presumably a burden of proof less than "beyond a reasonable doubt" would aid the state in discovering information in the investigative phase of case processing and minimize the number of false-positive outcomes (i.e., wrongful acquittals of the guilty) at trial. But although it would improve the ability of the criminal justice system to pursue and promote truthful outcomes, such an error-preference rule is fundamentally inconsistent with the government control model for the simple reason that *not all errors are created equal* in the adversary system. The American system is premised on a burden of proof that allows conviction only beyond a reasonable doubt precisely because it distrusts the uses to which the awesome powers of the state—whose resources vastly exceed those of any of its citizens—may be put if left unchecked or not put to the test in any given case. For these reasons, the adversary system creates obstacles to the pursuit of truth by permitting one type of error (the dismissal or acquittal of the guilty)in order to minimize another type of error (the wrongful conviction of the innocent).

The Assumptions of the Adversary System

The adversary system's assumed superiority over any other method of adjudication or type of legal system rests on several assumptions. The adversary system presumes the zealous partisan representation and sharply defined roles among lawyer, judge, and jury that have already been noted. It presumes not merely a division of labor, but also a division of the functions necessary to achieve its sub-goals. The investigative function is supposed to be separate from the prosecutorial function; the prosecutorial function is supposed to be separate from the adjudicative function; and the adjudicative function is supposed to be separate from the penal function. The adversary system also presumes relatively equal resources—financial and otherwise—between the disputing parties because without a level playing field the competition necessary to protect legal rights and promote truthful outcomes breaks down. Finally, in the context of criminal law the adversary system in theory holds the prosecution (unlike all other litigating attorneys) to the standard of dispensing justice, not merely winning its cases. This means that the prosecution is supposed to bring forward only those cases in which it believes that the defendant is factually guilty and that it can demonstrate this to an impartial jury beyond any reasonable doubt. Once this happens, however, the prosecutor may act just as adversarial as the defense within the existing rules of evidence and procedure (Givelber, 2001).

Criticisms of the Adversary System

The adversary system has been criticized for many reasons and from many sides (see, e.g., Frank, 1949; Strier, 1996; Pizzi, 1999). Perhaps the most salient criticism is that by privileging the role of partisan interests and the goal of winning, adversary criminal procedure fundamentally undermines any rational or purposive search for the truth. Instead, the adversary system creates incentives for the parties to distort or suppress unfavorable evidence in order to maximize their strategic advantage vis-à-vis one another—what comparative legal scholar John Langbein (2003) has called "the combat effect." A related criticism is that case outcomes are determined by which party has the most resources and the best lawyers in our highly unequal society. Such criticism of "the wealth effect" (Langbein, 2003) calls into question the adversary system's assumption that truth and justice are likely to emerge as by-products of intense partisan struggle. Another criticism is that the adversary system turns the pursuit of justice into a game—the so-called sporting theory of justice (Pound, 1909). Not only is the side with the most resources most likely to impose its agenda and win the contest, but, according to this view, the sporting approach breeds disrespect for legal institutions and the rule of law and undermines confidence in the integrity of the judicial process and the reliability of case outcomes. The sporting approach ultimately debases the quality of justice. One consequence is that it creates a kind of moral ruthlessness, or "role immorality," in which the parties and their representatives come to see the ends justifying the means, once again undermining the search for truth, if not the rule of law (Luban, 1988; Strier, 1996).

One could supplement each of these critiques with the empirical observation that the American adversary system in practice often fails to deliver anything remotely close to the kind of substantive or procedural justice it promises in theory. Some have argued that America is not so much an adversary system of criminal justice as a plea bargaining system, since 90 to 95 percent of all criminal cases are resolved through plea bargains. In deciding to plea, a defendant agrees formally to admit guilt (and thereby forego a trial) in exchange for a reduction in charging or sentencing by the prosecution (Pizzi, 1999). In a plea bargaining system, the defendant in effect trades away his many trial rights—including the presumption of innocence, the privilege against self-incrimination, and the right to confront adverse witnesses—as well as his right to appeal in exchange for prosecutorial leniency. Plea bargaining allows prosecutors to circumvent the evidentiary burdens, standards of proof, and due process requirements that would otherwise have been imposed on them by trial. The adversarial search for truth is, in effect, exchanged for bureaucratic efficiency. The public system of partisan adversary conflict that is supposed to protect individual liberties and result in superior fact-finding instead becomes a private system of compromise and deal-making. In a plea bargaining system, there is no record of the deal-making sessions that occur between the parties, and no right to appeal. Depending on one's perspective, the process of plea bargaining is either consensual or coercive, yet there is little dispute that plea bargaining results in malleable and inconsistent case outcomes.

Proponents and critics of the adversary system thus paint very different images of the administration of justice in America. Virtually all of the critics focus their animus on some aspect of the system's alleged failure to permit adequate case investigation or to produce fully accurate outcomes. These critiques make sense from the perspective of the truth model, but have limited applicability from the perspective of the government control model. They also make sense when applied to the civil adversary system. But in the criminal justice system, unlike in the civil system, the state is not merely an umpire over a private dispute but also the moving party and the most powerful adversary in a public dispute in which the stakes—potentially the deprivation of liberty, the stigma of criminal conviction, lengthy imprisonment, and possibly even execution—are much higher. Because the adversary system seeks to prevent the arbitrary or abusive exercise of governmental power, it necessarily subordinates unfettered case investigation by state officials to these larger, systemic objectives. If a society seeks to maximize the power of state officials to obtain the truth in its criminal investigations and prosecutions, then there is little point in having an adversarial system of criminal justice in the first place.

I do not seek to praise or criticize the adversary system for its own sake, but instead to empirically understand the structure of American interrogation practice and how it fosters or hinders the search for truth and the pursuit of justice. Regretfully, the adversary structure of American trial practice has, for the most part, been neglected in the empirical and criminological study of police investigation. Yet interrogation cannot be separated from its larger adversarial context: only when we see just how modern police have reinvented the structure of interrogation and confession-taking as part of an orchestrated adversarial strategy will we be in a position to fully understand the uniquely American practice of interrogation and its implications for the quality of criminal justice. Whether proponents or critics of the adversary system, virtually all scholars appear to agree on the propriety of separating key functions in the criminal justice system (investigative, prosecutorial, judicial) and on the importance of fact-finding as a prerequisite for the delivery of substantive justice.

But what happens when the police investigators act less like impartial fact-finders than committed adversaries? Or when the investigative function becomes adversarial and begins to approximate the prosecutorial function? As we will see, these are precisely the problems posed by the American practice of interrogation.

The Adversarial Nature of American Police Interrogation

In the American criminal justice system, the proper role of the detective is to collect relevant case information in a neutral and dispassionate manner *at the preadversary stage of the criminal process.* Based on the quality of information provided by police investigators, the prosecution must make what is arguably its most important decision: whether to charge the suspect and thus set in motion full-scale adversarial proceedings against him. If police act as partisans or become committed to a prosecutorial agenda in their investigations, it is not just prosecutors whose perceptions and decisions may be distorted. Defense lawyers, judges, and juries may also end up relying on biased, incomplete, erroneous, or one-sided information in forming judgments, making decisions, and dispensing justice. For the adversary system to work properly, the police should not identify with the function, purpose, or role of the prosecution. The police are fact-finders and investigators, not ministers of justice. When they act as partisans, they potentially undermine the three primary goals of the adversary system—the protection of legal rights, the control of government power, and the search for the truth—and thus risk contributing to unfair procedures and unreliable outcomes that may undermine the system's legitimacy.

In the American criminal justice system, however, police interrogators have turned the assumptions and logic of the adversary system on their head. American police interrogators are adversarial in the sense that they are committed to the goal of incriminating the accused in order to assist the state in its prosecution. Their partisanship is evident in four areas: their values, culture, and ideology; the goals of the interrogation process; the psychological methods they use to break down resistance and elicit confessions; and the impression management they engage in vis-à-vis suspects, judges and juries, and everyone else in the public domain.

The Adversarial Culture and Goals of Interrogation

One-Sided Skepticism

Police investigators tend to be skeptical about many things. They tend to assume that the rules of criminal procedure unduly restrict their discretion and authority. They tend to assume that that the rules are unfairly stacked against them in favor of the suspect. And they tend to assume that the rules inhibit discovering the truth, favor form over substance (or "technicalities" over "the truth"), and thus make little sense for the rational pursuit of justice. The rules of criminal procedure, they know well, sometimes impair their ability to obtain probative evidence of a suspect's guilt or even mandate the exclusion of such evidence. Anyone who spends a significant amount of time with detectives will be regaled with stories about cases in which seemingly arbitrary and nonsensical rules of procedure prevented them from apprehending a guilty suspect or obtaining the kind of evidence that would have resulted in a conviction.

Detectives also tend to be skeptical, if not downright cynical, about the integrity and character of the suspects they encounter, many of whom are repeat offenders. They doubt suspects' honesty and assume that suspects will lie to them reflexively, without compunction. They tend to be skeptical about suspects' motivations and assume that they are only self-interested and often beyond moral redemption or constraint. Influenced by the typically conservative worldview they bring to police work as well as their occupational experience before they became detectives (all police detectives have first worked as patrol officers, often for many years), interrogators develop a distinctive professional outlook that has been referred to in the police literature as a "working personality" (Skolnick, 1966). Perhaps as a result, detectives are also skeptical about the ability of suspects to experience genuine remorse or be meaningfully rehabilitated. The proper response to the social problem of crime, in their worldview, is to apprehend and incarcerate incorrigible offenders, preferably for a very long time.

But their skepticism is one sided. They tend not to be skeptical about the possibility of the criminal defendant being treated unfairly by the state; the potential for police discretion to be misapplied or even abused; or the potentially corrosive effects of their own trickery, deceit, and manipulation in the interrogation room. Perhaps most strikingly, American police detectives tend not to be skeptical about the possibility of the type of error that the adversary system, in theory, is designed to prevent: the wrongful prosecution and conviction of an innocent person. Rather, they complain that the guilty often escape punishment.

The one-sided character of their skepticism has important implications for how detectives interrogate suspects, the quality of the evidence they elicit during interrogations, and the potential for error. Because they see themselves as crime specialists, police detectives tend to believe that their investigative and factual judgments are superior to those of nonspecialists. As criminal justice experts, interrogators are trained to believe and tend to assume that they can distinguish truth-telling from deception by analyzing a suspect's verbal and nonverbal behavior (Inbau, Reid, Buckley, and Jayne, 2001). In other words, detectives believe that they can distinguish whether a suspect is telling the truth or lying by *how* he is acting and speaking. Detectives not only assume that they can separate the innocent from the guilty in the investigative process, but that they rarely make any sorting mistakes (Kassin and Fong, 1999).

Further, detectives are skeptical that their interrogation techniques can cause the innocent to confess or be convicted. Because of their belief in the near infallibility of their sorting judgments, American police detectives assume that, with rare exceptions, they only interrogate the guilty (Kassin, 2005). Modern interrogation is a method of influence that is designed only for the guilty (Inbau et al., 2001). American police are trained to interview the innocent (victims, witnesses, and individuals who may later become potential suspects), not interrogate them. If, however, an innocent suspect is somehow interrogated, police assume that they will realize their mistake during the questioning process and terminate interrogation (Inbau et al., 2001). Even if they do not, police interrogators, like other criminal justice officials and much of the public, assume that innocent suspects will not confess falsely—especially to serious crimes that carry lengthy sentences—unless they are physically tortured or mentally ill.

Conviction Psychology

An unmistakable conviction psychology underlies and animates the interrogator's methods, strategies, and goals. American detectives are, first and foremost, committed to the goal of convicting the suspects they interrogate. They understand their role as incriminating the guilty to help the state successfully prosecute and punish them. Since interrogation is confined to those whom police have confidently judged as deceptive and therefore guilty, interrogators tend to treat the possibility of an innocent man in the interrogation room as little more than an urban legend perpetuated by naive liberals, muckraking journalists, or self-serving criminal defense attorneys. Because of their one-sided skepticism and conviction psychology, interrogators tend to perceive the procedural safeguards accorded to the accused in our adversary system of criminal justice as little more than a shield for the guilty. They tend to be too skeptical about a suspect's procedural rights to see any inherent value in promoting or protecting them.

American police interrogators thus act and think like highly partisan, strategically oriented adversaries: once they have judged a custodial suspect guilty, they seek to incriminate him at every turn. Detectives often see the interrogation process as their best opportunity to build a case against a suspect by eliciting and constructing incriminating statements—ideally a full confession—that will undermine his defense at later stages of the pretrial and trial process. By incriminating the suspect, the interrogator aims to maximize the likelihood that charges will be filed against him, weaken the suspect's position in plea negotiations, and minimize the possibility of an acquittal at trial. Once police have decided to interrogate a suspect, they have, in effect, crossed the line that separates police work from prosecutorial work. They have aligned themselves with the prosecution in orientation and goal; their function at this point becomes more prosecutorial than investigative.

Police Interrogation as a Game

Perhaps not surprisingly, police treat interrogation as a game (Leo, 1996c). As in other games, the aim is to win. Winning involves outsmarting the suspect, overcoming his resistance, obtaining compliance, and eliciting an admission or confession. Contrary to the myths of American justice, *the goal of police interrogation is not necessarily to determine the truth.* From the detective's perspective, a confession ideally will consist of the truth and thus confirm the accuracy of his presumption of guilt, but the interrogation process does not always achieve its ideal result; it is structured to promote incrimination, if necessary, over truth-finding.

   Three examples support this point. First, detectives are trained that if they cannot get a confession, they should try to catch the suspect in lies (the more the better)—the exact opposite of the truth, of course, but incriminating nonetheless. As one detective told me: "A lot of times a good lie is invaluable . . . and is as good as a confession because all you need to do is just show that one aspect of what he said . . . and the jury is not going to believe anything the defendant says" (Interview of Michael O, 1993: 26). Second, to elicit incriminating statements, American interrogators frequently rely on the technique of suggesting "themes" (i.e., scenarios that recast the alleged crime as legally or morally justifiable or excusable, such as portraying an intentional murder as an act of self-defense or an accident). By its very nature, the theme technique intentionally distorts what interrogators believe to be the truth. Third, interrogators often are unconcerned with the errors a suspect may make in his postadmission narrative (the account he gives after saying the words "I did it") so long as he is incriminating himself. They frequently fail to acknowledge, investigate, or correct such errors.

Means–Ends Rationality

As a result of their one-sided skepticism, conviction psychology, and game approach to interrogation, America detectives are motivated by a means–end rationality in the interrogation room that is in tension, if not contradiction, with the role and function assigned to them by the adversary system. Once they commence interrogation, their goal, again, is to convict. They see their mission as delivering *substantive* justice to society and to crime victims despite the adversary system's emphasis on *procedural* justice. Weighed down by what they perceive to be irrational, burdensome and counterproductive rules and procedures, American interrogators seek to outsmart and outmaneuver a system of rules and restrictions that, in their view, would structurally advantage the criminal and thereby threaten to pervert the ends of justice.

Their means–ends rationality bears on a larger dilemma that criminologist Carl Klockars (1980) has famously called "The Dirty Harry Problem": When is it acceptable for police detectives to use bad means to achieve good ends? In American interrogation and confession law, the ends of justice do not always justify the means of achieving it. It is never permissible, for example, to torture suspects or psychologically coerce them no matter how important it may seem to the police to incriminate them. To focus on the extreme case—such as a "ticking bomb" (Dershowitz, 2002; but see Scheppele, 2006)—as the Dirty Harry comparison does, however, is perhaps to miss understanding the adversarial culture and goals of American police interrogation. With rare exceptions, contemporary American detectives do not torture, or even physically touch, their suspects (Leo, 1994). Nor do they often see themselves as violating any of the laws of criminal procedure or engaging in morally questionable behavior.

Yet in the culture of American interrogators the ends often do justify the means. Detectives seek to overcome the obstacles that the law and the criminal justice system have put in their way and adapt their methods to fit their goals of incrimination and case-building. In the last seventy years, American interrogators have developed a body of psychological tactics and strategies that are based on thoroughgoing manipulation and deception, and sometimes even psychological coercion. The adversarial culture of American police interrogation rewards and valorizes the detective who overcomes procedural restrictions on his discretion and successfully discovers or elicits the evidence that will seal the case against the criminal suspect. Treating the interrogation as a game in which the goal is to win and the ends justify the means (so long as, in the detective's mind, he has not violated the letter of the law) allows the detective to pursue his ends more effectively and to absolve himself of any doubts he may have about the ethics of the means through which he elicits incriminating statements. To those who are skeptical of the adversary system, however, the same criticism about the role immorality of one group of partisan advocates (the lawyers) may also extend to another group of partisan advocates (police interrogators).

The Adversarial Strategies and Techniques of Interrogation

American detectives assume that the suspects they interrogate will initially lie to them and deny their guilt. As one detective told me: "Suspects lie, their alibis lie, everybody's lying and . . . even if they truth would get them off, they will fabricate some story . . . Seldom does anybody come right off the top and say "I did this" or "I did that" (Interview of Charlie D, 1993: 1–2). Detectives assume that suspects will lie because it is not in their rational self-interest to provide the state with testimonial evidence that almost certainly will lead to his arrest, prosecution, conviction, and incarceration (Inbau et al., 2001). The modern methods of psychological interrogation have been designed to break down a suspect's denials of guilt by persuading him that he has no meaningful choice under the circumstances but to comply with detectives, and that contrary to all appearances, logic, and common sense he is better off by confessing (Ofshe and Leo, 1997b). To move a suspect from denial to admission, interrogating detectives must therefore convince the suspect of something that usually is far from the truth—that it is in his best interest to provide the police with a full confession.

Police interrogation in the American adversary system is firmly rooted in fraud. Modern interrogation is fraudulent not simply because police are legally permitted to–and frequently do–lie to suspects about such things as the seriousness of the crime or case evidence (e.g., fingerprints, eyewitnesses, or DNA results) that they do not possess. It is also based on fraud because detectives seek to create the illusion that they share a common interest with the suspect and that he can escape or mitigate punishment only by cooperating with them and providing a full confession. Although the suspect's self-interest would usually best be served by remaining completely silent, interrogators seek at every step to convince him that what is in their professional self-interest is somehow in his personal self-interest. The entire interrogation process is carefully staged to hide the fact that police interrogators are the suspect's adversary. While they portray themselves as seeking only to "collect the facts" and to help the suspect if he cooperates, they, of course, try to construct a damning case against him.

To understand the structure and logic of interrogation, it is important to see the whole as more than the sum of its parts. American interrogation is a multistage process that relies on a distinct logic of influence and deception to manipulate a suspect's perception of his situation, options, and ultimately self-interest (Ofshe and Leo, 1997b). Carefully orchestrated, it also involves isolation, role-playing, ambush, manipulation, inducements, and sometimes the sheer imposition of will. The interrogation process begins before the first accusation and typically ends well after the detective elicits the suspect's admission. It has essentially four distinct stages in the American adversary system: the softening up phase, the *Miranda* warning phase, the interrogation proper (i.e., from denial to admission), and the postadmission interrogation (i.e., from admission to confession). Although each will be discussed more fully in subsequent chapters, I describe them briefly here to show how they are integral to detectives' adversarial role.

1. Softening Up the Suspect

Detectives initially structure the interrogation to psychologically soften up the suspect. They must first establish a rapport with him. The interrogator asks background questions, engages in small talk, and may even flatter or ingratiate the suspect to create the illusion of a nonthreatening, nonadversarial encounter. The detective's appearance in plainclothes and his friendly demeanor are intended to put the suspect at ease and break down the social distance inherent in their different roles and statuses. At this stage, the detective seeks to minimize the significance or seriousness of the questioning by portraying the interrogation as a mundane interview. Indeed, the detective tries to create the illusion that he and the suspect will be engaged in a simple and nonthreatening information exchange designed to assist the investigator solve an important problem (the crime) that does not implicate the suspect. The softening-up phase of questioning is intended to divert the suspect's attention from the fact that he is about to be interrogated by a state official in police custody about a serious crime he is believed to have committed. By establishing a rapport, ingratiating himself, and obscuring his adversarial relationship to the suspect, the interrogator seeks to create the perception that he is fundamentally concerned about the suspect's welfare—a perception that may assist the interrogator later in trying to persuade the suspect that it is to his advantage to confess.

2. The Miranda Waiver

American police are legally required to issue the now-famous *Miranda* warnings before custodial interrogation, informing the suspect that he has constitutional rights to silence and state-funded defense counsel and that anything he says may be used against him in court. Interrogation may not legally commence unless the suspect waives these rights. If detectives fail to properly warn the suspect of his *Miranda* rights or fail to elicit a proper waiver, any statements the suspect makes cannot be used against him and should, in theory, be excluded from evidence at trial. The *Miranda* warning and waiver ritual, however, makes almost no difference in American police interrogation because virtually all suspects waive (or are legally constructed to have waived) their *Miranda* rights, and almost no confession is ever excluded from evidence at trial because of a *Miranda* violation. As we will see, American police have devised a number of strategies to obtain (or create the appearance of obtaining) the suspect's compliance at this stage in the interrogation process, thereby minimizing the impact of *Miranda* (Leo and White, 1999). As in the other stages, the detective's strategy is to "de-adversarialize" the interaction by creating the illusion that he and the suspect share the same interest and thus that it is in the suspect's best interest to waive his *Miranda* rights and consent to interrogation.

3. Interrogation: Preadmission

Once the interrogator has obtained the suspect's implicit or explicit waiver (typically memorialized by his initials at the bottom of a *Miranda* advisement form), the interrogation process becomes accusatorial, and the detective shifts from asking the suspect questions to accusing him of committing the crime and imploring him to confess. It is usually at this point that every interrogator must confront the dilemma of how to persuade a suspect that confessing is in his self-interest. As will be seen later, since the early 1940s the interrogation training industry has been devising techniques, methods, and strategies to overcome this dilemma. For example, interrogators will accuse the suspect of having committed the crime and repeat this accusation frequently and with unwavering confidence; ignore, cut off, or roll past the suspects' denials or objections; attack the suspect's alibi as inconsistent, implausible, contradicted by all the case evidence, or simply impossible; escalate pressure on the suspect to comply (e.g., by moving closer to him or reminding him of the gravity of the situation); confront the suspect with real (if they have it) or false (if they do not) evidence of the suspects' guilt (e.g., eyewitness reports, fingerprints, videotapes, DNA results, and so on); implore him to confess by presenting him with numerous inducements or scenarios suggesting that the benefits of admitting guilt clearly outweigh the costs of continuing to assert innocence; and pressure the suspect to believe that this is their only opportunity to explain or justify the allegations against him and make a statement that will mitigate his inevitable punishment and put an end to the interrogation.

If these techniques are effective, the suspect should come to perceive himself as caught, trapped, and utterly powerless to change a seemingly unchangeable situation. He will conclude that he has no choice but to comply with the detective's wishes. As I discuss subsequently, detectives elicit confessions not only by hiding their adversarial role but also by breaking down the suspect's self-confidence in his ability to deny the accusations and by strategically transforming the suspect's perception of his situation, his available options, and the likely consequences of each choice (Ofshe and Leo, 1997b). The genius or fraud of psychological interrogation (depending on one's perspective) lies in its ability to persuade (and sometimes coerce) the suspect to view the act of self-incrimination—and thus self-conviction—as both logical and rational under the circumstances. If successful, the interrogator will have caused the suspect to understand his situation in a way that confessing appears to make sense. Suspects typically make or agree to an admission because they view it as their best choice among the existing options, the only way to put an end to the interrogation, or simply inevitable.

4. Interrogation: Postadmission

Although it receives far less attention from scholars, lawyers, and the media, the postadmission portion of police interrogation is also important because here the investigator and suspect jointly create a narrative of the suspect's culpability. Since the suspect's postadmission narrative will ultimately be treated as his confession, we might conceptualize the postadmission portion as the confession-taking—or perhaps more accurately the confession-*making*—phase of interrogation. Contrary to popular mythology, police investigators typically do not take a "just the facts, ma'am" approach in this phase either. Instead, most make no distinction between preadmission interrogation and postadmission interrogation and often continue to use confrontational, suggestive, and manipulative interrogation techniques if the suspect's answers do not fit their expectations. The suspect's postadmission narrative or confession, then, is not something that is simply taken or elicited. Rather, it is actively shaped and constructed—with the suspect's participation, to be sure, but at the interrogator's direction.

Interrogators seek to orchestrate (some would say choreograph) suspect's postadmission narrative to advance their goal of incriminating him and ensuring his conviction. Once the suspect has been moved from denial to admission, interrogators often seek to confirm their theory of how and why the suspect committed the crime. If the suspect's postadmission narrative does not fit their expectations, interrogators may interrupt the suspect; accuse him of lying; and repeat the evidence ploys, scenarios, inducements, and other techniques that were used in the preadmission portion of the interrogation. Some interrogators will even suggest the correct answers to specific questions or format the desired postadmission narrative for the suspect through leading questions and explicit suggestions and declarations. Interrogators may thus purposefully seek to insert the presence or absence of specific facts, explanations, or motives into the suspect's postadmission narrative to make it appear more believable and to deflect any potential challenges to the confession's authenticity, voluntariness, or reliability.

Interrogation and Plea Bargaining

The Importance of Confession Evidence

"Incrimination," as Doreen McBarnet (1981: 26) has pointed out, "is the first step in the process of conviction." We might reorder this observation by noting that interrogation is often the first step in the process of incrimination. Police interrogation has traditionally been one of the primary strategies of criminal investigation in the American adversary system, for often there is no physical, witness, or other direct evidence linking a suspect to a crime. Instead, detectives may possess anything from indirect evidence to purely circumstantial evidence to suggestive leads to perhaps no evidence at all (only the most speculative of hunches). Regardless of how much or how little evidence they possess, detectives will formulate theories of the crime. The stronger the evidence in their possession, the more likely their theory is accurate; the weaker the evidence, the less likely. Even when the evidence is weak to nonexistent, however, detectives may be highly confident of the intuitive judgments, inferences, or speculations—what they sometimes refer to as their "sixth sense" (Leo, 1996c)—that lead them to focus on a potential suspect. Confessions are especially valuable to detectives when there is weak to nonexistent evidence against a suspect who fits their theory of the crime, as well as in high-profile cases where there is considerable social pressure to generate evidence.

Regardless of the strength of the other case evidence, however, confessions are *always* valuable to detectives because of the manifest and latent functions they serve. First and foremost, confessions allow detectives to "clear" crimes (i.e., close the file and classify the case as solved by arrest), the standard by which most police departments evaluate and reward their detectives. Confessions also make police detectives and departments look good to external audiences—other criminal justice officials, crime victims, the public, the media, and the politicians who determine their yearly budgets—thereby reinforcing the legitimacy and social importance of detective work. But confessions do something in addition that virtually no other type of evidence can do as authoritatively: provide a narrative account of the crime that, because it is presumably in the words of the offender, creates the appearance of authentic answers to existential questions about the crime, thus providing social closure for victims and others (Brooks, 2000).

Perhaps equally important, confessions preserve scarce resources of the criminal justice system because they are regarded as such powerful evidence of the suspect's guilt that they will almost always lead to a conviction, typically by plea bargain. Once a suspect confesses, his case is effectively over: his confession-driven plea bargain spares the state the cost of proving his guilt at trial. Confession evidence thus removes uncertainty from the criminal process while lending efficiency and predictability to the outcome. Confessions ease the workload of overburdened police, prosecutors, judges, and even defense attorneys, making everyone's job easier and, ironically, less susceptible to criticism. Hence confessions, like guilty pleas, are enormously valuable commodities in the American criminal justice system.

Coerced Incrimination and Judicial Leniency

American police interrogation has become very much like plea bargaining— in effect, a kind of backstage session that we might call "pre-plea bargaining" or what Yale Kamisar (1980) has described as plea bargaining without defense attorneys. For cases in which suspects make confessions (estimated to be between 45 and 55 percent of all criminal cases [Thomas, 1996]), interrogation may be even more determinative of case outcomes than plea bargaining because it occurs earlier in the criminal process. It contributes substantially to the amount and direction of plea bargaining by creating a strong disincentive for the suspect—who has already incriminated himself in the most damning of ways—to take his case to trial and risk being convicted of the most serious possible charges and receiving the harshest possible punishment. Like plea bargaining, interrogation is thus facilitative of expedient, negotiated case outcomes even as it represents an end run around adversary trial procedures.

To be sure, there are several important differences: American defendants are represented by counsel and make their confessions in open court, whereas the plea extraction process is recorded and overseen by a judge. Moreover, the criminal defendant who agrees to a plea bargain receives something tangible in return for his public confession—typically a reduction in the type or number of offenses he is being charged with and a corresponding reduction in the type or amount of punishment he will endure—whereas the interrogated suspect typically receives only the illusion of a reduction in charging or punishment in exchange for his private confession. And while the criminal defendant who plea bargains may feel coerced to accept the state's deal, he is not deceived—he understands his situation, the adversarial nature of the procedure, and his options—unlike the suspect in interrogation who is led to believe that incriminating himself is in his self-interest. Perhaps most importantly, the pre-plea bargaining practices of American interrogation offer the suspect no benefit (no charge or sentence reductions) in exchange for his admission of guilt. In this sense, then, interrogation is more like a plea without a bargain, since the suspect usually stands to gain nothing.

Nevertheless, the logic of American police interrogation and that of plea bargaining are remarkably similar: both are based on creating resignation, fear, and the perception that the only way to mitigate punishment is by accepting the state's deal. In both plea bargaining and interrogation, the state attempts to extract a confession to a crime scenario that it believes is at least partially untrue by persuading the suspect or defendant that the state already has strong enough evidence against him to win a conviction at trial; that if the state must take his case to trial, it will extract the maximum punishment possible; but that if the suspect or defendant spares the state the

time and expense of proving his guilt at trial, it will reward him with reduced punishment. The logic of the interrogation process is, in effect, repeated
at the plea bargaining stage in a criminal justice system that, as Rosett and
Cressey (1976: 31) pointed out a long time ago, "from beginning to end
threatens all defendants with severe punishment if they do not plead guilty."
Yet both create the appearance of allowing the accused to negotiate how the
facts of his crime will be constructed and how his culpability will be framed
in order to receive leniency. Both play on our culture's equation of confession with truth while hiding from public view how the truth was determined or constructed. And both interrogation and plea bargaining allow police and prosecutors to rationalize the accused's acceptance of the deal as an
act of contrition rather than a response to the state's coercive powers. The
American system of plea bargaining is fundamentally a system of deal-
making in exchange for self-incrimination—a process that begins during the
investigative stage of detective work, well before the filing of any charges by
the prosecutor, the negotiation of any reductions by defense counsel, or the
ratification of any two-party deals by the judge.

American police interrogation is therefore a kind of "pre-plea bargaining"
because it resembles the potentially coercive psychology of plea bargaining
but occurs prior in time. At the root of virtually every interrogation is the
message, whether implicit or explicit, that the suspect will receive intangible or tangible benefits in exchange for his confession, but that he must
act *now* or the opportunity to "tell his side of the story" will expire along
with the benefits. Psychological interrogation is, by necessity, based on the
appearance or reality of bargaining because the suspect can only come to
see the act of confessing as in his self-interest if he perceives that there is
something to gain from it or a harm to avoid. Although American detectives
do not possess prosecutorial powers, they often imply or overstate their
ability to influence the prosecutor's decision-making and negotiate a charge
or sentence reduction. Their exaggeration is not immediately obvious to un-
sophisticated suspects.

Normative Implications

It is useful to view interrogation as a kind of backroom pre-plea bargaining
because it gives us both greater insight into how police interrogation and
the American process of justice really work and more clarity about what is
normatively at stake in our ethical and policy discussions. Because of their

similarities, plea bargaining and police interrogation pose similar problems for the theory of the adversary system—both allow the state to circumvent adversarial procedures through largely hidden processes that are often regarded as coercive. Both essentially sacrifice the adversarial search for the truth in favor of negotiated outcomes that trade leniency for expedient case resolution. Both therefore threaten to undermine the protection of legal rights and the pursuit of reliable truth-finding that the adversary system, at least in theory, holds as central to its justification and superiority.

Despite these similarities, however, police interrogation may present the more serious problem for adversary theory because it is not only potentially coercive but also routinely fraudulent. The suspect who is induced to confess during interrogation typically not only fails to receive the deal that detectives implied or suggested in exchange for incriminating himself, but receives the exact opposite—more and higher charges, more and harsher punishment (Leo, 1996a). In modern interrogation, then, the suspect who confesses is deceived both about the true nature of the interrogation process and about the consequences of incriminating himself. Thus American police interrogation (like plea bargaining) risks not only eliciting involuntary and unreliable evidence, but also corrupting the integrity of the very adversary procedures that are intended to protect legal rights, check state power, and ensure truthful fact-finding.

Contradictions and Challenges for the Adversary System

The history, structure, and logic of American police interrogation have all been shaped by the culture and imperatives of the adversary system of criminal justice. The interrogation process is, in fact, thoroughly adversarial. This fundamental insight is at odds with the statements of criminal justice officials who treat interrogation as a value-free search for the truth. It is also largely overlooked by psychologists who study interrogation as a method of social influence, criminologists who study it as a method of criminal investigation, and legal scholars who study it as an instance of rule compliance or violation. Interrogators have internalized the values and goals of the adversaries (i.e., the lawyers) and emphasize case-building over impartial investigation and impression management over straight case reporting. By incriminating the suspect, interrogators aim to maximize the likelihood that charges will be filed against him, weaken his position in plea negotiations, and minimize the possibility of an acquittal at trial. Interrogation as practiced in the American adversary system is essentially a prosecutorial function, not an investigative one, even though it is carried out by police detectives.

Contradictions

FRAUD

As I will illustrate empirically in subsequent chapters, interrogation in the American adversary system is fraudulent in multiple ways. Besides obscuring the purpose of the interrogation, pretending that their motivation is really to help the suspect, and conveying that he is best served by confessing, detectives regularly lie to suspects about why they are being questioned, the seriousness of the crime, the evidence the police possess, and sometimes even about the consequences the suspect faces. Detectives also create deceptive and misleading appearances in their construction of the public narrative of the interrogation and the suspect's culpability. In all these ways, modern American interrogation is steeped in artifice, deception, and fraud.

Contemporary police interrogation is inherently fraudulent because of the fundamental contradictions and role conflicts detectives must manage to achieve their goals of incrimination and case-building. The contradictions are multiple and build on one another. On top of detectives' efforts to convince the suspect that it is in his self-interest to confess when that in fact is rarely the case, the American legal system requires that all confessions must be voluntary if they are to be used against a criminal defendant. But to be effective interrogators believe they must persuade a suspect that under the circumstances he has no meaningful choice but to confess. The American criminal justice system does not permit interrogators to threaten harm, promise leniency, or engage in deal-making, yet to be effective interrogators believe they must persuade the suspect that he will receive a tangible benefit in exchange for admitting culpability. The system treats the goal of interrogation as getting the truth, yet to be effective interrogators believe they must regularly rely on deception, outright lies, and sometimes sophisticated forms of trickery. The system permits only reliable evidence to be used against a criminal defendant, yet to be effective police interrogators believe they must actively construct, manipulate, and shape the narrative of the suspect's guilt. American interrogators thus engage in fraud and impression management to resolve the contradictions between their objectives and the legal principles and rhetoric of the adversary system.

Interrogators rationalize their use of fraud and impression management by emphasizing the importance of confession evidence in the criminal justice system. Although ours is an accusatorial system, it is almost entirely dependent on the word of the accused (i.e., in confessions and plea bargains) for solving crimes and convicting offenders. Hence interrogation is the primary investigative strategy in American detective work. Confession evidence possesses two qualities that make it especially attractive to law enforcement. It is socially generative: detectives can create confessions entirely through their social interaction with the suspect. They need not rely on victims, witnesses, crime scene technicians, or laboratories, and thus they can exercise more control over the conditions that lead to confession evidence than they can over virtually all other types of evidence. And, as we've seen, confessions are uniquely potent evidence because criminal justice officials and lay people tend to place more weight on them than on virtually any other type of evidence: confessions close police files, lead prosecutors to file more and higher charges, facilitate favorable plea bargains, sway judges and juries, and win cases (Leo and Ofshe, 1998a).

SECRECY

Another way that American interrogators have managed their role conflicts and contradictions is through secrecy. Secrecy not only serves to hide what occurs in the interrogation room from public view and thus to allow interrogators to avoid criticism, but also prevents a third party from undermining the police's ability to control the public narrative of the interrogation and confession. If there is no objective record of it, American detectives can construct what occurred, as well as how and why it occurred, in a way that most favorably advances their goals. If their account is disputed, the so-called swearing contest over what transpired will almost always be resolved in their favor, because, as they know, they typically have greater status and credibility and present themselves more favorably in courts of law than do most suspects (Kamisar, 1980).

The issue of secrecy runs like a thread throughout the history of American interrogation. It is particularly apparent during times of controversy or scandal, as when the Wickersham Commission in the 1930s focused attention on incommunicado interrogation and the third degree, or when the Warren Court in its 1966 *Miranda* decision focused attention on police-dominated custodial interrogation in secrecy, or when advances in DNA technology in the 1990s focused attention on police-induced false confessions and wrongful conviction of the innocent. The issue tends to disappear from public view once the controversy passes. The use of secrecy, however, may be the Achilles heel of contemporary American interrogation because in the era of inexpensive and reliable technology, police resistance to electronic recording can no longer be easily justified. As more states begin to require it, and as more police managers choose to impose it on their detective staff, electronic recording threatens to expose interrogators' adversarial strategies and thus undermine their ability to effectively manage the contradictions or control the public narrative of the interrogation and confession-taking process.

Challenges

The strategic use of fraud, impression management, and secrecy by American detectives does not, for the most part, violate the laws regulating police interrogation or the admissibility of confession evidence. Their interrogation practices do, however, raise a number of normative concerns about the process and quality of criminal justice in America, as well as evaluative questions about the extent to which the adversary system achieves in practice what it sets out to do in theory. As noted, the adversary system has three overarching objectives: the protection of legal rights, the control of unchecked governmental power, and the search for the truth. Contemporary American police interrogation frustrates each of these goals, to varying degrees, because of the contradiction between the nonadversarial expectations of investigators in theory and their adversarial behavior in practice. Although these issues will become clearer in subsequent chapters, I want to briefly highlight the dilemmas that police interrogation poses for the adversary system and the ideals of American justice.

PROTECTING LEGAL RIGHTS

The adversary system is designed to protect legal rights inside the interrogation room as well as in subsequent stages of the criminal process. The constitutional rights that apply specifically to the interrogation process are the *Miranda* rights, as part of the Fifth Amendment privilege against self-incrimination, and the Fourteenth Amendment right to due process, which is supposed to prevent prosecutors from using any statements police coerced or elicited involuntarily.[2] But *Miranda* is largely irrelevant to modern American police interrogation because detectives typically minimize and blow past the warnings in a moment (Leo, 2001a), and courts rarely suppress confessions on grounds of either it or the Fourteenth Amendment; defense attorneys do not bring suppression motions in most confession cases, and when they do they usually lose. Only a very small percentage of confessions are suppressed by courts as involuntary (Nardulli, 1987).

But there is a deeper sense in which the practice of American police interrogation undercuts the use of legal rights, particularly those a criminal defendant might exercise well after the interrogation has ended. Once the police-shaped narrative of the suspect's culpability has been entered into evidence against him, detectives have restricted his options in the adversary stage of the criminal process and thus weakened his ability to meaningfully exercise his trial rights. As legal scholars have long recognized (Wigmore, 1970; McCormick, 1972) and empirical studies have confirmed (Kassin and Neumann, 1997; Kassin and Sukel, 1997; Leo and Ofshe, 1998a; Drizin and Leo, 2004), because confession evidence is so damning and prejudicial, the subsequent trial (and thus the exercise of trial rights) is often superfluous. In other words, the legal rights that the adversary system seeks to protect at the trial stage of the criminal process may be rendered meaningless by what occurs at the pretrial stage. Trial rights that cannot be meaningfully exercised cannot be meaningfully protected.

CHECKING STATE POWER

Another primary goal of the adversary system is to impose appropriate checks and balances on the use of governmental power, particularly the state's legal powers to deprive citizens of liberty. Because of its historic distrust of concentrated state power, the adversary system creates presumptions, evidentiary burdens, and procedures that should, in theory, be more likely to let ten guilty suspects go free than wrongfully convict one innocent person. If practice is true to theory, there should be some mechanism for effectively regulating the state's power inside the interrogation room, and the balance of advantage should tilt in favor of the presumptively innocent suspect. However, interrogation in the American adversary system is an almost entirely state-dominated and state-manipulated process. Police enjoy a virtual monopoly of unchecked power in the interrogation room. They have the power to isolate, trick, deceive, and psychologically coerce through inducements that they can later deny without fear of contradiction or impeachment. They enjoy powers that the adversary system does not delegate to any other criminal justice official, including the prosecutor (usually regarded as the most powerful official of all). Perhaps detectives' most significant power, though, may be their virtual monopoly on the means of knowledge production about the interrogation, which allows them, in effect, to frame the confession evidence for the rest of the criminal justice system. Absent a third party monitoring the interrogation process or electronic recording of it, there is presently no adequate check on the power of American police interrogators.

PROMOTING TRUTH-FINDING

The third primary goal of the adversary system—which is subordinate to the first two—is the promotion of truth-finding. On the surface, contemporary American police interrogation appears to pose the fewest problems for the realization of this goal. In the age of psychological interrogation, most people tend to assume that all confessions are truthful—that is largely what makes them appear to be such potent evidence of guilt. Lay people typically do not believe that an innocent person would falsely confess to a crime unless the interrogators used physical coercion or the suspect was mentally ill. I call this *the myth of psychological interrogation* (Leo, 2001b: 36–37). Although there are no scientifically valid estimates of their incidence or prevalence, police-induced false confessions occur with troubling frequency in the American criminal justice system. Social scientists, legal scholars, and independent writers have documented numerous police-induced false confessions in recent years, many of which led to the wrongful prosecution, conviction, and imprisonment of the factually innocent (Drizin and Leo, 2004). Researchers no longer disagree about whether police-induced false confessions occur, but only about what should be done to prevent them.

But the problem of reliability in American interrogation is not limited to police-induced false confessions. As currently practiced, the interrogation process is fraught with the potential for unreliability and error, even from those suspects who were involved in the crime under investigation. To appreciate this point, we must remember that before any interrogation detectives have not only concluded that the suspect is guilty, but they have also formed a theory of his participation. The theory may be wrong about the big or small details of the crime (i.e., the suspect did not participate in the way or to the degree the interrogator theorizes), or detectives may not care whether they get all the details right so long as they elicit an admission of guilt. The interrogation process sometimes leads the guilty to comply with the detectives' wishes and *over-confess* to the crime for the same reasons that it sometimes leads the innocent to comply and falsely confess. Moreover, once detectives receive an erroneous admission from the guilty, they may manipulate and shape the partially false postadmission narrative to create the appearance that the suspect's confession is voluntary, reliable, and self-corroborating—even if it is none of these. The problem of partially false confessions from the guilty is compounded and reinforced by the secrecy in most American interrogations, thus preventing anyone from seeing the extent to which the erroneous postadmission narrative is the product of manipulation and suggestion. The problem of partially false confessions from the guilty may occur even more frequently than false confessions from the innocent. While most confessions in the American adversary system do not appear to be entirely false, many statements are at least partially unreliable.

These, then, are the central dilemmas for the practice of police interrogation in the American adversary system: how to structure or monitor the interrogation process in a way that simultaneously protects legal rights, checks police power, and promotes truth-finding. These dilemmas are aggravated by the deep-seated impulse of American interrogators to favor adversarial case-building over investigative fact-finding, secrecy over openness, and impression management over impartial case reporting. Critics of the adversary system tend to overlook the problem of zealous police investigation in the preadversary stage of the criminal process because they tend to focus their critiques almost exclusively on what occurs during the adversary stage. But what occurs at the preadversary stage may be even more influential on case processing and outcomes. When detectives intentionally fail to preserve a record of the process through which they obtained and shaped the most damning case evidence possible at the preadversary stage, there simply cannot be a level playing field between the state and the accused at the adversary stage.

FAIRNESS

Beyond the tripartite goals of the adversary system, there is also the enduring question of fairness that bedevils adversary criminal procedure and which in American legal discourse ultimately is framed as an issue of due process. Virtually all of the interrogation techniques that I have described in this chapter are not considered a violation of due process by American courts, but that does not resolve the issue of fairness. In most social contexts, the use of psychological manipulation and deception is regarded as unfair, if not unethical. Further, the use of fraud by interrogators is unique even in law: the American legal system does not permit other state officials to use fraud to achieve their objectives or dispense justice, nor does it permit police detectives to use fraud in other stages of the criminal process (such as when they are writing police reports or testifying in court). To many observers, police use of fraud and deception in the interrogation room is problematic not so much because of its effect on case outcomes but because of its corrupting influence on the integrity of adversary procedures and human interaction in the criminal justice system (Skolnick and Leo, 1992; Young, 1996).

The central moral questions for the study of American police interrogation are: What value should we place on confession evidence and what means should we permit police to use to elicit and shape it? How appellate courts and lawmakers answer these two questions will ultimately determine how the legal system confronts the inherent contradictions of psychological interrogation in the adversary system. These contradictions can be managed in different ways (some more favorable to the state, others more favorable to the accused), but they are not easily resolved. While courts and legislatures may impose more or fewer rules on police detectives, the contradictions at the heart of psychological interrogation are not likely to go away absent structural changes in the American process of justice.

But to ask these questions is to get ahead of the story of American police interrogation, which begins in the era of the third degree.

CHAPTER 2

The Third Degree

Against a hardened criminal I never hesitated. I've forced confessions—with fist, black-jack, and hose—from men who would
have continued to rob and to kill if I had not made them talk. The
hardened criminal knows only one language and laughs at the
detective who tries any other . . . Remember that this is war after
all! I'm convinced my tactics saved many lives.

    —Cornelius Willemse (1931)

If the Constitution be taken as law, it would be hard to find anything more illegal—if it be taken as defining Americanism, nothing
could be found more un-American—than the third degree.

    —Ernest Jerome Hopkins (1931)

Men will respect the law only when the law is respectable. The
method of administering justice is often more important than
justice itself.

    —George Wickersham (1931)

On August 1, 1930, Christine Colletti was murdered and left
lying on the side of an abandoned road with five bullet wounds (Wickersham Commission Files). Shortly after learning the next day of his wife's
death, Tony Colletti, an eighteen-year-old Cleveland resident, accompanied
plainclothes detectives to police headquarters for what he was told would
be routine questioning. During the car ride to the station, Detectives Corso
and Welch told Colletti that they knew "what really happened" and instructed Colletti to "come clean" and tell them about the murder. Colletti
responded—as he would many times over the next two days—that he did
not know what the detectives were talking about. He had last seen his wife

the night before and was as surprised as everyone else to learn of her murder, he said.

At the station house over the next twenty-six hours, Tony Colletti was questioned nonstop, lied to, threatened, screamed and cursed at, deprived of food and water, and made to stand for hours. He was slugged with bare fists, stripped naked, and beaten with a rubber hose. Finally, under this punishment, he stopped denying that he had killed his wife and agreed to sign a confession.

At the beginning of Tony Colletti's interrogation, Detective Hogan expressed sympathy for Colletti while commenting on Christine's bad reputation in the neighborhood. Hogan did not blame Colletti for killing his wife, he said—adding that he would have done the same thing. After twenty minutes of polite questioning, Detective Cody stormed into the interrogation room, slammed two guns down on the table, and falsely declared that they had been found at Colletti's house and been used to kill Christine. When Tony Colletti again professed his innocence, Detective Cody ominously replied, "I'm going to get permission to abuse this fellow like they do in Detroit, hang him up by his feet, beat him up and kick him in the testicles—that will make him talk" (Wickersham Commission Files). Colletti was then shuttled between rooms at the Cleveland Police Department and questioned incommunicado in relays by Detectives Corso, Welch, Cody, Wolf, and Hogan.

The detectives made Colletti stand facing a wall for hours as they questioned and fired accusations at him. They slapped him whenever he appeared to fall asleep. The detectives denied his requests for water and food, and refused to let him sit down or lean against the wall. They jolted him whenever his knees sagged or he sought support from the wall. Detective Welch repeatedly punched him just below the ribs on both sides and slapped him in the back of the head, causing Colletti's face to strike the wall. Although the rooms and detectives changed, the assaults and deprivation continued for hours. The detectives hit Colletti countless times—sometimes two detectives worked him over simultaneously—and threatened him with worse if he did not confess. They would eventually make him talk, they snarled. But Colletti continued to deny any involvement.

After hours of relentless grilling and frequent physical assaults, the detectives again moved Colletti to another room. This time they made him lie naked on a table. One of the detectives held Colletti's left arm while pushing his head down; another held his right arm, and a third held his two legs.

Detective Corso then pulled out a two-and-a-half-foot piece of rubber hose and proceeded to beat Colletti's bare back and the soft hollows above his ribs for about an hour. "Will you talk?" Corso intermittently asked. Each time, Colletti responded that he had nothing to say and reasserted his innocence (Wickersham Commission Files).

But eventually Tony Colletti had taken all that he could. With his back, kidneys, and sides swollen and bruised, he told the detectives, "I will say what you want me to say if you let up, stop beating me." As Colletti struggled to get up from the table, he added: "I don't know what you want me to tell you, but you can make up a statement and I will sign it" (Wickersham Commission Files).

Then, for the first time in more than twenty-four hours, the detectives provided Tony Colletti with food and water. He was taken to another interrogation room to wait with two of the detectives as his statement was being typed up. When, after a change in heart, Colletti told them that he would not sign it, one of the detectives responded: "If you don't sign it, we'll give you the works worse than we did before" (Wickersham Commission Files). Shortly afterwards, two detectives returned to the room and laid the typewritten paper in front of Colletti. It contained what he had told them, they said. Colletti hesitated momentarily, then quickly signed the statement without even reading it. He was then treated by a police nurse and doctor for his injuries and taken to jail.

Only when he read the local newspaper the next day did Tony Colletti discover the contents of the confession he had signed. The Cleveland Police Department subsequently denied beating or mistreating him. It claimed that his welts and bruises were caused by sleeping on his side.[1]

By the standards of the time, there was nothing unusual about the manner in which Cleveland detectives obtained a confession from Colletti (Hopkins, 1931). His interrogation was in many ways representative of the methods police generally used in the early 1930s in America. In fact, detectives frequently employed far more violent ways to extract admissions of guilt, and over even longer periods of time (Lavine, 1930; Hopkins, 1931; Wickersham Commission Report, 1931). What had come to be known in American popular culture as the "third degree"—the infliction of physical pain or mental suffering to extract information—was, by virtually all accounts, widely and systematically practiced (Wickersham Commission Report, 1931). Tony Colletti's case was unremarkable for yet another reason: it never became the subject of an appellate court ruling or published court decision, and, as in virtually every instance of the third degree in the era, the detectives were never disciplined or punished.

Yet only ten years later, W. R. Kidd, a former Berkeley police lieutenant, would condemn third-degree practices as "vicious and useless" (Kidd, 1940: 46-47) in the first police interrogation training manual ever published in America:

Third degree should never be used by the police because:

1. It does not produce the truth. Under sufficient torture, a man will tell you anything you want to know. If you build your case on this "confession" you may find in court the man could not possibly have committed the crime.
2. Evidence so obtained is not admissible in court, and defense attorneys are quick to develop the facts surrounding the securing of the statement.
3. Public confidence in the police is shattered if knowledge of such methods is publicized. Unless the suspect dies, it is difficult to prevent such publicity. If he dies, a terrific public protest is inevitable.

Under third degree, only three things can happen to the suspect:

1. He will tell anything desired.
2. He will go insane if the torture is severe enough.
3. He will die.

Perhaps the greatest harm done by third-degree methods lies in the eventual harm to the department. Once the public is convinced such methods are used, it becomes extremely difficult for the police to convict anyone, no matter how guilty, nor how good the police case. Judges and juries are ready to believe the defense contention that third-degree methods were used. The case goes out the window. The police, unable to obtain convictions, take it out "first hand" on the criminals, usually with the nightstick, and the cycle becomes more and more vicious.

In the decade separating Tony Colletti's case and the publication of Kidd's manual, the third degree had become a national scandal. Numerous media accounts and exposés, several Supreme Court decisions, and a well-known government commission report—the "Report on Lawlessness in Law Enforcement" from President Herbert Hoover's National Commission of Law Observance and Law Enforcement, which came to be known as "The Wickersham

Report"[2] after its chair, former attorney general George Wickersham—all had condemned strong-arm interrogation methods and called for immediate reform. The chorus of criticism included the voices of many police leaders and trainers whose larger agenda was to professionalize the occupation of policing. In the 1940s and 1950s, several more interrogation training manuals—all exhorting detectives to avoid third-degree practices altogether—would appear and circulate widely among the nation's police departments. Whereas in the 1920s many police leaders and detectives had publicly defended third-degree interrogation methods as necessary for controlling crime, by the 1940s police leaders universally condemned the third degree as unacceptable under all circumstances. With the spread of so-called scientific forms of crime detection as well as new training and education requirements, American police soon came to see the third degree as not only unprofessional and illegal but also as less effective at eliciting confessions than modern interrogation techniques, and thus dispensable. As one FBI agent aptly noted, "The special agent questioning a prisoner uses no special compulsions . . . The third degree isn't necessary when you've got the facts. Special agents get the facts" (Purvis, 1936: 102).

The third degree has long since become the exception rather than the norm in police work. It appears to have declined dramatically in the 1930s and 1940s, and further still in the 1950s, though violence sometimes persisted in some smaller and more rural departments. By the middle of the 1960s, the revolution in interrogation practices seemed complete: police methods became entirely psychological in nature. Indeed, as the President's Commission on Criminal Justice and the Administration of Justice declared in 1967, "Today the third degree is virtually non-existent" (Zimring and Frase, 1979: 132). Police interrogators in the 1960s were no longer criticized for the use of force or duress but for failing to give or properly announce the *Miranda* rights to silence and legal counsel before commencing any custodial questioning. Although the media occasionally report police violence and other physical abuse during interrogations (see, e.g., Conroy, 2000), third-degree practices appear to be rare in contemporary America.

In this chapter, I explore the practice and consequences of third-degree interrogation in the nineteenth and early twentieth centuries. My goal is not merely to document the history of the third degree in America but to deepen our understanding of the historical backdrop and larger context in which modern psychological interrogation emerged in the 1940s. The delegitimation and decline of the third degree represents a crucial turning point in the history of American police investigation. To understand fully the evolution and character of contemporary interrogation practices, it is essential to take a closer look at the third degree—modern psychological interrogation grew out of it and in many ways has been a response to its excesses, criticisms, and contradictions.

The Third Degree: Varieties of Extreme Interrogation

The term "third degree" connotes, in American folklore, extreme interrogation. The Wickersham Commission (1931: 19) defined the third degree as "the employment of methods which inflict suffering, physical or mental, upon a person in order to obtain information about a crime." But a broader definition may be necessary to appreciate fully the significance of the third degree as an institutional practice. From the hindsight of more than seventy years, it is clear that the third degree was, in essence, a totalitarian practice. That is, it was not simply the infliction of pain or suffering to extract incriminating information but the creation of an environment in which police could inflict punishment and terror virtually *without restraint*. Its characteristic features are that it occurs during custodial detention, involves use of physical force or psychological duress, and is primarily intended to extort admissions and confessions. Because there was no effective mechanism of restraint on police power inside the interrogation room, the third degree was fundamentally lawless.

The Wickersham Commission used "third degree" as an overarching term to refer to a variety of coercive interrogation strategies, ranging from psychological duress, such as prolonged confinement, to physical violence and extreme torture. As Hopkins (1931: 194) wrote in the heyday of the third degree: "There are a thousand forms of compulsion; our police show great ingenuity in the variety employed." There were purely physical techniques, purely psychological ones, and many that incorporated both physical and psychological elements. Some were simple and straightforwardly brutal while others were more sophisticated. Regardless, the third degree in all its forms contained a master psychological logic—the infliction of terror to elicit compliance and extract admissions. We can divide the third degree into several different subcategories. Each type was routinely and systematically practiced in most American police stations through at least the early 1930s (Wickersham Commission Report, 1931).

Physical Force and Physical Abuse

BLATANT PHYSICAL ABUSE

Most fundamentally, coercive interrogation entailed naked use of physical violence. Suspects were beaten and kicked all over their bodies. They were hit with nightsticks and blackjacks, pistol butts, leather saps loaded with lead, slabs of wood, chairs, and baseball bats. They were whipped with rubber hoses and leather straps, beaten on the soles of their bare feet with copper-bound rulers, and punched in the face, most commonly with clenched fists, sometimes with brass knuckles, less frequently with boxing gloves (Wickersham Commission Report, 1931). Sometimes suspects would be showered with blows while they were handcuffed or their hands were held or tied behind their backs. Other times they were kicked and stomped on by a group of officers, or clubbed and felled from behind with no forewarning (Lavine, 1930). Variations included holding up or hanging a handcuffed suspect over the top of an open door and pretending that he was a human punching bag, taking two or three running steps across the room and striking a suspect in his stomach, clubbing suspects repeatedly at the point of the knee-jerk reflex in order to cause temporary paralysis, and striking three direct punches directly over the heart. Suspects were knocked onto the floor, across the room, and down flights of stairs, and sometimes rendered unconscious (Wickersham Commission Report, 1931).

The injuries suspects received from such physical assaults frequently—though not always—left marks. Some police beatings ("hospital cases," in police jargon) were so vicious that suspects required immediate medical aid; some suspects spent days, even weeks, recovering from their injuries. In rare cases, suspects were beaten so severely that they subsequently died (Ageloff, 1928). Police reporters and prison personnel frequently observed healthy individuals entering police stations and later leaving with bloodied clothing, bruises, and swollen faces (Murphy, 1929). Judges sometimes asked suspects to remove articles of clothing and discovered that their bodies looked like raw meat (Wickersham Commission Files). One magistrate interviewed by the Wickersham Commission complained that some suspects would come into court with their faces so bandaged that only their eyes showed (Wickersham Commission Files).

Although nonpolice personnel were rarely allowed to witness interrogations, New York reporter Emanuel Lavine (1930, 1936) spent twenty-five years observing the police, including custodial interrogations. Lavine reported that the brute application of physical force—what the police referred to as a "shellacking," "massaging," or "workout"—was routine and systematic during station house questioning, estimating that 70 percent of criminal cases were solved by confessions wrung from in-custody suspects. Lavine (1930) witnessed one suspect who, with his head pulled back, was repeatedly beaten across the Adam's apple with a blackjack until blood spurted out of his mouth halfway across the room. In another interrogation, Lavine observed two suspects who were first beaten with a lead pipe and then transferred to another police station where they were beaten by a gang of officers as they lay prostrate on the floor; six nightsticks were broken on them. Lavine also witnessed police officers press both of their fists like a vise against a suspect's jaw with such force that it dislocated and in some instances broke the bone. The more intransigent the suspect, Lavine noted, the greater the punishment. But "there is nothing, from the police point of view, exceptional or startling in the application of the third degree; it is simply a part of the normal routine," he found (Lavine, 1930: 5). Lavine's account of rampant third-degree violence is corroborated by firsthand accounts of other sources, including other police reporters (Sedgwick, 1927), suspects who received the third degree (Sutton, 1976), and police officers who administered it (Fiaschetti, 1930a, b).

Still other documented forms of physical abuse included putting lighted cigars, matches, or red-hot pokers against a suspect's feet, arms, neck, or chest (O'Sullivan, 1928); tying a suspect's hands around a hot water pipe or placing his body against a furnace (O'Dwyer, 1987); banging a suspect's head against a wall (Wickersham Commission Report, 1931); and, in at least one instance, enlisting a dentist to drill into the nerves of a suspect's molars (Lavine, 1930). Sometimes blindfolds were employed (*Harvard Law Review*, 1930).

DENIABLE PHYSICAL ABUSE

Many physically abusive interrogation tactics were intended to be deniable in court, for police well knew that visible marks might arouse the sympathy of judges and juries, or perhaps even cause the district attorney not to use the confession at all. The most famous and probably the most common of these tactics was the use of a rubber hose, which did not break the skin (Wickersham Commission Report, 1931). A variation of this tactic, known as "the taps," involved tying a suspect to an armchair and then striking him on the side of the head at thirty-second intervals. Although the blows were not hard enough to bring on unconsciousness and although the welts disappeared within a few hours, they caused considerable pain and thereafter left the point of contact sensitive for as long as several months (Lavine, 1930).

Police also used garden hoses, pieces of tire, sausage-shaped sandbags lined with silk, and blackjacks soaked in water, wrapped in a handkerchief, or covered with soft leather (O'Sullivan, 1928). "An interesting Chicago discovery was that the local telephone book, weighing several pounds, would knock a man down if swung hard enough against his ear, yet would leave no marks, being soft," Hopkins (1931: 219) noted. This was a popular method of extracting confessions before the Wickersham exposure. Sometimes a suspect was seated on a bench between two detectives who questioned him alternately, jarring the suspect with an elbow to his ribs, a shove to his chin, or a slap on his face each time he provided a negative answer (Wickersham Commission Files). Another common method was hitting a suspect with a "fist to the wind," (i.e., blow to the solar plexus) not only because it weakened him without leaving marks but also because he quickly recovered (Wickersham Commission Files). Other prominent forms of deniable coercion included administering tear gas, sometimes into a large wooden box that had been placed over the suspect's head (Wickersham Commission Files); choking a suspect with a necktie; bringing a suspect to the morgue to view and touch the body of the victim (Willemse, 1931); bending a suspect's fingers or twisting his wrists or arms backwards (Henderson, 1924); forcing him to stand for hours on end, often while manacled (Wickersham Commission Report, 1931); and, of course, issuing threats.

Interrogators often focused on beating certain areas of the body—such as the back, the pit of the stomach, the kidneys, and above the hipbones—that were less likely to blister or bleed (Booth, 1930). An unwritten rule in many police departments was to avoid hitting suspects above the shoulders precisely because physical marks were more likely to show there. Sometimes detectives delayed letting a doctor see a suspect to give the bruises time to disappear. Other documented forms of deniable physical abuse included dragging or lifting a suspect by his hair, sometimes pulling the hair out of his head and stuffing it into his mouth (Murphy, 1929); hanging him out of a window or suspending him in a room by steel handcuffs around his ankles (Hopkins, 1931); forcing him to strip and placing him in an interrogation cell with sub-freezing temperatures (Willemse, 1931); and stripping and immersing him in a tub filled with crushed ice and cold water (O'Sullivan, 1928).

Interrogators frequently struck the suspect from behind so that he could not see the person who hit him and thus would be unable to identify him in court (Wickersham Commission, 1931). Occasionally detectives even wore masks. Or the arresting officer might turn the "rough work" over to another detective so that he could truthfully assert in court that he had neither touched the suspect nor seen him harmed by other police (Hopkins, 1931).

ORCHESTRATED PHYSICAL ABUSE

Some methods resembled downright torture. The famous Sweat Box treatment dates back to the Civil War and was a standard interrogation tactic in some police departments (Haller, 1976). It involved placing a suspect, sometimes for hours or days at a time, in a small, dark cell adjoined by a stove in which miscellaneous materials were used to stir a fire that produced scorching heat and pungent odors. Sickened, perspiring, and unable to endure the rising temperature, the suspect was compelled to confess (Sylvester, 1910). The Water Cure consisted of holding a suspect's head in water until he almost drowned; thrusting a water hose into his mouth or even down his throat; or forcing a suspect to lie on his back (if he was not already strapped to a cot or slab) while pouring water into his nostrils, sometimes from a dipper, until he was nearly drowned (O'Sullivan, 1928).

Another method of torture was to force suspects to walk barefoot on an electrically wired mat or carpet, causing sparks to fly and the suspect to scream and dance in agony until he confessed or fainted (Villard, 1927). A variation was to strap a suspect into a makeshift or real electric chair and administer electric shocks until he confessed (*International Police Magazine*, 1911). In one city, police invented a technique known as "the electric monkey" consisting of a storage battery connected to a device with two terminals: one pole was placed against the suspect's spine and another was held in his hands as currents were charged through his body (Hopkins, 1931).

Another ingenious instrument of third-degree torture was the cannonball. Police placed a heavy cannonball several feet above the floor in a box that was fastened to a wall. They closed the box with a sliding door, to which a trap was affixed and annexed to a cord. The trap, when sprung, opened the door and released the cannonball. The suspect would be bound and placed under the box. One of his legs would be elevated at right angles to his body, and the cord attached to the spring would be tied around his ankle. If he moved his leg toward the floor at all, the trap would be sprung and the cannonball released. The suspect would be taunted by police, who would insist that he was weakening—and thus that the cannonball would soon be dropped and crush his head (Villard, 1927).

Perhaps the most well known interrogation tactic in American culture is the so-called good cop/bad cop act or Mutt and Jeff routine (also known as the "hard and soft method"). Here a pair or team of detectives attempts to extract a confession by alternating between hostile and sympathetic appeals to the suspect. The good cop/bad cop act used to be routinely violent, involving the use of physical force as well as psychological appeals. Long after his conviction, one suspect named Schlager described this technique in detail to a police reporter who was subsequently interviewed by the Wickersham Commission (Wickersham Commission Files). After Schlager received beatings in his cell, the officers would disappear,

> and then would enter an officer named Burns—described as a grey haired, kindly-looking man—who posed as Schlager's "friend." Burns would hear Schlager's complaint of mistreatment and express indignation. "Who were they? Tell me and I'll report them—I'll have them thrown off the force." Schlager could not identify them because of the darkness. Burns would promise an investigation; also he brought Schlager coffee, cigarettes, etc., and then would disappear. Soon afterward the strong-arm squad would enter his cell again and "put him through" some more; then Burns would come in again.

After two to four nights of this, Schlager confessed to Burns.

Isolation, Deprivation, and Duress

INCOMMUNICADO INTERROGATION

According to the Wickersham Commission, the most common form of coercive interrogation consisted of prolonged incommunicado questioning under conditions of extreme psychological pressure. The Commission (1931: 111) noted that "the holding of a suspect *incommunicado* is regarded by police as essential to the entire process of obtaining a confession. Orders are given to permit no one, even an attorney, to see the suspect. This is admittedly illegal, but felt to be necessary." The purpose of incommunicado interrogation was to elicit a confession while hiding suspects from friends, family, and especially their attorneys and the courts. Suspects were detained for long periods—usually twenty-four to ninety-six hours, less frequently one to two weeks—and questioned continuously in relays, sometimes without rest or food or even a chance to sit down (Wickersham Commission Report, 1931). Some suspects were not even booked prior to questioning, their arrests unrecorded on the police blotter for days so that no attorney could locate them (a common police practice known as "losing" the suspect). Police might mislead counsel or friends as to the suspect's place of detention, charge him with a different unsolved felony every forty-eight hours, or book him on "vagrancy" or "open" charges. Sometimes suspects were forced or tricked into signing affidavits disavowing their attorneys altogether (Lavine, 1930). With such tactics, police frequently succeeded in delaying a suspect's arraignment before a magistrate for days, even weeks. Although defense attorneys sometimes filed habeas corpus writs requesting permission to see their clients, judges often delayed the operation of the writs (and thus the time when the suspect had to be returned) to permit police more time to obtain confessions (Hopkins, 1931).

During incommunicado interrogation detectives often "grilled" and "sweated" suspects in exhaustive relay questioning that frequently involved severe verbal bullying of the accused. One common tactic was to shine a bright, blinding strobe light continuously on a suspect's face, or to turn it on and off. Another strategy was to require a suspect to remain standing upright for hours on end, slapping or jolting him whenever his knees sagged or he started to fall asleep (Wickersham Commission Report, 1931). In some cities suspects were transferred between a dozen or more police stations, generally for two to three days at a time (or until there was a risk that an attorney might find them), an experience that could last up to six weeks and usually left them in terrible physical condition (Clark and Eubank, 1927). During such trips, suspects were often provided only short rations of food and water, and forced to sleep on hard benches or cement floors. They were confined in overcrowded, cold, damp cells, which were sometimes infested with cockroaches, mosquitoes, or rats (Limpus, 1939). As the Wickersham Commission (1931: 154) noted,

> through illegal detention, time is obtained for police investigation. . . . It may also be effective in "softening" the prisoner and making him more ready to confess. Especially is this so where, as in more than one city, many prisoners are jammed into the same cell, with the result that the air is vile, the sanitary facilities inadequate, the surroundings filthy and verminous, and sleep or rest

next to impossible. Illegal detention is at times definitely used for purposes of compulsion—prisoners are told they will be detained until they confess.

FOOD, SLEEP, AND OTHER DEPRIVATIONS

Many suspects were deprived of food, drink, sleep, or toilet facilities to obtain confessions. Food and drink could be withheld for days at a time, and a suspect could be kept awake to the point of acute exhaustion, or regularly woken and harassed after brief periods of sleep. Another tactic was to keep drugs—ranging from tobacco to heroin—from an addict until he confessed (Larson, 1932). According to Willemse (1931: 351):

> A drug addict is easy. Bring him into your office after he has been deprived for a long period of the drug he craves. Wild for a sniff or a jab, he sees on your desk a package of cocaine, heroin or morphine. "A sniff when you open up, not before!" Hours of that treatment, while he gets wilder by the minute, his whole body crawling for a shot. He breaks in the end, always.

Police also provided addicts with drugs (most commonly alcohol and marijuana) prior to interrogation to induce admissions (Booth, 1930). A variation was to starve a suspect and then place before him an elaborately prepared meal, permitting him to eat only after he confessed (O'Sullivan, 1928).

EXPLICIT THREATS OF HARM

Suspects were often threatened with death or severe bodily injury: they were hung out of windows, threatened with mob violence or violence to their families, or told at gunpoint that they would be shot and killed immediately if they did not confess (Larson, 1932). Lavine (1930) witnessed interrogations in which officers placed a gun against the temple of suspects and discharged blank cartridges until they confessed (known as the "black gun treatment"). Police sometimes threatened to pour acid on suspects' bodies, dig out their eyes with garden forks, or simply punch them in the face with brass knuckles (Wickersham Commission Report, 1931). At other times, suspects were merely threatened with incommunicado imprisonment or prosecution for additional crimes if they did not confess (Hopkins, 1931).

Interrogators also staged mock executions. A suspect might hear loud screams, groans of agony, the thud of falling bodies, and other bloodcurdling noises emanate from an adjacent room. The message: the suspect would get the same if he did not confess (Franklin, 1970), or an innocent party would continue suffering until then (Larson, 1932).

Cornelius Willemse (1931: 345–346) recounted his approach:

> I opened a drawer of my desk. The prisoner could see blackjacks and lengths of rubber hose. A careful selection, and I drew out a long, black piece of hose, testing it in my hands and then with a swish through the air before placing it on top of the desk. A loud moan from the next room, breaking off into sobs. The door opened suddenly. There stood the two detectives, ready for more action. Coats and vests off, shirt-sleeves rolled up, hair disarranged. "One minute boys. I'll call you if you're needed!" The sound of groans had swelled. As the door closed again there came a stifled shriek. At last I spoke to the prisoner.

The Third Degree and the American Process of Justice

Secrecy and Complicity

The third degree thrived on secrecy. Most third-degree interrogation occurred during secret detention in isolated or removed locations, including the patrol wagon, police basements, police garages, and sometimes even hotels or morgues (Wickersham Commission Report, 1931). But usually police administered the third degree at the station house in upstairs or back rooms. Most police stations had interrogation cells—known as "incommunicado" or "third degree" rooms—specifically designed for this purpose (such as the old "Goldfish" room in Chicago);[3] in some places, such as New York City, they were equipped with instruments of torture (Hopkins, 1931: 212–213). Police also "third degreed" suspects at outlying police stations so that journalists would be less likely to learn about it, friends and family would be less likely to intervene, the accused would be less able to contact a lawyer or bail bondsman, and high-ranking police officials could more easily deny any knowledge of the process.

In some cities, when police would "lose" the suspect by moving him from station house to station house, the third degree could be prolonged for days and even weeks. In Philadelphia, such movement was known as placing the suspect in "cold storage," and in Detroit as "sending a man around the loop." The Wickersham Commission (1931: 121) described the practice:

> The outlying stations are used in preference to headquarters because there are no outsiders around. The shifts are said to be generally made at midnight

in the patrol wagon. All told, there are 15 stations. In some cases, it is said, men go the entire circuit. In other cases, seven or eight stations are deemed sufficient. As a part of the process, the jailers have been ordered at times to jam as many men as possible into one cell so they have to squeeze the door shut with two jailers shoving the door. It has been said that the police order is that these men sent "around the loop" shall not be "overfed"; and that opportunities for keeping clean or for sleeping are poor. This is accompanied by the additional discomfort that arises from the knowledge that they are, to all intents and purposes, completely lost . . . In some instances the police have themselves been unable to find a man for some days because of the absence of records.

The police practiced the third degree in secret because it violated public and legal norms of acceptable police behavior. The third degree was never openly legitimate in America. Even in its heyday, most cases were not reported by the media. Police feared that if the veil of secrecy was lifted, the media would publicize the third degree, prosecutors would not use confessions, judges would bar confession evidence at trial, and juries would acquit defendants en masse. Moreover, criminal prosecution of the police who administered it could result, empowering their victims to file civil lawsuits. As Columbia law professor Raymond Moley (1932: 197) observed, "the essential problem of the third degree is not so much whether this method of securing evidence is actually used as whether the public believes it is being used." For this reason, the police were often careful to hide the third degree from the media, and it was less likely to be used in high-profile cases that garnered sustained media attention. Before publication of the Wickersham Commission Report in 1931, the police largely succeeded in keeping the third degree from becoming a major public scandal.

The third degree required the complicity of other criminal justice officials. Such officials might be regarded as "facilitators" of police violence for ignoring, excusing, supporting, or even rewarding it (Huggins, Haritos-Fatouros, and Zimbardo, 2002: xviii). A former police commissioner told the Wickersham Commission (1931: 196) how police managers facilitated the third degree without directly participating in or observing it:

Two detectives would take the suspect into a room and question him. The commissioner made it a point to be there at the start and listen to the first of the questioning, without taking part himself: "Suppose we had reason to believe a man knew something. I would then go out of the room and be absent for a while. Then I would return and ask, 'Has he talked yet?' Often enough the answer would be, 'Yes, he has talked.' In that case I wouldn't need to ask any questions, but I would know that probably the detectives had slapped him a few times, perhaps hit him with the fist, or twisted his arms a little."

Most criminal justice officials simply denied that the third degree existed (Larson, 1932). Jail keepers and bondsmen were silent. Prosecutors publicly denied any knowledge of the third degree, though they privately acknowledged its existence and sometimes even justified its use. One told the Wickersham Commission (1931: 45): "In case one is convinced that the accused is withholding information necessary to connect and discover the facts, then, in my opinion, threats, deprivation of food and sleep, and in fact anything short of absolute physical torture is justified. The 'rule of reason' should be applied, however, in order that injustice may not be done to an innocent man." Prosecutors almost always used confessions in their cases, regardless of the violent methods through which police had elicited them. In some instances, prosecutors even participated in "third degreeing" suspects (Wickersham Commission Report, 1931: 48). Trial judges were complicit too. As Hopkins (1931: 121) wrote, "judicial responsibility for this abuse is great." Trial judges did nothing to stop the third degree. Like other criminal justice officials, they were silent and seemingly indifferent to it (Wickersham Commission Report, 1931). Judges knowingly permitted the illegal detention and false imprisonment on which the third degree thrived, and virtually always upheld confessions that were alleged to be the product of third-degree methods (and in some instances bore the marks of violence). As Sedgwick (1927: 667) observed, "The third degree is known to all who have associated with policemen, but it is one of those things which is winked at and tolerated." Even defense attorneys sometimes failed to challenge it because of the difficulty of corroboration and judicial indifference to their claims.

The Consequences of the Third-Degree System

ADMINISTERING PUNISHMENT AND DISPENSING JUSTICE

Though an underground practice, the third degree significantly influenced police behavior both inside and outside the interrogation room as well as in the criminal justice system more generally. Perhaps most fundamentally, it expanded the range of objectives that police perceived they could accomplish through interrogation. In an adversary system, the purpose of interrogation in theory is to elicit truthful information that aids police in investigating crimes; under the third-degree regime, however, the purpose became primarily to incriminate the accused by forcing confessions. Police were not discovering case evidence so much as creating it through coercion.

Police also often used the third degree to exact punishment and retribution, unleashing "revenge beatings" (Lavine, 1930). Because some criminal suspects were connected to political machines, the police believed that they were, in effect, immunized from prosecution. Thus police would arrest them, beat them up, and then release them without charge (Franklin, 1970). Cops used physical force on them to enforce their own sense of justice, sometimes even hospitalizing suspects (Hopkins, 1930). "Many of the most dangerous and vicious criminals of the period had not a single conviction against them, but carried the marks and scars of police beatings to their grave," as one author wrote (Franklin, 1970: 57).

Police also used the third degree to extract confessions that justified baseless arrests or illegal detentions, protected the identity of their informants (who did not need to reveal their identity once there was a confession), induced plea bargains (thus covering up unlawful arrests, detention, and interrogation methods), and compelled "undesirables" to leave town (Lavine, 1930). The third degree became an entrenched system of administering punishment and dispensing justice. By formally accusing suspects of criminal activity, police partially usurped the prosecutorial function of district attorneys; by adjudicating the guilt or innocence of suspects, police partially usurped the fact-finding function of juries; and by employing physical force or psychological duress against suspects, police partially usurped the punitive function of courts. Hopkins (1931: 196) described the third degree as a "pre-trial secret inquisition" and argued (1931: 200–204) that "our police are getting not so much evidence as verdicts . . . The third degree is our predominating type of trial for crime. It tries more men, convicts more men, acquits more men, in felony cases, than the regular trial courts ever see." The former police lieutenant W. R. Kidd (1940: 15–16) would echo Hopkins nine years later: "We recognize that most defendants have, in effect, two trials. They are first tried by the police . . . This procedure has no basis in law. The policeman has no legal authority to act as the judge, but we know from practical experience that far more cases are disposed of in this manner than ever reach the court." The third degree thus expanded not only in quantity—by the 1910s and 1920s it had become a routine and integral part of everyday police work—but also in function (Conroy, 2000). It became a means through which police were able to transcend their limited fact-finding role, increase their power, and circumvent adversarial rules designed to prevent the concentration and abuse of police power. By the early 1930s, the third degree had become as much a police method of "grilling" and "sweating" as a police system whose purpose was to convict and, in some instances, punish the accused.

THE THIRD DEGREE AND THE QUALITY OF CRIMINAL INVESTIGATION

One consequence of the third-degree system was to degrade the quality of police work by encouraging laziness in criminal investigations. The police employed the third degree largely because it was the most expedient way to identify suspects, obtain evidence, and close cases. As one writer (Villard, 1927: 607) pointed out, if a detective "can pound a confession out of a man, it saves endless trouble in bringing about a conviction; it insures that conviction, and it results in a favorable entry upon the detective's service record, for not merely arrests but convictions count heavily in the policeman's favor." One journalist interviewed by the Wickersham Commission put it more bluntly: "The plain fact was that these men were both lazy and stupid. Applying the third degree is the easiest way out. In two or three hours, information or a confession could be secured which would otherwise take days of labor and planning" (Wickersham Commission Files). Not surprisingly, most cases were "solved" by confession, and interrogation became perceived as the heart of detective work. Some observers estimated that 90 to 95 percent of all cases were solved by third-degree-induced confessions. (Haller, 1976: 320). The use of the third degree led to an overreliance on interrogation to the exclusion of other methods that required more planning, effort, skill, or foresight. Even when detectives attempted other methods of criminal investigation, they often fell back on the relative ease of the third degree.

Another consequence of the third-degree system was that it encouraged a brazen disregard for truth. The use of third-degree methods repeatedly led innocent suspects to confess falsely to escape the violence and psychological duress of continuous interrogation. Some police publicly asserted that they did not elicit any false confessions because they interrogated only the guilty and accepted only confessions that provided accurate details. But their claims were not supported by the evidence. The Wickersham Commission reported that the main reason given by appellate courts for excluding confessions was the risk of third-degree-induced false confession. The Commission went on to conclude that false confessions were by no means rare, contrary to police claims. In fact, nothing placed the innocent at a higher risk for false confession than the third degree. The overreliance on the third degree for investigating crime caused police to make more errors in identifying suspects than if they had used more rational investigative methods. And the overreliance on the third degree as a means of interrogating suspects caused police to make more errors in eliciting confessions than if they had used methods that did not involve physical or psychological torture. As the Wickersham Commission (1931: 161) noted, "many things make it clear that a not inconsiderable portion [of suspects who underwent the third degree] are innocent."

Early American police also used the third degree to extract a postadmission narrative that fit their theory of the crime, one that could be used in plea bargaining sessions and at trial. As one judge told Wickersham Commission investigators, "The police decide on the details as well as the essentials, and give a man whatever treatment they think necessary in order to make him come through" (Wickersham Commission Files). Once they obtained those "details" and "essentials," police usually inserted the following words in the suspect's signed confession: "This statement is made freely and voluntarily and is not made by me as the result of any form of threat or inducement" (Hopkins, 1931: 283). Police sought to create the perception that the suspect's confession was both voluntary and reliable so that it would not be successfully challenged in court, a practice that continues to this day.

THE THIRD DEGREE AND ERRONEOUS CONVICTIONS

Police use of third-degree methods created multiple opportunities for wrongful conviction of the innocent. The third degree induced numerous false confessions because police mistakenly suspected an innocent individual, forced incriminating statements from him, and shaped his postadmission narrative. And no piece of evidence was more likely to lead to a wrongful conviction than a false confession. Though we lack quantitative data on how often police-induced false confessions led to wrongful convictions in the era of the third degree, the qualitative data gives us every reason to believe that it occurred frequently. Not only did American police use the third degree extensively in the early twentieth century, but a confession, even then, was also the strongest piece of evidence the prosecution could bring against a criminal defendant at trial. Absent records that confessions had been extracted through torture, judges and juries placed more weight on them than on any other type of evidence, as police and prosecutors well knew. Confession evidence could be so damning that it led some innocent suspects to take plea bargains to avoid the near certainty of a conviction at trial and a much longer sentence.

On top of contributing to wrongful convictions, the third degree also increased the risk of eliciting erroneous admissions and confessions from the guilty. When detectives correctly identified a culpable suspect but held an erroneous theory of his role in the crime, their use of third-degree methods sometimes caused him to "over-confess." As Hopkins (1931: 225) observed, there was "a serious danger of over-confession—especially since the confessions were written by office men, only signed by the suspect, and the 'blanket-confession' was used at times so that there would be a high statistical record of 'solved crimes.'" It is likely that the guilty were induced to over-confess frequently, and for the same reasons that coercive interrogation led to false confessions from the innocent.

Police error in both the selection and interrogation of suspects appeared to be rampant in the era of the third degree. If the police acted on a false hunch or theory in identifying a suspect, the use of third-degree methods almost certainly guaranteed an erroneous result, whether the suspect was wholly or only partially innocent. One judge told the Wickersham Commission (1931: 137):

It is the most dangerous and the most uncivilized practice imaginable to allow the police to go out and arrest a man or a boy upon mere suspicion that he has committed a crime and for days subject him to the sweating process and to violence until he finally gives up and confesses in order to escape the torture to which he is being subjected. The guilt or innocence of such a suspect would necessarily be determined by the first guess of the police as to who was the real criminal, and if the police made a mistake, conviction of innocent men and boys would necessarily result from such practice.

The third degree also contributed to erroneous convictions by coercing or intimidating witnesses into making false accusations against defendants. It is even easier to coerce witnesses to falsely implicate someone else than it is to coerce suspects to implicate themselves. In some cases, police threatened reluctant witnesses with perjury if they did not show up in court to repeat allegations that they had made or agreed to under the third degree (Hopkins, 1931). To the extent that it occurred, subjecting witnesses to the third degree created fertile ground for false accusations, fabricated evidence, and erroneous testimony at trial. Police error when identifying suspects was easily compounded when interrogating witnesses and preparing them for trial.

Further, use of the third degree encouraged police perjury, another factor in the wrongful conviction of the innocent and the over-conviction of the guilty. Police regularly perjured themselves in court by denying the use of third-degree methods, typically claiming that the suspect's injuries were caused by resisting arrest, trying to escape, accidentally falling down stairs or off a bench, banging his head on the cell door, or taking a beating from cellmates (Hopkins, 1931). One judge (Murphy, 1929: 526) commented in 1919: "When a man is taken to the police station in perfect health and several hours later is removed on a stretcher, something is decidedly wrong. If the explanation of police that prisoner's condition is caused by falling down stairs is true, then the stairs certainly need fixing. Prisoners always fall down stairs, but officers don't." Frequently a suspect's testimony would be contradicted by that of several officers and detectives who claimed that no third-degree methods had been used. As one defense attorney told the Wickersham Commission, "even a judge who leaned toward the defense was helpless in view of the preponderance of the evidence and the outright testimony given by the police." A judge more pointedly told a reporter (Murphy, 1929: 526): "It is not easy to decide who is telling the truth, with twenty patrolmen swearing against a bashed skull."

Police committed perjury to substantiate confessions obtained by the third degree and because it was "winked at and tolerated" by prosecutors, magistrates, and judges. Routine police perjury was an open secret in the American criminal justice system during the era of the third degree (Lavine, 1930). As Hopkins (1931: 278–279) argued, "The principal source of this practice is the policeman's customary abandonment of his legal role as a finder of fact, and his assumption of the role of advocate for one side or the other. He shades his testimony accordingly. . . . This leads to perjury and the subornation of perjury in the exact degree that zeal of advocacy replaces a rigid sense of honor."

The third degree, in its various manifestations, thus poisoned the stream of evidence that went from police to prosecutor to judge and jury. It undermined the evidence collection process as well as the pretrial and trial processes. Whether applied to suspects or witnesses, the innocent or guilty, it dramatically increased the risk of error at every step of the criminal process. If police used the third degree to identify suspects, they were more likely to build a case around the wrong individual; if they used it to interrogate suspects, they were more likely to extract false confessions; and if they used it to "interview" witnesses, they were more likely to manufacture false accusations and identifications. Each third-degree-induced error compounded the next. Once the innocent suspect was made to confess, it confirmed the detective's erroneous identification of him and theory of his culpability. Once a confession was given, police and prosecutors were more likely to treat weak, ambiguous, or mistaken evidence as corroboration of the suspect's guilt rather than as grounds for dismissal or pursuing another suspect. And once a confession was introduced at trial, it became far more likely that the defendant would be convicted. The erroneous evidence caused by the third degree exerted an enormous impact on the outcome of many cases. And the further along that a case based on erroneous third-degree evidence progressed, the more difficult and less likely the reversal of the errors.

Finally, the third degree poisoned the criminal process by creating incentives for police and prosecutors to ignore or cover mistakes born of it. In other words, the third degree was used not only to extract erroneous evidence but also to justify and perpetuate it. It was employed to justify false arrests, illegal detentions, and false confessions as it fueled police perjury. The institutional actors who were supposed to act as checks and balances on one another simply failed to do so. Instead, they, in effect, facilitated the third degree.

THE THIRD DEGREE AND POLICE LAWLESSNESS

The third degree encouraged police corruption and lawlessness at three distinct phases of the criminal process: arrest, interrogation, and trial. Police illegally detained suspects in order to apply the third degree; circumvented the law requiring immediate arraignment by not booking the suspect until they first interrogated him or not charging him so that they could hold him for forty-eight hours (Lavine, 1930); and violated the laws of arrest by "losing" the suspect for days, if not weeks, on end (Hopkins, 1931). By coercing false confessions and false accusations, police were illegally manufacturing false evidence. And the third degree encouraged police lawlessness in court as police perjured themselves to ensure that judges would allow coerced confessions to be used. Police also knowingly suborned perjury from witnesses whom they had coerced into making false accusations and identifications. Although police could be fined, suspended, sued civilly, or criminally indicted and prosecuted for their coercive methods, third-degree practices were almost always tolerated by police leaders, prosecutors, and judges. Coerced confessions were typically upheld in court, regardless of the methods police employed or the defendant's injuries (Booth, 1930). Only under exceptional circumstances were police punished for their brutal and illegal interrogation practices (Villard, 1927).

Although detectives regularly broke the law with impunity at multiple stages of the criminal process, the system of third-degree abuses eventually began to cast doubt on the legitimacy of criminal justice in America. The public increasingly came to question the accuracy of police investigative work and the credibility of detectives' testimony in court. Confession evidence began to fall into disrepute. Jurors complained about police in voir dire, expressed skepticism about prosecutions that relied on confessions, and discounted police testimony at trial. Prosecutors blamed acquittals and hung juries on discredited police work. Others lamented that the third degree had led to a crisis of confidence in a bedrock institution of American criminal justice, imperiling criminal prosecutions and the predictability of trial outcomes. As Moley put it in 1932 (199): "The third degree is an effective way of securing an acquittal. An increasing number of guilty people are escaping the consequences of their crimes because of lack of confidence in police." Lavine (1930: 144) observed: "True or false, juries are coming to believe anyone who accuses the police of using the 'third degree.' The result is that the reputation the police have won militates against their own efforts."

The crisis of confidence in the American process of justice was not just about the accuracy of police interrogations or criminal prosecutions. More was at stake. The third degree had precipitated a loss of trust in the legal system as a whole. The police were perceived in many quarters as not merely coercive but also dishonest and lawless. The third degree eventually translated into a fundamental distrust of police, as Hopkins captured well (1931: 208):

The requirement of secrecy has given the third degree one more of its obvious characteristics, and that is its sneakiness. There is always an air of furtiveness, an impression of covering-up. . . . The facts may be successfully concealed, but the sneakiness cannot; people sense it; it colors the work of policemen on the witness stand and has communicated itself, in a vague feeling of distrust, to judges and juries all over the country today. Policemen, the people's witnesses, are not trusted as they should be, and confession evidence, while still probably more impressive than any other class of evidence, certainly does not enjoy the unquestioned status it would have if presented with open integrity. Many trials are overshadowed by the haunting wonder as to what the police have previously done to the defendant, how much they are concealing. . . Sneakiness is a strange quality for our law enforcement to possess, but there is no question that in many of our cities this quality pervades. At the bottom of it is some form of third degree.

THE THIRD DEGREE AND POLICE IDEOLOGY

Police did not speak with one voice about the third degree. Publicly, they tended to deny that they used it, blaming "baseless" allegations on "shyster" defense attorneys, "yellow" journalists, and the "criminals" themselves (Van Wagner, 1938). Privately, however, most police believed that they could not effectively acquire information, solve cases, convict offenders, ensure that the guilty were convicted and punished, or prevent crime without the third degree. As Lavine (1930: 53) observed, police perceived that a suspect "is usually guilty but he will not talk and if the third degree is not applied, he will go unpunished . . . This is the police point of view: it is a necessary evil, but the police must not be caught using it." A Los Angeles police chief interviewed by the Wickersham Commission insisted that police investigators would be "helpless" if they could not use the third degree.

Police employed several different rhetorical strategies to deny the existence of the third degree. Some simply denied it outright: "there is no such thing as the third degree," one police official told the Wickersham Commission (1931: 40). Other police redefined the third degree as something other than coercive interrogation. San Francisco Police Captain Duncan Matthewson insisted that it consisted only of "the asking of a few simple, direct questions" (Wickersham Commission Report, 1931: 44). New York Police Captain Cornelius Willemse (Wickersham Commission Report, 1931: 169) suggested that the controversy over the third degree was no more than a semantic misunderstanding: "To the public, a mention of the third degree suggests only one thing—a terrifying picture of secret merciless beating of helpless men in dark cells of stations . . . To the detective the 'third degree' is a broad phrase without definition. To him it means any trick, idea, and stunt, risk or action that he may use to get the truth from a prisoner."

Some police denied the existence of the third degree by shifting the focus from the interrogation to the suspect's confession, an impression management strategy that continues to this day. The implication was that the interrogation could not be coercive if the confession was voluntary (Wickersham Commission Report, 1931: 39). If they openly admitted that the third degree existed, police usually rationalized it as either necessary to achieve their objectives or excusable given the circumstances in which police work occurred—all the while excoriating their critics for failing to understand the police point of view. Police most commonly justified the third degree by appealing to necessity. "At times heroic methods must be resorted to gain desired ends," one Memphis police chief stated. "You may call it whatever you please, the 'third degree' or any other kind of degree, but it had the desired effect" (Wickersham Commission Report, 1931: 41). One police commander told the Wickersham Commission that the third degree was also necessary to prevent crime and save lives: "The criminal hires the best lawyers; politics is used and he gets out easily enough. The detective has to have the goods on the man or else he is sure to go out and probably commit a dozen more murders" (Wickersham Commission Files). Cornelius Willemse (1931) went even further, declaring that police were at war with crime and criminals and that the third degree was their primary weapon. "All arguments openly stated in behalf of unlawful police work come down in the end to the phrase: this is war," Hopkins (1931: 318) pointed out.

Some police leaders suggested that public criticism of the police encouraged criminals (Wickersham Commission), thereby preventing police from engaging in efficient and effective law enforcement. When criticized for their third-degree practices, police were particularly contemptuous of the idea of constitutional rights. Many appeared to believe that a criminal had no constitutional rights (Wickersham Commission Report, 1931). One police leader proclaimed (Wickersham Commission Report, 1931: 103):

> If I have to violate the Constitution or my oath of office, I'll violate the Constitution . . . A policeman should be free as a fireman to protect his community. Nobody ever thinks of hedging a fireman about with a lot of laws that favor the fire . . . Shysters have turned the Constitution into a refuge for the criminal . . . I'm going to protect the community. If in so doing I make a mistake and trespass on somebody's rights, let him sue.

Some police even went so far as to suggest that the Fifth Amendment was the cause of any third-degree practices (Wickersham Commission Files). Others rationalized it as necessary for retribution. The Wickersham Commission (1931: 146–147) reported: "At the Academy of Criminology and elsewhere, the police and their advocates made such statements as . . . 'The thug who refuses to talk deserves to get his ribs rattled and his toes stepped on.' One former captain advocated the whipping post and the cat-o'-nine tails—'cut them deep and then rub handfuls of salt into the cuts.' "

Some police suggested that the third degree was used only against hardened criminals and repeat offenders or "individuals known to be guilty" (Wickersham Commission Files). Other police believed that police violence was an inevitable reaction to the violence of criminals, particularly in large cities, where organized gangs existed (Wickersham Commission Report, 1931). Some police suggested that preventing them from using the third degree would lower their morale and render them ineffective. The Wickersham Commission (1931: 178–179) described the following police lore:

> Some years ago, they say, a certain police department called in a lawyer, who educated the policemen as to the precise limitations upon their work; and the chief ordered every man in the department to live up to the law strictly or lose his job. The result, so the story goes, was that for about six months there were few arrests; the police were "afraid to lift their hands." Meanwhile crime mounted, and the public became aroused because nothing was done. At the end of this time the order was rescinded and the department went back largely to its old methods. This is regarded as a significant illustration that if the policeman obeyed the exact refinements of the law at every step of the arresting and evidence-finding process he would be powerless.

In short, American police developed a working ideology—based on the idea of a war on crime, appeals to necessity, and the belief that the investigator's objective was to apprehend, incriminate, and punish criminals— through which they justified their lawlessness.

The Third Degree in American History

The Nineteenth Century

Following their invention in England, modern police forces emerged in most American cities during the middle of the nineteenth century. Controlled by political machines rather than an independent judiciary, early American police departments typically were brutal and corrupt. The term "third degree" appears to have become synonymous with coercive interrogation in popular parlance around the turn of the century (Keedy, 1937), though its usage in police circles dates back at least to the 1870s (Walling, 1887). While there is some debate over the origins of the term, "third degree" appears to have originally referred to the rigorous tests necessary to attain the master rank in free masonry; it was subsequently transposed in police folklore to signify the third stage of the criminal investigation process, following arrest and custodial confinement (Franklin, 1970).

Given the paucity of direct historical evidence on interrogation practices in the nineteenth century, it is unclear whether the third degree was practiced systematically by American police from their inception or became a regular investigative method only in the later decades of the century. But there is evidence that the use of some third-degree tactics—such as the sweat box, the hanging of suspects by the neck, and the use of incommunicado detention—dates back to the middle of the nineteenth century (Sears, 1948). And it is likely that coercive interrogation was practiced regularly by American police throughout the century. As Lawrence Friedman (1993: 303) has written, "Thousands of nineteenth-century tramps and thieves were beaten, coerced, arrested, thrown into jail, all without lawyers. They confessed after long stretches of the third degree, and almost nobody uttered a murmur of protest—certainly not the tramps, and thieves; but neither did their advocates, if they had any." The third degree was a routine police practice toward the end of the century.

At least one police writer has credited Thomas Byrnes, a well-known New York police officer and ultimately chief inspector in the last several decades of the nineteenth century, with inventing the third degree (Larson, 1932). Others have suggested that the term "third degree" is a play on Byrnes's name (as in burns) (Scheck, Neufeld, and Dwyer, 2000). Byrnes regularly meted out violence on criminal suspects and others who overstepped social boundaries (Reppetto, 1978)—so much so that New York police chief George Walling referred to Byrnes's office as a star chamber (Lardner and Reppetto, 2000). After their interrogations, Byrnes's suspects regularly appeared in court badly injured, some so weak they could hardly stand (Johnson, 2003).

Newspapers and the popular media frequently reported allegations of third-degree violence in the closing decades of the nineteenth century. And police biographies and journalistic accounts by police reporters indicate that the third degree was rampant in New York City and elsewhere from the late nineteenth century through at least the first three decades of the twentieth century (Willemse, 1931).

The Early Twentieth Century

At the turn of the century, local media would frequently publish accounts of brutality during interrogations that were virtually always ignored or denied by police departments (Haller, 1976). The third degree did not become a national issue until 1910, however, when allegations of custodial violence in two widely reported cases prompted the United States Senate to appoint a select committee to investigate custodial abuses by federal law enforcement agencies (*Journal of American Institute of Criminal Law and Criminology*, 1912). At the annual meeting of the International Association of Chiefs of Police (the leading professional police organization of the time) in 1910, some police chiefs spoke of the need for tough methods in apprehending criminals, but most, notably President Richard Sylvester of Washingtun, D.C., denied the existence of third-degree practices altogether. They attributed "this time worn and antiquated unfair criticism" to "the product of sensations and romances" (Dilworth, 1976: 72). Nevertheless, the IACP resolved to "at all times condemn such practice and to punish those guilty, if possible." As Samuel Walker (1977: 58) has observed, the police chiefs mounted a scatter-shot defense that, ironically, included not only denying the use of third-degree methods but also blaming private detectives for abuses, just as later police writers would attribute allegations of third-degree methods to the fabrications and exaggerations of "shyster" defense attorneys, sensationalizing journalists, and the accused themselves (Mathewson, 1929).

The Senate Select Committee to Investigate the Administration of the Criminal Law by Federal Officials also mounted a shotgun defense, reporting that (1) convincing evidence of brutality would be difficult to obtain because no witnesses were present at police questioning; (2) their sole source of information on police practices came from interviewing federal officials; and (3) even had they discovered the existence of police abuses, Congress possessed the power to legislate only against third-degree practices employed by federal, not state, officials. The Senate committee seemed especially impressed by the testimony of then Attorney General George Wickersham, who (ironically, as it would turn out) testified that he believed no third-degree practices existed among federal officials.

However, in response to the heightened media attention and congressional investigation into police abuses, several states enacted their own statutes against the third degree (Keedy, 1937). Though they used forceful and sweeping language, these statutes were largely symbolic: only rarely was a guilty officer or detective actually convicted under one (*Harvard Law Review*, 1930). In the 1910s, not a single police official was prosecuted under the statutes (Chafee, 1931). And although Illinois had criminalized the third degree in 1874, this made no difference in Chicago, which had the most violent and lawless police department in America for decades: it was so infamous for its use of interrogation violence that in many places the third degree was referred to as "The Chicago Treatment" (Franklin, 1970).

By the time of the Wickersham Commission Report in 1931, twenty-seven states carried anti–third-degree statutes on their books, but they had no effect on the use of the third degree, revealing the limit, if not futility, of criminal law as a source of control over police investigative behavior at the time.

The Heyday of the Third Degree

The two decades following the IACP meetings and the Senate committee's investigation (roughly 1911–1931) appear to have been the heyday of the third degree in America. This was a time of changing crime patterns—notably the rise of gangland violence and a thriving criminal underworld following Prohibition—and thus the nation's first declared war on crime (Johnson, 2003). In response to the perceived threat of mounting crime, numerous crime commissions and crime surveys were established and undertaken in the 1920s. The crime commissions influenced policing in at least three ways, as Nathan Douthit (1975: 318) has noted:

> First, they fostered a climate of attitudes and ideas emphasizing crime control as the primary function of police forces and giving rise to a "war on crime." Second, they encouraged the use of the concept of efficiency as the principal criterion by which other parts of the criminal justice system came to be evaluated. Third, they emphasized the need for state and national coordination and leadership in the struggle against crime.

During the 1910s and 1920s, the third degree was frequently publicized by the media and civic organizations (Chisolm and Hart, 1922), and in some cities police complained that they were perpetually on the defensive against charges of improprieties. In the muckraking tradition of the Progressive era, newspapers regularly reported allegations of police abuses and decried violent interrogation practices in popular editorials, graphically describing the disfiguring injuries that sometimes resulted. Plays were written about the third degree and performed in theaters. In detective fiction and motion pictures, the third degree was treated as a standard police practice. Bar association committees, civil liberties groups, and grand juries investigated custodial police abuses and issued reports. Sometimes police officers joined the fray by publicly defending and justifying their third-degree methods in news stories, articles, and books (see Chisolm and Hart, 1922).

Popular criticism of police interrogation practices culminated in 1931 with the publication of Volume 11 of the Wickersham Commission Report, *Report on Lawlessness in Law Enforcement*. It created a national scandal.

After the Wickersham Commission

Thoroughly documented, the Wickersham Commission Report revealed that police brutality in general and the third degree in particular were practiced extensively and systematically in police departments across the country. Its findings were immediately popularized by journalist Ernest Jerome Hopkins's 1931 book, *Our Lawless Police*, and many national newspaper and magazine stories. Although journalists, grand juries, legislative committees, bar associations, and civil liberties groups had all leveled such charges against police in the past, none had provoked nearly as much public controversy or exercised nearly as much impact on public attitudes as the Wickersham Commission Report.

The history of third-degree interrogation would change dramatically in the decades following the Wickersham Commission Report. Some police departments and organizations initially attacked the report's legitimacy and accuracy. The IACP denounced it as "the greatest blow to police work in the last half century" and formed a special committee to refute its findings (Wickersham Commission Files). As Zachariah Chaffee, one of the authors of the Wickersham Commission Report, pointed out, it "was greeted by the police with two answers which they regarded as conclusive: first, there wasn't any third degree; and second, they couldn't do their work without it" (Smith, 1986: 10).

The graphic revelations of routine police misconduct in the report threatened the institutional legitimacy of the police. Police administrators, chiefs, and supporters quickly realized the need to eliminate flagrant abuses to enhance their status among the public. Police chiefs could no longer brazenly deny that the third degree existed. Police became increasingly concerned with their public image, especially in the media. The professional model of policing, long encouraged by progressive reformers, gained ascendance in police circles (Fogelson, 1977). Reform-oriented police chiefs and leaders capitalized on the changing atmosphere to enact or enforce departmental policies against abusive police behavior.

Following the report, Federal Bureau of Investigation Chief J. Edgar Hoover immediately launched both internal and external attacks on third-degree practices. Hoover actively promoted more professional (i.e., nonabusive) forms of interrogation. He realized that public perceptions of police abuse undermined not only the image of policing but also the goal of conviction. The F.B.I. emphasized "scientific" forms of criminal investigation so as to render coercive interrogation obsolete. "Third degree methods, the ill-trained officer might think, perhaps a severe beating, will force a confession," Hoover stated (Frank and Frank, 1957: 185). "But the trained officer, schooled in the latest techniques of crime detection, will think otherwise—he will go to work, locating a latent fingerprint, a heel-print in the mud, or a toolmark on the safe."

The Wickersham Commission Report had a profound influence on the police. Like other major police scandals (Sherman, 1978), this one became a significant agent for social change. Its impact would be felt for decades, as police struggled to overcome popular stereotypes of third-degree interrogation. Following the report, police departments began to reform their arrest and investigative practices, instituting greater levels of training as the occupation of policing became increasingly professionalized. The use of coercive methods began to decline in the 1930s and 1940s. The decline was uneven—third-degree methods persisted in some places longer than others—but by the mid-1960s custodial police questioning had become psychological in nature. In less than two generations of American policing, the third degree had virtually disappeared.

Ultimately, the third degree collapsed under the weight of its own contradictions: the use of totalitarian methods by democratic police, the production of "voluntary" confessions through coercion and force, the pursuit of prosecutorial objectives instead of investigative ones, and the dispensation of punishment and justice by police rather than courts. Police and criminal justice officials promoted confessions as the most trustworthy type of evidence against a suspect when, in many instances, it was among the least reliable. Perhaps the largest contradiction of all was the systemic lawlessness by the very police who were sworn to uphold a Constitution that sought to prevent precisely these types of abuses.

Two very different groups came together to eliminate the third degree as a regular practice in the 1930s and 1940s: police leaders and progressive social reformers. Within policing, the move to reform interrogation practices was part of a much broader agenda to professionalize the structure, function, and public image of policing (Walker, 1977). Police reformers recognized the need to change the public perception of police investigators as poorly trained, inefficient, thuggish, and corrupt in order to increase the social status of police work. They sought to transform policing from a politically dominated working-class occupation into a politically autonomous and respectable middle-class profession. And with the development of so-called scientific techniques of crime detection, American police began to perceive, for the first time, that violent interrogation tactics were no longer necessary to obtain confessions.

Progressive social and legal elites, who worked through organizations such as bar associations, civil liberties and civil rights groups, and ultimately the Wickersham Commission, would, in effect, join forces with police reformers, but with a different underlying agenda. They were concerned about due process and the larger consequences of a justice system that allowed the third degree and its abuses to flourish with impunity. Progressive elites sought to disperse police power and thus exercise more control over the police so as to remove the power structure that produced the third-degree system of abuses and erroneous outcomes. They wanted an end to coercive interrogations, false arrests, illegal detentions, policy perjury, wrongful convictions, and over-convictions. Progressive reformers sought to mobilize public and elite opinion against the third degree in order to hold police accountable to the Constitution and ensure the legally proper division of function and power within the American criminal justice system. Hopkins's book, *Our Lawless Police*, for example, repeatedly decried that the third degree was not about getting evidence so much as getting verdicts that usurped the fact-finding, trial, and punitive functions of judges and juries. It was this emphasis on the police monopoly of power at the front end of the criminal justice system and the structural consequences of the third degree that separated the progressive reformers from police leaders. Progressive reformers had a more ambitious and systemic agenda than police leaders: they sought to break the third-degree system of abuses by placing limits on police power and making it conform to constitutional due process requirements, not merely to prevent police from relying on coercive methods.

At the time, the differences between police reformers and progressive elites may not have seemed as salient as their similarities. One common objective was to fix the problem of police-induced false confession, which had over time come to be associated with the third degree in public consciousness. Even though many police investigators denied that they erroneously prejudged their suspects' guilt or that their interrogation methods had ever caused the innocent to confess and be convicted, police reformers and many police chiefs knew better. False confession cases (to which the Wickersham Commission dedicated many pages in its report) called into question the legality and professionalism of police interrogation methods in particular cases and their investigative competence more generally. Progressive elites also deplored the problem of false confessions for the obvious reasons: the innocent were unjustly made to falsely confess, and some (perhaps many) were wrongfully convicted while the actual offender went free. And progressive elites deplored the third-degree torture sessions that led the innocent to falsely confess. But they also had deeper concerns: police corruption, unregulated police power, and the perversion of fair legal procedure that produced false confessions and miscarriages of justice.

Despite their different agendas, police reformers and progressive elites mobilized opinion against the third degree in a relatively short period of time. That two socially opposite coalitions came together may obscure the larger significance of their very different visions of the proper structure and role of police interrogation in the American adversary system. The police reformers emphasized improving interrogation methods in order to produce more accurate, efficient, and acceptable case outcomes. They were not interested in changing the structure of interrogation so much as sanitizing its content. By replacing the third degree with so-called scientific methods, interrogation could remain police-dominated and secretive and more effectively serve the goals of incrimination, case-building, and conviction. By contrast, progressive social and legal elites emphasized limiting state power and creating mechanisms to bring police interrogation practices in line with constitutional guarantees of due process. Unlike police leaders, progressive reformers were interested in changing not only the content of police interrogation but also its structure. They sought to break the monopoly of power that police wield at the very point in the criminal process when the accused are most vulnerable to coercion and the evidence that police may elicit from them is most likely to determine their fate. Despite the decline of the third degree, these two diverging visions—which correlate roughly with the truth and governmental control models of the adversary system—have continued to influence the development, regulation, and practice of American police interrogation in the past seventy-five years and, in part, explain its underlying contradictions.

Professionalism was the most salient issue in police circles by the 1950s (Wilson, 1968). Police norms on the use of violence continued to change in subtle but profound ways. In response to adverse publicity and stereotypes, police training and education consciously sought to transform the attitudes and professional norms of policing to improve the image of police. The ethics of police work, as well as the constitutional rights of criminal defendants, were now widely discussed in police training courses. The third degree was no longer considered merely ineffective but unprofessional and unacceptable as well. Although police training manuals were outspoken in their condemnation of coercive questioning, police continued to receive adverse publicity for third-degree interrogation when it occurred. Police attitudes increasingly dictated that no end could justify coercive or abusive means during custodial questioning. The use of physical force had become generally disfavored, for police realized that it undermined public relations and believed that psychological approaches were generally more effective.

Police attitudes and behavior continued to change in the 1960s, as the police became more educated, training programs expanded, and the ideology of professionalism became more entrenched, especially among local police. Although the third degree was still practiced in some forms, it was by no means common. One study found that police interrogation practices changed significantly in New Haven, Connecticut, a medium-sized city, during the early 1960s: by 1966 its police no longer engaged in physically coercive interrogation (Wald, Ayres, Hess, Schantz, and Whitebread, 1967).

Psychologically manipulative techniques are now the standard means for eliciting incriminating information during custodial questioning. To be sure, instances of third-degree interrogation do still occur. There were major police scandals involving use of the third degree in Philadelphia in the 1970s (Skolnick and Fyfe, 1993), Chicago in the 1970s and 1980s (Conroy, 2000), New York City in the early 1990s (Mollen, 1994), and Los Angeles in the late 1990s (Bandes, 2001). There have also been credible allegations of violent interrogation in smaller police departments in recent years (Maier and Smith, 1986; Leo and Ofshe, 2001). But what was once a routine, widespread, and institutionalized police practice is now widely perceived as illegitimate and anomalous and thus occurs infrequently.

The Third Degree and the American Legal System

Once exposed by the Wickersham Commission Report, the third degree had provoked not merely a police scandal but also a system scandal that involved other key actors and institutions in the American process of justice. The application of law—which to the average citizen police embodied perhaps more than any other legal institution—and the administration of justice had come to be perceived as fundamentally unjust. The third-degree system of abuses clashed with the American sense of fairness. It was, in essence, a medieval institution, a throwback to the star chamber and trial by ordeal. Indeed, it resembled the kinds of state abuses in the sixteenth and seventeenth centuries that gave rise to the adversary system in the first place. It was therefore perverse that it flourished in that system. Yet the third degree was also modern in its total stripping of the individual's autonomy in the face of state power.

The third degree was fundamentally at odds with both the truth model and the government control model of the adversary system discussed earlier. It undermined the pursuit of truth in multiple ways. Most obviously, third-degree methods created overpowering incentives for the suspect to tell the interrogator anything he wanted to hear, whether true or not, to put an end to the torture of continued questioning. They led to lazy and sloppy investigations, which produced errors in suspect identification and theories of culpability, and overreliance on interrogation and confession evidence to "solve" crimes. The third degree also fostered perjured testimony to cover bad police work and to help the prosecution convict the defendant. Each of these results compounded the probability of two types of error: the wrongful conviction of the innocent and the over-conviction of the guilty. The third degree was fundamentally at odds with the pursuit of truth not only because the use of torture as a method of questioning can easily produce error, but perhaps more importantly because the police had exceeded their role as impartial fact-finders and case investigators. The third degree was not designed to get the truth or even find the facts so much as to allow police to incriminate the suspect expediently and thus build a strong case against him.

Yet the use of torture as an interrogation method is not necessarily incompatible with the goal of pursuing the truth. The Wickersham Commission estimated that in the great majority of cases it studied involving third-degree interrogation the suspects were guilty. But even the Commission acknowledged that the third degree led to numerous false confessions. This was mainly because of two police errors *prior* to the use of the third degree: developing an incorrect theory of the crime and misidentifying an innocent individual as a guilty suspect. If police had not made these errors, the third degree would not necessarily have led to untruthful outcomes (i.e., false confessions or wrongful convictions). To put it differently, if police correctly theorize the crime and identify the guilty suspect, they will interrogate only individuals who are factually guilty. And if they interrogate only guilty suspects, they cannot, as a logical matter, elicit false confessions from the innocent, regardless of the interrogation methods they employ. In this sense the investigative work that police do prior to interrogation may be more consequential than the interrogation itself in determining whether an innocent individual may confess falsely. If police interrogate only the guilty, contrary to the ideology of professional policing that would emerge after the third-degree scandal, physical torture may be the most effective means of eliciting the truth (Bowden, 2003; but see also Rumney, 2005 and Bowden, 2007).

The system of third-degree abuses, however, was even more fundamentally at odds with the government control model of the adversary system than with the truth model. Because police routinely exceeded their authority and violated the rule of law with impunity, the third degree literally turned the government control model on its head. As we have seen, the police exercised a virtually unfettered monopoly of power at the front end of the criminal process before any meaningful legal checks and balances could be imposed on their behavior or on the evidence they had created: they illegally arrested and detained suspects; coercively interrogated them; and forced involuntary, if not unreliable, confessions. By the time the suspect was able to exercise any legal rights to compel fair and balanced procedures (i.e., after he had been formally charged by the prosecutor), those rights had become all but meaningless, because police had already extracted or simply manufactured a confession, the most damning evidence the state could bring against him. For many defendants (especially those with prior criminal records, those against whom there existed other evidence, those facing lengthy prison sentences, or those with inadequate representation), the coerced confession inevitably led to a coerced plea bargain to avoid the near certainty of conviction at trial. Those who chose to take their case to trial had to contend not only with damaging confession evidence but also with police who routinely lied about their interrogation methods and prosecutors and judges who knowingly suborned police perjury.

The third-degree regime undermined the rationale of the governmental control model in two related ways. First, it prevented criminal defendants from meaningfully asserting their legal rights at that point in the criminal process—the creation of testimonial evidence—when they mattered most. Like a chain, due process is only as strong as its weakest link: once a suspect has been tortured to confess, it is largely futile. Second, the third degree poisoned the stream of evidence that the state would eventually use to prosecute, convict, and incarcerate the defendant. Both effects increased the risk of error. The third-degree system, in effect, allowed the police to circumvent adversarial rules and rig the process in favor of the prosecution so that conviction was almost a foregone conclusion. This system thus made a mockery of the idea of checks and balances on state power in the criminal process. By allowing police to enjoy unchecked power without any meaningful oversight, the third-degree regime nullified the legal mechanisms in place to hold police accountable to law.

The dramatic decline of the third degree is usually told as a story of norm change and a model of success in the professionalization of American policing (Walker, 1993). Yet the decline of the third degree is also a story about the persistence of police institutions and behavior. For the structure of early American interrogation remains largely intact to this day, even if the content has changed. American police interrogators still presume the guilt of the suspects they interrogate; still attempt to overcome their resistance and move them from denial to admission; still try to convince them—if by fraud rather than force—that they have no real choice but to confess; and still exert pressure to shape and manipulate their postadmission narratives. As in the era of the third degree, the primary goal of police interrogators is not to elicit the truth per se but to incriminate the suspect in order to build a case against him and assist the prosecution in convicting him. And interrogation still often occurs in secrecy. Contemporary American police have skillfully adapted to the norms of the adversary system, but like their predecessors, they do not aspire to be impartial fact-finders. Rather, they are still essentially agents of the prosecution. And they also continue to exercise a virtual monopoly of power at the front end of the criminal justice system, manipulating suspects to provide damning testimonial evidence against themselves before any of the adversary system's checks and balances can be meaningfully applied. The seeds of modern interrogation were sown in the era of the third degree, and they have left an indelible, if largely hidden, imprint on contemporary police methods.

CHAPTER **3**

Professionalizing Police
Interrogation

Shunning the third degree does not make us sissies. It takes more
guts to control yourself and fight it out brain to brain than it does
to slug it out. When it is necessary to battle, the battle of wits is
tougher than physical combat. If you resort to torture you admit
your victim is the better man. When you "break" a man by torture,
he will hate you. If you break him by your intelligence, he will
always fear and respect you.

—W. R. Kidd (1940)

Polygraphs? I don't know if the damn things work, but I do know
that they scare the hell out of anyone who has to take one.

—Richard Nixon (1974)

We get better results than a priest does.

—John Reid (1971)

By exposing the practice and prevalence of third-degree
methods in station houses across America, the 1931 Wickersham Commission Report had a profound impact on public attitudes toward the police. "The informed and articulate public was no longer willing to tolerate
the misconduct that had been part of American policing for so long," histo-
rian Samuel Walker (1980: 175) observed. The report, as we have seen, also
had a profound impact on police themselves. Though many angrily disputed its findings, police reformers understood that the third degree had
become a black mark on the image of policing. Following the report, police
were portrayed in the media as dumb, bumbling, and corrupt men who
routinely beat confessions out of helpless suspects. To repair the damage,
police reformers believed that they needed to abolish the third degree and

fundamentally transform how the public perceived police investigation and interrogation.

The reformers did not, however, want to undermine the interrogation function of police, which was still considered the primary method of investigating and solving crime. Nor, of course, did they want to compromise their ability to obtain confessions. They thus sought to change the process of interrogation from within, lest it be compromised from the outside by police critics in the legislature or courts—or, worse still, reallocated to another criminal justice agency such as judges, as some had suggested after the Wickersham Commission Report (Kauper, 1932). To shore up the practice of interrogation and to maintain their monopoly over it, reformers within policing turned to the rhetoric and ideology of professionalism and the newly emerging field of so-called scientific policing and crime detection.

A movement for police professionalization had existed well before the release of the Wickersham Commission Report. It sought to achieve professional status for the occupation of policing by removing it from partisan politics and implementing techniques of managerial efficiency—centralizing authority, rationalizing command and control structures, and raising the quality of police personnel (Walker, 1977). The release of the report and the controversy it stirred moved the issue of third-degree interrogation methods from the periphery of the movement for police professionalization—which by now had become aligned with the larger movement for progressivism—closer to the center. Because of the publicity generated about the third degree, reform-oriented police chiefs believed they could rely on public support to improve their departments and more rigorously enforce regulations against police abuse (Walker, 1998). Police leaders sought to reform interrogation practices as part of a much broader agenda (Fogelson, 1977). Increasingly concerned about their image, police reformers embraced professionalism as a managerial strategy for enhancing their social standing and the influence of police organizations. But they also understood that police professionalism could be a means of furthering their crime control objectives.

The professionalization movement introduced the idea of policing as a science within a broader vision that entailed formal training, higher educational requirements, and greater efficiency in police work. In the 1920s "scientific" crime detection techniques were first applied in criminal investigations. In 1922, August Vollmer, perhaps the leading proponent of scientific policing at the time, urged that police investigators replace "trial and error" methods of criminal investigation with "more efficient scientific techniques and crime laboratories, enlisting the aid of microscopists, chemical analysts, medico-psychologists and handwriting experts" (Carte and Carte, 1975: 57). Academic and business leaders came together to establish the Scientific Crime Detection Laboratory in Chicago in 1929, after the famous St. Valentine's Day Massacre (Winters, 2005).

But it was not until the early 1930s and the revelations of the Wickersham Commission that scientific and technical innovations began to take shape. F.B.I. Director J. Edgar Hoover created the first federal crime laboratory in 1932 and founded the National Police Academy in 1935. The F.B.I. pioneered advances in scientific crime detection and other technical innovations such as fingerprint technology, ballistic tests, national identification records, police journals, and the Uniform Crime Reports.

Reform-oriented police such as Hoover and Vollmer sought to remake police interrogation in the image of scientific crime detection not only to raise the social status of police by promoting a more professional force but also to improve criminal investigation. The chief symbol of modern scientific interrogation was the polygraph, informally known as the lie detector. Police reformers hoped it would replace the third degree as a means of investigating suspects and eliciting confessions. They considered it more effective than the third degree because it relied on a different psychology: suspects might harden their resolve against interrogators who physically abused them, but they could not fool the polygraph or deny its results. Reformers also believed that the polygraph would produce more accurate results and was not apt to induce false confessions. Further, confessions elicited by psychological methods were less likely to be challenged by defense attorneys, thrown out by judges, and questioned by juries than those exacted through the third degree. The polygraph and other modern "scientific" methods of interrogation would render the third degree unnecessary, a relic of the preprofessional era of policing.

Yet the polygraph by itself was not an adequate substitute for the third degree. Police reformers also turned to the field of psychology, which like the polygraph carried the symbolism and authority of modern science. From these overlapping influences, the house of modern psychological interrogation was built. Unlike the third degree, modern interrogation consists of two different parts: the studied detection of deception and the use of psychologically manipulative methods.

The signal event in the development of a modern psychology of interrogation was the rise of the police interrogation training manual. Since the early 1940s, these manuals have defined the structure, practice, and culture of American police interrogation. They have allowed police managers to socialize officers and detectives into the norms of professional interrogation and thereby define and police the limits of their discretion. Police manuals have also taught generations of detectives the tactics, techniques, and strategies of psychological interrogation. Along with in-house and national training programs, the interrogation training manual was the mechanism through which American police professionalized their interrogation practices and sought to overcome the stigma associated with interrogation in the era of the third degree.

The Foundations of Modern Police Interrogation: Creating Human Lie Detectors

The use of behavioral lie detection—the attempt to infer guilt from body language and physical demeanor—as an interrogation strategy did not begin with American police. Throughout history, humans have attempted to detect deception by observing physiological changes in criminal suspects during interrogation. Trials by ordeal, in which accused individuals were subjected to physical trauma in order to adjudicate their guilt or innocence, prevailed in some ancient societies and in Europe between 800 and 1200. In one well-known ordeal, the ancient Hindus (and later the Roman Catholic clergy) required suspects to chew and then spit out a mouthful of rice: suspects who successfully spit out the rice were judged innocent; but if grains stuck to their mouths, they were found guilty (Trovillo, 1938a, b). In another trial by ordeal, accused thieves were made to put a hand first in cold water and then in boiling water: if they lost skin or showed a blister, they were regarded as guilty; if not, they were considered innocent (Larson, 1932). Accused people were also made to hold or walk on a hot iron, bleed from a ritual incision, or be submerged in a pool of water (Bartlett, 1986). The purpose of trial by ordeal was to provoke the gods to reveal a suspect's innocence. It was believed that an innocent individual would be stronger and helped by the gods to survive the ordeal.

Trial by ordeal is the historical precursor of modern methods of behavioral lie detection (Skolnick, 1961). But the attempt to detect deception through behavioral observation was not part of the regime of American interrogation in the late nineteenth and early twentieth centuries. Rather, with the third degree, behavioral lie detection was simply unnecessary. Yet the technology that would later culminate in the polygraph was first developed during the heyday of the third degree. It was modified further in the 1920s and 1930s, and completed in the 1940s. Following the Wickersham Commission Report, police turned increasingly to the emerging "science" of lie detection to overcome problems with the third degree.

American police leaders embraced behavioral lie detection in general and the polygraph in particular for two reasons. First, they wanted to improve the image of policing by aligning it with the authority and prestige of modern science and technology. The thuggish and lawless brute who once beat confessions out of suspects was now recast as a modern detective who carefully tested the suspect's guilt through what on the surface appeared to be a medical procedure. The polygraph shifted the authority of the interrogation from the detective to the machine, just as it shifted the focus of police questioning from interrogation (with its connotation of rubber hoses and bright lights) to truth verification. Police turned to the methods of behavioral lie detection because they sought to eliminate the perception of human bias and replace it with the seeming neutrality and sophistication of the lie-detection machine (Skolnick, 1961). Like the scientific method itself, behavioral lie detection conveyed that the purpose of interrogation was an objective search for truth. By appropriating the authority and objectives of modern science, police sought to confer legitimacy on their controversial interrogation practices. The move to behavioral lie detection created an abstract body of specialized and technical knowledge over which police interrogators could claim exclusive expertise. The illusion outstripped the reality: the methods of "scientific" lie detection, after all, were not invented by actual scientists, but by the police themselves.

The second reason American police leaders turned to behavioral lie detection was to render the third degree unnecessary by creating more effective methods of interrogation. The function of behavioral lie-detection methods inside the interrogation room is to incriminate the suspect by inducing a confession. The methods are intended to persuade the suspect that he has no choice but to comply with the interrogators' wishes because the infallible lie-detector machine has conclusively determined his guilt and continued resistance is therefore futile. Behavioral lie-detection methods have created a whole new category of evidence—demeanor evidence—that detectives use to convince the suspect that he is caught and that there is no way for him to escape this predicament. As a method of persuasion, it makes no difference whether the interrogator is telling the truth or lying about the outcome of a particular lie-detection test. If the interrogator persuades the suspect that the lie-detector instrument can read his mind and that the accumulating "scientific" demeanor evidence irrefutably establishes his guilt, the suspect should become resigned to the idea of confessing. That, at least, is the theory.

Police reformers also turned to methods of behavioral lie detection to increase the rate at which confessions would lead to successful prosecutions. They understood that confessions regularly lead to convictions, typically with minimal fanfare, so long as they are perceived as legitimately obtained. Because confessions are regarded as strong prima facie evidence of guilt, they usually induce the defendant to accept a plea bargain—the most efficient means of conviction—to a lesser charge or sentence. They thus typically serve the goal of police and prosecutors while sparing them considerable time and expense. Moreover, if challenged by defense attorneys, confessions induced through behavioral methods of lie detection are far more likely to hold up in court than those based on the third degree. This was particularly true following the Wickersham Commission Report and the changing legal climate in the 1930s. Although the results of behavioral lie-detection methods (e.g., whether a suspect supposedly "passed" or "failed" a polygraph exam) are not admissible in court, the use of those methods as an interrogation strategy is regarded as acceptable by American courts. Confessions induced through behavioral lie-detection methods are therefore virtually always admissible if the defendant chooses to take his case to trial.

Behavioral methods of lie detection served another useful function for police in the 1930s: they allowed detectives to keep what occurred during interrogation hidden from scrutiny. Police believe that their interrogation techniques require some measure of secrecy to be successful (Weisberg, 1961), and methods of behavioral lie detection served to keep them hidden for two reasons. First, most people assume that the sole purpose of behavioral lie detection is truth verification, not the elicitation of confessions. By shifting the focus away from the interrogator and his techniques to the lie-detection machine and endowing it with oracular status in the name of modern science, the detective mystifies the interrogation process. He creates the illusion that he is not an adversary but merely a neutral investigator; that custodial questioning is merely an honesty test; and that the purpose of interrogation is not to incriminate the suspect but to pursue the truth. Through these illusions, behavioral methods of lie detection serve as an effective tool of persuasion. They also create the opportunity for impression management by allowing police to claim that the cause of the suspect's confession was his failure of the truth-verification exam rather than their manipulative or coercive interrogation methods.

The second reason behavioral lie-detection methods served to keep interrogation methods insulated from scrutiny is that even in cases in which a criminal defendant goes to trial, defense attorneys typically will not present an account of the lie-detection methods used to elicit their clients' confessions. They fear that if the jury hears from a police officer that a client failed a lie-detection test such as the polygraph, the jury will automatically convict the defendant—even if the interrogating detective was lying about the results of the test, as is often the case.

Behavioral lie-detection methods thus were a brilliant substitute for the third degree. Just as legitimately obtained confessional evidence typically keeps the interrogation out of public view by leading to a plea bargain, the use of lie-detection methods typically keeps the interrogation out of public view by, in effect, preventing a jury from fully learning exactly how the confession was elicited. Either outcome contributes to the mystification that is at the heart of modern psychological interrogation.

The shift to methods of behavioral lie detection in the 1930s also served the agenda of police management by making it easier for them to counter any effort to break the monopoly police held on the interrogation function. American police leaders had good reason to fear that the interrogation function might be reallocated to another criminal justice agency. Shortly after the Wickersham Commission Report was released, there were calls to transfer the interrogation function from police to the judiciary (Kauper, 1932). Interrogation had, after all, been the exclusive domain of judicial magistrates less than 100 years earlier (Kamisar, 1980). The Wickersham Commission Report itself had suggested that the judicial branch reassert authority over the pretrial interrogation function. The turn to methods of behavioral lie detection allowed police leaders to create the appearance that they were reining in their detectives as they were repudiating the third degree and professionalizing the interrogation function. The turn to behavioral lie detection, however, may have changed the content of police interrogation but it did not change its structure or function. Minus the ability to coerce the suspect physically, the detective retained as much discretion as before. The objective of securing a confession remained paramount. With only minor oversimplification, one might say that trial by third degree was replaced, in effect, with trial by behavioral lie detection. John Larson, one of the early police pioneers in the field of behavioral lie detection and polygraphy, would draw the analogy himself (Lykken, 1998: 28–29): "I originally hoped that instrumental lie detection would become a legitimate part of professional police science. It is little more than a racket. The lie detector, as used in many places, is nothing more than a psychological third-degree aimed at extorting confessions as the old physical beatings were. At times I'm sorry I ever had any part in its development."

Although the polygraph is the first and archetypical instrument that sought to turn interrogators into human lie detectors and successful psychological manipulators, it is only one among several such devices that police have developed since the 1920s and 1930s. In American police interrogation, the search for the magic lie detector is never-ending because of the real and imagined benefits that such an instrument promises to deliver. Each new idea holds out the hope that, with less effort, the detective can become an even more effective interrogator. The search has also made some public and private law enforcement individuals quite wealthy.

The Search for the Magic Lie Detector

THE POLYGRAPH

The polygraph, or so-called lie detector, continues to bear striking similarities to the trial by ordeal. But the polygraph is a distinctly twentieth-century phenomenon; steeped in the aura and rhetoric of scientism, it has taken on iconic status in American popular culture and mythology (Alder, 2007). The U.S. federal government and state law enforcement agencies subject thousands of individuals to polygraph testing each year as part of preemployment and postemployment screening and in criminal and forensic investigations. With blind superstition, the government relies on the results of polygraph examinations for decisions about national security (National Research Council, 2003), including whether to go to war (Drogin and Miller, 2004) and sometimes even about other life and death matters (Tucker, 1997). Here I am concerned primarily with the use of the polygraph and other modern truth technologies in criminal investigations.

The polygraph was invented to serve as a tool of criminal investigation that would both identify the guilty and elicit confessions. The invention and evolution of the modern lie detector can be traced to a few men. In

1915 William Moulton Marston, a psychologist and lawyer, first used a blood-pressure cuff and stethoscope to obtain intermittent recordings of changes in a suspect's systolic blood pressure during questioning. In 1921, John Larson, a psychologist employed by the Berkeley Police Department, constructed an instrument that could simultaneously and continuously record blood pressure as well as pulse and respiration during the interrogation of criminal suspects. In the late 1920s and the 1930s, Leonard Keeler refined the lie-detector machine, adding to Larson's instrument a galvanometer (also known as the galvanic skin reflex), which measures changes in a person's skin resistance to electricity during questioning. In 1945 John E. Reid, a lawyer by training and an employee of the Chicago Police Department's Scientific Crime Detection Laboratory, modified the Larson-Keeler polygraph instrument even further by appending an auxiliary unit that could record changes in a subject's muscular activity during questioning. Reid also introduced the idea of evaluating "behavior symptoms" (i.e., body language and demeanor) as a supplementary method of scoring polygraph examinations. Finally, Cleve Backster introduced a competing polygraph format that relied on strictly numerical scoring of polygraph charts.

As designed, the polygraph examination unfolds in three stages: the pretest interview, the examination itself, and the posttest interrogation. In pretest interviews, examiners typically introduce themselves, explain how the polygraph works, and then hook subjects up to the machine. The polygraph consists of a pneumograph, psychogalvanometer, and cardiophygmograph, which are connected to electrically driven ink pens and a moving chart that graphically registers changes in the subject's physiological responses as he answers questions. In the typical polygraph examination, one rubber belt or tube is strapped around a suspect's stomach and another around his chest or abdomen; a blood-pressure cuff is stretched around the person's bicep; and metal electrode wires are fastened to the ends of the fingers. Together these attachments measure signs of arousal in the autonomic nervous system, recording changes in blood pressure, depth and rate of breathing, pulse rate and strength, skin conductivity and temperature, and palmar sweating.

In the pretest interview, the polygrapher will also typically ask the subject medical questions—to create the appearance of scientific professionalism—provide a consent form, direct him to sign it, and go over the sequence of questions that will follow in the examination itself. At this stage, the polygrapher may ask the subject questions about his personal life or prior misconduct (having nothing to do with the crime at issue) or questions that seek to elicit information that the polygrapher can later use when trying to manipulate the suspect to confess. Perhaps above all, however, the purpose of the pretest interview is to persuade the subject both that the polygrapher's professionalism and impartiality are beyond question and that the polygraph machine is so technologically sophisticated and scientifically valid that it does not make mistakes. The polygrapher is, in effect, trying to preemptively disarm the subject should he later wish to dispute the results.

Polygraphers will go out of their way to explain that they are not detectives or affiliated with law enforcement (even if they are), that they are purely neutral technicians (even if they are not) whose singular goal is to get the truth (even if it is not). They may even tell the suspect that they are trying to help him pass the examination and thus establish his innocence. Polygraphers will actively seek to persuade the subject of the machine's infallibility, perhaps telling him that it is used by the Department of Defense, that it was developed at the nation's leading physics laboratory (invariably Johns Hopkins University), and that it has a 99 percent accuracy rate, with the only exceptions being individuals who are drunk or mentally retarded (the interrogator is then quick to confirm that the subject is neither drunk nor mentally retarded). In the pretest interview, the polygrapher may also run a "stim test" by asking the suspect to choose a card from a loaded deck (of which the suspect is unaware) and then pretend to determine from the polygraph charts which card was chosen (e.g., the queen of hearts), thereby creating the impression that the polygraph can read the subject's mind and detect even the slightest deception with near certainty.

Once the pretest interview is complete, the polygrapher will typically proceed to the examination itself and ask the subject the set of predetermined questions several times. A polygraph examination essentially contains three types of questions: *irrelevant* questions that ask about a topic that does not bear on the crime at issue (e.g., "Is today Wednesday?"), *relevant* questions (e.g., "Did you kill [the victim]?"), and *control* questions that seek to provoke the suspect to lie about a general matter (e.g., "Have you ever broken the law?"). The theory underlying the polygraph is that the act of lying induces fear and anxiety in the subject, causing internal tensions that produce involuntary and measurable physiological responses. If the subject is more physiologically aroused by the relevant questions than by either the irrelevant or control questions, the polygraph examiner scores his reactions as "deceptive." If the subject is more physiologically aroused by the control or irrelevant questions than by the relevant questions, the polygraph examiner scores his reactions as "truthful." And if the two sets (i.e., relevant and irrelevant or control) of reactions remain roughly equal, the examiner scores the subject's reactions as "inconclusive."

In practice, however, the criminal suspect is almost always told that he failed the exam, even if he did not. In the dozens of polygraphic interrogations that I have studied, I have never once seen a polygrapher tell a suspect that he passed the exam and then let him go. Instead, after the polygrapher informs the suspect that he failed, he repeats his earlier assertion that the machine does not make mistakes and then either barrels forward to the posttest interrogation (the object of the test in the first place) or leaves the room so that the detectives can directly interrogate the suspect. In the posttest interrogation, the polygrapher or detectives typically tell the suspect that the exam results conclusively demonstrate that he committed the crime, he can no longer deny this fact, and he should therefore admit to some version of the offense. As we will see in more detail in the Chapter 4, the polygraph and other truth technologies are one of the many "evidence ploys" that police interrogators use to convince a suspect that he is caught and has no choice but to consent to the interrogators' demand that he confess. Ironically, the polygraph is not so much an instrument of detecting deception by the suspect as it is of perpetrating deception by interrogators. Its stated purpose of detecting "truth" or "deception" aside, its primary function has always been to induce confessions.

The polygraph is a highly effective interrogation technique. David Lykken (1998: 271) estimated that "with the polygraph in action, as many as 25% of crimes may be solved neatly and efficiently by means of a confession." But the polygraph is not an accurate lie detector. It is based on flawed, if not completely implausible, assumptions. It does not and cannot measure deception because when humans lie (or tell the truth, for that matter) they do not react in distinctive, involuntary physiological ways. Rather, the polygraph can only measure the emotional arousal a suspect experiences in response to particular questions *as a proxy for deception.* There is no logical reason, however, why lying subjects will experience greater stress or arousal (and truth tellers will experience less) in response to relevant questions than irrelevant or control questions. Some people exhibit nervous symptoms when they lie, but many do not. And many truthful subjects will display signs of nervousness and stress when they are telling the truth—especially during an accusatory interrogation. As Lykken (1998: 60, 66) has pointed out:

> There will never be a Truth Verifier (lie detector) until a specific lie re-
> sponse can be identified . . . A polygraph examiner who asserts that a re-
> spondent "showed deception" or "gave a deception response" on a particu-
> lar question is making either a misstatement or a false statement. He may
> be entitled to say, based on the charts, that the respondent made a larger
> response to one question than to another, and the examiner may proceed
> to draw some inference based on this difference. But the myth of the spe-
> cific lie response should be laid at last, permanently, to rest.

The real lie detector is not the sophisticated truth-verifying machine, with its seemingly objective outputs, but, rather, the polygrapher administering the exam, with his subjective judgments and intuition.

The claims of proponents of the polygraph that it is accurate 95 to 99 per-cent of the time are simply wild exaggerations with no empirical basis and have been discredited by scientific critics (Kleinmuntz and Szucko, 1984; Ekman, 1992; Lykken, 1998). In fact, the few methodologically sound studies of polygraphy suggest that the so-called lie detector is accurate no more than 60 to 75 percent of the time (Lykken, 1998). However, poly-graph examiners are more likely to make false-positive errors (classifying a truthful subject as lying) than false-negative errors (classifying a lying sub-ject as truthful). According to the leading scientific critics of the polygraph, an innocent subject stands a nearly 50 percent chance of failing the exami-nation (Kleinmunz and Szucko, 1984; Lykken, 1998). As Kleinmuntz and Szucko (1984: 774) have concluded, "modern lie detection is no more sci-entific than King Solomon's sword."

THE TRUTH SERUM

In the early part of the twentieth century, physicians began to give the anes-thetizing drug scopolamine to women during childbirth. In the early 1920s, Dr. Robert House, a Texas obstetrician, observed that scopolamine, as well as chloroform, induced "twilight sleep" that caused women to lose their inhibi-tions and share their private thoughts without hesitation, but later to forget what they had said. Dr. House subsequently sought to extend the use of scopolamine to the interrogation of criminal suspects. In an article pub-lished in 1931, on the basis of two cases, he argued that "a person under scopolamine could not lie and that the drug could distinguish the innocent from the guilty" (Gottschalk, 1961: 112). Dr. House conducted several hundred experiments trying to prove this, frequently traveling the country to teach law enforcement about the interrogational benefits of the "truth serum" (Geis, 1959). In the 1920s and 1930s, police trainers and researchers at the Scientific Crime Detection Laboratory in Chicago also experimented with various truth serum potions as a means of extracting confessions (Muehlberger, 1951). Some evidence suggests that truth serum drugs were employed extensively during interrogations in this era (Geis, 1959).

Like the polygraph, the truth serum was a potential alternative to the third degree. As John Larson (1932: 215) observed, "if it can be shown that the proper use of scopolamine is without danger to the individual, certainly the method is to be preferred over the usual browbeating, the whipping, and the other large variety of methods usually used to break the will of the suspect." The truth serum was also praised as a method that would "add an element of scientific certainty to court hearings" (Geis, 1959: 355). Police professionals such as Larson, Leonard Keeler, John Reid, Fred Inbau, and others regarded the truth serum as a potentially invincible lie detector through which detectives could elicit reliable confessions (Geis, 1959; Winters, 2005). Interrogators directed physicians to inject suspects with a truth serum drug (typically scopolamine but also morphine, chloroform, sodium amytal, or sodium pentothal), waited for it to produce "twilight sleep," and then interrogated the suspect. The leader of one professional society asserted that under the truth serum a subject is "unable mentally to divert his brain from what he knows to be true. A true knowledge of the subject's mind is revealed, leaving the examiner in a position of knowing what knowledge the subject possesses on any topic" (Larson, 1932: 210). Although it prompted suspects to be talkative, once the truth serum drug wore off, suspects supposedly could not recall anything they said during interrogation. Because the truth serum depressed the brain almost to the point of unconsciousness, police believed that it prevented suspects from lying in response to questions or concocting stories and thus rendered them incapable of lying (Mulbar, 1951).

Though American police used the truth serum for many years, it was eventually abandoned after the 1963 U.S. Supreme Court decision *Townsend v. Sain*, which held that a truth-serum-induced confession was unconstitutionally coerced. The use of truth serums (sometimes referred to as narco-analysis, narco-interrogation, or narcosis) during interrogation has also been discredited because the serums are likely to induce a heightened state of suggestibility and thus cause suspects to make unreliable statements (Gottschalk, 1961; Piper, 1994).

VOICE STRESS ANALYSIS

Another interrogation technology dressed up as "scientific" lie detection is voice stress analysis. In the 1960s, Lieutenant Colonel Allan Bell, an army intelligence officer, and Lieutenant Colonel Charles McQuiston, an army polygrapher, designed an instrument known as the Psychological Stress Evaluator (PSE), which was the first commercially available voice stress analyzer (Segrave, 2004). In the 1980s, the PSE was replaced by the Computer Voice Stress Analyzer (CVSA), a modified notebook computer with an attached microphone that is produced by a company that calls itself the National Institute for Truth Verification (National Institute for Truth Verification Training Manual, 2003). The CVSA processes voice fluctuations into patterns and charts that it graphically displays on a computer screen. The theory of voice stress analysis is that the human voice emits inaudible vibrations known as micro-tremors when a human is lying and that the CVSA can reliably measure them. The voice of a truthful subject will supposedly display peaks on the computer screen, whereas the voice of a lying subject will display lines that are more blocked and squared off. According to the National Institute for Truth Verification, more than 1,700 law enforcement agencies across the country now use the CVSA (http://www. cvsa1.com, 2007).

The Computer Voice Stress Analyzer is fundamentally similar to the polygraph. Both operate on the theory that the individual who lies will experience stress that is involuntarily manifested in his physiological responses; that the subject's stress can be directly measured; and that examiners can infer whether subject's stress reactions indicate that he is lying or telling the truth. Both claim astonishingly high accuracy rates (95 to 99 percent for the CVSA too) (Lykken, 1998). The CVSA and polygraph are also administered in fundamentally similar ways. Like the polygraph, the CVSA uses relevant, irrelevant, and control questions, as well as "zone of comparison" and "modified zone of comparison" test formats. Like the polygrapher, the CVSA examiner relies on pattern and chart interpretation to infer deception or truth-telling. And the CVSA examination unfolds in the same sequence of stages as the polygraph: from rapport-building pretesting (in which the subject is directed to sign a waiver releasing the examiner from any liability) to the administration of the examination to the posttest interrogation.

Despite their similarities, however, the National Institute for Truth Verification markets the CVSA as superior to the polygraph. Unlike the polygraph, the CVSA does not require that wires be strapped to the suspect; indeed, it does not even require the suspect's knowledge. The CVSA can thus be used covertly and on recordings of the human voice, whether the individual is dead or alive. The National Institute for Truth Verification, as well as police proponents of the CVSA, point out that investigators can be trained to use the CVSA more quickly than the polygraph and that the CVSA is a far less expensive piece of equipment for departments to purchase (http://www.cvsa1.com, 2006; Wilkens, 1998). By using the CVSA, police departments can, in effect, "cut out the middleman" by having many of their criminal investigators trained to use the CVSA rather than training or having to rely on one or two in-house polygraphers. The National Institute for Truth Verification further asserts that, unlike the polygraph, the CVSA is not restricted to yes-or-no questions; that it never produces inconclusive results; that there are no known ways to fool the machine; and that it is not affected by the subject's age, medical condition, or drug use. They also claim that CVSA examiners can conduct three times as many exams per day (http://www.cvsa1.com, 2006). Perhaps not surprisingly, a bitter war of words has developed between the polygraph industry (including state and national polygraph associations) and the voice stress analysis industry, both of whom compete for a lucrative public and private law enforcement market.

Like the polygraph (and all behavioral lie-detection technologies, for that matter), the real purpose of the CVSA as an interrogation technique is to elicit confessions. Proponents of the CVSA are far more forthcoming about this function than are their polygraph counterparts (Lykken, 1998). Indeed, the CVSA training manual explicitly states that "the primary goal" of the CVSA is to "extract a confession or admission" (National Institute for Truth Verification Training Manual, 2003: 88). The National Institute for Truth Verification's training materials teach police how to use the CVSA as part of an interrogation strategy described as "Defense Barrier Removal" that "will increase your confession rates dramatically" (National Institute for Truth Verification Training Manual, 2003: i). According to this strategy, most guilty subjects have one or more fears (e.g., incarceration, public shame, financial loss, retribution from co-conspirators) that become barriers to confessing.

The CVSA interrogates suspects by breaking down their fears. But the so-called Defense Barrier Removal technique is little more than a repackaging of standard interrogation techniques—such as rapport building, the projection of sincerity and impartiality, appeals to authority, evidence ploys, and the use of minimizing scenarios "to give the suspect an out"—recommended by virtually all contemporary interrogation training manuals and firms.

Though effective at eliciting confessions, the CVSA arguably takes junk science inside the interrogation room to new heights. There is no evidence that inaudible micro-tremors even exist in the human voice, much less that the CVSA can measure them. Therefore there is no evidence or reason to believe that the CVSA can identify differences in stress reflected in the human voice or that a CVSA examiner can reliably infer truth or deception from the CVSA's charts. Even if the CVSA could measure identifiable stress in the human voice, there would be no way for the examiner to know whether deception or any number of other factors actually caused the stress. Not surprisingly, then, there is no empirical support for the CVSA as an instrument of behavioral lie detection or truth verification (National Research Council, 2003). In fact, existing studies suggest that the ability of the CVSA to detect deception is no better than chance (Lykken, 1998). A series of Department of Defense studies in the 1990s found no credible evidence that voice stress analysis is effective at determining deception (see National Research Council, 2003 for a review), leading the National Research Council to conclude (2003: 168): "overall, this research and the few controlled tests conducted over the past decade offer little or no scientific basis for the computer voice stress analyzer." Lykken (1998: 173) put it more succinctly: "The voice stress lie test has roughly zero validity."

BEHAVIORAL ANALYSIS

Like voice stress analysis, behavioral analysis also has its origins in the polygraph, both historically and conceptually. John Reid, one of the early pioneers of polygraph testing, first developed the idea of "behavior symptom analysis" as a supplementary criterion in the scoring of polygraph charts in the 1940s. He later introduced it as a structured pretest interview method, though it was not formally written up as a lie-detection interrogation technique until 1986 (see Inbau, Reid, and Buckley, 1986). According to Reid, truthful and deceptive subjects displayed different behavioral responses (i.e., body language) and attitudes to questions before, during, and after polygraph testing (Reid and Inbau, 1977). To decipher these behavioral responses, Reid might have his secretary observe the demeanor and actions of subjects waiting to be polygraphed, place them in interrogation rooms, and exam them directly through a one-way mirror, or interrupt a polygraph examination to observe subjects' demeanors and actions from an adjoining room. According to Reid and Inbau (1977), lying suspects attempted to postpone the examination date, were late for the appointment, or altogether failed to appear; acted worried and highly nervous; had a resentful attitude; were aggressive and evasive; tended to have a mental block; were prone to suffering an extremely dry mouth or gurgling stomach; continually sighed or yawned; refused to look the examiner in the eye; and were overly friendly or polite. By contrast, truthful subjects requested or were glad to be given the polygraph exam; had confidence in the accuracy of the polygraph and the examiner; and were sincere and straightforward, completely cooperative, and not overly polite or solicitous (Reid and Inbau, 1977). From these apparent observations, the practice of behavior analysis was born.

As with the polygraph, the underlying theory of behavior analysis is that a normally socialized person will experience inner conflict and anxiety when lying, which will then manifest itself in involuntary physiological stress reactions. The deceptive individual, the theory goes, displays certain nonverbal behavior symptoms (manifested in body posture, eye contact, gestures, and movements) as well as verbal behaviors (e.g., attitudes and statements) in order to reduce the anxiety or conflict associated with lying, while the truthful individual does not. This theory assumes, therefore, that only deceptive subjects will experience stress in the interrogation room; that, as a result, they will behave and speak differently from truthful subjects; and that a police officer trained in behavior analysis can visually recognize these stress reactions (or clusters of them) and correctly infer that the suspect is deceptive and therefore guilty.

The most prominent method of behavior analysis is the "Behavioral Analysis Interview" (BAI), which was created and is now marketed by the Chicago-based interrogation training firm John Reid and Associates (Inbau et al., 1986).[1] The BAI, according to its proponents (Inbau et al., 1986; Inbau, Reid, Buckley, and Jayne, 2001; Jayne and Buckley, 1999), consists of fifteen to twenty questions designed to evoke particular behavioral (verbal, nonverbal, and paralinguistic) responses from which the interrogator can allegedly discern whether a suspect is telling the truth or lying. The BAI questions are listed in Table 3.1.

Table 3.1. Behavioral Analysis Questions

Behavioral analysis interview (BAI) question	Truthful	?	Deceptive
1. What is your understanding of the purpose for this interview with me here today?			
2. We are investigating the (alleged crime). Did you commit the (alleged crime)?			
3. Who do you think did (alleged crime)?			
4. Who do you suspect may have done this?			
5. Is there anyone you feel certain who would not do this?			
6. Do you think that someone purposely did this?			
7. Who would have the best chance to do this?			
8. How do you feel about being interviewed concerning this (alleged crime)?			
9. Have you ever thought about doing (alleged crime)?			
10. Why do you think someone did (alleged crime)?			
11. What do you think should happen to the person who did this (alleged crime)?			
12. Do you think that the person who did this should be given a second chance?			
13. Tell me why you wouldn't do something like this?			
14. What do you think the results of our investigation will show with respect to your involvement in (alleged crime)?			
15. Who did you tell about your interview with me today?			

Source: Inbau et al. (2001).

The alleged responses of liars to these questions are listed in Table 3.2. In the introductory (three-day) and advanced (two-day) interview and interrogation training courses that I took in 1991, Reid and Associates advised police to treat as guilty and thus formally interrogate any suspect whose answers to four or more of the questions the detective felt were deceptive

Table 3.2. Alleged Responses of Liars to Behavioral Analysis Questions

BAI question	Alleged indicator of deception
1. What is your understanding of the purpose for this interview with me here today?	More evasive than truth-tellers
2. We are investigating the (alleged crime). Did you commit the (alleged crime)?	Less emphatic in their denials than truth-tellers
3. Who do you think did (alleged crime)?	More likely to deny knowledge
4. Who do you suspect may have done this?	Less likely to name someone who is innocent
5. Is there anyone you feel certain who would not do this?	Less likely to name someone who is innocent
6. Do you think that someone purposely did this?	Less likely to admit that a crime took place
7. Who would have the best chance to do this?	Less likely to admit they had an opportunity
8. How do you feel about being interviewed concerning this (alleged crime)?	More likely to voice negative feelings
9. Have you ever thought about doing (alleged crime)?	More likely to admit to having thought about committing a crime
10. Why do you think someone did (alleged crime)?	Less likely to give a reasonable motive
11. What do you think should happen to the person who did this (alleged crime)?	Less likely to suggest serious punishment
12. Do you think that the person who did this should be given a second chance?	More likely to give someone a second chance
13. Tell me why you wouldn't do something like this?	More likely to answer in the third person
14. What do you think the results of our investigation will show with respect to your involvement in (alleged crime)?	Express less confidence in being exonerated
15. Who did you tell about your interview with me today?	Less likely to have informed their loved ones

Source: Inbau et al. (2001). See also Vrij, Mann, and Fisher (2006).

(Reid training in 2001 included the same instruction) (Shertz, 2004). Investigators are cautioned to look for clusters of behavioral responses indicating deception rather than a single response; to search out deviations from the suspect's normal behavior patterns; to evaluate verbal, nonverbal, and paralinguistic behavior simultaneously; and to assess the timing and consistency of the subject's behaviors and responses before determining deception (Inbau et al., 2001). But in the Reid training that I received, interrogators were instructed that "the rule of thumb" should be that the suspect is "untruthful."[2]

Modeled after the polygraph in both logic and application, the BAI purports to turn the investigator into a human lie detector and to use the results—whether real, imagined, or invented—as a technique for successful interrogation. The BAI was invented as an acceptable substitute for the polygraph in situations where a polygraph exam was too costly, too time-consuming, or not legally permitted (Wicklander, 1979, 1980). As an interrogation tool, the BAI may be superior to the polygraph insofar as the detective needs far less training (one day or less will usually suffice), need not rely on any equipment or mechanical device, and can allegedly visually assess whether the subject is guilty. After the passage of the federal Employee Polygraph Protection Act of 1988, which prevents most private sector employers from requiring job applicants and current employees to take polygraph screening tests, the BAI has, according to its proponents, become a standard investigative technique (Jayne and Buckley, 1999: 1). Just as the polygraph was a functional alternative to the third degree, the BAI has become a functional alternative to the polygraph.

Like the polygraph, the real purpose of behavioral analysis is not to detect deception or verify truth-telling, but to assist the interrogator in developing an interrogation strategy and eliciting incriminating statements. Behavioral analysis essentially unfolds in three steps, just like the polygraph: the investigator engages in rapport-building observation, administers the questions (including so-called control questions), and then engages in posttest interrogation. Some of the test questions are designed to gauge the suspect's psychological weaknesses so that the investigator can more effectively manipulate the suspect's perceptions in the posttest interrogation. For example, the "Objection" question ("Why wouldn't you do something like this?") is intended to identify the suspect's fears of confessing so that the interrogator may fashion an interrogation strategy to overcome them, just as the "Motive" ("Why do you feel someone would have done this?") and "Second

Chance" questions ("Do you think the person who did do this would deserve a second chance under any circumstances?") are designed to elicit information that will assist interrogators in developing successful "themes" (i.e., invented scenarios that minimize, excuse, or justify the suspect's actions) in the subsequent interrogation. Like the polygraph (and all other magic lie detectors), behavioral analysis permits interrogators—in the absence of any objective evidence of innocence or guilt—to rationalize intuitions, guesses, and hunches about a suspect's culpability while invoking the aura of modern science. John E. Reid and Associates boasts that law enforcement officials trained in the BAI can accurately discriminate between truth-telling and deception 85 percent of the time (Meissner and Kassin, 2002: 470). But there is no credible empirical evidence to support this claim (Vrij, Mann, and Fisher, 2006).

There are both theoretical and empirical problems with the assumptions of behavior analysis and the assertions of its proponents. Because no physiological or psychological response unique to lying exists, the theory of behavioral analysis is simplistic, if not altogether implausible. Since there is no behavior unique to deception, there is no logical basis for asserting that the act of lying leads to specific or clustered nonverbal, verbal, or paralinguistic "behavior symptoms." The act of telling the truth may produce the very same "symptoms." As David Simon (1991: 219), who spent a year observing interrogations inside the Baltimore homicide squad, has written: "Nervousness, fear, confusion, hostility, a story that changes or contradicts itself—all are signs that the man in an interrogation room is lying, particularly in the eyes of someone as naturally suspicious as a detective. Unfortunately, these are also signs of a human being in a state of high stress." Kassin and Fong (1999: 511–512) have similarly pointed out: "Nonverbal behaviors such as rigid posture, grooming, covering the mouth while speaking, and averting gaze may well betray a state of anxiety or distress, but there is no solid empirical basis for the proposition that these same cues reliably discriminate between criminals and innocent persons accused of crimes they did not commit." And just as one cannot assume that the act of lying leads to certain behavior symptoms, so too one cannot reason backwards from the existence of such symptoms to infer the act of lying. This is the logical fallacy known as *post hoc ergo proper hoc.*

Numerous controlled studies have shown that people generally are not good intuitive judges of truth and deception (Miller and Stiff, 1993; Bond and DePaulo, 2006),typically performing at no better than chance levels of accuracy (Vrij, 2000; DePaulo et al., 2003). Controlled studies have also shown that even investigators and other supposed experts who routinely evaluate deceptive behavior are highly prone to error (Ekman and O'Sullivan, 1991; Vrij, 1994; Ekman, O'Sullivan, and Frank, 1999). Moreover, Kassin and Fong (1999) have shown that police interrogators and others specifically trained in the BAI not only fail to discriminate accurately between true and false denials much of the time, but also that behavior analysis training actually lowers the ability of police interrogators to discriminate accurately between true and false denials. Further, such training inflates their confidence in their judgments (see also Meissner and Kassin, 2004). Vrij, Mann, and Fisher (2006), who also empirically tested the Behavioral Analysis Interview, found that "the BAI questioning led to differences between liars and truth-tellers but the difference was in the opposite direction to that anticipated by Inbau et al. They expected liars to be less helpful in investigations and to exhibit more nervous behavior. In fact, liars were more helpful and displaced less nervous behavior."

By authoritatively claiming that police interrogators can somehow divine whether suspects are lying or telling the truth based on a post hoc assessment of their demeanor, attitudes, and gestures, police interrogation training manuals, courses, and firms prime investigators to believe that they are human lie detectors who can justify their presumptions of guilt and use them to effectively elicit confessions. As with the polygraph and voice stress analysis, the Behavioral Analysis Interview is an oracular method of lie detection that is dressed up as scientific but whose real purpose is to help police elicit confessions.

STATEMENT ANALYSIS

Police interrogators have also turned to the analysis of a suspect's written language to infer deception and then use the results as a basis for eliciting confessions. This method of human lie detection is generally referred to as "statement analysis," though it sometimes also goes by the names "content analysis" or the seemingly postmodern "investigative discourse analysis" (Rabon, 1994). In America, the primary method of statement analysis in police interrogation is known as "Scientific Content Analysis" (SCAN Handbook, 1990). SCAN was invented in the mid-1980s by Avinoam Sapir, an ex-polygrapher and former code breaker in the Israeli army who now teaches and markets SCAN through his Phoenix-based company, Laboratory for

Scientific Interrogation (Gordon and Fleisher, 2006). According to Sapir, SCAN is used not only by American state, military, and federal law enforcement, but also by police in Australia, Canada, Israel, Mexico, Singapore, South Africa, England, Belgium, and the Netherlands (http://www.lsiscan .com, 2004, 2006). In the United States, "training in statement analysis has been extensive, widespread, and lucrative in the field of law enforcement and private security," according to one author (Shearer, 1999: 41).

The assumptions of SCAN are relatively simple. First, most deceptive suspects do not explicitly lie so much as fail to tell the entire truth. In other words, most guilty suspects will lie by omitting truthful information rather than by providing false information. Second, a deceptive suspect writes and talks differently than a truthful one, and the structure and content of truthful and deceptive written statements differ in systematic and patterned ways. "The deceptive person is working from imagination, according to Sapir, and the truthful person is working from memory" (Lesce, 1990). Finally, investigators trained in the SCAN method can infer whether a suspect is lying or telling the truth by analyzing the content and structure of his written statements *independent of any case facts.*

SCAN and other forms of statement analysis parallel the three-stage process (administration, evaluation, interrogation) found in most behavioral lie-detection methods. The investigator obtains a "pure" written statement from thesuspect about his involvement or lack of involvement in the crime, then evaluates the language in the statement for deception or truthfulness; and then, if the suspect is judged to be deceptive, the investigator launches into the posttest interrogation. The investigator infers the truthfulness of deception by analyzing the structure and content of the words used in the written statement. More specifically, the investigator analyzes the four aspects of the suspect's written statement: the parts of speech used by the suspect, whether the statement contains extraneous information, whether it lacks conviction, and its balance. Focusing on parts of speech, for example, SCAN teaches that truthful people give statements using the pronoun "I" (Adams, 1996: 13) rather than the pronoun "we"; that deceptive suspects are more likely to omit the pronoun "we" or overuse it; that deceptive suspects are less likely to use possessive pronouns; that they are more likely to shift from singular to plural pronouns or vice versa; that truthful suspects rarely talk about themselves in the third person; and that deceptive people are less likely to use the past verb tense and more likely to switch from the past tense to the present tense (Adams, 1996; Hess, 1997). Deceptive suspects engage in these linguistic maneuvers to "dilute their own culpability," according to SCAN (Hess, 1997: 60). SCAN also teaches that deceptive suspects write statements full of extraneous information (i.e., more detail than is necessary to answer the question) and lack conviction (i.e., tend to use phrases such as "I don't remember" and "I can't recall" as well as other hedging and qualifying language that shows a lack of commitment to their story). SCAN teaches that an investigator can infer deception if the suspect's statement lacks "balance" too. As Adams (1996: 20) put it:

> A truthful statement has three parts. The first part details what was going on before the event occurred; it places the event in context. The second part describes the occurrence itself . . . The last part tells what occurred after the event, including actions and emotions, and should be at least as long as the first part. The more balanced the three parts of the statement, the greater the probability that the statement is true. A statement containing the same number of lines in the before, during and after parts, i.e., 33⅓ percent in each part, indicates truth . . . If any part of a statement is incomplete or missing altogether, then the statement is probably false.

The "psycho-linguistic differences between truthful and deceptive suspects" according to SCAN are listed in Table 3.3 (Gordon and Fleisher, 2006: 57).

The lie detection and interrogation claims made on behalf of SCAN are bold. Sapir boasts not only that SCAN's accuracy rate is above 95 percent but that "SCAN will solve every case for you quickly and easily. You only need the subject's own words, given of his/her free will . . . Scan will show you: whether the subject is truthful or deceptive; what information the subject is concealing; whether or not the subject was involved in the crime" (http://www.lsiscan.com, 2004). Sapir further boasts that SCAN is a "cold technique" that can be used to solve high-profile cases. Based on his own analysis, Sapir has declared that William Kennedy Smith was innocent of the rape of which he was accused; that both Clarence Thomas and Anita Hill were lying; and that John Ramsey killed his daughter, JonBenet Ramsey. Sapir advertises SCAN as the easiest and most accurate, objective, and conclusive of all the lie-detection interrogation methods, and the least expensive, intrusive, or likely to cause resentment among its subjects. In part, Sapir seeks to position SCAN as the lie-detection technology that is most effective at identifying deceptive suspects: "While others are out searching for physical evidence, you have already solved the case—using only the subject's own words," his company's website brags (http://www.lsiscan.com, 2004).

Table 3.3. Alleged Psycho-linguistic Differences between Truthful and Deceptive Suspects

Truthful	Deceptive
1. Rich in details	Lack of details
2. First person singular, past tense	Deviates from the first person singular, past tense
3. Proper introduction of victim: "My daughter . . ."	Improper introduction of victim: "She . . ."
4. Uses possessive pronoun: "My daughter . . ."	Lack of possessive pronoun: "The child . . ."
5. No gaps in time	Missing time: "Two hours later . . ."
6. Appropriate emotions in the right place (postincident)	No emotions
7. Will deny doing the crime before being asked	Only makes denials to direct question
8. Flow of story proper	Incorrect flow of story

Source: Gordon and Fleisher (2002: 43).

And "unlike the polygraph, it [SCAN] does not require attaching the subject to a machine, and obtaining a signed release . . . The subject is therefore unaware that his statement will be the object of specialized treatment and analysis." SCAN "transforms the investigator from an ordinary collector of information into a walking polygraph" (http://www.lsiscan.com, 2004).

Like so many other behavioral lie-detection technologies, the primary purpose of statement analysis is to assist interrogators in eliciting incriminating statements. As one proponent (Adams, 1996: 20) has argued, it can determine whether a statement is intended to "convey the truth or to convince through deception. Armed with this knowledge, investigators can enter the interview room with increased confidence to identify the perpetrator and gain a confession." Statement analysis allows interrogators to prejudge the suspect as deceptive and thus guilty before he even walks through the door. It affirms interrogators' hunches, suspicions, and judgments, thereby increasing their confidence in the accuracy of their presumption of guilt. Investigators then use the results of the statement analysis as an evidence ploy with which to confront the suspect and persuade him to confess (now that he has failed the "scientific" content analysis, investigators might intimate, no one will believe his claim of innocence).

Sapir alleges that SCAN is so effective as an interrogation technique that even "many polygraph examiners who use SCAN report a significantly increased rate of confessions either in the pretest or after it" (http://www .lsiscan.com, 2004).

But statement analysis is just another form of junk science. Despite its name, there is nothing scientific about so-called Scientific Content Analysis. Statement analysis in general and SCAN in particular are theoretically vague, if not vacuous (Miller and Stiff, 1993; Shuy, 1998; Shearer, 1999). The unstated theory of statement analysis appears to be that deceptive and truthful people use different types of language because they are drawing on different types of memory (i.e., real and nonexistent). Even if that is true, however, there is no reason to believe that this alone would cause deceptive and truthful individuals to write and speak differently, that they would do so in the specific ways that SCAN suggests, or that third parties could infer truth and deception from the speech patterns or language changes in a person's prewritten narrative independent of any case facts or knowledge of the individual's background or history.

If the theory underlying statement analysis is based on little more than speculation, the empirical evidence for its claims is no better. Simply put, there is no empirical validation for SCAN (Porter and Yuille, 1996; Shuy, 1998), just endless post hoc illustrations and testimonials by Sapir and his former students (http://www.lsiscan.com, 2004; Scientific Content Analysis Handbook, 1990). Nor is there good reason to believe that there will be any validation for SCAN or statement analysis any time soon (Miller and Stiff, 1993; Shuy, 1993;Shearer, 1999). As Roger Shuy (1998: 75) has pointed out, "the accuracy of the detection of deceitful language is . . . at about the level of chance." Moreover, SCAN completely ignores linguistic research on how people talk (Shuy, 1998). As with the other behavioral methods of lie detection analyzed above, the value of SCAN and statement analysis lies simply in its utility as an interrogation technique.

The Behavioral Ghost in the Machine

The polygraph was created, developed, and marketed by American law enforcement as an attempt to professionalize the image of criminal investigation and thus overcome the stigma associated with the third degree. The use of behavioral lie-detection methods is now central to American police interrogation. Despite their variety, they all reflect the same aspiration within

American police work: the search for a magic lie detector that, doubling as a thinly veiled interrogation technique, will assist police not only in identifying guilty suspects, but also in effectively eliciting confessions and publicly authenticating their voluntariness. Behavioral lie-detection methods have transformed the face of American interrogation in the last seventy-five years, even as its underlying structure—the presumption of guilt, the goal of incrimination, and the use of accusatorial methods designed to make suspects perceive they have no choice but to confess—remains similar to that of the era of the third degree.

Behavioral lie-detection methods serve three overriding functions: truth verification, incrimination, and impression management. The first function is highly problematic: all of these methods seek to detect deception by identifying the supposed telltale signs of lying through some bodily media (e.g., the suspect's heartbeat, voice, eye movements, use of language, and so on). But until a unique human lie response is discovered and can be measured, there will be no reliable lie detector machine or technology; the real lie detector will always be the investigator (Lykken, 1998), guided by intuitions, hunches, and stereotypes (see Meissner and Kassin, 2002). Modern human lie detection therefore typically amounts to little more than fancy guesswork, a process that is more akin to the witch-finding techniques of the late seventeenth century than the "scientific" methods of the early twenty-first century. Ironically, the most accurate of all the behavioral lie-detection methods may still be the polygraph, despite its high error rates.

Perhaps it is not surprising that law enforcement so fervently embraces modern truth technologies. American police are not behavioral scientists. They lack a background in modern science and are not trained to appreciate the fallibility of human perception, the social and cognitive biases in their clinical judgments, or the importance of systematic data gathering and analysis. As Paul Ekman (1992: 292) has pointed out: "While the police . . . may be well-intentioned, most are not well trained in how to ask unbiased and non-leading questions. They have not been taught how to evaluate behavioral clues to truthfulness and lying, and . . . they think that nearly everyone they see is guilty, and everyone is lying." Moreover, they do not appreciate how they "are made arrogant by the fact that they are protected from discovering their mistakes" because "the only feedback examiners typically receive is when a subject whom they have accused of lying actually confesses and thus corroborates their diagnosis" (Lykken, 1998: xv–xvi). There is nothing in the training of police detectives on why behavioral lie-detection methods are unreliable (Kassin and Fong, 1999; Vrij, 2000). Instead, these methods reinforce their belief in the superiority of their ability to detect deception. They allow investigators to confirm their preexisting suspicions, to impose certainty on ambiguous interactions and situations, and to exude confidence in the suspect's guilt, one of the most important traits in a successful interrogator, according to police training manuals (Inbau et al., 2001). As Meissner and Kassin (2004: 91) have observed, "police training in the detection of truth and deception leads investigators to make prejudgments of guilt, with high confidence, that are frequently in error."

Nor should it be surprising that law enforcement is always searching for the next great lie detector. Apart from the possible financial rewards, methods of behavioral lie detection are powerful means of manipulating and controlling human behavior. The second function of behavioral lie-detection methods—as a tool for inducing incriminating statements—is often paramount. As interrogation techniques, they can be extremely persuasive at disarming suspects, weakening their psychological resistance, and demoralizing them so that they comply with the interrogator and make a confession. Before administering the exam, interrogators will likely tell the suspect that "if you're telling the truth this machine will show it; if you're not, the machine will show that too,"—as if the machine can actually read the suspect's mind—in order to convince him that the results are indisputable (Hanson, 1993: 69). When told that he failed, the subject is thus placed in a cognitive bind: he can no longer deny his guilt without challenging the veracity of the results or the integrity of the interrogator, but neither response is socially acceptable. Most people presume police are trustworthy and therefore do not know that behavioral lie-detection methods are notoriously unreliable or that American law permits interrogators to lie about the test results.

The structure of the situation empowers interrogators by joining the rhetoric of scientific proof with their position of authority. But it disempowers the suspect by rendering him psychologically defenseless in the face of renewed accusations of his guilt. Like all evidence ploys, behavioral lie-detection interrogation methods are ultimately designed to convince the suspect that the evidence against him is so overwhelming that his only real option is to confess (Leo, 2001b). Though some of the truth technologies discussed here may be more powerful interrogation props than others, they are ultimately interchangeable once the interrogators convince the suspect of their infallibility. As one detective remarked, "If I put a spaghetti strainer on a suspect's head and he is convinced it is a device for detecting truth telling and it gets him to focus better, to tell me the truth, then I guess it worked" (Wilkens, 1998: E1). What Jerome Skolnick (1961: 705) long ago noted about the polygraph is equally true today of other behavioral lie-detection methods: "The chief function appears to be to induce confessions by deception, convincing the suspect that 'the machine doesn't lie'."

The third function of behavioral lie detection—impression management—is the least visible of all. The goal of psychological interrogation is not simply to elicit incriminating statements but to create the perception that they are both voluntary and reliable. The first step in the use of behavioral lie-detection methods is thus to orchestrate consent by directing the suspect to sign a waiver releasing the investigator from any liability and explicitly stating that the suspect is voluntarily answering questions. Relying on behavioral lie-detection methods, interrogators try to persuade the suspect that the questioning is not adversarial because both sides are committed to finding the truth—often telling the suspect that they are on his side and just want to help him pass the test—and therefore share the same interest. Behavioral lie-detection methods allow detectives to recast the interrogation as a mere honesty test and any admissions as freely given rather than as the product of intimidation or coercion. At the same time, the suspect's confession appears reliable because it seemingly corroborates the interrogators' initial diagnosis of deception. The larger impression management strategy, however, is to create the perception that the use of behavioral lie-detection methods have removed the problem of investigator bias and coercion from modern interrogation (Skolnick, 1961). These methods create the appearance of scientific neutrality and professionalism while masking the presumption of guilt, the reliance on deception, and the underlying goal of eliciting confessions. In this way, behavioral lie-detection methods perpetuate the fraud of modern American interrogation.

The Foundations of Modern Interrogation: Creating Psychological Manipulators

If one of the two pillars of modern American interrogation is behavioral lie detection, the other is psychological manipulation. Together they form its foundation. In the last seventy-five years, American police have developed a specialized body of psychological procedures, techniques, and strategies with which to interrogate criminal suspects. Instead of beating or torturing a suspect, they now rely on a variety of methods to influence, deceive, persuade, cajole, pressure, trick—in a word, manipulate—him to stop denying and start confessing. They also attempt to manipulate the perceptions of those who may evaluate the propriety of their procedures (e.g., prosecutors, judges, juries, the media) so that confession evidence can be used to prosecute and convict offenders. With the paradigm shift from physical coercion to psychological manipulation, police believe they have been able not only to more effectively elicit incriminating admissions from suspects but also to better shape these confessions so that they will be deemed "voluntary" and therefore legally admissible.

Central to the development of psychologically manipulative techniques are the police manuals, which have now been responsible for the training of several generations of American police detectives. Numerous scholars (Zimbardo, 1967; Leo, 1996a; Kassin, 1997a) and appellate courts (*Miranda v. Arizona*, 1966; *Oregon v. Elstad*, 1985; *Missouri v. Seibert*, 2004) have recognized the import and effect of these training manuals on police practices. Since the early 1940s, they have largely defined the structure, practice, and culture of American police interrogation. They have not only served as an antidote to the third degree, but also, along with behavioral methods of lie detection, created an alternative to it.

Although general police training manuals date back to shortly after the inception of urban police departments in the nineteenth century, interrogation training manuals did not emerge until the early 1940s. The first manual was Berkeley police lieutenant W. R. Kidd's 200-page pocket-sized book, *Police Interrogation*. Though largely overlooked by police historians and legal scholars, Kidd's manual was important for a number of reasons. With a foreword by August Vollmer touting it as "truly an epochal contribution to the police literature" (Kidd, 1940: v), *Police Interrogation* emphasized the importance of shifting to psychological interrogation methods as a means to achieving police professionalization. From the opening pages, Kidd announced that the goal of his book and interrogation training generally was to help establish police work as a profession that, like medicine and law, the public would come to respect and trust. Unlike virtually all subsequent police training manuals, Kidd discussed the problem of the third degree in some depth, arguing that it undermined the goal of eliciting truthful confessions and getting convictions. Kidd's manual enumerated many basic psychological interrogation techniques and strategies that would subsequently be repeated and elaborated by numerous other police manual writers. Kidd's pioneering manual was progressive for its time, criticizing the use of polygraphs for truth verification (though endorsing them as an effective interrogation technique), acknowledging the problem of false confessions, and even arguing for the recording of interrogations.

Two years later, in 1942, Fred Inbau, the former director of the Scientific Crime Detection Laboratory in Chicago and then a professor of law at Northwestern University, published *Lie Detection and Criminal Interrogation*, the first edition of what would later become the most well known manual in the history of American police interrogation. *Lie Detection and Criminal Interrogation* attempted to establish a "scientific" basis for police interrogation, educating investigators both about the behavioral methods of lie detection and the emerging psychology of interrogation. Though he mentions Kidd's name only once, Inbau repeated, without attribution, many of the same techniques that Kidd first created. Unlike Kidd, Inbau trumpeted the virtue of the polygraph as an instrument of truth detection. He also organized the interrogation techniques in an alphabetic sequence and included a section on the law of interrogation and the admissibility of confession evidence. Unlike Kidd, Inbau mentioned, mostly in passing, and sometimes with a defensive tone, the "so-called third degree" that produced "occasional miscarriages of justice" (Inbau, 1942: 46, 118). Like Kidd's, though, Inbau's manual was regarded by reformers as a significant advance at the time. As Skolnick (1982: 47) has written, it "was a reformist document, representing a kind of dialectical synthesis between the polarities of third degree violence and civil liberties for protection of human dignity: such a synthesis would have been progressive for the 1930s."

In 1947, John Reid, who had been one of Inbau's co-workers at the Crime Detection Laboratory, formed the police training firm John E. Reid and Associates in Chicago. In the 1953 edition of *Lie Detection and Criminal Interrogation,* Inbau would add Reid as second author and eventually Inbau and Reid would divide their book into two separate manuals on polygraphy and interrogation.

Following Kidd's and Inbau's interrogation manuals in the 1940s, several other training texts would appear—notably, Mulbar (1951), O'Hara (1956), and Arther and Caputo (1959)—as they began to redefine the practice and ideology of custodial police questioning. By the 1960s, numerous police manuals were on the market, though Inbau and Reid's (1962) *Criminal Interrogation and Confessions,* then in its first edition, had already become the most well known one. It would later be recognized by social scientists, legal scholars, and the U.S. Supreme Court as the industry leader. Based on the

Inbau and Reid manual, Reid and Associates first began teaching interviewing and interrogation courses in 1974.

By the 1980s and 1990s, there would be more than a dozen police interrogation training manuals on the market, as well numerous police agencies and several private firms offering their own interrogation programs, courses, and seminars. In the early twenty-first century, tens of thousands of police receive training every year in the methods of interviewing and interrogation. Reid and Associates alone claims to have trained more than 300,000 investigators in the last thirty years (www.reid.com, 2007).

The early interrogation manuals articulated for the first time an ideology of police interrogation that sought to replace third-degree practices with psychological methods. They were, in effect, an attempt by police reformers to assert ownership and control over the public problem of interrogation. Drawing on the rhetoric, symbols, and cultural authority of science, they sought to further the goal of professionalizing interrogation so as to insulate it from outside review or control. As Yale Kamisar (1980: 97) once wrote of Inbau, "he yearned for, and fought for, the day when criminal procedure would have no (or at least very few) constitutional dimensions."

Historically, the interrogation manuals served several functions for the police. They educated detectives about morally appropriate and inappropriate behavior, thereby defining contemporary professional standards of interrogation. They instructed detectives in the new "scientific" methods of interrogation. The manuals asserted that psychological methods were, in fact, far more effective at eliciting truthful admissions than the traditional physical methods they sought to replace. Moreover, the manuals argued that psychological methods—unlike the third degree—could not induce an innocent person to confess falsely. Finally, the manuals educated police about the changing and rather complicated law of criminal procedure that regulates police interrogation. The earlier manuals focused almost exclusively on the development of the Supreme Court's case-by-case "voluntariness" standard. After 1966, they also instructed police on the law of preinterrogation warnings and on the myriad legal issues generated by *Miranda* and subsequent case law. The manuals have interpreted and taught the police how to apply the Court's rulings, usually but not always correctly (Kamisar, 1980). The interrogation training manuals and courses have thus been the medium through which investigators acquire their working knowledge of the constitutional law of criminal procedure, the primary source of external restraint on their interrogation practices.

Developing a Psychology of Interrogation

THE ASSUMPTIONS OF PSYCHOLOGICAL INTERROGATION

As police leaders and trainers professionalized the interrogation function, they sought to create a studied and effective psychology of interrogation with which to reform police practices and advance their agenda. Like behavioral lie-detection methods, the new psychological techniques of interrogation would become increasingly sophisticated over time. But the underlying goals of psychological interrogation always remained the same: to elicit incriminating statements (ideally full confessions) that would be regarded as voluntary and thus be used by the state to successfully prosecute criminal defendants.

The new regime of psychological interrogation was based on several assumptions. First, police would only interrogate the guilty. The methods of interrogation were not designed for the innocent. In fact, police manual writers gave little thought to the possibility of psychologically induced false confessions (other than from pathological liars). Psychological interrogation was founded on a presumption of guilt. Interrogators were trained to interrogate only those suspects whom they were reasonably certain were guilty.

Second, guilty suspects did not usually make spontaneous admissions. It was the rare criminal who, stricken by conscience, would independently confess to police. Police believed that it is human nature to deny wrongdoing, particularly for serious criminal offenses that carry the possibility of felony charges and lengthy incarceration. Interrogators should thus expect the suspect to deny his guilt, perhaps even to try to manipulate him to shift blame from himself. Hence it was necessary for police to use psychological interrogation techniques to overcome a suspect's resistance and move him from denial to admission. These techniques would involve the use of pressure, control, deception, and manipulation. Confessions were something that had to be induced from suspects. As Inbau (1942: 71) put it, "ordinarily it is no simple matter to obtain a confession of guilt . . . The task is one that usually requires considerable patience and effort."

Third, interrogators were not born but made. Detectives had to be trained in psychological interrogation techniques. It was thus necessary for experts to emerge who could lay out the techniques in training manuals and eventually teach them in training seminars. The manuals and classes provided a written body of instruction whose larger purpose was to create the human lie detectors and psychological manipulators necessary for effective interrogation and confession-taking.

Fourth, the psychological techniques were neither morally nor legally objectionable. The manual writers recognized that the techniques were deceptive and manipulative and even required that the interrogator "deal with a criminal offender on a somewhat lower moral plane than that in which ethical, law-abiding citizens are expected to conduct their everyday affairs" (Inbau, 1942: 118). But the manual writers steadfastly claimed that their methods were justified because they were not psychologically coercive and therefore would not produce involuntary or false confessions. As Inbau (1942: 117) asserted in his first manual (and repeated many times in subsequent editions), "It can be stated with the utmost confidence that none of the methods are apt to induce an innocent person to confess [to] a crime he did not commit." That assertion would later be repeatedly disproved by considerable research (Leo and Ofshe, 1998a; Gudjonsson, 2003; Drizin and Leo, 2004).

Finally, interrogation was often the only method available to solve a crime. As Inbau et al. (1986: xiv) put it, "Many criminal cases, even when investigated by the best qualified police departments, are capable of solution only by means of an admission or confession from the guilty individual or upon the basis of information obtained from the questioning of other criminal suspects." As a result, police trainers believed that interrogation was usually more important and more effective than other methods of criminal investigation. The manuals consequently are infused with a higher moral purpose and make clear that the ends of psychological interrogation justify the means.

THE TEXTBOOK PSYCHOLOGY OF INTERROGATION

The interrogation training manual is now standard fare in American police work and integrated into introductory and advanced police training. Although W. R. Kidd invented many of the psychological techniques that subsequent manual writers (including Fred Inbau and John Reid) would repeat as their own, Kidd never updated or expanded his 1940 manual. Perhaps as a result, it never became institutionalized in police training and eventually fell out of print. By contrast, Inbau's 1942 manual would be updated twice (1948, 1953), then expanded into a separate series (1962, 1967, 1986, 2001) that now is in its fourth edition. Inbau and his co-authors (for many years John Reid, more recently Joseph Buckley and Brian Jayne too) have produced the longest running, most well known, and most influential police interrogation training manual in America. For better or worse, the Inbau–Reid series has set the standard for other interrogation training manuals and unpublished training materials. It has largely defined the culture of police interrogation training in America in the last half-century. It has created a textbook psychology of interrogation that goes by the name of the "Reid Method." Empirical studies show that American police employ many of Inbau and Reid's tactics and techniques (Wald, Ayres, Hess, Schantz, and Whitebread, 1967; Simon, 1991; Leo, 1996a; Feld, 2006a, 2006b).

In his first manual, Inbau (1942) laid out the rudiments of this psychological approach. First, the suspect needed to be isolated from all friends, family, and other social support. "The principal psychological factor contributing to a successful interrogation is privacy," Inbau (1942: 71) wrote. By isolating suspects who are in police custody, detectives could more effectively dominate the interaction, influence the suspects' perceptions of their situation, break down their resistance, and pressure them to confess.

Also, the interrogation room needed to be structured to maximize the opportunity for exerting psychological control and influence. Inbau (1942: 74) advised interrogators to question suspects in "a quiet room with few or none of the usual police surroundings." They were to seek out barren rooms, without windows, pictures, ornaments, or anything else that could distract the suspect. In subsequent editions, Inbau and his co-authors (1986, 2001) would more explicitly spell out the optimal room conditions: besides having privacy, detectives should "remove all distractions" (such as telephones), "select proper lighting," "minimize noise," and "arrange chairs properly" (four to five feet apart), among other things. The purpose was to increase the suspect's anxiety and prevent him from releasing tension while diminishing his sense of control over the situation (Kassin and Gudjonsson, 2004). In addition, Inbau et al. (1986, 2001) advised interrogators to "set up an observation room" adjoining the interrogation room with a two-way mirror so that the suspect could be seen without seeing the observers. This adjoining room was to be equipped with a concealed microphone so that the suspect could be surveilled "for signs of fatigue, weakness, anxiety and withdrawal" (Kassin, 1997a: 222) before, during, and following the interrogation.

Further, interrogators were to "display an air of confidence," accusing the suspect of committing the crime and pointing out "the circumstantial evidence of guilt" as well as the subject's "symptoms of guilt." They were to remind him of the "futility of resistance." They were also to suggest "themes" (i.e., psychological, moral, and legal excuses and justifications that minimized the crime or the suspect's culpability) that permitted the suspect to "save face." For example, the interrogator might downplay the moral seriousness of the offense, or blame the victim or the suspect's alleged accomplice for the crime. He might also suggest that the victim's exaggerated account would be taken as fact if the suspect did not confess. There were many other techniques as well, including the good cop/bad cop routine (which Inbau dubbed the "friend and enemy act"), flattering the suspect, pointing out the "incriminating significance" of the suspect's silence, playing one suspect against another, and even making explicit threats and promises. For example (Inbau, 1942: 100):

> You know what will happen to you if you keep this up, don't you? This time you've taken a relatively small amount of money; next time it will be more, and then you'll do it more often. You'll finally decide it's easier and more exciting to get what you're looking for at the point of a gun. You'll begin packing a rod. Then someday you'll get excited and pull the trigger when the muzzle's resting against somebody's belly. You'll run and try to hid [sic] out from the police. You'll get caught. There'll be a trial, and when it's all over, despite the efforts of your parents and relatives who in the meantime have probably spent their last dime on trying to save your neck, you'll either have to spend the rest of your life in the penitentiary or else sit down on the hot seat and have a lot of electricity shot through your body until your life's been snuffed out. Listen, fellow, take my advice; now's the time to put the brakes on before it's too late.

Inbau and Reid's recommended techniques would expand over the years and grow increasingly deceptive and manipulative. By 1986, Inbau, Reid, and Buckley would move away from the earlier scattershot approach, reorganizing their interrogation method into a nine-step psychological process that emphasized a sequential logic of influence and persuasion. In this model, each step of the interrogation process builds on and reinforces the previous one so as to systematically neutralize the suspect's resistance, render him passive and compliant, persuade him to agree to a minimizing scenario of how he could have committed the crime, and then transform his compliance into a full written statement. The nine-step method emphasizes that interrogation is a lengthy and repetitive process in which the interrogator establishes psychological control over the suspect and gradually elicits a confession by raising the suspect's anxiety levels while simultaneously lowering the perceived consequences of confessing.

The nine-step method is summarized in Table 3.4. Setting an accusatorial tone and seeking to disarm the suspect, interrogators begin by forcefully confronting him with his guilt (step 1). Interrogators do not allow the suspect to deny his guilt as they move into a monologue, suggesting various "themes" (step 2). As this is the heart of the Reid method, Inbau, Reid, Buckley, and Jayne (2001) recommend numerous "themes" for each crime (see also Senese, 2005). For example, the interrogator might suggest to a child-molestation suspect that he "was merely showing love and affection toward the child," that he was "teaching the child about sex because her parents failed to do this," that "the child was engaged in all of the sexual contact," not the suspect, or that the suspect "was molested as a child and was brought up to believe this was normal behavior" (Inbau, Reid, Buckley, and Jayne, 2001: 250). The interrogator cuts off and suppresses the suspect's denials or assertions of innocence (step 3). He also recognizes and overcomes the suspect's emotional, factual, or moral objections to his accusations while ensuring that the suspect does not mentally withdraw or "tune out" the "themes" (step 4). The interrogator seeks to retain the attention of the suspect—perhaps by invading the suspect's physical space, establishing eye contact, and asking hypothetical questions—who by now should be withdrawn and confused (step 5). Recognizing the suspect's passive mood, the interrogator continues to develop a specific "theme," invade the suspect's physical space, display sympathy, and urge the suspect to confess (step 6). The interrogation culminates in step 7, in which the interrogator presents the suspect with "an alternative question" consisting of two "themes" or choices (one good, the other bad), both of which incriminate the suspect. Inbau et al. (2001: 360) illustrate the use of the "alternative question" in a homicide interrogation this way:

Table 3.4. The Reid Nine-Step Method

Step 1: The Direct Positive Confrontation
Step 2: Theme Development
Step 3: Handling Denials
Step 4: Overcoming Objections
Step 5: Procurement and Retention of Suspect's Attention
Step 6: Handling the Suspect's Passive Mood
Step 7: Presenting the Alternative Question
Step 8: Bringing the Suspect into the Conversation
Step 9: The Written Confession

Source: Inbau et al. (2001).

Joe, was hurting this guy part of your original plan, or did it just happen on the spur of the moment? If you went in there with the full intention of pulling that trigger, it tells me that you have no regard for human life and that you are capable of doing anything. If that's the case we might as well end this right now because I know that people like that are not capable of telling the truth. But, Joe, I think that the gun just went off. I think all you wanted was a few bucks; you didn't want to hurt him, Joe. But because this is out of character for you, you panicked and the darn thing went off. Gosh, if that's what happened you've got to let me know, because I'm no mind reader. The guy who plans something like this for months in advance and walks into a store knowing full well that he's going to shoot and kill any possible witness looks the same to me as the fellow who acts out of desperation and, on the spur of the moment, finds himself with a gun in his hand and in the heat of the moment panics and ends up doing something he really regrets. Joe, this wasn't part of the plan, was it? It just went off, didn't it, Joe?

According to Inbau et al. (1986: 337), the "alternative question" presents the suspect with an opportunity to confess with either "minimum anxiety or maximum anxiety." After the suspect agrees to the positive "theme" in step 7, the interrogator directs him to reveal the details of the offense (step 8) and, finally, converts his oral statements into a full written confession (step 9).

In an appendix in the third edition of *Criminal Interrogation and Confessions*, Inbau et al. (1986) spell out what they believe to be the psychological theory of influence underlying the Reid nine-step method. Because they presume that suspects are guilty, they posit that "interrogation is the undoing of deception" (1986: 332). According to Inbau et al., the suspect's deceptions cause him to experience inner conflict, frustration, and anxiety during the interrogation, which he seeks to release through verbal and nonverbal behavior. The psychological techniques underlying the nine-step model are designed to increase his anxiety while decreasing the perceived consequences of confessing. Interrogators increase the suspects' anxiety by directing statements at his perception of himself; by not allowing him to verbalize his denials, express anger or hostility, smoke, or engage in any other tension-relieving activities; and by feigning anger or impatience, invading the suspect's personal space, staring at him, and referring to a thick investigative folder (whether real or contrived) of evidence implicating him.

Interrogators reduce the perceived consequences of confession by using "themes" that should distort the suspect's perception of reality. Although it may not be an accurate statement of law, Inbau et al. (1986: 333) have written that:

> During a legal interrogation reality cannot be changed. A confession will be inadmissible as evidence if the interrogator takes away the consequences of the confession (promises), or physically adds anxiety (threats, abuse) during interrogation. However, the interrogator can legally change the suspect's *perception* of the consequences of confession or the suspect's *perception* of the anxiety associated with deception through influencing the suspect's beliefs.

Inbau et al. theorize that if the interrogation process is successful, the suspect will go through several stages of expectancy—from actively rejecting the interrogator's message to ultimately accepting and internalizing it—before his initial belief that confessing is the worst thing he can do is transformed to a belief that confessing is acceptable.

Conclusion

The origins of modern American police interrogation are to be found in the emerging "science" of behavioral lie detection and police-invented techniques of psychological manipulation. They are the two master strategies through which police have replaced the third degree and created an alternative practice of interrogation. Put differently, the modus operandi of modern interrogation is to create human lie detectors and psychological manipulators through which police can wear down a suspect and elicit confessions that will later be deemed voluntary and reliable. The various lie-detection technologies and psychological strategies have professionalized the image and practice of interrogation while simultaneously improving the ability of police to solve crimes.

Though the assault on the third degree in the 1920s and 1930s involved a coalition of police professionals and progressive reformers, the subsequent transformation of American interrogation reflected the interests and priorities of the police professionals only. The progressive reformers, who earlier had played so prominent a role in delegitimizing the third degree, expressed virtually no interest in what came next. The new behavioral and psychological methods of interrogation would thus be largely insulated from outside scrutiny for several decades to come. The progressive reformers had moved on to other issues as police developed one truth-detection technology after another and eventually a full-fledged psychology of interrogation. With the shift from physical to psychological approaches, the progressive reformers were, in effect, missing in action. As a consequence, their concerns with due process, limited government, and political legitimacy would not serve to check the development of psychological interrogation practices in the immediate decades following the Wickersham Commission Report.

The new strategies of police interrogation were an alternative to force but not to manipulation or deception (Marx, 1988). The training manuals taught police a kinder and gentler way to interrogate while still creating the opportunity to overbear the will of suspects. Indeed, the new techniques sought to project an image of total control in which detectives wore down the suspect's ability to deny culpability, rendered him passive if not helpless, and then compelled him to confess. The authors of the emerging interrogation training texts made no pretense of neutrality or fairness—there would be nothing even-handed about police strategies and maneuvers. Rather, the manuals recommended police behavior that progressive reformers would have in other contexts regarded as an unjustifiable exercise of state power in a constitutional democracy. Interrogation manual writers and trainers continued to push the envelope of psychological interrogation as their techniques became increasingly manipulative and sophisticated. It fell solely to appellate courts—through their mostly weak and ambiguous rulings—to act as a source of restraint on the interrogation techniques.

Psychological interrogation has always had low visibility. In the 1940s and 1950s, there was little public mention of it. There were no crusading journalists, no exposés, no government commission reports, no studies by lawyers or political scientists. For more than twenty years after the first interrogation manual appeared in 1940, no one studied or wrote about the new techniques. It was not until 1961 that Bernard Weisberg first proposed analyzing police interrogation training manuals as a window into what actually occurred during police interrogation. Five years later, the Warren Court, in its famous *Miranda* decision, would call the training texts "the most enlightened and effective means presently used to obtain statements through custodial interrogation" (*Miranda v. Arizona*, 1966: 449). Interrogation training manuals would thereafter become the subject of scholarly study (see, e.g., Zimbardo, 1967; Gudjonsson, 2003; Leo, 2004a).

Those manuals could only tell us part of the story of modern interrogation, however. For they represented the police establishment's theory of interrogation but not necessarily its practice. Police secrecy remained the main obstacle to understanding how investigators interrogated criminal suspects in practice, as the Warren Court recognized: "interrogation still takes place in privacy. Privacy results in secrecy and this in turn results in a gap in our knowledge as to what in fact goes on in the interrogation room" (*Miranda v. Arizona*, 1966: 448).

Much has changed since the Warren Court identified the "gap problem" more than forty years ago. Studies and records of interrogation have now made it possible to describe empirically the process of interrogation and why suspects confess. Since *Miranda*, scholars and writers have been able to study the process through participant observation (Wald et al., 1967; Simon, 1991; Leo, 1996a) and analysis of audiotapes, videotapes, and transcripts of interrogations (Katz, 1999; Leo and White, 1999; Feld, 2006a, b). As a result, the picture is now much clearer.

CHAPTER 4

The Structure and Psychology of
American Police Interrogation

At the core of the detective role is the paradox that those people who have [the] most information about criminal activities are the criminals themselves, but they also have the least incentive to provide any such information to the police.

—Martin Innes (2003)

Interrogation may be thought of as an extended "anti-*Miranda*" warning, in which the suspect is led to believe that *failure to tell* his version of the events in question can and will be held against him in a court of law, and that, conversely, everything he does tell the investigators can and will work to his benefit.

—Deborah Davis and William O'Donahue (2003)

Believe it or not, and I know you're going to have trouble believing this, ah, I'm actually here to help you.

—Los Angeles police detective interrogating Jose Jacobo (1999)

Police portray modern interrogation as an informal give-and-take "interview" that involves little pressure and results in voluntary confessions. The image of the third-degree inquisitor has been replaced by that of the neutral information collector who is concerned only with discovering the truth. But psychological interrogation is not a simple or unbiased information-collecting exercise. It is a strategic, multistage, goal-directed, stress-driven exercise in persuasion and deception, one designed to produce a very specific set of psychological effects and reactions in order to move the suspect from denial to admission. Confessions, especially to serious crimes, are rarely made spontaneously. Rather, they are actively elicited, and often demanded of the suspect, then jointly shaped, typically after sustained psychological pressure.

We cannot understand how modern interrogation works without first explaining its structure and psychology. Many scholars have researched and written about the social psychology of police influence and suspects' decision-making during interrogation (Kassin and Wrightsman, 1985; Ofshe and Leo, 1997b; Davis and O'Donahue, 2003; Costanzo and Leo, 2007). Here I take the analysis one step further by linking the social psychology of interrogation to the imperatives of the American adversary system. For we can fully grasp the structure and psychology of interrogation only by seeing it as integrally connected to the logic and workings of the adversary system. A social psychological analysis can explain the police strategies, methods, and micro-moves of interrogation, but to understand the larger picture—which is particularly important when considering policy alternatives—one must understand the adversarial context in which interrogation operates. I argue here that police interrogators resort to manipulation, deception, and fraud to secure admissions precisely because they view themselves as agents of the prosecution and thus the suspect's adversary. The use of fraud is an adaptive strategy that American police have developed over the years to move away from the third degree and achieve maximum strategic advantage over the suspect while remaining within the mostly vague and highly discretionary legal guidelines that constrain them. It is employed to rationally achieve their goals of incrimination and conviction.

The use of fraudulent methods, however, creates two irresolvable contradictions that lie at the heart of psychological interrogation in America. First, to be admissible in court, a confession must be legally voluntary—freely given by a suspect whose will was not overborne by police detectives. But if interrogation works as designed and the suspect comes to perceive that he has no real choice under the circumstances but to confess, then his statements cannot, by definition, be strictly voluntary. Second, under the individualistic assumptions of the adversary system, it is almost never in the suspect's self-interest to incriminate himself because it will inevitably lead to harsher punishment. But psychological interrogation is designed to persuade a suspect that under the circumstances it is rational to admit to committing the crime (or at least some version of it). Both of these contradictions clash with the underlying assumptions about the separation of functions and power in the criminal justice system, yet neither can be eliminated without overhauling American interrogation as it is presently practiced. To elicit confessions that are admissible in court, police must successfully negotiate the tensions created by these two contradictions.

In this chapter, I analyze the structure and psychology of American police interrogation and show how it is designed to overcome a suspect's resistance and obtain his compliance. I also show how it relies on fraud, misrepresentation, and deceit to create the illusions believed to be necessary to elicit confessions. By emphasizing incrimination and conviction, I argue, American police interrogation turns the truth and government control models of the adversary system on their heads. By presuming the suspect's guilt, interrogators merely seek to confirm what they believe they already know. And by pretending to be the suspect's advocate when in fact they are his adversary, interrogators wield enormous power that is largely unchecked. They assume a prosecutorial function, although the suspect is not yet entitled to the rights or due process protections that he would receive at trial. Even though interrogation may be the most adversarial moment in the entire criminal process, police enjoy a virtual monopoly of power inside the interrogation room.

Adversarial Strategies and Tactics of Interrogation

American detectives, as we have seen, assume that every suspect they interrogate is guilty but will initially deny his guilt. Suspects will lie because it is not in their rational self-interest to provide the state with potent testimonial evidence that almost certainly will lead to their arrest, conviction, and incarceration. Modern methods of psychological interrogation have been designed to persuade suspects that—contrary to all appearances, logic, and common sense—it is actually in their self-interest to confess. American interrogation relies on a distinct logic of influence, deception, and sometimes psychological coercion to manipulate a suspect's perception of his situation, options, and self-interest (Ofshe and Leo, 1997b; Leo, 2001b). It has essentially four distinct stages: the softening up phase, the *Miranda* warning phase, the interrogation proper, and the postadmission phase.

Softening Up the Suspect

The process of police interrogation in America often begins in ambush. If the suspect is not already in custody, detectives will typically call and ask him to "voluntarily" come into the police station for some questioning, offering an escort if necessary. Investigators will not tell the suspect that they believe he committed a crime or that they seek to interrogate him. In fact, they will go out of their way not to use the word "interrogate" at all, which threatens to put into plain view the power differential between interrogators and the suspect and the true nature of what is to follow. They prefer "interview" instead. They will tell the suspect that they need only to ask him a few questions or that they need his help in solving a crime, invariably promising not to take much of his time. In some cases, investigators may explicitly tell the suspect that they do not consider him a suspect at all or that they need to eliminate him as a "potential" suspect and are confident that a few minutes of questioning will accomplish this. Detectives misrepresent the nature and purpose of the questioning to catch the suspect off guard and thus disarm him.

Detectives intentionally ask the suspect to come to the police station so that they can isolate the suspect from any familiar environments, friends, family, or any other source of social support that might psychologically empower the suspect to resist the interrogation process. Detectives also wish to get the suspect on police territory, in an interrogation room, in order to exercise control over the timing, pace, and strategy of interrogation. By isolating the suspect, stripping him of any social support, and questioning him on police turf, investigators believe that they maximize the suspect's vulnerability to police pressure. Their goal is to create the structural and psychological conditions most conducive to compliance and confession.

Once the suspect is in the interrogation room, detectives initially structure the interaction to psychologically soften him up. The first step is to establish a rapport. Interrogators ask background questions, engage in small talk, and maybe even flatter or ingratiate themselves with the suspect to create the illusion of a nonthreatening, nonadversarial environment. The detective's appearance in plainclothes and friendly demeanor are intended to put the suspect at ease and decrease the social distance between them. At this stage, the detective seeks to minimize the significance of the questioning by portraying the interrogation as a mundane interview. Indeed, the interrogator tries to create the illusion that he and the suspect will be engaged in a simple information exchange that does not implicate the suspect and is designed to assist police solve the crime.

By establishing rapport with the suspect and creating the impression that they need the suspect's help, interrogators seek to hide the fact that they have prejudged the suspect to be guilty of a serious crime, that their singular goal is to incriminate the suspect, and that the suspect is about to be interrogated. They attempt to portray the questioning as a friendly joint problem-solving exercise and to convey that they are fundamentally concerned about the suspect's welfare—a perception that may assist them later when they are trying to persuade the suspect that it is to his advantage to confess. As in other stages of the interrogation process, detectives seek to gain strategic advantage and control over the suspect. As one detective told me, "I don't care whether it is rape, robbery or homicide . . . the first thing you need to do is build rapport with that person . . . I think from that point on you can get anybody to talk about anything" (Interview with Frank D., 1993: 5).

Moving Past the Miranda Moment

American police are legally required to issue the famous *Miranda* warnings prior to interrogation, informing the suspect of his constitutional rights to silence and state-funded defense counsel and notifying him that anything he says may be used against him in court. In a typical interrogation, the detective reads the suspect the following *Miranda* rights from a card or form:

1. You have the right to remain silent.
2. Anything you say can be used against you in a court of law.
3. You have the right to an attorney.
4. If you cannot afford one, one will be appointed to you free of charge.

In some departments, the rights form may contain additional statements, such as: "If you agree to answer questions, you may stop at any time and request a lawyer, and no further questions will be asked of you."

In addition to the fourfold warnings, the 1966 U.S. Supreme Court decision *Miranda v. Arizona* also mandated that the state bears a "heavy burden" to demonstrate that police detectives elicit a "knowing, voluntary and intelligent" waiver of the *Miranda* rights before an interrogation may legally commence. Detectives thus often follow up the fourfold warning with two questions:

1. Do you understand these rights?
2. Having these rights in mind, do you wish to speak to me?

Detectives then typically ask, direct, or attempt to persuade the suspect to sign a rights waiver form. If detectives fail either to properly warn suspects of their *Miranda* rights or to elicit a proper waiver, any statements the suspect makes should, in theory, be excluded from evidence at trial.

At first blush, the *Miranda* requirements might appear to present a major obstacle to American interrogators. After all, *Miranda* requires detectives to inform asuspect that his statements can incriminate him, that police must obtain his consent in order to question his, and that he has the right to terminate interrogation. Perhaps most fundamentally, *Miranda* requires the detectives to inform the suspect that he stands in an adversarial relationship to police. By telling suspects that they do not share common interests with police, the *Miranda* warnings threaten to strip detectives of the strategic advantage that modern interrogation is structured to achieve and to expose the adversarial role that they assiduously seek to hide. In this sense, the *Miranda* requirements, though they pass quickly, may be the most honest moment in the entire interrogation process.

As we will see in more depth later, however, the *Miranda* ritual makes almost no practical difference in American police interrogation. Virtually all suspects waive their *Miranda* rights, or are legally constructed to have waived them (Leo and Thomas, 1998). Moreover, almost no confession is ever excluded at trial because of a *Miranda* violation (Leo, 2001a). American police have minimized the impact of *Miranda* by successfully adapting to it (Leo and White, 1999). They have developed multiple strategies to avoid, circumvent, nullify, and sometimes violate *Miranda* and its invocation rules in their pursuit of confession evidence. Because American police have learned how to "work *Miranda*" to their advantage (i.e., to issue the warnings in strategic ways that will result in legally accepted waivers or to interrogate without the necessity of providing warnings), *Miranda* exerts minimal restraint on police interrogation. *Miranda* has become a "manageable annoyance"—the anti-climax of custodial questioning—to American police that once waived does not affect the subsequent interrogation because it does not prohibit any post-waiver interrogation techniques, and suspects rarely invoke their rights following the warnings.

AVOIDING *MIRANDA*

Recasting Interrogation as a Noncustodial Interview
Perhaps the most fundamental police strategy to successfully negotiate *Miranda* is to do an end run around its requirements by taking advantage of the definitions, exceptions, and ambiguities in *Miranda* doctrine. Because *Miranda* warnings are required only when a suspect is legally in custody (i.e., either under arrest or not free to leave), police often redefine the circumstances of questioning so that the suspect technically is not in custody (*Berkemer v. McCarty*, 1984). They do this by simply telling the suspect that

he is not under arrest and is free to leave. For example, they might say (Interrogation transcript of Henry Rodriguez, 1998: 2):

> You're here on a voluntary basis. You elected to come in here on your own and I appreciate that, okay? And I told you on the phone I had no intention of arresting you.

In California, detectives refer to this strategy as issuing "Beheler warnings," named after a Supreme Court case from California that legally permits them to do so (*California v. Beheler*, 1983). Once detectives have issued "Beheler warnings," they can proceed to interrogate the suspect without giving *Miranda* warnings or eliciting a *Miranda* waiver, thereby avoiding the risk that the suspect will terminate the interrogation by exercising his right to silence or counsel. Detectives sometimes issue "Beheler warnings" instead of *Miranda* warnings even after they have transported the suspect to the station house with the express purpose of questioning and eliciting incriminating statements from him.

Constructing "Implicit" Waivers

To obtain an "implicit" waiver of *Miranda*, interrogators simply read the suspect the fourfold *Miranda* warnings and then move directly into the interrogation without asking the suspect for an explicit waiver of his rights. In other words, they do not ask him whether he understands his rights and wishes to act on them (the twofold invocation rules). If, after hearing the warnings, the suspect responds to interrogation without invoking his rights (that is, by saying nothing or answering the interrogator's queries), he is said to have implicitly waived his rights and thereby consented to interrogation, according to *North Carolina v. Butler* (1979). For example (Leo and White, 1999: 437):

Interrogator: Okay. You can call me Mark, all right, if you want. What I want to do is ask you some questions, all right? And I want to get your side of the story. And you're right, maybe you never could do something like this. But since you've been handcuffed and all that stuff, I've got to read you your rights. Have you ever had them read to you before?

Suspect: Uh-huh.

Interrogator: Yeah? You have the right to remain silent. You do not have to talk to me or answer any questions. You have the right to have an attorney and have an attorney present if you wish. If you cannot afford to hire one, one will be appointed to represent you free of charge. Do you understand those rights?

After the suspect nodded, the detective immediately launched into the interrogation, without asking the suspect whether he wished to waive his rights or even whether he was willing to speak to the police. Often, interrogators do not even ask whether the suspect understands his rights or wishes to waive them but simply launch into interrogation directly, as if the issue of a waiver did not even exist. The courts have upheld implicit waivers as satisfying the *Miranda* waiver requirements even though an implicit waiver is really no waiver at all.

NEGOTIATING *MIRANDA*

Even when they issue the *Miranda* warnings and ask suspects whether they wish to respond to questions, police are enormously successful in moving past the *Miranda* moment and eliciting signed waivers. In the last forty years, they have learned to skillfully deliver the warnings and invocation rules in ways that will not lead the suspect to invoke his rights or terminate questioning. The two primary ways are playing down or deemphasizing the significance of the *Miranda* warnings and persuading the suspect to waive *Miranda* and thus consent to interrogation.

Deemphasizing the Significance of the Miranda *Warnings*

Interrogators often minimize, downplay, or deemphasize the import of the *Miranda* warnings (Leo, 2001a). The purpose is to trivialize the legal significance of *Miranda*, create the appearance of a nonadversarial relationship, and convey that the interrogator expects the suspect to passively execute the waiver and respond to questioning. The interrogator's hope is that the suspect will not see the *Miranda* warnings as a crucial transition point in the questioning and an opportunity to terminate the interrogation, but as something akin to standard bureaucratic forms that one signs without reading or giving much thought to them.

Interrogators may attempt to deemphasize the *Miranda* warnings in several ways. One is by ingratiating themselves with suspects prior to the reading of the *Miranda* rights, engaging in extensive rapport-building small talk, and personalizing the police–suspect interaction in order to establish a norm of friendly reciprocation and the expectation that the suspect will comply. In conjunction with this, interrogators may portray the reading of the warnings as an unimportant bureaucratic ritual and communicate, implicitly or explicitly, that they anticipate the suspect will waive his rights and make a statement. One strategy is to camouflage the warnings by blending them into the conversation. Detectives who employ this approach often become less animated when they read the warnings. Some deliver them in a perfunctory tone and bureaucratic manner, implicitly suggesting that the warnings do not merit the suspect's concern, that they are a necessary but insignificant technicality, and that his passive acceptance of them is a foregone conclusion. Other detectives read the warnings without pausing or looking up at the suspect, sometimes even a little quickly, before requesting the suspect's signature on the waiver form, all the while implying that the warnings are merely a matter of standard routine.

Another way in which detectives deemphasize the significance of the *Miranda* warnings is by explicitly telling the suspect that the warnings are unimportant and a mere formality that they need to dispense with before questioning (Leo and White, 1999: 434):

Interrogator: Let me go ahead and do this here real quick. . . . Don't let this ruffle your feathers or anything like that, it's just a formality that we have to go through, okay. As I said, this is a *Miranda* warning and what it says is that you have the right to remain silent, anything you say can be used against you in a court of law, you have the right to the presence of an attorney to assist you prior to questioning and to be with you during questioning if you so desire, and if you cannot afford an attorney you have the right to have an attorney appointed for you prior to questioning. Do you understand these?
Suspect: Yeah.
Interrogator: Okay. Any questions about those at all?
Suspect: (Shakes head)
Interrogator: Okay. Now, as I've said . . . our main objective is to try and get some answers . . . for things that . . . we're looking into. . . . What we try to do as I've said before is . . . go to people that can . . . help us and . . . lead us in a direction, okay. Otherwise we'll roll around aimlessly and . . . end up talking to people that . . . don't make any difference, okay. We know that you probably, most definitely have some information that can help us out in this regard. That's why I want to talk to you, okay? Do you know what I'm talking about?

Suspect: Yeah.
Interrogator: Okay, so do you know what I want to talk to you about?
Suspect: (Nods head)

Interrogators may also deemphasize the significance of the *Miranda* warnings by referring to their dissemination in popular American television shows and cinema, perhaps joking that the suspect is already well aware of his rights and probably can recite them from memory. Before giving the *Miranda* warnings in one interrogation, for example, the interrogator said to the suspect, "You've probably seen it on TV a thousand times. I know I've said it about ten thousand times" (Leo and White, 1999: 435).

Still another approach is for interrogators to portray themselves as the suspect's friend, confidant, or guardian whose goal is not to obtain incriminating statements but to help the suspect improve his situation. If interrogators personalize the interaction and convince the suspect that they are trustworthy, the suspect will almost inevitably view the *Miranda* warnings as insignificant. Interrogators here clearly imply that waiving *Miranda* rights will be to the suspect's advantage.

If the Supreme Court in *Miranda* sought to "level the playing field" by having detectives notify the suspect that they are his adversary and that the suspect's best interest may not be served by making statements that will be used against him, then the strategies that American interrogators use to obtain signed waivers have, in effect, turned *Miranda* on its head. *Miranda* is often little more than a continuation of the softening up phase of the interrogation. As in other stages, the detective's strategy is to create the illusion that he and the suspect share the same interest and that continued compliance is to the suspects' advantage.

Persuading Suspects to Waive Miranda
Sometimes interrogators simply tell suspects the alleged benefits of waiving their *Miranda* rights and consenting to interrogation. For example, interrogators may state that they can inform the suspect of the charges against him and the likely disposition of his case only if the suspect waives his rights, or that interrogators can portray the suspects' accounts in their most favorable light to the prosecutor (and thus describe the suspect as cooperative, remorseful, and helpful) only if the suspect waives his rights. Or interrogators may state that the charges against the suspect will be reduced if he gives some explanation for what he has done, that the suspect will be in

greater jeopardy if he does not waive *Miranda* and receive more lenient treatment if he does, or that waiving his rights and consenting to interrogation is the only way the suspect will be able to prove his innocence.

Detectives sometimes also accuse a suspect of committing a crime, confront him with real or alleged evidence, and then suggest that the range of possible punishments depends on how favorably his actions are portrayed. The implication is clear: if the suspect waives his *Miranda* rights, the police can help him (such as by talking to the prosecutor or testifying on the defendant's behalf); but if the suspect invokes his right to silence or counsel, they cannot. Sometimes detectives explicitly tell the suspect that they can only help him or that the criminal justice system will treat him more leniently if he waives his rights. Following the *Miranda* warnings, interrogators may seek to persuade the suspect further of the benefits of waiving his rights by modifying part of the traditional phrasing of the invocation rule from "Having these rights in mind, do you wish to speak to me"? to "Having these rights in mind, do you want to hear what I have to say?" Or, "Having these rights in mind, do you want to tell me your side of the story?" Or even, "Having these rights in mind, do you want to hear how I can help you?"

One of the most subtle ways of persuading a suspect that it is in his best interest to waive his *Miranda* rights is by focusing his attention on the benefit of telling his "side of the story." Detectives sometimes state that he will be able to tell it only if he first waives *Miranda*, implying that the suspect will not be able to clear things up unless he first answers their questions.

The interrogation of McConnell Adams for two murders in Detroit in the mid-1990s illustrates a masterful employment of this strategy. Before questioning Adams, the interrogators tell him that the answers he gives over the next few minutes are "going to change [his] life." At this point, Adams likely believed that he could help himself by giving the "right" answers. The interrogators then make it clear to Adams that they know what he did, but that they need to get "the whys and an explanation so that the world knows that McConnell isn't a cold-hearted, stone killer" (Leo and White, 1999: 443). The benefit Adams will receive by telling his story is clear: He can show that he is not a "cold-hearted" killer but rather someone who did not intend to kill the victims, and as a result he will be treated as someone who simply made a mistake. To take advantage of this opportunity, however, Adams must first waive his Miranda rights. Not surprisingly, he did and made a statement admitting the killings.

In the interrogation of Alex Garcia, a juvenile, for mass murder the interrogators suggested that Garcia's explanation might not only lead to less serious charges but perhaps to no charges at all. While the detectives read Garcia his *Miranda* rights, Garcia asked what he was being charged with. One of the detectives responded that there was a "possibility" that Garcia's case would be handled by an adult court, a determination that would be made by the juvenile court judge on the basis of, among other things, the seriousness of the offense. After Garcia signed a card stating that he understood the rights that had been read to him, the interrogation proceeded as follows:

Interrogator: Okay, Alex. What we're investigating, like I told you and your father out there, [is] a very serious situation, okay?
Garcia: Uh hm.
Interrogator: I don't know what your exact involvement in it [is] at this time, okay?
Garcia: Uh hm.
Interrogator: Obviously, uh, you know that we've been talking to other people about this situation, okay?
Garcia: Uh hm.
Interrogator: We're gonna give you the opportunity to clear this whole matter up and, uh, that's gonna entail you answering some questions to us. Okay? You feel comfortable with that?
Garcia: Pretty much, yeah.

Based on the interrogator's statement that Garcia would have "the opportunity to clear this whole matter up," Garcia could have reasonably believed that his answers to the interrogator's questions might lead to no charges or at the very least being charged as a juvenile. And based on the warnings that had just been read to him, he would understand that to "clear this whole matter up" he would first have to waive his *Miranda* rights.

NULLIFYING *MIRANDA*

If interrogators fail to elicit an implicit or explicit waiver of the suspect's *Miranda* rights, they may try to persuade the suspect to reconsider or simply continue to question him in direct violation of *Miranda*. In the last two decades, particularly in California, numerous police have been trained to question suspects "outside *Miranda*." In this situation, police continue questioning suspects, though they have invoked their right to silence or counsel, after falsely telling them that anything they say is now off the record, that nothing they say can be used against them since they have invoked their constitutional rights, and that their answers will be used only to help the interrogator understand what happened (Weisselberg, 1998). The purpose of questioning suspects outside *Miranda* is to capitalize on the Supreme Court's ruling in *Harris v. New York,* which established the impeachment exception to *Miranda.* As a result of *Harris,* prosecutors can use statements elicited in violation of *Miranda* to impeach the defendant at trial should he take the stand. Further, regardless of whether the defendant testifies at trial, prosecutors can use information and evidence that police discovered from the suspects' statement—such as the names of witnesses, the identities of accomplices, the suspects' modus operandi, or even the fruits of the crime— against him at trial even though it was obtained during an interrogation that violated *Miranda.*

Sometimes police ignore the *Miranda* requirements altogether. They may simply tell the suspect to sign the waiver form as if he had no choice, perhaps without even reading the rights. Or if a suspect asks for an attorney, they may try to talk him out of one. One suspect recalled, "When he told me I could have a lawyer present, he advised me against it because all a lawyer would do is drag things out and tell me not to do or say things that would prove my innocence" (Statement of Kevin Mohr, 1999: 2). Other suspects who requested an attorney have reported being told that they could not have a lawyer during questioning but would be provided one at trial. In some instances, detectives have flippantly handed the suspect a phone or phone book when he requested an attorney, implying that he could get one only if he already knew one to call.

When suspects actually request attorneys or are silent following the *Miranda* warnings, their responses often tend to be ambiguous, however, and they sometimes even ask the interrogator whether they should talk or seek counsel. Interrogators may either try to talk the suspect out of getting an attorney or persist in seeking to elicit a waiver. In one case, after the suspect indicated that he did not wish to give up his right to counsel, the interrogator pressed forward nonetheless (Interrogation of Dontay Weatherspoon, 1998: 4):

Interrogator: "You know what that means? Okay. That means you can talk to us right now without a lawyer present. Is that correct? Because the way it's phrased, it's a little tricky. So it's—you know, it's asking you to give up something, but actually what that means is, you can talk to us right now without a lawyer about what's happened. Can we talk about what's going on here?

Suspect: I guess.

Another response to a suspect's attempt to request counsel might be to imply or state that the suspect can go home (and thus be free) if he agrees to waive his *Miranda* rights and answer questions, but that he will be arrested if he does not.

Perhaps the ultimate charade, however, is eliciting the confession first, then attempting to sanitize the interrogation by providing the *Miranda* warnings after the fact. As one suspect described it:

> As the evening progressed, I had been there several hours—must have been three or four hours, at least. I was very tired. I had been up several days over at the city jail. I was just literally exhausted. . . . They showed me the rifle, and they showed me Ms. Smith's purse, and then they kept telling me that Joe said that I did all these things, and finally I said, "If Joe said it, show me his statement, if he has given a statement." And, finally, Mr. Johnson showed me a statement, and let me hold it and pointed out certain things in the statement that said that I did these things, and it was at that time that I felt that I needed to give a statement, and that is when I started telling them what happened, and Mr. Davenport said: "Hold it. Hold it. We have got to read him his rights and things." That is when I signed the rights waiver. (Testimony of Terry King, 1995: 200)

Moving the Suspect from Denial to Admission

Once the interrogator has obtained the suspect's implicit or explicit waiver (typically memorialized by his initials at the bottom of a *Miranda* advisement form), the tone, content, and force of the interrogation may change dramatically. It is typically after the *Miranda* moment that the interrogation process becomes accusatorial—detectives shift from asking the suspect questions to telling him the answers and imploring him to confess. To be sure, there are different styles of interrogation. Some detectives remain as friendly as they were in the softening up phase even as they begin to employ calculated psychological techniques. Others become more assertive and controlling yet retain a nonthreatening demeanor. Still others become outwardly aggressive, sometimes even badgering. Regardless of the detective's interpersonal style, however, the modus operandi of the interrogation process remains the same: to obscure the detective's adversarial role and goal of incrimination by creating the illusion that he and the suspect share a mutual interest, to lead the suspect to perceive that the interrogator's role is to help him achieve this interest, and to persuade the suspect that he can do so only by complying with the detective's requests. At the root of virtually every interrogation is the message, communicated implicitly or explicitly, that the suspect stands to receive intangible or tangible benefits and avoid harms in exchange for an admission—ideally a full confession—to some version of the offense.

Every interrogator must confront the dilemma of how to persuade a suspect that confessing is in his rational self-interest. Compared to salesmen in even the most despised of industries, interrogators are at a distinct disadvantage because the product they are selling—incrimination and incarceration—would top just about anybody's list of undesirables. But at the same time interrogators possesses institutional powers (and the corresponding ability to deceive, manipulate, and coerce their targets) that most salesmen can only dream about. As we have seen, since the early 1940s the interrogation training industry has been devising techniques, methods, and strategies to overcome the inherent dilemma of interrogation and move the suspect from denial to admission and then ideally to a full confession. Detectives do this not only by hiding their adversarial role but also by transforming the suspects' perception of his situation, his options, and the likely consequences of each choice such that he comes to see the act of confessing as offering the easiest escape from a hopeless situation and as in his self-interest (Ofshe and Leo, 1997b). Interrogators seek to persuade the suspect that he is trapped and powerless, to diminish his self-confidence to deny the detectives' accusations, and to offer him a way to seemingly minimize his culpability and mitigate his punishment if he provides a statement. The suspect's admission is, in effect, his quid pro quo for an end to the interrogation and avoidance of the worse-case scenario—harsher treatment or punishment, for example—that the detectives want him to believe will occur if he persists in denying their accusations.

It is important to see modern interrogation as a structured, cumulative, and goal-directed process with a distinct logic of persuasion to induce compliance and confession (Ofshe and Leo, 1997b). It is not merely a conversation or a give-and-take interview, as police may claim. Nor is it a random set of approaches or single-mindedly focused on getting the truth. It has a multistep, repetitive, and layered psychology and structure, which explains why it often succeeds. Although there are hundreds of interrogation techniques, the essence of American police interrogation can be reduced to a few basic overarching strategies and methods that usually occur in predictable sequences.

Police interrogators use *negative incentives* to break down suspects' resistance, reverse his denials; lower his self-confidence; and induce feelings of resignation, distress, despair, fear, and powerlessness (see Leo, 1996a). Once a suspect is broken down, police use *positive incentives* to motivate him to see the act of complying and admitting to some version of the offense as his best available exit strategy and option, given his limited range of choices and their likely outcomes (Leo, 1996a). Together, the use of negative and positive incentives are meant to make the suspect view the interrogation as a negotiation in which he has little meaningful choice but through which he can put an end to this distressing process and gain a better outcome before it is too late. The logic of this approach is pithily captured in a Los Angeles Police Department interrogation training manual, which exhorts detectives to tell suspects: "You did it. We know you did it. We have overwhelming evidence to prove you did it. But the reason makes a difference. So why don't you tell me about it" (Papke, 1995: 1).

NEGATIVE INCENTIVES: MOTIVATING SUSPECTS TO STOP DENYING

Accusations
Elsewhere I have defined negative incentives as tactics that suggest the suspect should confess because no other course of action is plausible (Leo, 1996a). The purpose of interrogation is not to evaluate the suspect's denials, claims, alibis, or assertions of innocence, but to overcome his anticipated resistance and elicit an incriminating statement. Perhaps the foundational technique of modern psychological interrogation is the accusation, which usually triggers the start of the actual interrogation. Put differently, the accusation ushers in the moment when the process becomes confrontational. Interrogators make two general types of accusations: accusations of committing the offense and accusations of lying. Both are typically interspersed throughout the interrogation and repeated over and over again. It would be only a slight oversimplification to say that repetition is the essence of accusation in American police interrogation.

Although accusations may be delivered in different styles (ranging from polite to hostile), they have several common functions and effects. First, they signal a shift in the nature and seriousness of the interaction. The suspect now stands accused of a crime and thus is put on notice that he is no longer merely engaged in a simple conversation or joint problem-solving activity with police.

Second, accusations communicate the interrogators' unwavering belief in the suspects' guilt and in the untruthfulness of his denials. Interrogators typically express accusations with unyielding confidence, exactly as they are trained to do and as the logic of American interrogation demands. A common strategy is to tell the suspect that the purpose of the interrogation is not to debate whether he committed the crime, but why: "Well, let me tell you something, okay? I didn't bring you down here to ask you if you did it. Okay? I brought you down here to tell me why you did it" (Interrogation of Brandon Blackmon, 1996: 9). The accusation is thus presented as a fait accompli. If a suspect denies that he committed the crime, interrogators frequently accuse him of lying: "I'm gonna be real honest with you. Probably the last, I don't know how long it's been, maybe 30 or 40 minutes that we've been talking to you, I can probably tell you about 30 lies you've already told me" (Interrogation of Peter Gonzalez, 1996: 54).

Third, accusations exert psychological pressure on the suspect, especially as they are repeated over time. They carry the demand that the suspect stop denying, bend to the will of the interrogator, and confess (Interrogation of Duane Johnson, 1998: 5): "We told you we were gonna check out your story. You got a problem, man. You're either gonna tell us the truth or you're gonna bury yourself."

Fourth, accusations create the social expectation that the suspect must persuade the interrogators of his innocence to put an end to the accusations. This informal shifting of the burden of proof from the state to the accused is one of the most subtle, yet ingenious, psychological aspects of American interrogation. Rarely do suspects in the interrogation room appreciate that, from a legal standpoint, the state must prove their innocence. Rather, police interrogators create the impression through their repeated accusations that the suspect must prove his innocence to their satisfaction before the process can terminate. But because suspects rarely realize that interrogation presumes their guilt, they are unaware that their interrogators are unwilling to consider the possibility that they are innocent. The impossibility of proving their innocence often helps break down a suspect's resistance and create a perception of resignation and despair, especially as the length of interrogation grows.

Fifth, accusations are a constant reminder that the interrogation will not cease until the suspect complies with the demand to confess or actively terminates the interrogation. Only rarely does a suspect tell his interrogators that he wishes to end the interrogation, however. Instead, accusations typically put the suspect in a defensive mode in which he is constantly trying to deny his guilt or explain his innocence—only to be met with more accusations.

Finally, interrogators sometimes communicate through accusations their beliefs about how and why the suspect committed the offense. In other words, they educate him about the police's theory and the details of the crime. Interrogators who are poorly trained, inexperienced, or under pressure to solve a crime are particularly prone to this. They might accuse a suspect of lying by telling him that the details he is offering are incorrect and then provide him the correct ones. Sometimes interrogators will show a suspect evidence—such as crime scene photographs—when accusing him of lying, in effect educating him about the crime.

Like any other interrogation technique, accusations, by themselves, rarely lead to admissions. Nevertheless, they are the most basic American interrogation technique and tend to be employed the most frequently because they may be repeated whenever the detective disagrees with the suspect. In this sense, accusations are the engine that carries interrogation forward, laying the foundation for what follows. In combination with other interrogation techniques, accusations allow interrogators to confront and challenge a suspect while communicating that it is futile for him to resist.

Attacking Denials

Attacking a suspects' denials is the logical extension of making accusations. Together, the two form a kind of one–two punch. Just as detectives presume a suspect's guilt when they initiate interrogation, so too do they expect the rational suspect to immediately and repeatedly deny guilt once accused. As the leading police interrogation manual puts it (Inbau, Reid, Buckley, and Jayne, 2001: 303–304): "Confessions are not easily obtained. Indeed, it is a rare occurrence when a guilty person, after being presented with a direct confrontation of guilt, says: 'okay, you've got me; I did it.' Almost always, the suspect, whether innocent or guilty, will initially make a denial." Moreover, police interrogators assume that it is more difficult to elicit admissions from suspects who successfully persist in their denials (Inbau et al., 2001: 304). It is therefore necessary, they believe, to aggressively challenge a suspect's denials, especially early in the interrogation, before the suspect can establish a pattern of denial.

Police interrogators view terminating a suspect's denials as essential to eliciting an incriminating statement. They thus use a series of techniques to attack, challenge, overcome, and ultimately reverse denials. The most basic way interrogators attack a suspect's denials is by preventing them from being voiced or cutting them off. Interrogators do this either by anticipating and discouraging a suspect's denials or by interrupting the suspect, sometimes by raising their hands or arms. They also sometimes talk over him or maintain a monologue so that the suspect has no opportunity to make denials. One suspect recounted (Declaration of Derek Niegemann, 1999: 4):

> On several occasions . . . I tried to deny I had set the fires, but Agent Lafayette would not let me speak or explain myself. Agent Lafayette berated me continuously in an angry tone. He said . . . I was lying and that I had set the fires. Whenever I tried to respond or deny his accusations, he would talk over me, point his finger at me and glower at me. I interpreted this to mean that I should not even bother denying my involvement.

Once the suspect begins to utter denials, interrogators attack them in one of several ways. Often, they simply assert that the suspect's denial is not true, that he is lying, or implore him to stop denying (Interrogation of Marcos Ranjel, 1997: 6):

Suspect: I never been there.
Interrogator 1: No-no . . . don't tell us, "No sir."
Interrogator 2: We know you've been there.
Suspect: No, I never been there.
Interrogator 2: We wanna know, we wanna know.
Suspect: I never been there, I promise.
Interrogator 1: No-no, no-no.
Interrogator 2: Stop denying this, OK?

Or interrogators might attack a suspect's denials by telling him that the denials are logically impossible. Sometimes they tell the suspect that his denials are implausible or simply not believable, or that they are inconsistent with the existing case evidence or some aspect of the suspect's previous account.

Interrogators often will make more general attacks on a suspect's denials, saying that they do not add up or make sense and thus no one—especially prosecutors, judges, and juries—will believe or credit them. Invoking such third parties can be a particularly persuasive interrogation strategy because it may be joined with a discussion of the potential unfavorable consequences to the suspect if he continues to deny. As one interrogator warned a suspect: "All the lying that you're telling me is going to come back and haunt you." (Interrogation Transcript of Jackson Burch, 1973: 12)

Often interrogators will try to stem denials by employing the accusation strategy discussed earlier of telling the suspect that they are not there to discuss whether he committed the crime but why. They thereby attempt to persuade the suspect that his fate has been determined and thus to shift his response from denial to explanation.

Sometimes an attack on the suspects' denials will take the form of undermining the suspect's confidence in his memory. This occurs when a suspect says that he has no memory of committing the crime. Because they assume that the suspect's claim is a lie and a facade, interrogators will attempt to cut off his denials by trying to persuade him that he does, in fact, remember committing the crime. One suspect recalled: "Special Agent Krause then asked me over and over again how I did it, and I kept saying, 'I don't remember.' He said he didn't believe that I couldn't remember something like that. 'When something as tragic as this happens you remember every little detail, don't tell me you don't remember, I don't believe it. You know something that happened that night. Now what is it?'" (Interview of Stephanie Traum, 1999: 7). Interrogators sometimes suggest that the suspect could have committed the crime despite having no memory of it—for example he was in a drug-induced blackout or experienced amnesia—and urge that the suspect find the memory and confess. Or they might claim that his supposed lack of memory clashes with the guilt he is feeling over the crime.

The psychological purpose of attacking a suspect's denials is to cause him to perceive that no one will believe his claims of innocence regardless of what he says; that he is completely powerless to resist the interrogators' accusations; and that there will be serious consequences if he continues to deny guilt or remain silent. More generally, the combination of multiple and repetitive accusations and attacks on a suspect's denials, especially in conjunction with other interrogation techniques, is intended to break down the suspect's resistance by silencing him, rendering him passive and ultimately inducing resignation and despair.

Evidence Ploys

An evidence ploy is any attempt by interrogators to make the suspect believe they possess incriminating evidence against him (Ofshe and Leo, 1997b). Like accusations and attacking denials, evidence ploys are one of the most fundamental and common techniques of modern psychological interrogation (Leo, 1996a). Repeated often, they are also one of the most effective (Moston, Stephenson, and Williamson, 1992; Kebbell and Hurren, 2006). Evidence ploys may be either true or false: if interrogators possess actual evidence against a suspect (e.g., eyewitness identifications, accomplice statements, DNA, etc.), they will confront him with it as they press him to confess; these are known as true-evidence ploys. If interrogators do not possess any actual evidence against a suspect, they will often pretend that they do and confront him with it as if it exists; these are known as false-evidence ploys.

Evidence ploys are used to make a suspect perceive that the case against him is so overwhelming that he has no choice but to confess because no one will believe his assertions of innocence. Whether the evidence ploys are true or false, the psychological effect should be the same so long as the suspect believes that the alleged evidence is real. Most suspects, after all, do not know that police can lie about evidence when questioning people, and many are shaken when police tell them that evidence exists that proves their guilt and then begin to enumerate it. Even more than accusations and attacking denials, evidence ploys informally shift the burden of proof away from the detectives to the suspect. As one suspect related, the detective "held up his ink pen and said, 'This is your worst enemy. Whatever I write, you gotta prove you didn't do" (Interrogation of William Laughlin, 2000: 12). Evidence ploys communicate that the suspect is caught, that his guilt is beyond dispute, that his fate is now certain, and that the case against him will not go away no matter how hard he tries to resist the interrogators' accusations or argue against the evidence (Ofshe and Leo, 1997b). As one suspect told me, "[They] made me believe I was going to get convicted whether I did it or not" (Interview of Emile DeWeaver, 1998: 7).

There are many different types of evidence ploys. "Simple" evidence ploys are those in which interrogators confront the suspect with one or more pieces of real or false evidence while expressing confidence in their belief in the suspect's guilt. "Orchestrated" evidence ploys are those in which interrogators confront the suspect with evidence from a situation that has been socially orchestrated, typically by moving the suspect through a testing or examination process that is intended to create the appearance of more potent and thus irrefutable incriminating evidence. Within these two general categories, there are many different types of evidence that interrogators may draw on in their ploys.

Simple Evidence Ploys. Simple evidence ploys generally rely on three different types of evidence: demeanor evidence, testimonial evidence, and real or alleged scientific, medical, or technological evidence. As we have seen, American interrogators are trained that they can accurately interpret whether a suspect is lying or telling the truth from his body language, speech, and nonverbal behavior. They will sometimes treat a suspect's body language and demeanor as if it is evidence of hisguilt, and then confront him with their perceptions as conclusive evidence of his guilt. For example: "You're lying. I could see it right in your eyes" (Interrogation of Farrell Wildcat, 1999: 26). Or, "Your body is screamin'. Your body is screamin' at me, your face is screamin' and your body language, everything is screamin' at me, telling me I have knowledge, I know something. So, if you didn't do it, you sure know what happened" (Interrogation of Sean Harrill, 1999: 65). Sometimes interrogators will tell a suspect that his body language is an indication of remorse. The second and perhaps most common type of simple evidence ploy relies on testimonial evidence.

Testimonial evidence may be the easiest type for interrogators to gather against a suspect when it exists and among the easiest to fabricate when it does not: investigators simply attribute statements to others implicating the suspect and confront him with them. Typically there are four types of testimonial evidence: statements incriminating the suspect made by victims, eyewitnesses and bystanders, co-perpetrators or accomplices, and other relevant third parties.

Confronting a suspect with real or alleged statements from victims can be powerful, in part because interrogators typically present victims as pure, with no involvement in the crime, and with no reason to lie. Interrogators often present the accusation by the victim as overwhelming evidence of the suspect's guilt. The suspect's repeated denial is thus pitted against the inherently more credible victim. As one interrogator told a suspect (Interrogation of Stanley Vaughn, 1998: 11): "Why would these kids all say that you are . . . touching . . . their vaginal or their private areas, as well as . . . your older daughter's breasts? Why would they say that? Why would they make up something? Are they lying?" The implication is clear: the suspect is the one who is lying, the victim's statement will prove it, and therefore no one will believe the suspect. Interrogators shift the burden of proof onto the suspect, but then refuse to credit his denials. Often there is no way for the suspect to dispute the veracity of the victim's accusations or identification other than to say that the victim is lying or mistaken. But interrogators will typically counter that the victim has no reason to lie and cannot be mistaken.

Police interrogators routinely confront suspects with real or alleged eyewitness evidence, especially for crimes in public places or when it is possible for the police to make up an eyewitness. Interrogators often tell a suspect that an eyewitness, sometimes multiple eyewitnesses, witnessed the suspect commit the crime and accurately identified him. Typically interrogators tell a suspect that the eyewitness or eyewitnesses picked him out of a photo line-up or array; occasionally, interrogators will conduct live line-ups. Interrogators represent eyewitness testimony as potent and irrefutable, never mentioning the well-known fallibility of eyewitness memory or the possibility of eyewitness errors (Doyle, 2005). As evidence ploys go, eyewitness testimony tends to be additive, especially when it is false, as interrogators can simply reference one eyewitness after another. Eyewitness evidence ploys are also often buttressed by technological supports, such as hidden surveillance cameras or videos, which allow interrogators to tell the suspect that there is corroboration for the eyewitness identification.

In multiperpetrator crimes, interrogators often confront suspects with real or alleged statements by co-perpetrators or accomplices. Typically interrogators tell the suspect that his co-perpetrators or accomplices have identified him as participating in or even masterminding the crime. This can have a powerful effect on a suspect who was either involved in the crime, knows who was involved, or was present at the scene. It can also have a strong effect on a suspect who is innocent but who comes to believe that he is being falsely identified or framed by the true perpetrators. Co-perpetrator evidence ploys can be especially potent because, unlike most other evidence ploys, interrogators can use the real or alleged statements by co-perpetrators to attribute knowledge of the crime, a motive, and specific activity to the suspect, thus implying that his conviction and punishment are certain. Interrogators who confront the suspect with co-perpetrator statements tend to suggest that if the suspect does not confess, he will go down for the crime alone and foreclose his only opportunity to make a deal. This posture is intended to feed the fear of exposure and the distrust of others that someone who actually co-perpetrated a crime may have. It is sometimes buttressed by supports—such as a co-perpetrator's recorded or written statements implicating the suspect—if police actually possess such evidence.

Interrogators will also confront suspects with opinion evidence of a third party whose views may matter to the suspect. It is common for interrogators to tell suspects not only that they do not believe his denials, but also that his family, parents, spouse, children, or close friends do not believe them either. In a case in which a suspect was accused of sexually molesting his daughter, the interrogators told him that his wife's opinion constituted evidence of his guilt (Statement of Kevin Mohr, 1999: 5):

> He stated my wife didn't even believe me. I just wanted to die, my own wife thought I was a child molester. I said I was going to talk to my wife Monday and he said I wasn't . . . I felt my world crashing down all around me. I couldn't talk with my wife and daughter until this was over. I told him again I didn't do it, he held up two videotapes and said they were of my daughter saying what I did to her.

In addition to demeanor and testimonial evidence, simple evidence ploys often involve real or invented forensic, medical, or technological evidence. This may be the most persuasive type of simple evidence ploy because it tends to carry the weight, authority, and presumed certainty of modern science and technology. Perhaps the most common type is print evidence, typically real or alleged fingerprints (Interrogation of Jackson Burch, 1973: 8): "Jack, let me explain something. We have beer cans, beer cans with fingerprints on them, and we are going to compare your fingerprints with everything that we found, including the palm frond, wood . . . and with the comparison we are going to make, we are going to charge you with the crime, do you understand that?" Interrogators may allege that they have print evidence from virtually any part of the body, such as palm or hand prints, foot or shoe prints, head prints, teeth prints, and sometimes even penis prints. Police interrogators will occasionally tell suspects of "special laser techniques" that allow them to remove prints from any part of the human body. In one case, interrogators told a suspect who was alleged to have pushed her baby's head into a couch and smothered it that they had retrieved her fingerprints from the baby's head. This type of evidence ploy trades on the popular mythology that print evidence is unique to each individual, never wrong, and therefore dispositive of the suspect's guilt.

Police interrogators also routinely confront suspects with other types of forensic evidence, such as ballistic or scent evidence. As interrogators told a suspect in a murder case (Interrogation of Anthony Cain, 2004: 105):

That dog just did what any witness could do in court. He just identified you. They can bring the dog to court. They can bring the evidence to court. That dog just identified you by what he just did right now. From your car to the bench that you sat on out there in the lobby, right in here. Followed your scent. The scent that we obtained from the house. The scent that we got from the towel that's covering Lamar's head. Which is why I wanted you to see that because the towel covered his head. The scent that we got off of that towel had your scent on it. Doesn't matter if you were wearing gloves, some type of medical suit, some type of hazardous materials suit. Doesn't matter if you were wearing a mask. Doesn't matter if you were covered— covered to make sure you didn't leave any DNA. You leave scent. That dog got that scent. That dog followed that scent to your house a long time ago. Right up to your front door. Right up to your front door. And now has also connected that towel with you. That's why you're in a lot of trouble.

Interrogators will often confront suspects with real or alleged medical or scientific evidence, ranging from the opinions of doctors and other medical personnel (e.g., in sexual molestation cases where there is no actual evidence of sexual activity or assault) to physical evidence such as hair, blood, semen, and other bodily fluids. In many of the cases that I have studied, interrogators will falsely tell the suspect that they have DNA evidence against him because of the aura of the infallibility of DNA evidence, even though many suspects do not even know what DNA is.

Police interrogators will confront suspects with evidence ploys that rely on modern or imaginary technologies. Such technologies often involve surveillance and photography of one sort or another that is alleged to have captured the suspect in the commission of the crime. Interrogators also tell suspects of technologies that supposedly allow police to retrieve evidence that the suspect does not know could exist. In murder cases, for example, interrogators may falsely tell suspects that through the use of modern technology they were able to retrieve images of the suspect killing the victim (Interrogation of Erwin Young, 1997: 32, 49):

Have you ever heard of scanning electron microscopy? It's a big old microscope, okay. And when people die, their images of what they see, like if you died right now and you saw him and I in your eyes. What happens is in the autopsy we take out the lens and we put it in the microscope and look at it, right before they die, that image is saved forever . . . When we get those at the autopsy and pull those lenses out, we aren't going to see you pointing the gun, right?

Orchestrated Evidence Ploys. The evidence ploys that interrogators represent as the most sophisticated tend to rely on so-called lie-detector technologies. Interrogators represent these technologies as scientific, sophisticated, and infallible. Investigators orchestrate an examination process, sometimes lasting several hours, after which the suspect is confronted with the results of the test—invariably, that he failed—and again pressure him to confess based on this new information. Sometimes interrogators will ask suspects to take a lie-detector test early in an interrogation. When this happens, they usually portray themselves as wanting to help the suspect and tell him that the purpose of the examination is to eliminate him from suspicion. As one interrogator told a suspect (Interrogation of Jerome Denny, 2005: 196): "I'm trying to clear you of what's going on with you. My job is not to convict you of any crime, okay? My job by giving you the test is to clear you of this, and that's my whole intention, okay?" It is far more common, however, for interrogators to ask the suspect to take a lie-detector test *after* he has repeatedly denied the interrogators' accusations and refused to make an admission, usually one or more hours into the interrogation. At this point, detectives typically represent the lie-detector test as an opportunity for the suspect to prove his innocence, implying that if he does not take the test people will think he is guilty. Interrogators usually either assert or imply that this outcome will put an end to the interrogation and allow the suspect to go home. Not surprisingly, virtually all suspects consent to the lie-detection examination.

Lie-detector ploys are more orchestrated than the other types of evidence ploys mentioned above partly because interrogators need to involve third parties to administer the examination. Detectives typically either must pause the interrogation to find the administrator or reschedule this portion of the interrogation for a time when he is available. Interrogators tell suspects that the third party is a trained scientist or specialist in lie detection, or a neutral civilian or police employee who has no stake in the outcome of the test, and therefore is concerned only with finding the truth. More often than not, however, the lie-detection specialist is a police officer or detective dressed in civilian clothes, whose goal is to get a confession.

There are two primary variants of lie-detection evidence ploys: the first relies on the traditional polygraph, or so-called lie detector, the second on the Computer Voice Stress Analyzer (CVSA). With both, there are three phases: (1) the pre–lie detection phase in which the interrogating detective or technician educates the suspect about the supposedly scientific nature and near infallibility of the instrument, goes over the questions he is going to ask, and tries to impress upon the suspect the importance of telling the truth (sometimes even telling the suspect what he believes the truth to be); (2) the actual administration of the examination; and (3) the postexamination interrogation in which the administrator of the exam or the interrogators confront the suspect with the alleged results and reinterrogate him. The postexamination reinterrogation is more forceful than before because the interrogators now confront the suspect with seemingly scientific results that they represent as error-free—"It's 100 percent accurate. There's no fault in it," as one interrogator told a suspect (Interrogation of Juan Diaz, 1998: 27)—and thus indisputable evidence that his denials are false and cannot withstand scrutiny. Like their counterparts, lie-detection evidence ploys are intended to break down a suspect's resistance by persuading him that he has been exposed, that his denials are futile, and that there is no escape from the necessity of admitting guilt. As one suspect recounted (Statement of Ronald Suzukawa, 1999: 8):

> He said that the test showed that I was not cooperating with them. I was being deceptive in my responses to the questions that we had agreed on. I was asked to explain why I would show deception on the questions then. Another agent came in and showed me his badge. He explained that he had been monitoring the examination and it was obvious that I was being deceptive. He started in on this line that there is a bad Ron that is maybe doing things that the good Ron would not do. I should stop covering up for the bad Ron. The guilt from what the bad Ron had done was tearing me up inside and it was obvious from the charts that I wanted to get the truth out.

The primary lie-detection instrument is the polygraph. Although many suspects have not heard of the word "polygraph," most know what a traditional lie detector is from television and cinema. Consistent with its portrayal in American popular culture, most suspects appear to believe in the near infallibility of polygraph results. The polygraph may be administered in its traditional form or in its more modern computerized version, both of which involve attaching wires and straps to a suspect and generating graphically driven printouts of his physiological responses to different types of questions. When interrogators confront the suspect with his alleged failure of the test, they invariably tell him about the test's accuracy rate (99 to 100 percent, they will say), sometimes showing the suspect the actual charts. Interrogators often represent the results of a polygraph as a pivotal point in the interrogation from which there is no turning back: "If you would have passed the polygraph, I'd be sitting here shaking your hand, and you'd be walking out the door, and I'd say, 'Okay, Mr. Vaughn, we'll get this part up to the District Attorney's Office regarding your daughter.' But you failed the polygraph" (Interrogation of Stanley Vaughn, 1998: 9) When the suspect learns that he failed, the impact can be powerful (Interview of Stephanie Traum, 1999: 24): "It said I was 99 percent lying and so I figured I must have . . . killed Caitlyn, even though I . . . told him, I don't remember killing Caitlyn."

Though used less frequently than the polygraph, the Computer Voice Stress Analyzer has become increasingly popular among police interrogators in the last decade. It is not well known among the public, however, and therefore is seen as more mystifying than the polygraph, a fact interrogators use to their advantage. Unlike the polygraph, the CVSA is said to measure inaudible micro-tremors in the voice that register different decibels of stress based on whether a suspect is telling the truth or lying. Although no such micro-tremors actually exist, it is the perception, not the reality, that determines the success of evidence ploys during interrogation. The underlying principles and application are the same as with the polygraph: police have a third party (again, usually another police officer or civilian employee whom they represent as neutral and concerned only with finding the truth) administer the exam, they tell the suspect he failed the exam, and then represent the results as scientific, infallible, and thus conclusive of the suspect's guilt. As with the polygraph, sometimes interrogators will tell the suspect that the results of the CVSA are error free (Interrogation of Oscar Macias, 1999: 10):

> What this instrument is, it's called a voice stress analyzer. Basically what it does, it's a computerized instrument. It has a little microphone. You just clip the microphone on a tie or a shirt or something like that. You and I, we'll talk about some questions. We'll go over 'em and you just answer "yes" or "no" in just a normal tone of voice, okay? And then what it does is it can identify through the computer. It's 100 percent accurate, it will tell, without error, what is truthful and what's a lie. As a matter of fact, I'll even

ask you a question like, "Is this wall white?" . . . and then when I ask you that question, you say "no" and I'll show you that it shows that, you know, you can tell when somebody's lying.

Whether the orchestrated lie-detection evidence ploy is based on alleged polygraph or CVSA results, the effect is likely to be the same. Police use lie-detection instruments during interrogation because they are believed to be the most potent evidence ploys available when the suspect refuses to stop denying his guilt. With both polygraph and CVSA results, interrogators strive to create the impression that the evidence against the suspect is indisputable. As one interrogator told a suspect (Interrogation of Prudenzio Sanchez, 1997: 28): "You can lie to us but you can't lie to the machine."

Regardless of their source, evidence ploys are powerful interrogation techniques because they can authoritatively back a suspect into a corner from which he cannot escape through denial. Used repetitively and in combination with other interrogation techniques, evidence ploys often help eliminate resistance to getting a confession (perhaps more than any other interrogation technique). Some evidence ploys, of course, are more persuasive than others, and their persuasiveness will also vary by the type of crime under investigation, the context in which the evidence ploy is used, and its timing and repetition. True evidence ploys are one of the primary techniques that lead suspects to confess in routine cases (Moston et al., 1992; Leo, 1996a). False-evidence ploys often cause innocent suspects to perceive their situation as hopeless (Ofshe and Leo, 1997b) and thus are a significant factor in virtually every police-induced false confession in America (Drizin and Leo, 2004; Leo and Ofshe, 1998a).

Evidence ploys are also highly successful at eliciting confessions because they are part of a general strategy of communicating omniscience, exposure, and capture. Interrogators often tell a suspect they know all the facts but just need to hear what happened from the suspect, or that they know more than the suspect knows or thinks he knows, or even that they possess evidence against the suspect of which he is unaware. It is not uncommon, for example, for interrogators to tell a suspect, "Every single question that we asked you we knew the answer to, and we do that for one reason, to see if you're going to lie to us" (Interrogation of Daniel Blank, 1997: 36), or "We know a lot of the answers to the questions that we're asking you, okay? We just want to get your side" (Interrogation of Dontay Weatherspoon, 1998: 13). Evidence ploys are embedded in representations about omniscience because interrogators want to communicate their full knowledge not only of the incriminating evidence against the suspect but also of what he did and how he did it, so that he comes to perceive that he cannot escape detection. Combined with appeals to omniscience, evidence ploys communicate that a suspect has been captured and therefore is powerless to resist the interrogators' accusations or demands to confess.

Pressure, Repetition, and Escalation

In addition to accusations, attacks on denials, and evidence ploys, interrogators rely on pressure, repetition, and escalation to weaken the suspect's resistance and increase the likelihood that he will confess. From the minute the interrogation begins, police apply psychological pressure to get the suspect to stop denying and start confessing. The conditions of modern interrogation are designed to be inherently stressful and anxiety-producing and thus create constant background pressure. Prior to interrogation, the suspect is isolated, put into a police environment (typically a relatively small and windowless interrogation room), and either informally detained or formally arrested. Before any accusation or confrontation, police seek to increase the suspect's anxiety by removing him from any social setting in which others could provide psychological support. They want him to perceive that he is at the will of the interrogators. Police structure the physical environment of interrogation to "promote feelings of social isolation, sensory deprivation and a lack of control" (Kassin, 1997a: 222).

Psychological pressure is also inherent in the techniques of accusatorial interrogation. Interrogators escalate the pressure in a variety of ways. In addition to repeatedly confronting and interrupting the suspect, they sometimes raise their voices, scream at, or relentlessly badger him. As one suspect recounted (Statement of Bobby Benton, 2000: 25):

> They just kept on and on. Hounding and hounding and hounding. Finally, I just said yes, so they'd just leave me alone. . . . I don't even know what they said. . . . I tried to repeat what they said. I try to ask them. "I don't know what you're talking about." I was just tired. It was just like arguing with her. Finally . . . they told me I was done. . . . I thought I was going home. I didn't go home. It was just like a big dream, just like something that just never happened. . . . I was so tired. It was like being so confused.

Interrogators step up pressure partly through repetition. They seek not only to distress and wear down the suspect, but to create the perception that the interrogation will not cease until the suspect says "I did it" (Ofshe and Leo, 1997b).

Another technique interrogators use to exert pressure on suspects is to manipulate their perceptions of time. They use time pressures in several ways to get suspects to comply. One is to make the suspect perceive that the interrogation works like a time-limited sales offer—he has an "opportunity" that is available now but will expire once the interrogation ends. If the technique is successful, the suspect will think that his situation will worsen, perhaps irreversibly, if he does not act now and comply with the interrogators' demands. Or interrogators may try to make the suspect perceive that the interrogation will go on much longer, if not indefinitely, if he does not comply with their wishes. As interrogators told one suspect: "If you tell me the truth, it'll be a piece of cake. If you don't tell me the truth, we'll be here awhile" (Interrogation of Howard Allen, 1987: 5). Another suspect was advised: "If you walk out of here tonight and don't tell us the truth, it's not gonna go away, it's only gonna get worse" (Interrogation of John Lopez, 1993: 4). Sometimes interrogators use time as a lure, suggesting that the interrogation is almost over, only to keep prolonging it, creating the expectation that if the suspect just complies it will at long last end. As one suspect reported (Declaration of Derek Niegemann, 1999: 6):

> Each time I was left alone time seemed to drag. I was frustrated because I did not know what was going on and being escorted to and from the bathroom by an agent convinced me I was not free to leave. I felt physically, mentally, and emotionally off balance. Throughout the interrogation, agent Lafayette periodically told me the questioning was almost over. Each time he returned after leaving the room, he would say he just had a few more points to clear up and that the questioning was almost over. This further confused and disoriented me because I kept thinking the questioning would soon be over, but it continued on and on, even after his constant reassurances that it was almost over.

Interrogators also employ a number of other strategies to increase a suspect's anxiety and exert pressure on him. They might invade his personal space. As one suspect recounted (Interview of John Irvin, 2000: 16):

> I was sitting like right here and he was sitting right beside me. You know, real close. It kinda made me uncomfortable somebody sitting that close. . . .
> I scooted over just a little bit, he scooted over towards me. I was just

uncomfortable. Because everytime that I scooted, he scooted with me. I ended up starting at the middle of the table and by 10:00 I was almost over to the edge.

Interrogators may also alternate displays of sympathy with displays of hostility, positively reinforcing the suspect with friendliness when he says what they want to hear but negatively reinforcing him with anger when he does not. Further, they will sometimes try to prevent the suspect from responding to them (e.g., denying involvement) or engaging in an activity (e.g., smoking a cigarette) that would allow him to release anxiety. Regardless of the specific strategy, interrogators understand that pressure and repetition are almost always necessary to overcome a suspect's denials. As with other negative incentives, interrogators exert and escalate pressure on the suspect so that he will perceive himself as trapped and thus will be desperate to escape a stressful situation.

POSITIVE INCENTIVES: MOTIVATING SUSPECTS TO START ADMITTING

Inducements

While interrogators use negative incentives to motivate a suspect to stop denying, they use what I have elsewhere called *positive incentives* to persuade a suspect that he will in some way feel better or benefit if he confesses (Leo, 1996a). Interrogators use a variety of positive incentives to persuade a suspect that he will obtain some psychological, material, or legal reward and avoid a corresponding harm if he makes an incriminating statement. Ultimately they seek to persuade the suspect that making an admission is the most desirable and rational course of action for someone in his situation, just as continuing to deny is the least desirable and rational course of action (Ofshe and Leo, 1997b).

Ofshe and Leo (1997a) have argued that the incentives interrogators use "can be arrayed on a continuum ranging from legally permissible psychological benefits . . . to the strongest coercive threats and promises." They have identified three general types of positive incentives: *Low-end* or *moral* incentives are interpersonal or moral appeals to convince a suspect that he will feel better if he confesses; *mid-range* or *systemic* incentives refer to appeals intended to focus the suspect's attention on the functioning of the criminal justice system in order to get him to believe that his case will likely be processed more favorably if he complies and confesses; and, finally, *high-end* incentives, which are implicit or explicit promises and threats, communicate that the suspect will receive less punishment or some form of police, prosecutorial, or juror leniency if he confesses, but that he will receive greater punishment if he does not (Ofshe and Leo, 1997a, b; see also Hilgendorf and Irving, 1981). The essential psychological point about these incentives is that interrogators use them to persuade the suspect that it is to his advantage to comply and confess and to his disadvantage to remain silent or continue to deny. In the remainder of this section, I use the broader term "inducements" to cover the kinds of incentives interrogators use to motivate suspects to make admissions.

Suggestions and Offers of Help
Early on in many interrogations, sometimes even before giving the *Miranda* warnings, interrogators tell the suspect that this is "your opportunity to present your side of the story"—sometimes adding, "before it is too late." This opening move is an attempt to motivate the suspect to talk by leading him to believe that his version of what occurred will only be entered into the official record if he speaks to police, and that he will forego this "opportunity" if he chooses not to speak.

Implicit in the interrogators' assertion is the idea that the suspect can put an end to any questioning or detention by convincing the interrogators of his innocence. With this bait, the investigators most immediate goal is to lock the suspect into an account that they can subsequently attack as implausible, inconsistent, or untenable. Even if they do not obtain an admission or confession, however, interrogators know that any account the suspect gives is likely to advantage the state because it increases the probability that the prosecution will be able to impeach him at trial if he takes the witness stand and thus increases the likelihood of securing his conviction.

Police seek to reframe the interrogation as an "opportunity" not only because they wish to divert the suspect's attention from its true purpose (i.e., incrimination), but also because they seek to persuade him that they can only help him if he continues to talk. An interrogator may tell a suspect, for example: "For me to help you, I need to hear your side of the story. . . . I need to understand what happened" (Interrogation transcript of Paul Miller, 1999: 3). Interrogators present themselves as the suspect's friend, supporter, ally and even advocate. Their role, police want the suspect to believe, is to assist him. "We're here to help you. I want to help you, I really do, you need to talk to somebody professionally to help you deal with this and we can arrange that" (Interrogation of Daniel Blank, 1997: 100).

Apart from how they represent their role, interrogators also offer to help the suspect—implicitly or explicitly as part of the quid pro quo for his compliance—through their actions and statements. Most fundamentally, interrogators will try to persuade the suspect that they can help him frame his culpability for the underlying act of which he is accused and thus help him minimize the social or legal consequences of his crime. For example, they may tell a suspect: "Michelle, I want to be able to help you and I can't help you if you can't tell me what happened, and you know what happened . . . Help me so I can help you, because there are people who would think, with the facts that we have and those things, there are people who would want to make you out to be a monster. You are not a monster" (Interrogation of Michelle Davis, 1999: 112, 136).

Interrogators may also tell a suspect more specifically how they can help. For example, with a favorable report: "I'm trying to help you, okay, to show in my report that, again, there was not any intercourse, okay. But for you to sit here and say there wasn't anything, I'll tell you, is a lie, okay? . . . The ball's in your court—and you can sit here and you know deny everything, but that's not going to help you out, Ricky" (Interrogation of Ricky Ford, 2000: 9). In addition, interrogators may indicate that they can help by what they tell the prosecutor prior to the filing of charges and what they testify to at trial. Offers of help can be very persuasive in getting a suspect to confess, as one reported: "They said that they would help me if I would. They said they would help me in my defense if I wrote another statement so that's the reason I wrote it" (Interview of John Irvin, 2000: 10). Interrogators' implicit and explicit suggestions and offers of help are designed to persuade the suspect that he can negotiate the best possible outcome if he complies with the interrogators' demands for an admission.

Constructing Scenarios

When using negative incentives to get a suspect to stop denying, interrogators will commonly tell him "the issue is not whether you did it but why." When using positive incentives to get a suspect to start admitting, interrogators will emphasize the "why," commonly saying that the only way he can help himself is by providing the reasons he committed the crime. Usually, however, interrogators will first suggest possible reasons or scenarios to get him to admit to it. This interrogation technique is known as using "themes" (Inbau et al., 2001; Senese, 2005), which, as we have seen, are scenarios or rationalizations that morally, psychologically, or legally downplay, excuse, or justify the suspect's act. Interrogators advance scenarios to persuade a suspect that if he admits to the act he can—with the interrogators' help—control how that act is framed to other audiences (e.g., prosecutors, judges, juries, his friends and family, the victim, the victim's friends and family, the media, and so on). In other words, he can explain his motive in a way that will portray him in the most sympathetic light and minimize his social, moral, and legal culpability.

Suggesting minimizing scenarios is one of the most fundamental methods of psychological interrogation. Every modern interrogation training manual recommends "themes" or scenarios of one sort or another; one manual even provides a list of more than 1,600 scenarios for police to use when interrogating suspects in more than 50 possible crimes (Senese, 2005). Regardless of the department, training firm, or part of the country in which interrogators work, the use of minimizing scenarios to motivate admissions is widespread. The reason: "themes" can be a subtle yet powerful inducement. They work by shifting the blameworthiness of the act from the suspect to another person; by attributing the blameworthiness to the social circumstances that allegedly led to the act; or by redefining the act in a way that appears to minimize, reduce, or even eliminate the suspect's culpability because the act now seems less criminal or no longer criminal at all. Scenarios seek to place the locus or motivation of the act outside the suspect's conscious intent or will.

Interrogators use a variety of scenarios to induce the suspect to admit to the act. They may construct scenarios that appear to excuse or justify the suspect's alleged crime by suggesting morally acceptable or understandable reasons why he did it. For example, interrogators may suggest a suspect committed a robbery because he was unemployed or needed to feed his family. Interrogators regularly use scenarios that suggest psychological excuses or explanations. For example, they may suggest that a suspect assaulted his wife only because he was under stress. Interrogators also use scenarios that suggest physiological excuses—for example, that a rape suspect was under the influence of drugs or alcohol. They may even use scenarios that suggest existential reasons that appear to minimize the suspect's culpability. One of the most prominent "themes" that interrogators are trained to use, for example, is that the suspect did not plan to commit the act but that it occurred "in the spur of the moment" (Inbau et al., 2001).

Ofshe and Leo (1997b) have argued that the most significant and effective scenarios are those that offer the suspect legal excuses or justifications for his alleged behavior. These types of scenarios redefine the suspect's mens rea (i.e., mental state) and thus the formal elements of the crime such that the suspect's legal culpability is reduced or eliminated. For example, it is common in murder investigations for interrogators to suggest that the suspect killed the victim in self-defense. Because self-defense is not a crime, the scenario suggests that the suspect will not be charged or punished for admitting to it. It is also common in murder investigations for interrogators to suggest that the suspect killed the victim accidentally, again mitigating the criminality of the act and seemingly lowering the punishment if the suspect agrees to the accident scenario (Ofshe and Leo, 1997b). These scenarios are effective because they "pragmatically" communicate that the suspect will receive a lower charge or lesser punishment if he agrees to the suggested scenario (Kassin and McNall, 1991; Ofshe and Leo, 1997b).

The scenarios discussed so far seek to minimize the seriousness of the alleged act and its consequences by portraying the suspect's intent and the cause of the act in their most sympathetic light. We might call these "good" scenarios because they seek to minimize the suspect's moral and legal blameworthiness. Interrogators often couple and contrast these good scenarios with their opposite: "bad" scenarios that portray the suspect's intent in its worst possible light, thus exaggerating the seriousness of the act or its consequences. Interrogators use this strategy to persuade the suspect that if he fails to minimize his culpability by adopting the good scenario, everyone who matters (e.g., his friends and family, the victim, the prosecutor, the judge and jury) will come to believe the bad scenario, as it will become the official narrative of his crime—and he will suffer the consequences. For example, homicide investigators often tell the suspect that if he does not adopt their accident or self-defense scenario, he will be perceived as committing the killing intentionally, with premeditation, as in the following example: "You know what I'm saying. Even if you admit to things doesn't mean that you get convicted of things. Cause like you can kill somebody, it can be justified homicide later on or self-defense" (Interrogation of Donald Perry, 1999: 88).

The good scenario/bad scenario technique is a cerebral or intellectualized version of the well known good cop/bad cop technique that was more common in an earlier era. Delivered against the backdrop of the techniques that have preceded them—isolation, accusations, attacks on denials, evidence ploys, and so forth—these scenarios are intended to motivate the suspect who already feels trapped and powerless to confess because he is being offered a chance to mitigate his punishment by choosing the better of his two remaining choices. Like all inducements, scenarios portray the act of complying with the interrogators' demands as in the suspects' rational self-interest given his situation. Interrogators use scenarios so that the suspect will perceive the essential, if illusory, quid pro quo of psychological interrogation: in exchange for his compliance and admissions, they will attempt to negotiate the best possible outcome for him.

Negotiating Punishment Outcomes: Promises and Threats

All inducements seek to persuade the suspect that he will benefit by confessing. Yet not all inducements are created equal; some offer more tangible benefits than others (Ofshe and Leo, 1997b). From the interrogator's perspective, the ideal inducements are those that most subtly convey the benefit the suspect can or will receive, because the more subtle the interrogator's negotiation with the suspect the less likely a court is to later throw out the suspect's statement as inadmissible. Subtle inducements, however, do not always work to motivate suspects to make admissions. Sometimes more powerful inducements are necessary.

The most powerful types of psychological inducements are promises and threats. Promises and threats too come in degrees. The essential aspect of a promise is that it offers or suggests a benefit or deal—typically some form of police, prosecutorial, judicial, or juror leniency—in exchange for an admission. The essential aspect of a threat is that it threatens harsher treatment—typically higher or more prosecutorial charges and a longer prison sentence—in the absence of an admission. Promises and threats can be delivered implicitly or explicitly (Kassin and McNall, 1991; Ofshe and Leo, 1997b; Solan and Tiersma, 2005). They often go together because they imply one another: a promise of leniency implies a threat of harsher treatment if the suspect fails to comply with the interrogators' wishes, just as a threat of harsher treatment implies a promise of leniency if the suspect complies.

Kassin and McNall (1991) have demonstrated that certain techniques such as scenarios communicate promises of leniency through "pragmatic implication" (i.e., indirectly or implicitly). Ofshe and Leo (1997b) have illustrated how some of the scenarios widely used by American interrogators, such as accident and self-defense scenarios, communicate and create expectations of leniency in exchange for admissions. Homicide investigators routinely contrast an accident with an intentional murder, signaling that if the suspect adopts the accident scenario it will drastically lower the charges and sentence he is likely to face. For example (Interrogation of Harold Kramer, 1999: 41):

> You get no help cuz your gonna look like a murderer, whereas if you tell us now what happened and it was an accident, I'll write it that way. I mean, Ken, we can write it that it was an accident. You shook the kid, if that is true, shaken-baby syndrome, what I was telling you about contraconcussion with the brain and stuff and where you just shook him, that is truth and that's an accident. Or if you held your hand over his mouth, that's an accident, okay? But intent, and the intent is lying—I meant that when I said before that if you lie that fixes intention. We walk outa here today and your straight with this story and then we show something else that fixes intent, then your looking at first-degree intentional homicide which carries an automatic life without possibility of parole.

The accident scenario technique may be formatted or unformatted (Ofshe and Leo, 1997b). Interrogators sometimes encourage the suspect to fill in the story of how he committed the act accidentally. Other times they structure the scenario for the suspect by making clear how he needs to tell the story in order to receive the deal, as in the following example (Interrogation of Jose Luna, 2000: 40):

> But I think maybe you might of touched her with your hand, maybe on the outside of her vagina. Okay? And I know it happened more than once, so it couldn't have been only one time that it happened. Okay? But I have to get everybody's side of the story and for us to understand it and you are to be a stand-up guy and say, Okay, shit, I made a goddamned mistake, it was the worst fucking . . . thing that has ever happened to me. All right, she came on to me. I was drunk. I screwed up. I didn't screw up, I fucked up. I'm a man. I'm gonna tell what happened like it happened and be done with it. . . . I don't think you put your penis inside of her. I think you put your finger or your tongue inside of her vagina. And you can tell me yes or no. Okay? So did you rape her? You're shaking your head no.

Lawyers and judges often draw sharp distinctions between what they believe does or does not constitute a promise or threat, but promises and threats exist in degrees and like all inducements range from weak to strong. The most important thing to understand about the promise–threat dynamic is its psychological logic: police interrogators use promises and threats—whether implied or direct, subtle or explicit—to persuade the suspect to perceive that he is far better off by confessing and far worse off by continuing to deny guilt. More specifically, American police interrogators use the promise–threat dynamic to manipulate the suspects to believe that (1) although the evidence irrefutably establishes his guilt, the investigators' decision whether to continue to detain him, the prosecutor's decision whether to charge him (as well as with what and how many counts), and the judge's or jury's decision whether to sentence him (and for how long) have not yet been determined; (2) these decisions are negotiable, not fixed; (3) if he agrees or admits to some version of the act, he can negotiate more favorable decisions; and (4) if he continue to deny that he committed the act, he will be treated and punished more harshly. This is the logic that underlies the use of promises and threats. There are numerous varieties of this promise–threat dynamic.

American police investigators are trained that promises of leniency and threats of harm violate the law that governs the admissibility of confession evidence and therefore may lead trial courts to suppress the defendant's statements. However, most detectives receive brief and superficial training about what constitutes a promise or threat, and are typically told only to avoid the most extreme examples (such as explicitly threatening physical violence or promising a suspect that he can avoid the death penalty). Perhaps for this reason, the most common promise–threat dynamic in American interrogation is more subtle and indirect: while detectives seek to communicate that the suspect will be treated more leniently if he confesses, they also want to be able to plausibly deny that they issued any promises or threats. Detectives often accomplish this by focusing the suspect's attention on the various actors in the criminal justice system (police, prosecutors, expert witnesses, judges, and juries) and the roles they play in determining the suspect's fate, and by contrasting how they will react to the suspect's denials versus how they will react to his admissions. For example, detectives may tell a suspect that what he says to them will determine what they testify to in court or put in their report. As interrogators told one suspect (Interrogation of William Ethridge Hill, 1997: 150): "The bus is leaving, my friend, the bus is leaving. You don't want me to have to put in my final investigation report that I flew to Baltimore, I gave William Ethridge Hill, Jr., every opportunity to tell the truth, and he would not do it." If the suspect is on probation or parole, interrogators may threaten to "violate" the probation and thus send him back to prison if he does not cooperate.

Interrogators may also tell a suspect, "You're giving us nothing to take to the D.A.'s office on your behalf" (Interrogation of Victor Lee, 1995: 49). Another suspect recounted: "They just kept telling me about the prosecutor will go easy on me if I just cooperate. If they tell the prosecutor that I cooperated, it will look good for me" (Interview of Beverly Edwards, 1998: 25). Or interrogators may suggest that the judge will sentence the suspect more leniently if he cooperates. As one interrogator wrote in a police report (Police Report of R. F. Armstrong, 1998: 4–5):

> The subject was told that I knew he had been involved in the judicial system and knew how it worked. The subject was told that it was always better to tell the truth. He was told that he had been taught to tell the truth by his parents and when he was a child and did something wrong he got in more trouble for lying about what happened than he did for what ever it was that he did. He agreed. The subject was told that nothing changes when a person grows up. He was asked to visualize two people standing in front of a judge, one of the people saying that he did not do it when everyone knew that he had, and the other admitting that he had made a mistake, was sorry and wanted to make sure that he did not do it again. The subject was asked if he would treat the two people differently.

Interrogators often focus on juries as well. One told a suspect (Interrogation of William Ethridge Hill, 1997: 158–159): "You can fill in the blanks here or the jury is going to fill in the blanks down the road. And what they're going to fill in the blanks with is going to be the worst possible scenario." In another case, a suspect was advised (Interrogation of John Lopez, 1993: 7–8):

> The sooner you confess to this, the better it is for you. Like we brought up to your attention earlier this afternoon, that this is how the jury looks at it. Either, well, geez, the cops had to do all the work on this, he never had any remorse whatsoever, or he must of really felt bad if this thing went bad. I mean, he confessed to the cops, he really wants to get this taken care of. It's just something, Johnny, you go, you're helpin' yourself out. The longer you wait, the deeper the hole gets.

Sometimes interrogators will imply that if the suspect complies with their demands he can go home and will not be charged. They may communicate this message in a number of ways, perhaps the most common of which is through the use of scenarios that redefine the act as not criminal. For example, some suspects have been led to believe that by admitting to consensual sex in a rape investigation or self-defense in a murder investigation they would not be charged, and thus were shocked when police arrested them. Another was told (Interrogation of Donald Perry, 1999: 118): "Let's cut right to the chase. Flat out. Do you want to take care of it tonight and get it over with or do you want to drag it out in court? That's basically your decision. You're completely in control of it." It is not uncommon for suspects to describe some version of the following (Testimony of Thomas Battle, 2001: 670): "On numerous occasions when I requested to go home . . . I was told that . . . as soon as we're done, we can all get out of here. I hadn't been told I was under arrest at the time . . . When they said we can all get out of here once we're done, I was just, okay, I'll just tell them whatever they want me to say, and we can all go."

Sometimes interrogators will tell a suspect that he can choose which role they will assign him—principal, accessory, co-perpetrator, innocent bystander, or witness, for example—in the narrative they are completing for the prosecution. The implication, of course, is that if he agrees with these assertions he will be cast in the noncriminal role that carries no punishment, but that if he continues to deny their claims he will be cast in the criminal role and thus arrested and prosecuted. Sometimes interrogators suggest or promise immunity or amnesty in exchange for compliance and confession. One suspect recounted (Declaration of Derek Neigeman, 1999: 7):

Agent Lafayette said words to the effect, "You are now at the point of amnesty." He asked if I knew what amnesty was, and I replied that I did. I understood him to mean that If I admitted setting the fires, I would not be arrested or prosecuted. Agent Lafayette followed what I perceived as an amnesty offer with an ominous threat. He said something like, "You are now at the point of amnesty, but that amnesty is fading fast." Agent Lafayette kept repeating that he wanted to get these fires "out of the way" so that he could focus on the problems at the center.

Interrogators may use the promise–threat dynamic to educate the suspect about the various types and degrees of charges that might follow from how the state frames the crime, perhaps even using wall charts that show the penalty the suspects face if convicted (Douglas, 1995). If the suspect complies with the interrogators' demands, they might suggest, he will receive a more lenient charge and thus a lower sentence. For example (Interrogation of William Ethridge Hill, 1997: 142): "Let me . . . go back and talk about the difference between murder and the difference between manslaughter and the difference between this was an accident and, you know, I'm sorry that it happened. A lot of what I'm going to be able to do from this point on, almost everything to help you out, depends on what you tell me right now." In another case, interrogators told the suspect: "A judge can also understand, like I can and him and anyone else, that we all make mistakes, right? And that . . . if it's consenting sexual contact, it's a whole lot different . . . I can read you in the California Penal Code, there's a big difference between consenting sexual contact and forced intercourse" (Interrogation of Ricky Ford, 2000: 10).

Sometimes interrogators pull a legal book on the penal code off the shelf and either show or discuss the various degrees and elements of the crime and the corresponding punishments. A murder suspect remembered (Statement of Tony Ringer, 2001: 4–5):

> I told him that I couldn't do that; he said it was my only way out of there tonight. At that time his partner walks back in the room and they both began to discuss my options out of there, so they showed me a law book which describes what different crime penalties are. They told me that if an accidental shooting occurs that is called negligent homicide and it was a misdemeanor and that I could come home tonight. Seconds later the same detective left the room again and the other began to tell me a story on how I could say I accidentally shot Ms. Betts. He said because they were charging me with aggravated murder . . . if I said the story he gave me that his boss would lessen the charges to negligent homicide and I could go home to see my mother tonight. . . . So I told the story the way the detective said to.

Sometimes interrogators use the promise–threat dynamic to suggest that the suspect's loved ones will benefit if he cooperates and confesses, but that they will be worse off if he continues to deny. For example, the following exchange occurred in one case (Interrogation transcript of Jose Jacobo, 1999: 65–67):

Interrogator: How many children do you have?
Jacobo: Two.
Interrogator: How old are they?
Jacobo: Four and five years old.
Interrogator: And do you want some other person to . . . see them grow? Do you want someone else to support them? . . . You have to think exactly

of your future, okay? . . . Do you want to see your wife? Do you want to still be able to see your wife?

Jacobo: Sure.

Interrogator: . . . Your children? What happened here was a mistake. It was a mistake, Jose.

Jacobo: It was a [unintelligible].

Interrogator: It was a very big mistake, okay? But now, here, right this moment you have to tell these police exactly what happened. Now forget about all the lies, about everything you said before

Perhaps the ultimate psychological threat involves the death penalty in murder cases. Even though police interrogators are taught that death threats are coercive and should be avoided, it is not uncommon for homicide suspects to report that they were threatened with the death penalty. Occasionally one even sees such threats in recorded interrogations. Interrogators may make the threat implicitly or explicitly. One suspect recalled (Statement of William Schofield, 1997: 10): "They told me that their boss did not believe what I was telling them. They said she thought I was lying. They said she thought I murdered Adam and that I did it premeditatedly. I told them no. Detective Jones told me that their boss wanted to charge me with premeditated murder. I remembered what he said about premeditated murder and murder one. It was life in jail or death." In another case, two interrogators told the suspect repeatedly that the only way he could avoid the death penalty was by confessing to the murder. The interrogators told him that if he did not confess, the killing would be framed as a cold-blooded act of first-degree murder, but that if he did it would be charged as second-degree murder because it would be seen as an act of passion (Interrogation of Jimmie Thomas, 1998: 39): "There's a big difference between not getting out of jail and getting the death penalty, and see, that's the reason why I'm talking to you. And one of the things I want to get to in this conversation is your side of the story makes a big difference in what happens."

Or consider the FBI's interrogation of Wen Ho Lee (2001: 81):

Agent: Do you know who the Rosenbergs are?

Lee: Yeah, I heard.

Agent: The Rosenbergs are the only people that never cooperated with the federal government in an espionage case. You know what happened to them? They electrocuted them, Wen Ho.

Lee: Yeah, I heard.

Agent: They didn't care whether they professed their innocence all day long. They electrocuted them. OK. Aldrich Ames. You know Aldrich Ames? He's going to rot in jail.

Lee: I see.

Agent: OK? John Walker! Okay, he's another one. He was arrested for espionage. OK? Do you want to go down in history? Whether you're professing your innocence like the Rosenbergs to the day that they take you to the electric chair? . . . Do you want to go down in history? With your kids knowing that you got arrested for espionage?

Lee: I don't.

Agent: The Rosenbergs professed their innocence. The Rosenbergs weren't concerned either. The Rosenbergs are dead.

Conclusion: Why People Confess

Why do suspects confess? The short answer, of course, is police interrogation, since suspects almost never confess spontaneously but virtually always in response to police pressure. As Inbau et al. (1986: xvi) has written, "It is impractical to expect any but a very few confessions to result from a guilty conscience unprovoked by an interrogation." However, this does not explain why some suspects confess more quickly than others, why some never confess at all, and why some confess truthfully while others confess falsely. There may be multiple reasons why suspects make admissions. Here I focus only on why suspects make true, or partially true, confessions; in Chapter 6 I address false confessions. Suspects who make true confessions in response to interrogation do so for at least three broad and interrelated reasons: they wish to terminate the interrogation and escape from the stress, pressure, and confinement of the interrogation process; they come to perceive that they have no meaningful choice but to comply with the demands of the interrogators; or they come to perceive that the benefits of admitting to some version of the offense outweigh the costs of continued denial (Ofshe and Leo, 1997b).

Some suspects confess simply because the stress and pressure become too overwhelming. The stress and pressure come from multiple sources: social isolation; confinement in an unfamiliar setting; physical discomfort; perceived lack of control, even helplessness; fear; confusion; uncertainty; the detectives' interpersonal style; the aversive, manipulative, and threatening nature of accusatorial interrogation techniques; and the fear of being caught, arrested, and prosecuted. Interrogators are often relentless. They may badger the suspect; question him intensely; raise their voices in anger; move in closer; misrepresent the case against him; issue threats and promises; and prolong the questioning process as they pursue his admission. Interrogators negatively reinforce the suspect when he denies their accusations and positively reinforce him when he complies with them. They strive to create the impression that the questioning is not going to end until he bends to their will—that confession is the only way out.

Although different people can withstand different levels of stress and pressure, for many the interrogation becomes intolerable at some point. For suspects who are already sleep deprived, fatigued, distressed, or suffering from physical discomfort (e.g., drug withdrawal), interrogation exacerbates these conditions. Accusatory interrogation is a highly unpleasant experience for just about every suspect, however. The need to escape may become so overwhelming that it overpowers any rational considerations about the effects of confessing. Interrogators, who know this well, attempt to focus the suspect's attention on the immediate benefits of confession and divert it from the long-term consequences. Some suspects confess because they come to perceive it as the best or only means available to put an end to the process (Ofshe and Leo, 1997b).

A second, related reason why some suspects confess is that the interrogation causes them to perceive that they have no meaningful choice but to comply with the interrogators' demands. At first glance, it may not appear rational for suspect to perceive that he has no choice but to confess, especially since he had been told of his rights to silence and counsel beforehand. However, as the pressures and stresses mount, they may deplete him of cognitive resources, divert his attention, and compromise his ability to think clearly, process and retrieve information, and form reasonable conclusions (Davis and O'Donahue, 2003). The Supreme Court recognized this when, in *Miranda v. Arizona* (1966: 466), it wrote, "The entire thrust of police interrogation . . . [is] to put the defendant in such an emotional state as to impair his capacity for rational judgment." The suspect's cognitive functioning and responses may be further undermined by the time pressures that interrogators exert on him to cooperate.

Moreover, the psychology of interrogation is structured to promote and reinforce feelings of helplessness, futility, and inevitability. Investigators communicate that they control all aspects of the interrogation process and consequently the suspect comes to perceive that he is entirely dependent on them. Investigators control where the interrogation takes place; when it begins and ends; the suspect's freedom of movement; the content, speed, and intensity of the questions; the acceptability of his responses; and his access to restroom facilities, food, and breaks. Interrogators also seek to control the information the suspect receives and how he interprets and acts on it. If they succeed in convincing him that he is irreversibly caught and powerless to change his situation, he may easily come to feel that he no longer possesses the will to resist.

Finally, some suspects confess because the interrogators persuade them that confessing is their *relatively* best choice among the available options. As Ofshe and Leo (1997b: 985) argue:

> Psychological interrogation is effective at eliciting confession because of a fundamental fact of human decision-making—people make optimizing choices given the options they consider. Psychologically-based interrogation works effectively by controlling the alternatives a person considers and by influencing how those alternatives are understood. The techniques interrogators use have been selected to limit a person's attention to certain issues, to manipulate his perceptions of his present situation and to bias his evaluation of the choices before him . . . Police elicit the decision to confess from the guilty by leading them to believe that the evidence against them is overwhelming, that their fate is certain (whether or not they confess), and that the evidence against them and that there are advantages that follow if they confess.

Some suspects comply because interrogators have reversed their subjective confidence of escape and, instead, persuaded them that the moral, social, psychological, or legal benefits of confessing outweigh the costs of denial (Irving and Hilgendorf, 1980; Ofshe and Leo, 1997b). Suspects who perceive that there is little likelihood of escaping conviction are more easily led to see the act of confessing as a way to minimize the consequences that follow. As Drizin and Leo (2004: 919) noted, "the genius or mind trick of modern interrogation is that it makes the irrational (admitting to a crime that will likely lead to punishment) appear rational. . . ."

CHAPTER 5

Constructing Culpability

Interrogations are best understood therefore as social encounters fashioned to *confirm* and *legitimate* a police narrative. In this sense they are similar to the trial—the event which interrogations traditionally lead up to and feed into, but which they increasingly *replace*.

> —Michael McConville, Andrew Sanders, and Roger Leng (1991)

Do I have to tell you the story before you tell me the story?

> —San Diego Police Detective Bruce Pendleton interrogating suspect Deron Ford (2005)

A police-induced confession is like a Hollywood drama: scripted by the interrogator's theory of the case, shaped through questioning and rehearsal, directed by the questioner and enacted by the suspect.

> —Saul Kassin (2005)

It is often assumed that once the detective has moved the suspect to say the words "I did it," the interrogation is effectively over. Analytically, it would be more precise to say that those words signal that the *preadmission* portion of the interrogation process is over. The preadmission portion is the focus of most social psychological research on the methods of social influence and their effects during interrogation (Ofshe and Leo, 1997b; Davis and O'Donahue, 2003; Kassin and Gudjonsson, 2004). It is also the focus of pretrial suppression motions in which prosecutors and defense attorneys argue over whether the interrogation was coercive and the resulting admissions involuntary. It is the focal point of their arguments over the interrogation and confession evidence at trial too. Moreover, the preadmission phase is the dramatic high point of police interrogation scenes in television, movies, and cinema.

Though it has received far less attention from scholars, lawyers, and the media, the postadmission portion of police interrogation is enormously important for a number of reasons. As scholars have pointed out, it can be useful in analyzing the reliability of the suspect's admissions (Ofshe and Leo, 1997b; Leo, Drizin, Neufeld, Hall, and Vatner, 2006). The postadmission narrative portion of the interrogation process is also important because it reveals how the interrogator and the suspect jointly create a persuasive narrative of the suspect's culpability that transforms the fledgling admission into a full-formed confession. Since the suspect's postadmission narrative will ultimately be treated as his confession, we might conceptualize the postadmission narrative portion as the confession-taking—or perhaps more accurately, the confession-*making*—phase of interrogation. As Hepworth and Turner (1982: 148) have pointed out, "Confessions are constructed not discovered." Contrary to popular mythology, just as police investigators are neither neutral nor impartial in the preadmission phase of interrogation, they are not neutral or impartial in the postadmission phase either. If they were, their postadmission questioning would shift from interrogation mode to the interviewing format that detectives often use with victims and witnesses: their approach would no longer be accusatorial, their questions would be open ended, they would let the suspect do most of the talking (without interruption), and their objective would be to collect the unadulterated truth, regardless of the suspect's responses.

Instead, most detectives in practice make no distinction between preadmission interrogation and postadmission interrogation, and therefore often continue to use confrontational, suggestive, and manipulative interrogation techniques if the suspect's responses and account do not match the detective's expectations or theory of the crime. The suspect's postadmission narrative or confession, then, is not something that is simply taken or elicited. Rather, it is actively shaped and manipulated—with the suspect's participation to be sure, but at the interrogator's direction. The interrogators' strategic orientation and behavior in the postadmission stage are no different than they were in earlier phases of the interrogation process. Their primary goal continues to be to incriminate the suspect in order to assist other state actors prosecute and convict him. The interrogators' modus operandi remains the same as well: to persuade the suspect of the illusion that he and the interrogators share a common interest and that the suspect can only advance his self-interest by complying with the interrogators' wishes. Interrogators also seek to manipulate the suspect's postadmission narrative to confer legitimacy on the police procedures through which the admissions were obtained, and to deflect any eventual challenges to the confession's authenticity. In short, the postadmission phase of interrogation is crucial to understanding how confessions are made, how investigators seek to control the public narrative of the interrogation, and why confession evidence is so persuasive and difficult to overcome in court.

Postadmission Interrogation and Confession-Making

As in the preadmission phase, investigators in the postadmission portion of interrogation will accuse a suspect of lying, cut off and roll over denials or explanations that they believe to be false, confront a suspect with real or invented evidence that supports their position, and feign omniscience. And, again, they will use incentives to convey the benefits of giving or agreeing to a particular account, and even suggest minimizing scenarios that explain how and why the suspect committed the crime or could have done so. But while investigators in the preadmission phase seek to move the suspect from denial to admission, in the postadmission phase they strive to elicit an account that explains how and why he committed the crime.

Yet the postadmission interrogation process in the American adversary system is about more than merely eliciting information. Interrogators seek to shape the suspect's narrative to incriminate and build a case against him that will ensure his conviction. To do so they usually try to elicit an account that is consistent with their theory of the crime. If the suspect's postadmission narrative does not fit their preexisting expectations about how and why he committed the crime, they continue to interrogate him. While there are some detectives whose only goal in the postadmission phase is to get an uncontaminated account (Napier and Adams, 2002), many others seek to influence the suspects' narrative to create the appearance that his confession is believable, if not compelling; that it comes entirely from the suspect and thus is voluntary; and that it is self-authenticating and therefore reliable. Police interrogation in the adversary system is arguably as much about constructing and managing the public narrative of interrogation and confession as it is about getting the suspect to say "I did it."

Constructing a Persuasive Narrative

An admission is a statement, but a confession is a story. Like all stories, some confessions are more plausible than others. Police interrogators instinctively understand this. As one writer has pointed out, "detectives' occupational consciousness is much more narrative than analytical" (Jackall, 2005: 13). To build a case against a suspect, interrogators must elicit a believable account of his participation in and knowledge of the crime. Sometimes this involves little work for interrogators in the postadmission phase: some suspects will, with little prompting or pressure, provide a detailed narrative of how and why they committed the crime. Others, however, may only reluctantly give interrogators the account they are looking for, or they may lie, or appear to be lying, about crime facts or details. And, as we will see later, some innocent suspects from whom interrogators have coerced a false confession do not provide accounts that interrogators believe to be accurate or legitimate.

There are essentially five elements investigators focus on in postadmission interrogation to make sure that the suspect's confession appears authentic, compelling, and self-corroborating: (1) a coherent, believable story line, (2) motives and explanations, (3) crime knowledge (both general and specific), (4) expressions of emotion, and (5) acknowledgments of voluntariness. Interrogators attempt to influence suspects to provide each of these elements in their postadmission narrative in order to construct a persuasive account of their culpability and build a successful case. Interrogators also seek to confer legitimacy on the police procedures through which the admissions were obtained and to deflect any eventual challenges to the confession's validity. Even though formal charges have not even been filed and the suspect is not yet represented by counsel, interrogators are already thinking about the possibility that his future lawyer will attack the confession's voluntariness or reliability. They therefore often seek to build into the suspect's narrative the kinds of statements and cues that those who will later evaluate it—prosecutors, judges, and juries—associate with individual volition and truth-telling.

THE STORY LINE

For interrogators, the first step in transforming the "I did it" statement into a confession is to elicit the who, what, when, where, how, and why of the suspect's alleged involvement in the crime. As with preadmission interrogation, postadmission interrogation varies in the amount of time and effort necessary for detectives to obtain their goal. The postadmission interrogation process may require little additional pressure or prompting to elicit the details of the crime. Once suspects—especially guilty ones—are moved from denial to admission, they may readily supply the details because they do not understand the difference between an admission and a confession. In other words, they may see little difference between telling the police that they committed the crime and telling them how and why. Since the suspect perceives that the jig is up, the details may seem no more incriminating than the admission.

In other cases, however, the postadmission interrogation process may require substantial additional pressure and prompting to move the suspect from admission to confession. This typically occurs when either the interrogators perceive that the suspect is refusing to provide details of the offense or his account does not fit with their expectations or beliefs about how or why the crime occurred. This process is most acute in false confession cases when the interrogators are having difficulty getting the details from the suspect because he simply does not know them.

Whether or not they encounter resistance, interrogators need to elicit more than a telling of the details in the postadmission phase: they need a story or narrative so that the confession is persuasive to important third parties such as prosecutors, judges, and juries. The narrative should organize the details of the admission in a way that makes sense of the crime and the suspect's participation in it. To be plausible and persuasive, the confession narrative requires a coherent story line, characters, an unfolding plot (with a beginning, middle, and end), a description of actions and events in sequence, and explanations. When third parties recognize a story line developing, they are cued to interpret subsequent information as consistent with that story (Amsterdam and Bruner, 2000). As Steven Lubet (2002: 5) has put it, "Once a juror begins to envision events in a certain context, new information will tend to be evaluated in that same context."

Interrogators instinctively recognize this and often try to influence the suspect to supply information that will make his narrative cohere into a convincing story. They sometimes do so by telling the suspect what happened (including, in multiperpetrator crimes, who did what), suggesting or filling in missing details, correcting statements, directing the suspect to particular conclusions, and suggesting how and why the crime occurred. Moreover, interrogators sometimes pressure the suspect to provide a persuasive narrative of his culpability by focusing on how judges and juries are going to react to his account. In some cases, interrogators may even suggest that they can only help the suspect or deliver the promised benefit (and avoid the anticipated harm) if his account contains particular facts. In most cases, however, this is not necessary because the interrogators have clearly and repeatedly communicated their theory of the crime, the information or evidence that supports their beliefs, and the kinds of answers they except to receive from the suspect in the preadmission portion of questioning.

MOTIVES AND EXPLANATIONS

A crime narrative requires a description of why the suspect committed the crime to be plausible and persuasive. Crimes happen for a reason. In American society, a crime story without a motive is inherently incomplete. Some suspects may, in the postadmission phase of interrogation, freely supply their interrogators with a description of their motive or motives. Others may not offer one so readily (because, for example, they were in a drug-induced state and do not know why they committed the crime) or even resist providing an explanation altogether. If the interrogators do not agree with the suspect's description, they may try to challenge his account. In addition, they may pressure a suspect to build a particular motive into his narrative to make it appear more believable or to ensure that he is more likely to be prosecuted and convicted. Interrogators may also seek to exclude or deemphasize some aspect of the suspect's narrative that would make him appear more sympathetic to a prosecutor or jury, less likely to be convicted, or perhaps more likely to be convicted of a lesser offense.

In many cases, investigators will suggest, and pressure suspects to accept, certain motives in the preadmission phase of interrogation. As we saw in Chapter 4, one of the primary preadmission interrogation techniques is to suggest various possible minimizing and/or exculpating scenarios to the suspect to induce him to confess. These scenarios invariably contain motives for why the suspect committed the offense: for example, that he committed the act because he was stressed out; that he was in a drug- or alcohol-induced state and thus experienced a lapse of judgment; or that he just made an honest mistake. Many scenarios (and suggestions of motive) are crime specific: for example, that the suspect assaulted or murdered the victim because he was provoked or acting in self-defense; that a parent hit his child to teach the child discipline or because his wife was too permissive; or that the suspect had sex with the rape victim because she was she came onto him or because his wife was not satisfying his sexual needs; or that the suspect committed the burglary because he lost his job or needed to feed his family (Senese, 2005). Often suspects repeat the motives in their confessions that the investigators first suggested to them in the preadmission portion of the interrogation.

CRIME KNOWLEDGE

To be persuasive, the suspect's confession must also contain both general and specific crime knowledge. In the postadmission phase, interrogators press suspects to provide details about the crime, the crime scene, the victim, and other relevant aspects of the offense. Some suspects may reveal or know more than others, however, and some interrogators will expend more time and energy eliciting details than others. Suspects may also learn crime facts and details from police or other third parties (e.g., community gossip, overheard conversations, the media, etc.). The presence of detailed knowledge of the crime gives the suspect's confession verisimilitude. It is this kind of knowledge that important third parties find compelling (Leo et al., 2006), especially if it is perceived as vivid, accurate, and unique (Kassin, 2006). Interrogators realize that judges and juries will often treat the details in a confession as corroboration of the admission.

Interrogators do not merely elicit detailed crime knowledge from suspects; they also suggest it. Because they presume the suspect's guilt, interrogators typically assume that the suspect knows most, if not all, of the details of the crime. As a result, interrogators are usually blind to the process through which they communicate crime facts and details to suspects. Moreover, much preadmission interrogation is by its very nature suggestive and involves explicitly (through declaration) and implicitly (through leading questions) telling the suspect the details in order to move him from denial to admission. When interrogators accuse suspects of committing the offense, for example, they often communicate many of the specific details of the crime. When the suspect resists or denies, interrogators not only repeat their accusations but also correct his answers and tell him their theory of the case—which is authoritatively presented as fact—including many of the details that support their accusations. This tends to be especially true in cases in which the only evidence against the suspect is the alleged victim's accusations (such as those involving allegations of sexual abuse). In these and other cases, interrogators also educate the suspect about the details of the crime when they confront him with real or fictitious evidence of his guilt. In some cases, interrogators have shown suspects autopsy and crime photographs, brought suspects to the crime scene itself, and even set up entire "prop rooms" containing photographs, reports, charts, and other visual information that may have the effect of educating the suspect about the crime.

While guilty suspects may know many or all of the details of the crime, innocent suspects usually do not (unless they witnessed the crime or learned the crime facts from a third party). For innocent suspects, then, the detailed crime knowledge in their confessions usually first came from the police. The process of suggesting crime facts to the suspect occurs as part of the standard techniques of preadmission interrogation, but may also occur in the postadmission phase when the suspect is not providing interrogators the account they seek. Consider the following example from a detective's report:

> Avis remembers committing a number of pepper spray robberies, along with her sister, Rhonda. She could not remember times or dates so we provided them for her, along with some minor details of the cases, in order to jog her memory. (Police Report of Dale Fox, 1999: 12)

As we'll see in more detail in Chapter 6, in false confession cases interrogators often feed nonpublic facts to the suspect that they claim originated with him and thus proves his guilt. For example, Chicago detectives coerced from Corethian Bell a false confession to murdering his mother, Netta Bell (Drizin and Leo, 2004), in which he regurgitated numerous nonpublic details that he could have learned only from the detectives. They included that (1) the stabbing of his mother had occurred in the bedroom of the apartment; (2) after the attack, she had walked from the bedroom to the bathroom where she died; (3) a murder weapon had been recovered in a dumpster in the alley behind her apartment; (4) the murder weapon was a standard-sized kitchen knife; (5) his mother had been stabbed in the face, including through the eye, and on the torso; (6) the knife blade had broken off inside his mother's body; and (7) blood spatters had been found on the bathroom walls of the apartment. According to the detectives, these details originated with Bell. But we know that the detectives falsely attributed them to him because DNA evidence identified the true killer, a violent sex offender, who was eventually convicted of raping and murdering Netta

Bell. In the Bell case, as in many others, the detectives even rehearsed the details before turning on the tape recorder and taking Bell's confession. According to Bell: "Like he would say 'when I tell you who murdered your mother, say you'; and I was like 'okay.' I said yes. You know, questions like, 'Did you like have a pack of hot dogs with you?' And I would say 'yeah'; and after we was done practicing, then they filmed the video" (Deposition of Corethian Bell, 2005: 212–213).

EMOTIONS

Persuasive confessions also include the expression of emotions such as anger, fear, sorrow, remorse, shame, and regret. Confessions that are textured with these and other emotional expressions—such as crying (Katz, 1999)—humanize the admission, seemingly rendering it the natural product of lived experience. Remorse, shame, and regret make the confession appear authentic and thus seemingly beyond dispute. Recognizing the probative force of emotion-laden confessions, interrogators sometimes try to get suspects to express remorse and regret—by implying, for example, that it could result in more sympathetic or favorable treatment by the decision-makers who hold the key to a suspect's fate. The interrogators might ask a suspect, "Now what do you want me to tell the DA? Do you want me to tell him that you did this with no remorse?" (Interrogation of Sean Harrill, 1999: 160). In the same vein, investigators sometimes even implore the suspect to write an apology note to the victim (even when the victim is dead)—a brilliant technique for corroborating (or creating the appearance of corroborating) the authenticity of the suspect's postadmission narrative.

In their police reports, pretrial and trial testimony, and interviews with the media in high-profile cases, investigators also impute emotions such as relief and catharsis to suspects. For example, in one case an interrogator wrote in his report: "Cobb stated that he felt so warm and so good admitting involvement that he now would be able to sleep better" (Affadavit of Raymond Lundin, 1999: 3) even though the videotape did not bear this out. In another case, the interrogator testified: "I think [the defendant] was pleased with the fact that he had finished the statement. He seemed to be happy with it. He seemed to be relieved to have it written down . . . He appeared to be at ease with what he had said, with the fact that he had been allowed to say it and get it off his chest" (Testimony of L. Bradlee Sheafe, 1999: 69,

163). In another case, the interrogator declared that the suspect was so relieved when he confessed that it was as if he had gone through an exorcism: "After the statement was completed, the way I would characterize it, it was like almost like he was a different guy. . . . It was almost like to me like he excised a demon or something" (Testimony of Martin Devlin, 1993: 52).

These kinds of representations are often the product of confirmation bias: the confession confirms the interrogators' presumption of guilt, and the interrogators interpret, accurately or not, the suspect's body language and statements about his emotional state as expressions of guilt. These kinds of representations are also intended to make the confession appear corroborated and thus serve the interrogators' larger goal of incriminating the suspect.

VOLUNTARINESS

The process of scripting the interrogation so that the suspect's confession appears voluntary begins in the preadmission portion of the interrogation. Investigators will report, for example, that they told the suspect that the door was open, that he was able to leave at any time, and that it was his choice whether to cooperate and participate in the interrogation. They will then write this up in their reports and testify to it in court. When the interrogation is unrecorded, there is, of course, no way to objectively prove or disprove the investigators' assertions. They will also relate, for example, that they solicitously read and the suspect freely waived his *Miranda* rights; that they offered the suspect frequent bathroom, cigarette, and food breaks; and that they used no improper interrogation techniques (e.g., no threats or promises) that would have overborne the suspect's will or made him feel compelled to confess. Sometimes investigators will report that the suspect brought up the question of whether he should get an attorney, and that they expressly told him that he was entitled to one and that they would stop all questioning immediately if he exercised this choice, but that he decided against it. The investigators' goal is to portray the suspect as a rational agent who is freely choosing to participate in the interrogation and making statements to police with foreknowledge of his legal rights and options.

Interrogators also try to influence the suspect's postadmission narrative so that it appears voluntary and thus reliable when the suspect and his lawyer challenge it in court. Committed to the goal of conviction, they seek to elicit and construct an account that the prosecutor will readily incorporate into his charging decision and use to maximum advantage in plea negotiations; that will convince the judge to deny any motions brought by defense attorneys to suppress or exclude the confession from evidence; and that the jury will put maximum weight on in their deliberations. Interrogators seek to shape the suspect's postadmission narrative not only so that it is persuasive in the ways described above but also so that it is impregnable against future challenges, thereby increasing the likelihood that the suspect will be convicted.

There are a number of elements that interrogators may try to build into the suspects' postadmission narrative to create the appearance that it is voluntary. For example, they will often direct the suspect to explain why he is confessing. Usually, interrogators suggest or pressure the suspect to agree that he is admitting his culpability to expiate his guilt over the crime and to seek forgiveness from others—even though most American detectives (like prosecutors) are too cynical to believe the truth of such an explanation in most cases (Johnson, 2002). Formatting the suspect's narrative so that he locates the cause of his confession in his individual psyche rather than the structural conditions of interrogation allows detectives to divert attention from other possible causes, such as their interrogation methods and strategies. So long as the suspect's confession appears to emanate from his individual will or conscience rather than from any potential source of physical or psychological coercion, the interrogators can portray it as freely given, and it will almost always be deemed voluntary and thus admissible in an American court of law. For this reason, interrogators will often represent that the suspect provided his confession spontaneously, in response to open-ended questions, and without any pressure or prompting.

Interrogators will often ask the suspect—typically toward the end of the postadmission phase, well after his resistance has been broken down and he has been motivated to believe that he will benefit by incriminating himself—whether they made any threats or promises or in any way coerced him. As all seasoned interrogators know, the suspect will invariably answer "no"—even if he later reports (or the record clearly indicates) that he was threatened or offered promises of leniency in exchange for the confession. Once again, the purpose of this postadmission influence technique is to create the appearance of a legally voluntary and factually reliable confession and thereby divert attention from the manipulative and potentially coercive interrogation methods that may have been used to elicit it.

Another postadmission influence technique that interrogators use to create the appearance of a voluntary confession is known as the "Error Insertion

Trick" (Maple, 1999; Kassin, 2006). In this ploy, interrogators will write out the suspect's confession (rather than letting the suspect compose it himself), intentionally inserting spelling and other trivial errors into the statement. The interrogator will then ask the suspect to correct and initial the errors so that the written confession appears not only to be the product of the suspect's free will but also reliable and correct (or at least corrected). One suspect described how police used the Error Insertion Trick in shaping his statement: "He goes 'I screwed up some dates on here,' and he says, 'so just change, whatever you need to change, just make sure you initial it,' and he says 'your birthday is wrong, so fix your birthday,' and he goes 'Frank's already gone over your rights so just initial those and don't worry about those'" (Interview of Walter Casper, 2000: 53–54). Interrogators also use the Error Insertion Trick in their courtroom testimony to represent that the suspect confessed voluntarily, as occurred in the following testimony: "He made some corrections as to names like where Sergeant Neighbours' name was placed in error and he put in Baldwin's and initialed it" (Testimony of Anthony Belovich, 1987: 146).

The Error Insertion Trick, as Kassin (2006) has pointed out, creates the appearance of voluntariness by suggesting that the suspect read, understood, and verified the contents of his statement. It also increases the perceived reliability of the statement by falsely creating the impression that only the true perpetrator would know of or be able to spot these errors.

Even the act of directing the suspect to sign the police-written statement can be used to create the appearance of voluntariness. As police interrogation trainer Albert Joseph (1995: 131) has exhorted:

> *Get the confession signed.* Don't *ask* the suspect to sign the confession. You have just honored his request for additions and/or changes and he has told you that it is true. Say, "Good, I just need your signature." Put it in front of him and hand him the pen and point to where you want him to sign. The majority of the time the suspect will sign the confession. Then you and the other Officer witness the changes and the suspect's signature. You are now done. What could the defense attorney say about this confession? We can show that the suspect knowingly, voluntarily, and intelligently gave the confession. We can show that we went over the confession with the suspect. We can show that the suspect actually participated in the confession.

Related to the Error Insertion Trick, the Inbau, Reid, Buckley, and Jayne (2001) police interrogation training manual also advises interrogators to incorporate into the suspect's written confession "a number of more or less irrelevant questions calling for answers known only to the offender. For instance, the suspect may be asked to give the name of the grade school he attended, the place or hospital in which he was born, or other similar information" (Inbau et al., 2001: 383). The purpose of this postadmission technique is to create a false illusion of credibility (Kassin, 2006). The same is true of soliciting an apology note, which appears to further corroborate the suspect's admission, though in reality it only repeats it.

Case Studies

If the primary goal of preadmission interrogation is to incriminate the suspect, the primary goal of postadmission interrogation is to build a persuasive case against him. Both goals converge into the larger prosecutorial objective of securing his conviction. The cases of Eddie Lowery and Bruce Godschalk illustrate how American police interrogators use preadmission and postadmission influence techniques to first elicit and then subtly but effectively shape the suspect's narrative in order to establish a seemingly irrefutable account of his guilt. Both Lowery and Godschalk falsely confessed and were exonerated many years later by DNA testing. The process of postadmission influence is most evident in false confession cases because the suspect did not commit the crime and thus typically does not know most or all of the crime facts, had no motive, feels no remorse or regret, and most likely did not confess voluntarily.

Eddie Lowery

On July 27, 1981, Arta Wright Kroeplin, a seventy-four-year-old woman who lived in Ogden, Kansas, was raped and assaulted by a man who broke into her house in the early morning hours. The assailant had cut the screen on her back door before entering her bedroom, then held a knife to her head, covered her face, and struck and raped her. Following the sexual assault, Ms. Kroeplin was unable to describe the rapist; she could not identify his height, weight, or race, and did not hear what he said to her. Police did not have any evidence linking anyone to the crime. Nevertheless, Riley County Police officers Harry Malugani and Douglas Johnson assumed that Eddie Lowery, a twenty-one-year-old member of the U.S. Army, had committed it because he had been involved in a minor automobile accident near Ms. Kroeplin's home that night.

Malugani and Johnson interrogated Lowery over the course of two days. They did not record the interrogation. Malugani and Johnson repeatedly accused Lowery of committing the crime and told him that they had the evidence to prove it. Lowery continually denied any involvement. When Lowery asked to see a lawyer, Malugani denied his request, telling Lowery that he did not need one because he was not under arrest—despite the fact that Malugani and Johnson had previously read Lowery his *Miranda* rights. Malugani and Johnson asked Lowery to submit to a polygraph, telling him that it could prove his innocence.

Riley County Sergeant Allen Raynor administered the polygraph and interrogated Lowery afterward. Raynor and then Malugani and Johnson told Lowery that he had failed the examination and that it provided conclusive evidence of his guilt. Raynor, Malugani, and Johnson again repeatedly accused Lowery of committing the burglary and rape and accused him of lying whenever he denied their allegations. Malugani and Johnson continued to attack his assertions of innocence, repeated that the polygraph results established his guilt, and pressured him to confess. In the same loud voice he had used throughout much of the interrogation, Malugani threatened that he was going to prove Lowery's guilt even if it took him ten years to do so. Malugani told him: "We're going to lay the hardest conviction at you that we can, send you to prison as long as we can" (Testimony of Eddie Lowery, 1981b: 12). Malugani's threat was coupled with an explicit promise of leniency: if Lowery admitted to the crimes, they would get him the psychological help that they said he needed. As Mr. Lowery described it: "They asked me to cooperate with them and everything would go a lot easier, and I said okay" (Testimony of Eddie Lowery, 1981a: 97).

Eventually Lowery broke down, cried, and began to agree with the officers' accusations. He believed that they would not let him leave the interrogation room unless he told them what they demanded to hear. Lowery, who had been provided nothing to eat all day and who thought that if he got up and tried to leave the officers would throw him in jail, was upset and confused: "I didn't know what to do and I just wanted to get away from it all" (Testimony of Eddie Lowery, 1981a: 87). He sought to escape the pressure and stress of the intense, hourslong polygraph and postpolygraph interrogation; he started to comply with the officers' demands in order to put an end to what had now become an explicitly coercive interrogation. Malugani "kept saying, 'Well, we know you did this, Lowery. All you got to do is admit that you did this and the whole thing will be over with' " (Testimony of Eddie Lowery, 1982: 535–536).

Once Lowery started agreeing with their accusations, Malugani and Johnson supplied him with the facts of the crime. Prior to the interrogation, he did not know anything about Ms. Kroeplin's assault or rape. He had never met her, been to her house, or even heard of the crime. In their preadmission and postadmission interrogation, Malugani and Johnson, in effect, told Lowery what to say, feeding him the details of the burglary, assault, and rape through leading questions, cuing, explicit suggestions, and forced-choice questions (e.g., "Did you hit her with the vase or did you hit her with the butt of a knife?" [Testimony of Eddie Lowery, 1981b: 12]). Lowery repeated back and incorporated into his confession numerous nonpublic details of the crime that he had learned—and could only have learned—from Officers Malugani, Johnson, and Raynor. They included

That the true perpetrator stopped in front of a house that is white;
That the true perpetrator knew the house was on a corner;
That the true perpetrator entered the house through the back door;
That the true perpetrator busted open a screen door with his hands and went inside;
That the true perpetrator picked up a knife in the kitchen;
That the true perpetrator heard a noise and so walked down a hallway;
That the true perpetrator stopped at a bedroom door;
That the true perpetrator entered a room where he saw a person lying in a bed;
That the true perpetrator startled that person;
That the true perpetrator noticed that the victim was wearing a nightgown;
That the true perpetrator jumped on the bed;
That the true perpetrator placed a pillow over the victim's head when she began to sit upright;
That the true perpetrator struck the victim with the butt of a knife;
That the true perpetrator noticed that the victim was wearing underwear; and
That the true perpetrator committed a rape.

Many of these facts Lowery simply nodded in agreement with or verbally assented to. Nevertheless, Malugani and Johnson denied in their pretrial and trial testimony in 1981 and 1982 (as well as in their civil depositions in 2005) that they ever suggested or supplied any details to Lowery. Contrary to Lowery's testimony, Malugani and Johnson have claimed numerous times that they merely asked open-ended questions of Lowery, and that he freely volunteered a narrative of the crime without any prompting or pressure. For example (Testimony of Harry Malugani, 1981: 8):

Malugani: Again he would stop. Again, we would ask Mr. Lowery, "And then what did you do?"
Prosecutor: Is this roughly the way that you were doing this?
Malugani: This was exactly the way we was doing it.
Prosecutor: In other words, the conversation was, "what did you do next?" or then, "what did you do?" and then he would respond?
Malugani: Yes.
Prosecutor: Did you at any time suggest to him what the appropriate answer to the question should be?
Malugani: No, sir, not at any time.

In addition to providing Lowery numerous facts of the crime, pressuring him to incorporate these facts into his confession, and then testifying that he volunteered a detailed postadmission narrative without any pressure or prompting from them, Malugani and Johnson used multiple strategies to construct Lowery's culpability in their pretrial and trial testimony. First, they attributed to Lowery a seemingly plausible motive for why he committed the crime: "He said that he had just recently discovered that his wife had had an affair with another man and that she had left him because of that, and that he was having some emotional problems to deal with" (Testimony of Douglas Johnson, 1981: 7). Officers Malugani and Johnson added that Lowery had not planned to rape Ms. Kroeplin, but once he entered the residence and saw her sitting up he got scared and decided to rape her.

Second, they represented Lowery's emotional state in a way that created the impression of corroborating his guilt (Testimony of Douglas Johnson, 1981: 5): "He was somewhat upset. I would say that he was feeling or acting guilty and ashamed . . . Appeared to be the outward sign. He hung his head and refused to look at either myself or Investigator Malugani."

Third, they claimed that they did not employ any promises, threats, or other coercive interrogation techniques. They did not even subject Lowery to any accusatorial interrogation at all, they testified, but merely pointed out inconsistencies in his account and asked him to tell the truth—thus creating the appearance that his confession was thus voluntary (Testimony of Douglas Johnson, 1981).

Fourth, they testified that Lowery restated his confession narrative a second time (Testimony of Douglas Johnson, 1981), again creating the misleading appearance of corroboration, though Lowery emphatically insisted that this never occurred.

Fifth, they asserted that Lowery invoked his *Miranda* rights and asked for an attorney only *after* he made his alleged second confession, and that Lowery only cried shortly before he confessed. But Lowery insists that he repeatedly requested an attorney and was crying throughout the preadmission portion of the interrogation. He refused to sign a written statement.

Although the jury hung at Lowery's first trial, he was convicted of rape, aggravated battery, and aggravated burglary at his second trial in January 1982 and sentenced to eleven years to life in prison. He served out a ten-year sentence and was released on parole after agreeing to participate in sex-offender treatment and register as a sex offender. In 2002 DNA testing excluded him as the rapist, and based on that the District Court of Riley County vacated his conviction in 2003 (Garrett, 2005).

Bruce Godschalk

On July 13, 1986, Elizabeth Bednar, a white, middle-aged widow, was attacked and raped in her bedroom by a stranger who entered her home through an open window at the Kingswood apartment complex in King of Prussia, Pennsylvania. On September 7, Patricia Morrissey, a young single woman who lived in the same apartment complex, was also assaulted and raped in her bedroom. Based on the similarity of the descriptions provided by the victims, the police concluded that the same person—whom newspapers dubbed "the mainline rapist"—had perpetrated both attacks. After a composite sketch was prepared and published in the newspapers and on television, the adopted sister of Bruce Godschalk, a twenty-three-year-old landscaper, called the police suggesting that the sketch resembled him.

On January 5, 1987, Morrissey positively identified Godschalk in a photo array. Bednar told police she did not get a good enough view of the rapist to make an identification. On January 13, Upper Merion Township Detectives Bruce Saville and Michael Karcewski interrogated Godschalk for three hours. Again the interrogation was not recorded. Detectives Saville and Karcewski repeatedly accused Godschalk of assaulting and raping Bednar and Morrissey. Although Godschalk pleaded that he had not raped anyone, the detectives refused to credit his emphatic denials; instead, they told him that they had witnesses and fingerprint evidence that proved his guilt. The detectives also yelled at and threatened Godschalk; blocked the interrogation room door and refused his requests to leave; and promised to release him if he admitted his guilt, telling him that "the sooner you tell us what happened, the sooner we will take you home" (Statement of Bruce Godschalk, 1999: 2). Frightened, upset, crying, and believing that he was not free to leave, Godschalk eventually succumbed to the detectives' pressure and admitted to the rapes.

In the postadmission portion of the interrogation, the detectives asked Godschalk numerous leading and forced-choice questions from which he guessed and inferred the correct details of the two crimes. Believing that he would be released if he cooperated and told the detectives what they wanted to hear, Godschalk incorporated those details into his confession. He did not want the confession taped, but the detectives prevailed, telling him that it would make him feel better if he got it off his chest. The detectives and Godschalk rehearsed the answers to their questions before making the tape. After the detectives turned on the tape recorder, they read to Godschalk the *Miranda* warnings for the first time.

The Godschalk case is a dramatic illustration of the process through which interrogators can construct a suspect's culpability in the postadmission phase to build a case against him that will be persuasive to prosecutors, judges, and juries. Godschalk did not know or have any interaction with either Ms. Morrissey or Ms. Bednar; he had never been to either crime scene; and he had no preexisting knowledge of the crime facts. As a result, his confession narrative came wholly from the interrogation and postadmission influence techniques of Detectives Saville and Karcewski. They suggested when, where, how, and why he committed both crimes; had him rehearse their account before turning on the tape recorder; invented a supposed motive ("that he had a very bad drinking problem"); and then pressured him to accept and repeat it back to them.

Saville and Karcewski also fed numerous crime details to Mr. Godschalk, including nonpublic ones, which he incorporated into his confession. For the sexual assault of Patricia Morrissey, Godschalk's confession included the following nonpublic crime facts (Memorandum from Bruce Saville to Bruce Castor, 2001):

That the assailant had been outside the bedroom window watching her;

That Ms. Morrissey had been reading a magazine while she was lying
in bed;

That there was a light next to her bed, which was on, allowing the
assailant to see in;

That the assailant had sex with her on the bed;

That she had been wearing underpants;

That she was on her stomach during intercourse;

That prior to having sex the assailant removed her tampon and tossed it
to the side;

That she was a brunette with a medium build;

That the assailant had been very gentle with her;

That the assailant left the apartment by going out the door;

That the assailant was chased off a patio by a man prior to the assault.

For the sexual assault of Elizabeth Bednar, Godschalk's confession included
the following nonpublic crime facts (Memorandum from Bruce Saville to
Bruce Castor, 2001):

That the assailant watched Ms. Bednar while she was in the rec room
reading a book;

That she was wearing a robe;

That the assailant entered through a rec-room window;

That the assailant waited until she went upstairs before entering the
townhouse;

That the assailant went up two sets of stairs before finding her bedroom;

That the assailant took a pillow from another room before entering her
room;

That she told him others lived in the home and that someone could
come home;

That she was nude;

That the assailant told her he had been drinking prior to the incident
and that his beverage of choice was beer; and

That the assailant had sex with her on the floor.

Saville and Karcewski had suggested all of these nonpublic crime facts to
Godschalk, yet the detectives repeatedly claimed—in their police reports,
pretrial and trial testimony, memos and public statements—that these facts
had originated with Godschalk. At the suppression hearing, for example,

the following exchange occurred (Testimony of Detective Bruce Saville, 1987: 95–96):

Prosecutor: Did you suggest in the course of taking these statements any information to him that would have only been known to the victim, the police, and perpetrator?

Det. Saville: No, sir. As I stated before, when he would ask a question of us, I would then ask the question directly back to him. If he would say, "Was she blond?" I would look at him and say, "You tell us, was she blond or not?" And he would say, "Yes, she was blond." And I would say, "Okay, then tell us what else happened." So never did I offer anything to him.

Prosecutor: Did he in fact make some admissions regarding information that would have only been known to the police, the victim, and the perpetrator?

Det. Saville: Yes, sir, numerous.

The detectives also claimed—as did the prosecutor who charged Godschalk, the jury that convicted him, and an appellate court that denied his claim for postconviction relief[1]—that the presence of these nonpublic crime facts in Godschalk's confession proved that he committed both sexual assaults. As Detective Saville succinctly stated in a memo, "The facts mentioned in the Bednar and Morrissey cases were never released to the press, prior to arrest, and therefore could not have been known by Godschalk without his participation in the crimes" (Memorandum from Bruce Saville to Bruce Castor, 2001).

Detective Saville's and Karcewski's construction of Godschalk's culpability did not end there, however. They also elicited from Godschalk the oral equivalent of an apology note in his rehearsed audio-taped confession (Confession of Bruce Godschalk, 1987: 35):

Det. Saville: Okay. Is there anything that you would like to add to this tape at all?

Godschalk: Yes.

Det. Saville: What would you like to add?

Godschalk: Truly sorry for what happened, and it's all caused from my drinking problem. That's gotten out of hand. And I wish to, I'm seeking help desperately, and I'm very sorry for what I've done to these two nice women.

Saville and Karcewski publicly claimed that the emotions Godschalk showed during the interrogation were an expression of his remorse and guilt. Saville testified (Testimony of Detective Bruce Saville, 1987: 103):

> When his eyes welled up, it wasn't because of any kind of attack by us or anything even verbal or anything. He had come to the realization, in my opinion, knowing what the conversation was at the time and reading his actions, that he was now facing the truth that he did it and he was finally getting it off his chest and it was like, "I'm letting everything go here," and it was like, "I've done it," you know, "I'm glad I've got it over with," and he was emotional about it. There's no question about that.

The case that Detectives Saville and Karcewski were building against Godschalk was not complete until they established—in their police reports, memos, and pretrial and trial testimony—that he had confessed voluntarily. Saville repeatedly stated in his police report and testimony that Godschalk had come to and remained at the police station on his own free will; that the detectives had not detained him but had left the door open; and that they had told him that he was free to leave. Moreover, Saville testified multiple times that Godschalk had stated that he wanted to stay at the station and answer the detectives' questions. Detective Saville even wrote in his report, and testified under oath, that when Godschalk brought up the subject of an attorney prior to his admissions, he asked Godschalk whether he wanted an attorney and Godschalk said no, but that he wanted to cooperate with the police. After Godschalk made his admissions but before the detectives turned the tape recorder on, according to Saville, they solicitously read Godschalk his constitutional rights and he freely waived them. The following entry, from Detective Saville's Police Report, describes how he represented what occurred during the interrogation (Police Report of Bruce Saville, 1987: 7):

> At this time this reporter began taping the interview. This reporter at the beginning of the interview again gave Godschalk his constitutional rights and asked him if he was willing to give me a statement, whether he was giving it of his own free will, whether he had come to Upper Merion Police upon his own free will, whether he had felt that the Upper Merion Police had treated him fairly, whether we had cohoarsed (sic) him into saying anything, all of which were negative answers, except for the fact that Godschalk stated that he was there on his own free will and that he wanted to cooperate with police and was willing to give me a statement on his own free will.

Detective Saville also asked Godschalk on tape whether he was coerced into incriminating himself, and he received the rehearsed answer he sought (Confession of Bruce Godschalk, 1987: 24):

Saville: Am I putting words in your mouth?
Godschalk: No.
Saville: Am I enticing you to say any of this?
Godschalk: No.
Saville: Am I forcing you to say any of this?
Godschalk: No.
Saville: Are you saying this on your own free will?
Godschalk: On my own free will.

Saville and Karcewski's claims about Godschalk's motive, extensive knowledge of nonpublic crime facts, emotional expressions during the interrogation, and reason for incriminating himself were all effective at constructing Godschalk's culpability, building a persuasive case against him, and securing his conviction. In May 1987, a Montgomery County jury convicted Godschalk of two counts of forcible rape and two counts of burglary, sentencing him to twenty years in prison. In January 2002, however, DNA testing conclusively determined that the semen from each of the two rapes had come from the same individual, but that person was not Bruce Godschalk. In February 2002, his conviction was vacated and he was released from prison after serving fifteen years.

The Audiences of Interrogation

If interrogations and confessions are social productions, then for whose benefit are they intended? The primary audience of interrogations is, of course, custodial suspects. But there are other audiences as well: police managers (who review the detectives' performance), prosecutors (who decide whether to file charges and, in most cases, the terms of a plea bargain), magistrates (who decide whether the evidence is sufficient to hold suspects), judges (who decide whether to admit or exclude confession evidence), juries (who decide whether to convict or acquit), and in some cases the media (who write about high-profile cases) and the general public. Detectives know that how the narrative of the interrogation is represented and how the suspect's words are interpreted will largely determine whether the confession leads to a conviction.

Historically, American detectives have managed this narrative by controlling the production of information about their interrogations and confessions. One strategy for controlling information is to keep secret their practices. Police interrogation in America for the most part remains a hidden, low-visibility practice. Detectives keep their methods and strategies hidden by questioning suspects inside closed interrogation rooms that are secluded from the potential view or intrusion of nonparticipants. They also keep their practices hidden when they fail to create an objective or reviewable record of the interrogation. Despite the ease and widespread use of video technology in American society (and in many areas ·of police work), most detectives in America still do not electronically record their interrogations. Those who do are often required to by state law, and many only selectively record the suspect's brief confession statement, not the interrogation that produced it, as we saw in Bruce Godschalk's case.

American detectives keep their practices hidden to avoid exposure or criticism, particularly in high-profile or morally charged cases. They worry that opening up the interrogation process to outside scrutiny could lead reporters to write articles criticizing the fairness of their techniques, prosecutors to report criticism to their superiors or to decline to file charges, judges to suppress confession evidence, or juries to fail to convict. Detectives understand that police interrogation in the American adversary system is inherently morally problematic (and therefore always potentially controversial), because it often involves behavior—psychological manipulation, trickery, and deceit—that is regarded as unethical in virtually all other social contexts. Perhaps it should not be surprising, then, that interrogation remains one of the most secretive of all police activities, despite the fact that police solve more crimes with interrogation-induced confessions than they do with virtually any other type of evidence.

But there is a second, related reason why detectives seek to keep their interrogation practices hidden: to engage *without contradiction* in impression management about what occurred during interrogation or about their motives and methods. Like the salesmen to whom they are often compared, American interrogators are manipulators par excellence. They work in an adversary system that rewards strategic behavior and the successful manipulation of appearances, and they understand that to obtain favorable case outcomes they must often persuade others of the legitimacy of the interrogations they conduct and the confessions they obtain. Detectives thus seek to control the public narrative about what occurred in the interrogation room and why the suspect confessed. They attempt to portray their behavior in its most favorable light—deemphasizing their presumptive and partisan bias, preadmission incentives, and postadmission suggestions, for example—while portraying the suspect's behavior and statements in their least favorable light.

Police interrogators' impression management strategies can be divided into two parts: how they represent themselves to suspects *during* interrogation and how they represent themselves to everyone else *afterward*. During interrogation, as we have seen, detectives engage in impression management through the use of manipulative and deceptive techniques that seek to persuade the suspect of a reality that does not exist. For example, detectives work to manage the suspect's impressions of their relationship through a number of guises. They build rapport and may act sympathetic with the suspect's situation. They strive to create the illusion that they are the suspect's ally and supporter in the criminal justice process, and that they have a cooperative and mutually beneficial, rather than adversarial, relationship that will advance the suspect's self-interest. Detectives also try to persuade the suspect that he will obtain moral redemption, social approval, systemic benefits, or more lenient treatment by cooperating and agreeing to an inculpating scenario of the crime, if not by providing a full confession. In the end, it is the interrogators' impression management strategies and skills that lie behind their ability to persuade the suspect to believe that the act of confessing is in his rational self-interest.

But the impression management practices of American interrogators are also directed to external audiences. Detectives engage in scripting and persuasion to create the appearance that the interrogation process is completely legitimate and that a confession is both voluntary and reliable. Their goal is to maintain the appearance that the interrogation was conducted with the utmost professionalism so that any future inquiry about it will focus on the suspect's state of mind, his culpability, and the fact of his confession, rather than on the interrogation process or the police methods. Detectives may have to answer critical questions about their interrogation practices and the suspect's statement at various pretrial hearings or later at trial. In some states, they can also be formally deposed or interviewed by criminal defense attorneys prior to any court hearings. And, particularly in high-profile cases, the media may seek to question them and attend the court hearings.

Detectives' public narratives about what occurred during their interrogations usually follow a familiar pattern. On the prosecutor's direct examination at hearings or trial, detectives will usually state that they "interviewed" the suspect. They will neither use the word "interrogation" nor mention the use of any interrogation techniques or strategies. They will state that their goal was merely to get the truth, sometimes adding that they made no assumptions about the suspect's guilt or innocence prior to questioning. The admonition by the police trainers Inbau, Reid, and Buckley (1986: 36) to "avoid creating the impression of an investigator seeking a confession or a conviction" applies not only in the interrogation room but also on the witness stand. If asked, detectives will insistently deny that they used any psychologically coercive interrogation methods. If possible, they will assert their belief in the suspect's guilt and the voluntariness of his incriminating statements. On cross-examination by defense attorneys, they may acknowledge that they used some interrogation techniques, but will deny any impropriety. They will attribute the suspect's incriminating statements not to their persuasive or deceptive methods, but to the suspect's desire to stop lying, tell the truth, or relieve a guilty conscience, or to some other psychological reason that emanates from the suspect's will. If asked why they failed to audiotape or videotape the interrogation, detectives will respond that it is not their department's policy to record, or they will declare that it was not necessary: after all, the suspect confessed and signed a written statement. The more successfully that detectives shift the focus of the public narrative about interrogation away from their use of psychologically manipulative or coercive methods, the less likely the confession's admissibility or credibility will be effectively challenged, either inside or outside the courtroom, and the more likely the defendant will be convicted.

Investigators' attempts to construct and control the public narrative that emerges from the interrogation process illuminate the workings of the American adversary system. Psychologists, criminologists, and legal scholars have focused almost entirely on the drama that occurs inside the interrogation room. While it is widely recognized that detectives use manipulative methods inside the interrogation room, no one has looked at their manipulative practices outside the interrogation room and its effect on pretrial processes—most significantly, plea bargaining—or the trial itself. Detectives' attempts to shape the public narrative of interrogation is, of course, consistent with their role as partisan adversaries who seek to incriminate the suspect and help the state build the strongest possible case against him. These attempts reveal, once again, the blurred line between the investigative and prosecutorial functions in the adversary system.

Conclusion: Deception in the Interrogation Room

Police use of deception during interrogation has long been a source of controversy and debate (White, 1979; Skolnick and Leo, 1992; Magid, 2001). For the most part, appellate courts have permitted interrogators to use deception so long as their misrepresentations have not deceived suspects about their *Miranda* rights or constituted threats or promises (see *Frazier v. Cupp*, 1969). Following the unproven assertions of Fred Inbau and John Reid (1962), many American courts have for years simply reasoned that police deception during interrogation is legally permissible because it is not "apt to lead an innocent suspect to confess" (Young, 1996). Courts currently assess the permissibility of deceptive interrogation techniques by evaluating the totality of the circumstances on a case-by-case basis to determine whether they overbore the suspect's will, and American courts almost always find that police lying during interrogation does not render a confession involuntary. There have been a few exceptions, though. One court, for example, held that false verbal assertions of evidence were permissible, but that confronting a suspect with fabricated written documentation (false scientific reports prepared on the stationery of the state department of criminal law enforcement and that of a private testing organization) was unacceptable (*Florida v. Cayward*, 1989). Another court distinguished between deception intrinsic to the facts of the charged offense (e.g., misrepresenting the existence of incriminating evidence) and deception extrinsic to those facts (e.g., promises of mental health treatment in exchange for a confession), finding that the former was a fact to be considered in the totality of circumstances analysis but that the latter was impermissible (*State v. Kelekolio*, 1993). As Young (1996: 455) has noted, however: "Courts, with rare exception, have declined to prohibit confessions obtained with police lying. Rather, courts have displayed deep ambivalence toward police lying. They repeatedly have affirmed convictions based, at least in part, on confessions obtained with police lying, while simultaneously criticizing that lying."

Legal scholars have been divided about the permissibility of police deception during interrogation. Some have argued that police lying should be permitted because it is necessary to elicit confessions that are essential to solving many cases; without it, there would be a significant number of lost convictions, and thus many guilty criminals would remain free to perpetrate additional crimes (Inbau, 1961; Grano, 1993; Magid, 2001). Like the appellate courts, these legal scholars simply declare, without any supporting empirical evidence, that police lying during interrogation is not likely to lead to false confessions. In their view, the benefits of police lying clearly outweigh the costs. But other legal scholars have opposed police lying during interrogation on multiple grounds: that it is not necessary to solve most crimes; that it infringes on the suspect's dignity and autonomy while breaching social trust; that it corrupts the integrity of the fact-finding process and thus may diminish public confidence in the criminal justice system; that it has a tendency to expand into other areas of police work (i.e., it inevitably leads to police lying in other contexts, such as at trial); and that it does produce false and unreliable confessions (Paris, 1995; Young, 1996; McMullen, 2005; Gohara, 2006). Other legal scholars and social scientists have taken a more nuanced view of the empirical and moral complexity of lying during police interrogation (Skolnick and Leo, 1992). Welsh White, in particular, has suggested that some types of interrogatory deception by police should be permissible (e.g., telling a suspect that they are confident the evidence will establish his guilt or that eyewitnesses will testify against him) while others should not be (e.g., misrepresenting forensic or scientific evidence, or fabricating false polygraph results) because the latter, unlike the former, are "substantially likely to produce untrustworthy statements" (White, 2001b: 1243).

Many psychologists of law tend to take an even stronger stand against police lying during interrogation. Based on experimental studies that involve falsely accusing subjects of noncriminal acts such as accidentally hitting a specifically prohibited computer key while typewriting, some psychologists have argued that lying about evidence increases the risk that innocent subjects will confess falsely (Kassin and Keichel, 1996; Forest, Wadkins, and Miller, 2002; Horselenberg, Merckelbach, and Josephs, 2003; Redlich and Goodman, 2003). Other psychologists, however, have questioned the real-world validity and generalizability of these experiments. Loftus (2004: xi) has pointed out, for example, that "the 'destroyed computer' studies are steps removed from the kinds of crimes to which some actual suspects have falsely confessed." Social psychologists whose research is based on case materials and other documents tend to be less opposed to police lying during interrogation, if at all, because of its value in eliciting true confessions (Ofshe and Leo, 1997b; Davis and Leo, 2006; Costanzo and Leo, 2007). Ofshe and Leo (1997b) have argued that false-evidence ploys are one of the primary interrogation techniques that lead innocent suspects to perceive their situation as hopeless, a necessary, but not sufficient, condition for eliciting false confessions. Kassin and Gudjonsson (2004), in effect, have argued the opposite: that confronting a suspect with false evidence is a sufficient, but not necessary, condition for eliciting a false confession. All psychologists of law agree, however, that police deception during interrogation increases the likelihood of eliciting false confessions.

The debate about the propriety and effects of police lying during interrogation has focused almost exclusively on preadmission deception and in particular on how investigators use false-evidence ploys to elicit admissions. Scholars and courts have debated whether it is appropriate, for example, for interrogators to confront suspects with nonexistent evidence (e.g., false eyewitness identifications of them, nonexistent fingerprints, or bogus confessions by alleged co-conspirators or accomplices); to confront suspects with real evidence that is false (e.g., a composite sketch intentionally drawn to match the suspect, a fictitious eyewitness's identification of the suspect in a staged line-up, or false failed polygraph results); or to exaggerate the strength of the existing evidence (e.g., telling a suspect that the assault victim is dead). To my knowledge, however, no scholar or appellate court has analyzed the propriety and effects of police deception during the *postadmission* phase of interrogation and how investigators use it to construct a compelling narrative of the suspect's guilt. This is a remarkable omission, which may be related to the fact that only recently have scholars and courts begun to gain access to interrogation tapes and transcripts.

Yet the use of deception during the postadmission phase may be more pernicious than during the preadmission phase, because it is less transparent. When interrogators deceive in the preadmission phase, they usually lie to the suspect about evidence they possess and the benefits of confessing; when they deceive in the postadmission phase, they usually suggest, script, and construct a compelling narrative of the suspect's guilt. That is a far more subtle type of deception. Moreover, when interrogators lie in the preadmission phase, they usually describe their deception (and euphemistically refer to it as a "ruse") in their police reports and pretrial and trial testimony. This is because false-evidence ploys are legal and because detectives believe they are necessary to elicit true admissions and thus justifiable. When interrogators deceive in the postadmission phase, however, they rarely describe it in their police reports or testimony. This is because it may be viewed as illegitimate, especially if it involves suggesting the details of a suspect's confession.

Postadmission deception is therefore far more difficult to detect than its preadmission counterpart. Unlike the goal of preadmission deception, which is to create the perception that the suspect is caught and therefore should confess, the goal of postadmission deception is to shape the suspect's confession so that a judge and jury will perceive it to be voluntary and reliable. The investigators' postadmission techniques may make the narrative seem so authentic that virtually no one will question its validity. While it may not be easy to disprove an individual false fact, it is far more difficult to disprove a false but compelling story. As Donald Spence (1982: 182) has pointed out in another context, a narrative "is almost infinitely elastic, accommodating almost any new evidence that happens to come along." Absent the extraordinary advent of DNA testing, for example, almost no one would have believed that either Eddie Lowery or Bruce Godschalk could conceivably be innocent; their confession narratives simply appeared too persuasive and too damning to be false.

Postadmission influence and deception thus threaten to corrupt the integrity of the fact-finding process because they may lead to the creation— some would say fabrication—of false evidence that is not easily detected (Garrett, 2005; Gohara, 2006). Without a record of the interrogation, the detectives' postadmission influence may be so subtly woven into the suspect's narrative that it appears invisible to third parties. Indeed, as both the Lowery and Godschalk cases illustrate, a fictitious but scripted postadmission narrative may sometimes seem more real than a truthful but unscripted one. This should especially concern us in high-profile prosecutions that rely primarily or exclusively on confession evidence that is the product of unrecorded interrogations.

For these reasons, the postadmission interrogation process deserves more scrutiny by scholars, courts, and policymakers. The exclusive focus on preadmission deception has caused us to pose incomplete questions. In addition to asking whether preadmission police deception is "apt to make an innocent person confess," appellate courts should also ask whether postadmission police deception is "apt to make an innocent person's confession appear true." These questions must be answered empirically, not rhetorically. While in many cases there may be a legitimate purpose for preadmission lying (i.e., moving a suspect to admit to his crime), there is usually no legitimate purpose for postadmission lying or suggestion (i.e., narrating how and why he committed the crime).

There is no worse error in the American adversary system of criminal justice than the wrongful conviction of an innocent person, and thus no outcome that the system is, in theory, more engineered to prevent. DNA testing has shown us, however, that many people convicted of crimes are, in fact, innocent. The Lowery and Godschalk cases were not anomalies: we now know that the problem of police-induced false confession is more prevalent than almost anyone previously imagined. And when the wrong person is convicted, the true perpetrator usually remains free to commit additional crimes. This should be of heightened concern when police interrogation causes the error, because most documented false confessions are to the most serious crimes—murder and rape (Drizin and Leo, 2004).

CHAPTER 6

False Confessions

It is . . . the common-sense view that physically uncoerced false confessions are made by freaks and occur freakishly.

—Corey Ayling (1984)

I would have said anything to get out of that room.

—Corey Beale (2001)

A confession without corroborating evidence is worthless.

—Mark Frank, John Yarbrough, and Paul Ekman (2006)

In 1998 two young boys—ages seven and eight—in Chicago were charged with murdering an eleven-year-old girl named Ryan Harris who had been badly beaten around the head. Her underpants had been stuffed into her mouth and she appeared to have been sexually assaulted. After an unrecorded interrogation, the two boys had "confessed" to hitting Harris in the head with a brick (and then stuffing leaves and grass in her nose) in order to steal her bicycle. Largely because of the boys' ages, the case attracted national media attention: the country was horrified that two prepubescent boys were capable of committing so savage a crime. Although the evidence pointed to an adult sex crime, the police insisted that the two boys were not too young to have done it and that they knew details that could be known only to the detectives or the perpetrators.

Months later, however, the Illinois State Crime laboratory discovered semen on Ryan Harris's underpants—evidence that the crime could not have been committed by suspects that young—and prosecutors dismissed the charges. The collected DNA was later shown to match the DNA of Floyd Durr, an adult already charged with sexually assaulting three other young girls in the same neighborhood. Durr subsequently admitted being present and committing a sex act over Harris's body (Drizin and Leo, 2004).

The Ryan Harris case is not an isolated one. Nor are false confessions limited to children or teenagers. In recent years, police have elicited a substantial number of demonstrably false confessions from adults (Gudjonsson, 2003). Many of these false confessions have led to erroneous prosecutions, and some have led to wrongful convictions and incarceration (Leo and Ofshe, 1998a; Drizin and Leo, 2004). Some of the wrongfully convicted false confessors have spent many years unjustly incarcerated before being exonerated and released; others remain behind bars (Leo and Ofshe, 1998a, 2001; Drizin and Leo, 2004). A number of exonerated false confessors were convicted of capital crimes and sentenced to death (see Cohen, 2003). One false confessor, Earl Washington, spent almost ten of his more than seventeen years of imprisonment on Virginia's death row and came within nine days of being executed before being exonerated in 2001 (Edds, 2003). Leo and Ofshe (1998a, 2001) have argued that another false confessor, Barry Lee Fairchild, was executed in 1995 (Leo and Ofshe, 1998a, 2001). Lofquist and Harmon (2005) argue that two other false confessors (Edward Earl Johnson and Leo Jones) have also been wrongfully executed, and Sister Helen Prejean (2005) adds a third (Dobie Gillis Williams).

Throughout American history, police-induced false confessions have been among the leading causes of miscarriages of justice (Bedau and Radelet, 1987; Borchard, 1932). It is easy to understand how beatings, torture, sleep deprivation, and threats of violence may lead an innocent suspect to confess falsely. Yet with psychological interrogation methods, the idea that an innocent person would confess to a crime he did not commit—particularly to a felony that carries the possibility of a lengthy prison sentence or even the death penalty—is highly counterintuitive (White, 1997).

Most lay people believe in what I have elsewhere called the *myth of psychological interrogation:* that an innocent person will not falsely confess to police unless he is physically tortured or mentally ill (Leo, 2001b). The logical corollary is that suspects who confess are guilty. This belief has been noted by numerous social scientists and legal scholars (Johnson, 1997; White, 1997; Gudjonsson, 2003). Recently, a survey of one thousand potential jurors in the District of Columbia found that the majority of respondents discounted the possibility that confessions may be false. Sixty-eight percent indicated that they believed a suspect would confess falsely "not very often" (40 percent) or "almost never" (28 percent). This quantifies the perception of trial attorneys who report that the vast majority of potential jurors insist in their questionnaires that it is not possible for someone to confess to a crime he did not commit (Sauer and Wilkens, 1999).

Many criminal justice officials also believe in the myth of psychological interrogation. Police interrogators themselves frequently say that innocent people do not confess—sometimes after the interrogators have elicited false confessions. Maryland Detective Roger Thomson has asserted (Carlson, 1998: 23), "An innocent person never confesses to something he didn't do—unless he's crazy." Indiana prosecutor Michael Cosentino has stated, "If somebody tells you to confess to murdering your daughter, keep you there a week in the jail and you wouldn't confess to it. Keep me there a month and I wouldn't confess to it if I didn't do it" (NBC Dateline, 1997). Another prosecutor, Christie Stanley of Santa Barbara, California, has put it more succinctly: "Reason and common sense dictate that innocent people do not confess to crimes they did not commit" (Stanley, 2005: 19).

The myth of psychological interrogation is even expressed by so-called experts in the criminal justice system. Commenting on Gary Gauger's now proven false murder confession, which I discuss later in this chapter, Debra Glaser, a psychologist with the Los Angeles Police Department, stated that "no amount of badgering [would prompt the average, sober person to] admit to doing something that awful—or to admit to any crime" (Becker and Martin, 1995: 1).

The myth of psychological interrogation persists for several reasons. Most people do not know what occurs during interrogations because they have not experienced it firsthand and do not know anyone who has. They are also not familiar with how police are trained to interrogate suspects or with studies that describe actual interrogation practices. Most people are therefore unaware of the highly manipulative, deceptive, and stress-inducing techniques and strategies that interrogators use to elicit confessions. Nor are they aware that these methods have led to numerous false confessions.

Further, most people assume that individuals do not act against their self-interest or engage in self-destructive behaviors. They therefore assume that an innocent person would not confess to a crime he did not commit. Thus most people cannot imagine that they themselves would falsely confess, especially to a serious crime.

There is no single cause of false confession, and there is no single logic or type of false confession. Police-induced false confessions result from a multistep process and sequence of influence, persuasion, and compliance; they usually involve psychological coercion (Zimbardo, 1971; Ofshe and Leo, 1997b). Police are more likely to elicit false confessions under certain conditions of interrogation, however, and individuals with certain personality traits and dispositions are more easily pressured into giving false confessions. There is also a particular sequence of errors that occurs in the social production of every false confession: investigators first misclassify an innocent person as guilty; they next subject him to a guilt-presumptive, accusatory interrogation; and once they have elicited a false admission, they pressure the suspect to provide a postadmission narrative that they actively shape, often supplying the suspect with the (public and nonpublic) facts of the crime.

Police-induced false confessions occur for well-studied and well-understood reasons. In this chapter, I debunk the myth of psychological interrogation and explain why police sometimes induce innocent suspects to confess falsely.

Varieties of False Confession

The social scientific study of police interrogation and false confession dates back almost a century to Hugo Munsterberg's classic study *On the Witness Stand* (1908). Since then, psychologists, criminologists, sociolegal scholars, and others have researched and written hundreds of articles, books, case studies, treatises, and other publications on police interrogation practices, coercive influence techniques, and false confession (Davis and O'Donahue, 2003; Gudjonsson, 2003;Kassin and Gudjonsson, 2004). Empirical studies on false confession have been primarily conducted through two different methods: experimental manipulations in the laboratory (see, e.g., Russano, Meissner, Narchet, and Kassin, 2005; Redlich and Goodman, 2003; Horse-lenberg, Merckelbach, and Josephs, 2003) and documentary or archival analyses of actual cases (see, e.g., Ofshe and Leo, 1997b; White, 2001a; Drizin and Leo, 2004).

Experimental studies of the causes of false confession have been limited because researchers are ethically and legally prohibited from exposing research subjects to the types of highly stressful and psychologically coercive interrogation techniques that typically lead to false confessions. Researchers also cannot replicate the real-world consequences of making a false confession in a laboratory setting (Loftus, 2004). Thus much of the research on the causes and consequences of police-induced false confession has been based on actual cases. Nevertheless, researchers have used experimental designs in innovative ways to study many other issues related to false confession, such as the extent to which observers (both lay people and trained law enforcement professionals) can distinguish between truthful and false statements made in a criminal interrogation (Kassin and Fong, 1999; Hartwig, Granhag, Stomwall, and Vrig, 2004; Bond and DePaulo, 2006); the cognitive and behavioral response biases that increase the likelihood of eliciting a false confession (Meissner and Kassin, 2002); how common interrogation techniques implicitly communicate promises of leniency and threats of harsher punishment (Kassin and McNall, 1991); and how mock jurors evaluate and weigh confession evidence (Miller and Boster, 1977; Kassin and Neumann, 1997; Kassin and Sukel, 1997). Together, the experimental and documentary studies on police interrogation and false confession have produced a triangulated and consistent set of research findings (Leo, 2001b; Davis and O'Donahue, 2003; Kassin and Gudjonsson, 2004).

Perhaps the most influential publication in the modern study of police interrogation and false confession has been Kassin and Wrightsman's 1985 book chapter "Confession Evidence." Synthesizing the psychological and legal literature on interrogation and confessions, Kassin and Wrightsman's chapter effectively set much of the research agenda in this area for the next two decades (Lassiter and Ratcliff, 2004). Perhaps most importantly, Kassin and Wrightsman were the first to see that false confession is not a unitary phenomenon but caused by a combination of factors (Davis and O'Donahue, 2003). Drawing on case studies and social psychological theories of attitude change, Kassin and Wrightsman suggested three distinct types of false confession: voluntary, coerced-compliant, and coerced-internalized.

Kassin and Wrightsman (1985: 76) defined *voluntary* false confession as occurring "in the absence of elicitation." They defined *coerced-compliant* false confession as occurring when "the suspect publicly professes guilt in response to extreme methods of interrogation, despite knowing privately that he or she is truly innocent" (Kassin and Wrightsman, 1985: 77). And they (1985: 78) defined a *coerced-internalized* false confession as one in which the suspect "actually comes to believe that he or she committed the offense." This threefold typology has provided a useful conceptual framework for studying the antecedents, causes, and consequences of false confession (Ofshe and Leo, 1997a; Gudjonsson, 2003).

In the last two decades, virtually every researcher who has studied false confession has relied on Kassin and Wrightsman's typology (Kassin and Gudjonsson, 2004). Several scholars have critiqued, modified, and extended it. Notably, Davison and Foreshaw (1993) suggested that Kassin and Wrightsman's distinction between voluntary and coerced confessions is simplistic and that coerced-internalized false confessions are not necessarily the product of coercion. Ofshe and Leo (1997a) have argued that the underlying psychological process at work in coerced-internalized false confessions is persuasion, not internalization, and have thus renamed this category *coerced-persuaded* false confessions. Echoing Davison and Foreshaw, Ofshe and Leo (1997a) have also argued that not all police-induced confessions are coerced. Ofshe and Leo (1997a) have divided compliant ones into *stress-compliant* and *coerced-compliant* false confessions and persuaded ones into *coerced-persuaded* and *non-coerced persuaded* false confessions. More recently, Gudjonsson (2003: 211–212) has proposed changing Kassin and Wrightman's original terminology from "coerced" to "pressured," thus renaming the latter two categories *pressured compliant* and *pressured internalized* false confessions, a change that Kassin and Gudjonsson (2004) have endorsed.[1]

Social scientists rely on typologies to condense vast amounts of information, capture variation in a phenomenon, and create a vocabulary of concepts. Many of the proposed changes to the initial Kassin and Wrightsman typology have sought either to capture more variation in the phenomenon of false confession or to use concepts that more accurately describe it. However, a tension remains in any typology between inclusiveness and parsimony. So many new categories and subcategories have now been proposed that researchers run the risk of losing the clarity of the original Kassin–Wrightsman typology. What is important to understand are the three conceptually distinct psychological processes at work in the production and elicitation of false confession. For simplicity, I will drop the various prefixes and simply refer to voluntary, compliant, and persuaded false confessions.

Voluntary False Confessions

Kassin and Wrightsman (1985) initially defined a *voluntary* false confession as one that is offered in the absence of police interrogation. Voluntary false confessions are thus explained by the internal psychological states or needs of the confessor (Gudjonsson, 2003) or by external pressure brought to bear on the confessor by someone other than the police (McCann, 1998). Most voluntary false confessions appear to result from an underlying psychological disturbance or psychiatric disorder. As Kassin and Wrightsman (1985) point out, individuals volunteer false confessions in the absence of police questioning for a variety of reasons: a desire for notoriety or fame, the need to expiate guilt over imagined or real acts, an inability to distinguish between fantasy and reality, or a pathological need for acceptance or self-punishment. But voluntary false confessions need not be rooted in psychological maladies. A person may, for example, provide a voluntary false confession out of a desire to aid and protect the real criminal (Wagenaar, van Koppen, and Crombag, 1993), to provide an alibi for a different crime or norm violation (Radelet, Bedau, and Putnam, 1992), or to get revenge on another person (Gudjonsson, 2003). High-profile crimes—such as the Lindbergh kidnapping in the 1930s, the Black Dahlia murder in the 1940s, and the JonBenet Ramsey and Nicole Brown Simpson murders in the 1990s—tend to attract large numbers of voluntary false confessions (*Indiana Law Journal*, 1953; Corwin, 1996). Detectives tend to be far more skeptical and less accepting of voluntary false confessions than of police-induced false confessions. Put differently, police more readily recognize and discount voluntary false confessions than those they elicit (Gudjonsson, 2003).

Compliant False Confessions

A compliant false confession is one given in response to police coercion, stress, or pressure in order to achieve some instrumental benefit—typically either to terminate and thus escape from an aversive interrogation process, to take advantage of a perceived suggestion or promise of leniency, or to avoid an anticipated harsh punishment (Ofshe and Leo, 1997a). Perhaps the most distinct aspect of compliant false confessions is that they are made knowingly: the suspect admits guilt with the knowledge that he is innocent and that what he says is false. Compliant false confessions are typically recanted shortly after the interrogation is over.

There are a number of reasons why suspects give compliant false confessions. Kassin and Wrightsman (1985: 77) first suggested that compliant false confessions arise "through the coerciveness of the interrogation process." In the premodern era of American interrogation, the third degree was their primary cause. Innocent suspects knowingly gave false confessions to avoid or end physical assaults, torture sessions, and the like. In the modern era, psychological coercion is the primary source of compliant false confessions. Psychologically oriented interrogation techniques are just as capable of resulting in compliant false confessions as are physical ones. Ofshe and Leo

(1997a) have identified "classically coercive influence techniques" (i.e., threats and promises, explicit or implied) as the root cause of most compliant false confessions in the modern era.

Coerced-compliant false confessions are the most common type of false confession. As Kassin (1997a: 225) notes, "the pages of legal history are filled with stories of *coerced-compliant* confessions." Compliant false confessions occur as a result of the sequenced influence process through which detectives seek to persuade a suspect that he is indisputably caught and that the most viable way to mitigate his punishment and escape his situation is by confessing (Ofshe and Leo, 1997a; Davis and O'Donahue, 2003). As we have seen, interrogators use negative incentives to convince the suspect that it is futile to deny the crime, and positive incentives to motivate him to perceive that it is in his self-interest to confess.

The most potent psychological inducement is the suggestion that the suspect will be treated more leniently if he confesses and more punitively if he does not. Unlike negative incentives, promises and threats are neither standard nor legal; rather, they are regarded as coercive in both psychology and law (Ofshe and Leo, 1997b; White, 2001a). It is not hard to understand why such threats and promises in combination with standard interrogation techniques may cause a suspect to knowingly confess to a crime he did not commit. Put simply, he comes to perceive that the benefits of confessing (e.g., release from custody, mitigated punishment, etc.) outweigh the costs of denial (e.g., arrest, aggravated punishment, etc.). This may be especially true for suspects who naively believe that the fact of their innocence will, in the end, exonerate them (Gudjonsson, 2003; Kassin, 2005).

Though psychologically coercive threats and promises may be the primary sources of compliant false confessions, they are not the only ones. Stress (Ofshe and Leo, 1997a) and police pressure (Gudjonsson, 2003) are also causes. As discussed, custodial interrogation is inherently stressful, anxiety-provoking, and unpleasant; it is the paradigmatic example of the use of psychological pressure and manipulation by state authorities to extract damning information from reluctant subjects. As David Simon (1991: 201) observed,

> A good interrogator controls the physical environment, from the moment a suspect or reluctant witness is dumped in the small cubicle, left alone to stew in soundproof isolation . . . Control is the reason a suspect is seated farthest from the interrogation room door, and the reason the room's light

switch can only be operated with a key that remains in possession of the detectives. Every time a suspect has to ask for or be offered a cigarette, water, coffee or a trip to the bathroom, he's being reminded that he's lost control.

Interrogators' interpersonal styles may also be a source of distress: they may be, by turns, confrontational, insistent, demanding, overbearing, deceptive, hostile, and manipulative. Their accusatorial techniques are also designed to induce distress by attacking the suspect's self confidence, by not permitting him to assert his innocence, and by causing him to feel powerless and trapped. The interrogation may span over hours—as often occurs with compliant false confessions—weakening a suspect's resistance, inducing fatigue, and heightening suggestibility.

The combined effect of these multiple stressors may overwhelm the suspect's cognitive capacities such that he confesses simply to terminate what has become an intolerably stressful experience. Facing overbearing interrogators who refuse to take no for an answer, he may reason that telling interrogators what they want to hear is the only way to escape (Ofshe and Leo, 1997b).

There are several important things to note here. First, compliant false confessions are caused by a combination of factors. Typically, no one factor alone is sufficient to induce compliant false confessions. Second, their primary causes—psychological coercion, stress, and pressure—are external to the individual. Though the capacity of people to endure pressure and stress varies, false confessions are primarily caused by coercive and overbearing interrogation practices, not deficient psyches or personalities. Whether compliant or persuaded, police-induced false confession is thus a phenomenon to be explained by social psychology, not psychiatry or clinical psychology. Third, regardless of its source, the underlying psychological logic of a compliant false confession remains the same: the custodial environment and police techniques create an intolerable or punishing experience from which the suspect seeks release. Whether he aims to put an end to the questioning, to avoid a harsher punishment, or to gain leniency, the suspect chooses the immediate benefits of falsely confessing over the perceived costs of continued denial. Coerced-compliant confessions have been recognized in law as potentially overbearing a suspect's will more than any other category of police-induced statements (Ofshe and Leo, 1997b; Kassin and Gudjonsson, 2004).

Two recent cases illustrate the psychological logic of compliant false confessions.

Case Studies

David Saraceno

On August 25, 1994, Connecticut State Police Detectives Reinaldo Ortiz and James Thomas and Sergeant Scott Martin went to the house of eighteen-year-old high school student David Saraceno and arrested him for the midnight burning of a fleet of fifteen school buses in Haddam, Connecticut. The burning was one of the worst cases of vandalism ever in the region. While patrol officers stayed behind and executed a warrant at his house, the detectives brought Saraceno back to the station and interrogated him for more than ten hours. The detectives did not record the interrogation or even write out his confession, though two days later they reconstructed it from memory and wrote it up in a police report.

Saraceno describes a classic coerced-compliant false confession. Detectives Thomas and Ortiz repeatedly accused him of setting the bus fires, he recalls. They made their accusations aggressively and forcefully. Saraceno repeatedly denied involvement, explaining that he was at his girlfriend's house that night. But each time Saraceno professed his innocence, the detectives either cut him off or repeated their accusations. "We are not idiots," they told him. "Don't bother wasting our time" (Interview of David Saraceno, 1998: 8). They also demanded that he stop bullshitting them. As the detectives grew frustrated with Saraceno's denials, they raised their voices, yelled at him, and moved in closer. They knew that he had been involved, they told him. Saraceno describes them as menacing and repetitive: " 'You know you did this. . . . Just admit it to us. . . .' The whole repetition was running down on me. The guy is not stopping" (Interview of David Saraceno, 1998: 21). Saraceno was upset, shocked, confused, and scared.

The detectives repeatedly confronted Saraceno with false or mistaken evidence of his guilt. His accomplices had identified him, they claimed. The detectives told Saraceno that beer cans left at the crime scene bore his fingerprints. They also presented him with items taken during the search at his parents' home that they believed to be evidence of his guilt; some of those items did not even belong to him. For example, they showed him what they believed to be the hiking boots that he had worn at the time of the arson because one of their dogs had allegedly sniffed out an accelerant on them. The boots, however, belonged to Saraceno's father, as Saraceno repeatedly tried to tell them. When they refused to believe him, Saraceno put his head down in despair: "I was just thinking this is unreal. They are never going to let me leave here" (Interview of David Saraceno, 1998: 49).

Earlier in the interrogation Saraceno had requested an attorney, but he was told that that would be taken care of later. Saraceno subsequently asked to call his parents, but again the detective denied his request, informing him that calling his parents was a privilege, not a right. Unbeknownst to Saraceno, at around the same time his father had shown up at the police station and requested to speak to him, telling the officers that he wanted to make sure that his son had actually waived his right to counsel. The detectives falsely assured Mr. Saraceno that his son had.

Throughout the interrogation, the detectives promised Saraceno freedom or leniency if he confessed and threatened that he would be physically harmed if he did not. The detectives even implied that Saraceno could go home if he confessed. Saraceno recounted, "He never explicitly said 'you can go home if you sign this confession or admit to this crime.' He never said those exact words, but he said 'why don't you make this easy'—you know, 'we will let you go.' I took that as meaning, if you let me go, I can go home. Where else will I go?" (Interview of David Saraceno, 1998: 23). In addition, the detectives told Saraceno several times that if he confessed to the bus fires they would put a good word in with the prosecutor, that he would only get probation and likely only have to do community service. But if he did not confess, they said, he would be looking at jail time (Interview of David Saraceno, 1998).

The detectives made their most dramatic threats later in the interrogation. They told Saraceno that if he continued to deny that he torched the buses they would make sure he went to jail, where, they said, he would not survive. It would be like "throwing a lamb to the lions," they told him. He would "be raped by a big black nigger" (Interview of David Saraceno: 38). Terrified, and believing this was a "done deal," Saraceno started to shake uncontrollably. He started to see spots; twice he felt like he was going to pass out. He told the detectives that he felt nauseous and asked them if he could receive medical attention, but they denied his request and responded that his feelings of nausea were really just feelings of guilt and would pass once he confessed. "I never felt like this ever," Saraceno recounted later. "Ever in my whole life. This physically shaken, emotionally upset. I did feel like I was going to pass out. I never felt these things before. I wanted some sort of medical attention. They told me I didn't need it" (Interview of David

Saraceno, 1998: 40). As he had throughout earlier portions of the interrogation, Saraceno cried, this time uncontrollably.

Eventually, Saraceno asked the detectives: "Do you want me to lie? Is that what you're telling me I should do?" (Interview of David Saraceno, 1998: 65). One of the detectives responded that Saraceno should do whatever he felt was necessary and right. At this point Saraceno began fabricating a story, repeating the details the detectives had told him and agreeing to their suggestion of the facts:

> I remember very vividly standing there thinking, what am I supposed to do? How am I supposed to get out of this? What's going to be my way out of this? What? Nothing has worked so far. Denying hasn't worked. Asking for an attorney hasn't worked. Asking to call my parents hasn't worked. I believed their threats that they could ship me down to the New Haven jail . . . So I figured maybe I can just kind of start bullshitting and see where that would go . . . I am reaching a conclusion in my own mind that telling them something will be my only way out. My only way to avoid them yelling at me. It's going to be my only way to avoid getting beat up and possibly raped, you know. My only way out. I can't call my parents. I don't have any numbers to any attorneys, you know. I have no phone book. Nothing. So I am starting to reach this conclusion that this is going to be my only way out. I give them whatever they want.
>
>   . . . I was mentally exhausted, physically exhausted. Scared. I felt very threatened. I felt like I had no options available to me whatsoever . . . What the hell am I going to do? How do I end the situation? All I wanted to do is get back home, you know. The safety of my home and my parents (Interview of David Saraceno, 1998: 57, 59, 66).

Saraceno finally confessed that he and several accomplices had torched the buses. Although Saraceno quickly recanted and there was no evidence supporting his confession (indeed, there was exactly the opposite), he was eventually convicted of arson and four related felonies. He faced a possible sentence of thirty-five years in prison.

While Saraceno's appeal was pending, private investigators learned of the true perpetrators. The state had chosen to protect them rather than disclose their identities to the defense or the court, although one of them had confessed in detail in a privately sealed affidavit and offered to testify against the other three if given immunity. But now it was too late to prosecute them because the district attorney had let the statute of limitations run out.

Although the judge set aside Saraceno's conviction, prosecutors threatened further prosecution unless he pled "no contest" to a lesser bus-fire charge. When Saraceno refused, they, incredibly, offered him a deal requiring that he plead guilty to the misdemeanor of "hindering prosecution by falsely confessing" and receive a suspended sentence. To put an end to this "surreal prosecution," stop draining his family finances, and get his life back on track, Saraceno took the deal (Drizin and Leo, 2004).

Corey Beale

On August 11, 1998, a daycare worker and five children out for a walk discovered the badly decomposed body of Michael Harley in Brandywine, Maryland. Friends said the last time they had seen Harley was outside the Waldorf Hotel—where they had been with him at a party—walking a white female home. Prince George County police suspected seventeen-year-old Corey Beale of killing his good friend Harley because a pager belonging to Beale was found in Harley's possession.

Shortly after the discovery of Harley's body, the police contacted Joanne Beale, Corey's mother, a former federal law enforcement officer. They told her that they had found a note with Corey's name on it next to a dead girl, and that they wanted to speak to Corey about it. That was a lie. Once she and Corey arrived at the station, the police told her that the real reason they wanted to speak to Corey was because Harley had been found dead.

Mrs. Beale informed the detectives that Corey suffered from a learning disability, comprehension problems, and a seizure disorder, and that she did not want the police to speak to him without her present. The police verbally agreed to her request, then separated her from Corey, asking her to write out a statement about when she last saw Harley. The police then escorted Mrs. Beale from the detective station into the lobby, where they told her that Corey was free to go and waiting for her. By that ruse they had locked her out of the area where they were, in reality, holding and interrogating Corey.

Mrs. Beale pounded on the doors to the detective station, yelling at the police to stop questioning Corey outside her presence and to provide him with seizure medication. But her attempts to regain entry were to no avail. She waited in the lobby for hours, eventually falling ill and suffering chest pain. An ambulance had to take her to the hospital, where she was admitted for three days due to a heart condition. Meanwhile, her sister and a family attorney both came to the police station to intervene, all unsuccessfully.

Beginning on the evening of August 13 and ending more than fifty-one hours later on August 15, eight Prince George County homicide detectives detained and interrogated Corey Beale. Because the Prince George County Police Department failed to electronically tape the interrogation, there is no objective record of what occurred. According to Beale, the detectives were friendly to him during the brief initial interaction when his mother had been present. Once they removed her, however, their demeanor and tone changed dramatically.

The detectives repeatedly accused Corey of killing Harley, screamed and swore at him, and demanded that he confess. Beale repeatedly declared his innocence. The detectives accused him of lying. Terrified, Beale asked to see his mother many times, as well as a lawyer, but his requests were denied. According to Beale (Witt, 2001: 4): "I asked for a lawyer. They wouldn't give me one. They kept saying I was a witness, not a suspect; when you are not a suspect you are not appointed a lawyer. I ain't never been in trouble. I didn't understand what they was talking about. I was like, 'I want a lawyer.' They were like, 'You don't need a lawyer.'" After approximately four and a half hours of interrogation, the detectives asked Beale to sign a release form. They told him that if he signed it he would be released back to his mother. "I just went along with him . . ." Beale recalled. "He told me it was a releaser form. You don't think like police will lie to you, you know" (Deposition of Corey Beale, 2005: 220). The detectives had actually directed Beale to sign a *Miranda* waiver, which he had not read.

The detectives kept telling Beale that the evidence proved beyond any doubt that he had killed Harley. They claimed that they had found Harley's blood in Beale's car. They were lying. The detectives also gave Beale two Computer Voice Stress Analyzer (CVSA) examinations, both times telling Beale that he had failed and that the test put an end to any possible questions about his guilt. Subsequent detectives would tell Beale, over and over, that the CVSA demonstrated his guilt—it was no longer a question of whether he killed Harley, but how and why.

Corey Beale's marathon interrogation included numerous deprivations— of food, medicine, and sleep—that are indisputably regarded as coercive. The detectives allowed him to sleep for less than an hour, despite his repeated requests. As for food, they gave him only a soft drink and donut the evening of August 13 and one or two McDonald's meals on August 15. In addition, Beale repeatedly asked the detectives to allow him to get his seizure medication, but they responded that they would call an ambulance if he had a seizure. The detectives made it clear to Beale that he could not leave until the interrogation was done. At one point, they handcuffed Beale to the wall during their questioning; at another, one of the interrogators grabbed him by the shirt and slammed him up against the wall. "The cop started getting violent," Beale recounted. "He started jacking me up. He snapped me out of the chair and he threw me up against the wall. He was short and white. He was like, 'We ain't got time to be playing games with you. Just confess so we can all go home' " (Witt, 2001: 4).

The detectives promised Beale prosecutorial leniency and freedom in exchange for an admission. The detectives offered to help Beale because his mother was a U.S. marshal and they did not want to see a good kid go down, they said. "They told me 'we're trying to help you out. If you just say you did it, we can let you go right now on pretrial,' " Beale remembered (Witt, 2001: 4). The detectives also told Beale that he would be treated more leniently—as a witness rather than a suspect—if he confessed to killing Harley, and they promised to allow him to go home. "They said they were going to send me home," Beale recalled. ". . . Then after I done it, they were, 'Okay, we're about to send you home now.' I guess by 'home' they meant jail" (Witt, 2001: 5).

The detectives also told Beale that agreeing to particular scenarios (such as killing Harley in self-defense) would help reduce his charge and sentence, and earn his release from their interrogation: "it was my only—like this is my only chance to—for me to come home is to confess. And if I confessed, it would be a lesser charge, like it was self-defense, like I was protecting myself and I'd be home with my mother the next day, which never happened" (Deposition of Corey Beale, 2005: 296).

The detectives threatened Beale with harsher treatment and extreme punishment if he did not confess. The detectives told Beale that he was going to be sent to the gas chamber and executed or spend the rest of his life in prison without the possibility of parole if he did not admit to killing Harley. According to Beale (Deposition of Corey Beale, 2005: 175): "They [detectives] picked me up and they took me back to the questioning room, and then at that time they told me like this was my last chance before I get the gas chamber or spend my life in jail." They threatened him with the death penalty several times, leaving Beale shaking and crying. Not knowing how the criminal justice system worked, Beale assumed that the police had the power to carry out their threats immediately.

As the interrogation progressed, the detectives essentially coerced Beale into agreeing with a number of scenarios in which he either witnessed or participated in the killing of Michael Harley; each scenario was more incriminating than the one before it. For example, in Beale's initial police-written statement, he says that Harley and a friend, Jurwand "Posey" Riley, got into a fight after they left the party (which presumably resulted in Harley's death), but that Beale drove off while they were still fighting. In a subsequent police-written confession, Beale said he was involved in the fight between Harley and Riley. And in his final police-written confession, Beale admitted to killing Harley. He ultimately provided five different conflicting statements.

According to Beale, the homicide detectives supplied him with the details of his confessions and coached him through the confession-taking process. They told him what happened and what to say, including where the body was located. Beale says the police also attributed a number of things to him that he did not state, and that he just initialed what they wrote.

Beale was charged with Harley's murder and spent the next ten months in jail—where he was assaulted, raped repeatedly, and even gang-raped—before detectives in neighboring Charles County discovered that the killer was actually Kenneth Shirell Williams. During his incarceration, Beale missed his entire senior year of high school. Prosecutors eventually dropped charges against Beale and released him in June 1999. In July 2002, Williams pled guilty to Harley's murder and was sentenced to thirty years in prison.

Persuaded False Confessions

INTRODUCTION

Persuaded false confessions occur when police interrogation tactics cause an innocent suspect to doubt his memory and he becomes temporarily persuaded that it is more likely than not that he committed the crime he is being accused of, despite having no memory of committing it (Ofshe and Leo, 1997a). When this occurs, the false confessor reasons from inference—rather than actual knowledge or memory—that he must have committed the crime and, as a result, accepts responsibility for it. Unlike the compliant false confessor who knows he is innocent, the persuaded false confessor is in an uncertain belief state about his guilt: in light of what he has learned during the interrogation, he comes to believe that he probably committed the crime even though he cannot remember doing so because it is the only explanation that makes sense to him. Reflecting his uncertain belief state, the suspect confesses in language that is tentative, speculative, and hypothetical ("I must have done it," "I probably did it," "I guess I did it," "I could have done it." Ofshe and Leo (1997a) have called this the grammar of confabulation; this language of uncertainty is present in all persuaded false confessions. Usually, the persuaded false confessor recants either during the interrogation or shortly after being removed from the interrogation environment.

Persuaded false confessions are the most troubling and difficult to understand of the two types of police-induced false confession. Below I briefly describe two cases of persuaded false confession, and then explain the three-stage psychological process that leads to a persuaded false confession.

Case Studies

Michael Crowe

After twelve-year-old Stephanie Crowe was found stabbed to death in her bedroom in Escondido, California, on January 21, 1998, police took her fourteen-year-old brother, Michael, into custody. They interrogated him for more than ten hours over three days. The interrogations were recorded almost in their entirety. The detectives repeatedly accused Michael of killing his sister and confronted him with false evidence that they said conclusively established his guilt. For example, they told Crowe that they had found blood in his room and that his sister had been found with his hair in her hand.

After repeatedly denying that he killed his sister, Crowe was directed to take a Computer Voice Stress Analyzer exam. The detectives told him that the test was scientific and accurate and that it would allow him to prove his innocence. Not surprisingly, after he took it, they informed Crowe that he had failed the exam and that it established his guilt conclusively. Crowe, who recalled being asleep at the time of Stephanie's murder, began to doubt his memory (Deposition of Michael Crowe, 2002). He was devastated and started to sob almost uncontrollably. But the detectives continued to accuse him of killing his sister while claiming they were trying to help him. They said that "the evidence can't be argued with. So what happened is not an issue any longer." Rather, "why it happened and how we're going to help you get through this" was "really all this is about," they told him. "We need to help you get through this" (Interrogation of Michael Crowe, 1998a: 88). After Crowe said he didn't think he did it and couldn't remember it, the detectives suggested that he may have blacked out.

Crowe pleaded dozens of times that he did not know how he could have possibly committed the murder because he did not remember doing so. But the detectives continued to accuse him of lying or of having a selective memory. They also told him that they could not accept "no" or "I do not know" for an answer. Crowe felt boxed in: "Everything I do, you don't believe me. Everything. You don't believe a thing I'm saying" (Interrogation of Michael Crowe, 1998b: 46).

The interrogators told him there were "two Michaels"—a good Michael and a bad Michael—and that the bad Michael might have committed the crime without the good Michael realizing it. "You're going to be treated just as if this was an unconscious act," they said (Interrogation of Michael Crowe, 1998b: 73). As Crowe continued to protest his innocence, the detectives told him to make up a story: "Use your imagination. What do you imagine could happen?" (Interrogation of Michael Crowe, 1998b: 76). Crowe responded: "I can't answer any questions because I don't have any answers. . . . I have no memories" (Interrogation of Michael Crowe, 1998b: 82).

But Crowe began to seriously entertain the possibility that he had killed his sister. "If I did it, I hope she forgives me," he said (Interrogation of Michael Crowe, 1998b: 94). The detectives kept telling Crowe that they were trying to help him remember his actions. Crowe began to allow that he could have done it without remembering it: "If I did this, then I must be subconsciously blocking it out or something like that" (Interrogation of Michael Crowe, 1998b: 104). The interrogators shattered Crowe's confidence in his memory. "The very fact anything happened—the only reason I know is you've been telling me I did this," Crowe said. "That's the only way" (Interrogation of Michael Crowe, 1998b: 132–133).

The detectives told Crowe that if the system had to prove his guilt, he would be charged as an adult and go to prison. But if Crowe admitted it, he would be treated as a juvenile and would instead be taken care of and rehabilitated by the system. There were two "roads" or "paths," they said: "There is the path of punishment, which is jail. And that's really all that jail's good for. Jail doesn't rehabilitate anybody. You're too young for that. Or there's the path that says, 'Hey, I'm sorry for what I did' " (Interrogation of Michael Crowe, 1998b: 148). One path would lead to a murder charge, formal punishment, and perhaps even homosexual rape in an adult prison. But if he took the other path and confessed, the detectives said, he would avoid prison and the possibility of homosexual rape by older offenders. They sought to convince Crowe that one of these two fates was inevitable. He had to choose which path to take. And they wanted to help him choose the right one.

Crowe eventually cracked, but still could not retrieve any memories of committing the crime. "I know I did it, but I don't know how," he cried (Interrogation of Michael Crowe, 1998b: 163). Apparently agreeing with their memory repression theory, he speculated on why he suppressed the memory: "I think the reason I don't remember was rage. All I know is I'm positive I killed her" (Interrogation of Michael Crowe, 1998b: 173). Crowe was substituting the interrogators' assertion for his own discredited memory: "The only way I even know I did this is because she's dead and because the evidence says that I did. You could find that someone else did it—and I pray to God someone else did. I think it's too late for that. I think I did it" (Interrogation of Michael Crowe, 1998c: 6).

Some years later in a civil deposition, Michael Crowe (Deposition of Michael Crowe, 2002: 193–194) was asked whether at that moment he doubted if he killed his sister:

Yes, I did . . . for a few reasons. One of them was I had been asleep at the time [of the murder], and they had told me that I could have done it and not remembered it. So since I didn't remember anything, I thought they were telling the truth that that could have happened. They also told me they had found all this evidence that pointed towards me and said I did it, and I believed them when they told me that. As well as the truth verification machine. It put some doubt in my mind when he told me I was lying . . . they told me flat out that I could have blacked out and done it and not remembered it.

Following his confession, local prosecutors charged Crowe with the murder of his sister, and he spent over seven months in juvenile hall awaiting trial. The charges were dismissed, however, when his sister's blood was found on the shirt of Richard Tuite, a mentally ill drifter who several people had seen acting suspiciously in the Crowe neighborhood the night of the murder. Eventually state prosecutors filed charges against Tuite and he was convicted of the killing.

Gary Gauger

At approximately 11:30 on the morning of April 9, 1993, forty-year-old Gary Gauger called 911 to report that he had found his father, Morris Gauger, dead on their 200-acre farm near Richmond, Illinois, and that his mother, Ruth Gauger, was missing. Paramedics and McHenry County

Sheriffs' deputies arrived at the farm shortly thereafter, and at approximately 1:40 P.M. Mrs. Gauger's body was located. Both of Gary Gauger's parents had been murdered.

Sheriffs detained Gary Gauger inside a squad car until 4 P.M., when they drove him to the sheriffs department for questioning. Over the next eighteen hours, Gauger would be interrogated by three sheriffs' deputies and a polygrapher. Gauger's marathon interrogation—unlike Michael Crowe's—was not recorded, and Gauger was never asked to sign a statement, a departure from standard procedure.

During the first eight hours of the interrogation, one detective questioned Gauger. He asked Gauger about his activities on the previous days, his parents' routines and habits, and various aspects of his life. Gauger told the detective that he had had an alcohol problem in the past but had been sober for more than thirty days. Though he said nothing incriminating and there was no evidence that he had killed his parents, the detective believed that his account "raised a lot of suspicions" (Marshall, 1994: 9). He asked Gauger to submit to a polygraph examination. The polygrapher found that the test results were inconclusive due to "flat polygraph records usually associated with fatigue" (Marshall, 1994: 9).

Following the polygraph, three detectives interrogated Gauger in rotating teams of two for the next ten hours. The detectives repeatedly told Gauger that he had failed the exam and that it proved his guilt. One of the detectives claimed that his answers had "jumped the needle right off the graph" (Gauger, 2005: 94). The detectives also told Gauger that there was a stack of evidence against him four or five inches tall, and that they had found clothes soaked in his parents' blood in his room, blood on his pajamas, bloody fingerprints, and the murder weapon (Cohen, 2003; Gauger, 2005). When Gauger denied that he had killed his parents, the detectives kept accusing him of committing the crime and restated the evidence that they claimed to have against him. At one point, they threw pictures of his parents' dead bodies in front of him (Gauger, 2005). Gauger disputed the detectives' claims, but they convinced him that they were not lying about the evidence against him because, they said, they would lose their jobs if they lied to him.

By this point, Gauger had become confused and exhausted, but his requests to go to sleep were denied. The interrogators asked him to construct a hypothetical scenario of how he could have killed his parents and reenact the crime (Gauger, 2005: 95): "I'm thinking if I killed my parents, I want to know about it . . . They're not asking me if I killed my parents, they're telling me that I did kill my parents and they wanted to know what happened, and if I would go through a hypothetical account with them, using facts they'd fed me about what I must have done, it might jog my memory."

Gauger constructed an account of sneaking up behind each parent and slashing their throats. Gauger began to wonder if he had killed his parents, despite having no memory of it. The detectives suggested that he had killed his parents in a blackout (Gauger, 2005), making it sound like such blackouts happen "every day." Gauger now "really started to think that I had killed my parents" (Marshall, 1994: 15).

Every time Gauger told the detectives that he had no memory of killing his parents, however, they reminded him that he had failed the lie-detector test and that they had that stack of evidence against him (Gauger, 2005: 97): "You did it. We know you did it. There was no struggle. It was someone they trusted. We've got the clothes. We've got the bloody knife. We can see it in your eyes. You killed your parents. We know you did."

The detectives wanted to know why he had killed his parents and constructed a number of scenarios. Gauger agreed with their suggestion that he had disappointed his parents with his alcohol problem. Although he told the detectives again that he did not believe he killed his parents, they continued to accuse him, attacking his denials and confronting him with false evidence, and refused his requests to be allowed to go to sleep. At approximately 6 A.M.—fourteen hours into the interrogation—Gauger repeated the hypothetical scenario that he had offered earlier in the evening, then followed it with "but I don't remember doing any of this" (Marshall, 1994: 18). All the detectives wanted to hear was a confession, however. "They wouldn't let me say anything else," Gauger testified later. "Every time I would say something else, he was just hollering at me. I couldn't stand being hollered at anymore" (Marshall, 1994: 18).

Sometime between 6:00 and 7:30 A.M., Gauger came to believe he must have killed his parents. Gauger testified, "I still couldn't believe it. I mean, I thought I had done it," he testified later. "I didn't see how I could *not* have done it, but I still couldn't believe it" (Marshall, 1994: 20, emphasis added). Like every other persuaded false confessor, Gauger ultimately trusted the detectives and assumed they were telling him the truth about the allegedly overwhelming evidence that supposedly established his guilt against him. He came to believe that he must have killed his parents, even though he did not remember doing so, because that explanation made the most sense to him in light of what the police were telling him. Gauger (2005: 97) explains:

> I thought I'd actually killed my parents, and there was all this evidence. I
> said I would have gone out to the garage, come up behind my father,
> grabbed his hair, cut his throat, and let him fall. They said, "What did you
> do with the weapon?" And I said, "I would have left it there," cause I had
> no memory of doing anything. Immediately upon saying it, I said, "But this
> is just a hypothetical. I have no memory of this." But they've got me
> thinking now that I did it . . . I'm believing that I actually killed my parents
> in a blackout."

Gauger's interrogation ended at approximately 10:22 A.M.

Gauger was immediately charged with the capital murder of both of his parents, though his confession was inconsistent with many facts of the crime and not a single piece of evidence linked him to the murders (Leo and Ofshe, 1998a). "To the extent that Gauger got any facts about the murders right, these were facts that detectives (and the polygrapher) admitted to having told Gary prior to his confession" (Marshall, 1994: 35). In just three hours, a jury convicted Gauger of two counts of first-degree murder in October 1993. The trial judge initially sentenced him to death in January 1994, but nine months later the judge vacated the sentence and resentenced him to life in prison. An Illinois appeals court reversed Gauger's conviction in March 1996, however, after ruling that the sheriffs had improperly obtained his confession (Leo and Ofshe, 1998a). Gauger was released from prison in October 1996 after spending three and a half years behind bars (and almost a year on death row). In June 1997, Randall Miller, a member of a Wisconsin motorcycle gang, was heard on tape confessing to the crime. A federal grand jury indicted Miller and James Schneider, another gang member, for the murders of the Gaugers. Schneider pled guilty in 1998, and Miller was convicted in 2000 (Cohen, 2003).

UNDERSTANDING PERSUADED FALSE CONFESSIONS

The Three Stages
Persuaded false confessions typically unfold in three sequential steps. It is important to understand each of these steps because they identify the necessary conditions and psychological logic of the making of a persuaded false confession. First, the interrogator causes the suspect to doubt his innocence.

As in the cases of Michael Crowe and Gary Gauger, this is typically a by-product of an intense, lengthy, and deceptive accusatorial interrogation. It involves three standard interrogation techniques used in combination over and over again: First, interrogators repeatedly accuse the suspect of committing the crime, never wavering in their confidence or acknowledging the plausibility of the suspects' protestations of innocence; second, they relentlessly attacks the suspect's denials as implausible, illogical, contradicted by the known facts, or simply wrong because of the interrogators' alleged superior knowledge or authority; third and most importantly, they repeatedly confront the suspect with multiple forms of fabricated but allegedly irrefutable evidence of his guilt. The most potent false-evidence ploys are orchestrated ones involving rigged polygraph and Computer Voice Stress Analyzer examinations.

The innocent suspect enters the interrogation with no foreknowledge of what is about to occur: he typically has never been interrogated before, he instinctively believes he has no reason to be concerned because he is innocent, and he does not even realize that he is a suspect in a felony investigation. He naively trusts the police, assumes that they are acting in good faith, and does not know that they can or will lie to him. When first accused, the innocent suspect thinks that the interrogators are genuinely mistaken, and he counters by attempting to reason with them and persuade them of his innocence. Anticipating this, the interrogators simply repeat and escalate their accusations, attacks on his denials, and false-evidence ploys. At some point, however, the suspect realizes that they are not going to credit his assertions of innocence. He may then begin to experience dissonance because he cannot reconcile the obvious contradiction between his knowledge that he is innocent and his belief that the police are truthfully reporting unmistakable evidence of his guilt. The asymmetry of the situation puts the suspect at a psychological disadvantage of which he is unaware: The interrogators can simply invent false evidence of his guilt to refute his assertions, but the innocent suspect, who does not realize the police are lying to him, cannot simply invent false evidence of his innocence to refute their assertions. Instead, the suspect offers up the remaining basis for his belief in his innocence: that he has no memory of committing the crime.

The interrogators, however, continue to press forward with their onslaught of accusations and challenges. The suspect may resolve his dissonance by accepting the interrogators' repeatedly and forcefully stated belief in his guilt as more likely to be true than his declining belief in his innocence, and thus abstractly acknowledge the possibility that he may have committed the crime. But the resolved dissonance gives way to a different type of confusion: even if it is hypothetically possible that he committed the crime, the suspect still cannot make sense of his lack of memory of it. The interrogators have caused him to doubt his belief in his innocence, but his confusion persists. For even though they have convinced him that his guilt is *possible*, they have not convinced him that it is plausible. Even though he credits the interrogators' evidence and their reasoning, he still does not understand how he could have done it given his lack of memory.

To convince the suspect that it is plausible—and likely—that he committed the crime, the interrogators must supply him with a reason that satisfactorily explains how he could have done it without remembering it. This is the second step in the psychological process that leads to a persuaded false confession. Typically, the interrogators suggest one version or another of a "repressed" memory theory. They may suggest, for example, that the suspect experienced an alcoholic or drug-induced blackout (as in Gary Gauger's case), a "dry" blackout, a multiple personality disorder (as in Michael Crowe's case), a momentary lapse in consciousness, posttraumatic stress disorder, or, perhaps most commonly, that the suspect simply repressed the memory of committing the crime because it was a traumatic experience for him. Because they believe the suspect is lying when he claims to have no memory of the crime, the interrogators usually are the first to suggest that the suspect may have blacked out; they then provide the explanation for how this could have occurred. Sometimes, as in Gauger's case, the suspect may first inquire about the possibility of a blackout, after which the interrogators affirm the suspect's suggestion—often telling him that it "happens all the time"—and supply the explanation.

The suspect can only be persuaded to accept responsibility for the crime if he regards one of the interrogators' explanations for his alleged amnesia as plausible, however. Once this occurs, the suspect come to believe that it is *more likely than not* that he committed the crime. But the suspect still remains in an uncertain belief state. His inability to retrieve any memories of his act explains his inability to be certain of his guilt (Ofshe and Leo, 1997b). The suspect has been persuaded that he must have committed the crime because in light of his changed beliefs it is the explanation that makes the most sense to him at this point in the interrogation and thus appears to resolve his confusion. But even though he has credited the interrogators' purported evidence of his guilt, accepted their explanation for his alleged amnesia, and been persuaded to confess, he still has no memory of committing the crime.

Despite his lack of memory, once the suspect is "over the line" (Ofshe and Leo, 1997b), he is ready for the third and final step in the making of a persuaded false confession: the construction of the postadmission narrative. Once the suspect has accepted responsibility for the crime, interrogators push him to supply the details of how and why he did it. The suspect does not know them, however; he is in the paradoxical situation of believing he committed an act that he wants to confess to but cannot remember. He may believe that if he thinks hard enough, searches his mind, or tries to imagine himself committing the crime that he will somehow be able to remember it and supply the desired details. But this does not happen. Instead, the suspect either guesses or confabulates about how the crime could have occurred, repeats back the details that the police have suggested to him, knowingly makes up the details, or tries to infer them from the interrogators' suggestions.

Usually the persuaded false confessor's postadmission narrative is replete with errors. Reasoning from inference rather than actual knowledge, he confesses in largely hypothetical, tentative, and speculative language (Ofshe and Leo, 1997b; Gudjonsson, 2003) that reflects his uncertain belief state, confusion, and lack of memory. Assuming the suspect is lying, however, the interrogators sometimes reject his speculations and pressure him to use declarative, rather than conditional, language and provide the details of the crime that they continue to believe he knows. Some persuaded false confessors will bend to the demands of their interrogators and confess in declarative language (e.g., "I did" instead of "I must have done"), even though they lack any knowledge or memory of the crime; others will continue to use equivocal and uncertain language, insisting that they still do not know or remember the details.

Persuaded false confessions appear to occur far less often than compliant false confessions. They also tend to occur primarily in high-profile murder cases and be the product of unusually lengthy and psychologically intense interrogations (as in the Michael Crowe and Gary Gauger cases). Once removed from the interrogation environment and its attendant influences and pressures, the persuaded false confessor typically recants his confession (Ofshe and Leo, 1997a; Gudjonsson, 2003). Some will even recant before the interrogation terminates. Police interrogation is not usually a strong or long enough process of influence to produce permanent belief change (Ofshe and Leo, 1997a).

The Myths of False Memory

Persuaded false confessions have been poorly understood by many researchers for several reasons. The problem begins with both terminology and conceptualization. Kelman (1958) famously distinguished between three processes of social influence (identification, compliance and internalization) in order to specify "the conditions under which influence attempts are temporary and superficial and, by contrast, those under which such changes are lasting and integrated into the person's belief and value systems" (Kelman, 1974: 125). Following Kelman's distinction, Kassin and Wrightsman (1985) named the second type of police-induced false confession *coerced-internalized*. As Ofshe and Leo (1997a) have pointed out, however, this naming misapplies the concept of internalization, which, as the Kelman quote above indicates, refers to lasting belief change that endures over time and across a variety of situations. The empirical data simply do not support the application of Kelman's concept to this type of false confession.

Despite Ofshe and Leo's (1997a) correction to the literature, many scholars continue to misleadingly refer to persuaded false confessions as *internalized* false confessions. The misuse of the concept of internalization creates and reinforces the imagery that may be responsible for a second misconception in the literature: that persuaded false confessors are certain in their belief of guilt and sometimes or often acquire false or distorted memories during the interrogation process. Kassin and Wrightsman (1985: 78) initially conceived of this type of false confession as one in which "the suspect comes to believe that he or she committed the offense," but as we have seen this formulation is only partially accurate: The suspect typically comes to believe only that it is more likely than not that he committed the offense and thus reasons from inference—not memory—that he must have committed the crime. Kassin (1997a: 226) has further suggested that "the suspect's memory of his or her own actions may be altered, making its original contents potentially irretrievable. This phenomenon is closely related to recent laboratory and field studies involving the creation of false memories," and more recently has written that "an innocent person . . . sometimes form[s] a false memory in the process" (Kassin, 2005: 221). Kassin (1997b) has also likened this type of false confession to the creation of false memories in recovered memory therapy (see McNally, 2003), an analogy that Ost, Costall, and Bull (2001) have attempted to extend. Most recently, Henkel and Coffman (2004: 568) have posited that "the literature is replete with case studies and compendiums of reports showing that innocent people can come to believe in their own guilt and even create "memories" for their alleged crimes," and have gone on to argue that these "vivid memories" are the product of memory distortions that may be explained as a source monitoring error (i.e., confusing real and imagined events).

These arguments, however, are simply not borne out by the real world persuaded false confession cases and have thus created a misplaced emphasis on, and analogy to, (false) memory in the literature. As we have seen, the persuaded false confessor does not acquire or encode a memory but rather comes to falsely believe *in the absence of any memory* that he has committed a crime and agrees to accept responsibility for it because doing so seems like the most reasonable explanation to him in light of his newfound belief about the plausibility of his guilt. As Mazzoni, Loftus and Kirsch (2001: 58) point out in a different context: "believing that an event is likely to have occurred is not the same as remembering it occurring" (see also Scorboria, Mazzoni, Kirsch, and Relyea, 2004). This distinction between belief and memory is crucial to understanding the psychological logic, development and consequences of persuaded false confessions. As Gudjonsson (2003: 201) noted: "It is important to distinguish between a false belief and a false memory . . . confessors can be persuaded, or may have convinced themselves, that they have committed a crime without their developing a recollection of the offense. This is in my experience what typically happens."

Contrary to Henkel and Coffman's assertion, the research literature is *not* replete with case studies showing that innocent people create false memories for their alleged crimes. I have analyzed approximately forty American cases of persuaded false confession, and there is no evidence that any of the confessors except one, Paul Ingram, ever recovered any "memories" of committing the crime; rather they all came to believe that they must have committed the crime in the absence of memory.[2] Moreover, there is no evidence of which I am aware in any of these cases that supports the hypothesis that the contents of the persuaded false confessor's original memory were permanently distorted (Gudjonsson, 2003). As Ofshe and Leo (1997a: 209) have noted: "Ordinary police interrogation is not sufficient to produce transformative or internalized belief change." To properly understand the psychology of persuaded false confessions, researchers must focus on how and why interrogation techniques induce belief change, not on the acquisition, distortion, or implanting of false memories.

Persuaded false confessors do not acquire false memories unless the environment and conditions producing the belief change is so extreme that it no longer resembles an ordinary police interrogation. The case of Paul Ingram—the single American case in which there is unequivocal evidence that the confessor eventually acquired false memories during the interrogation process—illustrates this point. But there are at least three significant aspects about the environment and conditions of Ingram's interrogation that distinguish it from the interrogations of the other persuaded false confessors (or for that matter from any ordinary American police interrogation). First, most false confessors are interrogated in one or two sessions in a one- or two-day period. Ingram, however, was interrogated at least three to four times a week (sometimes seven days a week) over a six-month period of incarceration. After Ingram's first interrogation, he was persuaded of his guilt but he still had not formed any false memories. As Leo and Ofshe (2001: 339) have noted: "Ingram's supposed first session confession . . . was never really a confession. Instead, in response to the interrogators' false claims that it was common for sexual abusers to repress knowledge of their acts, Ingram agreed on sixteen separate occasions that if his daughters said he sexually abused them, then he must have done so—even though he had no memory of any improper act." Ingram would only begin to form false memories (of sexually abusing his daughters for seventeen years and being the leader of a satanic cult that murdered hundreds of babies) after multiple interrogation sessions.

Second, most persuaded false confessors are interrogated only by one or more police detectives. Many of Ingram's interrogations were conducted not only by police detectives, but also involved a religious pastor, a psychologist, and Ingram's own lawyer, all of whom were pressuring him to admit guilt and confabulate the details (Ofshe, 1992; Wright, 1994; Interview with Paul Ingram, 2005).

Third, unlike the other persuaded false confessors,[3] the interrogators used relaxation techniques that induced trance and ultimately led to Ingram's hypnotically induced false memories (Ofshe, 1992; Ofshe and Watters, 1994). All three factors show why Ingram's interrogation was truly exceptional and simply cannot be compared to the interrogations that led the other persuaded false confessors to accept responsibility for their crimes. Despite the extreme circumstances of Ingram's numerous interrogations, however, Ingram's hypnotically false memories were temporary and thus were never "internalized"; four to six weeks after his last interrogation, Ingram recanted his hypnotically induced memories and proclaimed his innocence (Interview of Paul Ingram, 2005).

In addition to overgeneralizing from Paul Ingram's unique case, scholars sometimes cite the impressive experimental literature on distorting true memories with misleading postevent information (Loftus, 1979; Roediger and McDermott, 1995) to suggest (by analogy) that the police interrogation process can produce false memories. This argument, however, is flawed. First, for ethical and practical reasons, researchers cannot meaningfully simulate inside university laboratories the kind of coercive and highly consequential interrogation process leading to a persuaded false confession. Second, even if researchers could, the misleading postevent information studies—such as Kassin and Keichel's (1996) experiment in which students falsely confessed to (and a significant percentage falsely remembered) the noncriminal act of striking the Alt computer key in a simulated learning experiment—logically do not analogize to *persuaded* false confessions. The misleading postevent in-formation studies distort previously encoded true memories for an event the subject already experienced (i.e., participating in the experiment), whereas the interrogated suspect is pressured to generate memories wholesale for an event he did not experience (i.e., the crime of which he is being accused).

In addition to these memory-distortion studies, there are also memory-implanting studies in which researchers have induced a minority of experimental subjects to falsely remember events as disparate as being lost in a shopping mall, spilling punch at a wedding, or being the victim of a vicious animal attack (Hyman, Husband, and Billings, 1995; Loftus and Pickrell, 1995; Porter, Yuille, and Lehman, 1999). Some scholars have also cited these studies to argue by analogy that police interrogation can lead suspects to create false memories. Although they are logically more relevant than the memory-distorting ones, the memory-creation studies still do not establish that it is possible for ordinary police interrogation to cause suspects to create false memories of committing crimes. Not only are these studies limited by the ethical and practical constraints mentioned above—the same inability to expose research subjects to a coercive and highly consequential interroga-tion process—but the memories they have induced in subjects do not analo-gize to the kinds of memories detectives are seeking to elicit in interroga-tions that lead to persuaded false confessions. The differences are significant: the false memories that have been created in the laboratory are of events that (1) are immediately plausible because the subjects may have had the experience at some point in his life (e.g., being lost in a shopping mall) whereas detectives are seeking to elicit memories to events that are imme-diately implausible (e.g., murdering someone you've never even heard of);

(2) occurred a long time ago (in the memory-creation studies) rather than very recently (in the real-world police interrogations); and (3) for which the experimental subject will experience trivial as opposed to significant personal consequence (e.g., the research subject does not go to prison and get charged with first-degree murder).

I am not suggesting here that the experimental method is unimportant or that it cannot be used to gain significant insights into the psychology of police interrogation and confession evidence. Rather, I am suggesting that the experimental studies specifically demonstrating the distortion and creation of false memories in the laboratory are not directly relevant to and thus misconceive the psychology of persuaded false confessions.

To the extent that this literature distinguishes between false memories and false beliefs, however, it can help us better understand the psychology of persuaded false confessions. For example, Mazzoni, Loftus, and Kirsch (2001) have suggested a three-stage model of social influence through which coercive or suggestive procedures can lead to false beliefs or false memories for implausible events. In the first stage of this model, the techniques cause the person to accept the plausibility of the event. As we have seen, American police interrogation can produce this specific belief change through the repeated and escalating use of three interrogation techniques: accusation, attacking the suspect's denials, and false-evidence ploys. In the second stage, the techniques cause the person to acquire the autobiographical belief that it is likely that the event happened to him. As we have seen, American police interrogators produce this belief change by proposing explanations for the suspect's alleged amnesia that he comes to regard as plausible. In the third stage, the techniques cause the person to interpret his thoughts or images about the event as memories. This stage may occur in the laboratory but has not yet been observed in ordinary American police interrogations. Mazzoni, Loftus, and Kirsch's (2001) model is thus helpful not only in understanding the conditions necessary to experimentally create false memories for implausible events, but also in recognizing that false beliefs fall far short of false memories (the difference between stage 2 and stage 3 in their model).

Case Characteristics

Analyzing known persuaded false confession cases tells us not only about the psychological techniques and processes that lead to the temporary belief change, but also gives us a window onto patterns present in these types of cases. There are three observations in particular that are briefly worth mentioning. First, persuaded false confessions do not come easily. In virtually all of the persuaded false confession cases that I have studied, the suspect confessed only after lengthy and intense interrogation. The typical interrogation ranged from approximately five to eighteen hours. Compliant false confessions do not appear, on average, to take nearly this long to elicit. Second, in almost all persuaded false confession cases, the suspect was interrogated for and falsely confessed to murder (Paul Ingram's exceptional case started out as a sexual abuse interrogation, but eventually he confessed to mass murder). Third, virtually all of the known persuaded false confession cases were either locally or nationally high-profile cases. These are the types of cases in which police investigators are most likely to be motivated to invest the extraordinary time, energy, and pressure necessary to break down an innocent suspect's belief in his innocence. Together, these observations also cast doubt on individual level explanations of why people give persuaded false confessions, for persuaded false confessions appear to be the product not so much of personal vulnerability as of unusually lengthy interrogation and extraordinary psychological pressure. It is a well known observation in psychology that if situational forces are extremely powerful they are likely to overwhelm individual differences (Ross and Nisbett, 1991).

Pathways to False Confession

The First Mistake: The Misclassification Error

As we have seen, false confessions are typically caused by a combination of factors. Scholars have primarily focused on psychologically coercive interrogation techniques (Ofshe and Leo, 1997b) and vulnerable personality traits to explain why innocent people confess (Gudjonsson, 2003). I will discuss both of these in more depth below. However, there are three sequential errors that lead to a false confession: elsewhere, I have called these the misclassification error, the coercion error, and the contamination error (Leo and Costanzo, 2007).

The first occurs when detectives erroneously decide that an innocent person is guilty. As Davis and Leo (2006: 123–124) point out, "the path to false confession begins, as it must, when police target an innocent suspect . . . Once specific suspects are targeted, police interviews and interrogations are thereafter guided by the presumption of guilt." Whether to interrogate or not is therefore a critical decision point in the investigative process.

Absent a classification error at this stage, there will be no false confession or wrongful conviction. Put another way, if police did not erroneously interrogate innocent people, they would never elicit false confessions.

Because misclassifying innocent suspects is a necessary condition for *all* false confessions and wrongful convictions, it is both the first and the most consequential error police will make. Yet it is also one of the least studied and thus least well understood.

There are several related factors that lead police to mistakenly classify an innocent person as a guilty suspect. The first stems from poor and erroneous interrogation training. As we saw in Chapter 3, American police are taught, falsely, that they can become human lie detectors capable of distinguishing truth from deception at high rates of accuracy. Detectives are taught, for example, that subjects who avert their gaze, slouch, shift their body posture, touch their nose, adjust or clean their glasses, chew their fingernails, or stroke the back of their head are likely to be lying and thus guilty. Subjects who are guarded, uncooperative, and offer broad denials and qualified responses are also believed to be deceptive and therefore guilty. These types of behaviors and responses are merely a few examples from lengthy laundry lists of so-called nonverbal and verbal "behavior symptoms" of lying that police manuals, training materials, and trainers instruct detectives to look for when deciding whether to prejudge a suspect as guilty and subject him to an accusatorial interrogation (see, e.g., Inbau, Reid, Buckley, and Jayne, 2001). Although police trainers usually mention that no single nonverbal or verbal behavior is, by itself, indicative of lying or truth-telling, they nevertheless teach detectives that they can reliably infer whether a subject is deceptive if they know how to interpret his body language, mannerisms, gestures, and style of speech. In the absence of any supporting evidence, some police trainers boast of extraordinarily high accuracy rates: the Chicago-based firm Reid and Associates, for example, claims that detectives can learn to accurately discriminate truth and deception 85 percent of the time (Kassin and Gudjonsson, 2004), though this rate seems to be represented in their training seminars as 100 percent (Davis and Leo, 2006).

The deeply ingrained police belief that interrogators can be trained to be highly accurate human lie detectors is both wrong and dangerous. It is wrong because it is based on inaccurate speculation that is explicitly contradicted by the findings of virtually all the published scientific research on this topic (Vrij, 2000; DePaulo, Lindsay, Malone, Muhlenbruck, and Cooper, 2003). Social scientific studies have repeatedly demonstrated across a variety of contexts that people are poor human lie detectors and thus highly prone to error in their judgments about whether an individual is lying or telling the truth. Most people get it right at rates that are no better than chance (i.e., 50 percent) or the flip of a coin (Bond and DePaulo, 2006). Social scientific studies have also shown that even professionals who make these judgments on a regular basis—such as detectives, polygraph examiners, customs inspectors, judges and psychiatrists—(Ekman and O'Sullivan, 1991)—typically cannot distinguish truth-tellers from liars at levels significantly greater than chance. Even specific studies of police interrogators have found that they cannot reliably distinguish between truthful and false denials of guilt at levels greater than chance; indeed, they routinely make erroneous judgments (Kassin and Fong, 1999; Hartwig et al., 2004; Vrij, 2004). The method of behavior analysis taught by Reid and Associates has been found empirically to actually lower judgment accuracy, leading Kassin and Fong (1999: 512) to conclude that "the Reid technique may not be effective—and, indeed, may be counterproductive—as a method of distinguishing truth and deception." According to Kassin and Gudjonsson (2004), police detectives and other professional lie catchers are accurate approximately 45 to 60 percent of the time.

The reasons police interrogators get it wrong so often are not hard to understand. As we saw in Chapter 3, there is no human behavior or physiological response that is unique to deception, and therefore no tell-tale behavioral signs of deception or truth telling (Lykken, 1998). The same behaviors, mannerisms, gestures, and attitudes that police trainers believe are the deceptive reactions of the guilty may just as easily be the truthful reactions of the innocent. As Kassin and Fong (1999: 501) note, "part of the problem is that people who stand falsely accused of lying often exhibit patterns of anxiety and behavior that are indistinguishable from those who are really lying." Police detectives acting as human lie detectors are therefore relying on cues that are simply not diagnostic of human deception (Vrij, Mann, and Fisher, 2006). Instead, the manuals are replete with false and misleading claims—often presented as uncontested fact—about the supposed behavioral indicia of truth-telling and deception. At least one prominent police trainer, Reid and Associates President Joseph Buckley, continues to insist "we don't interrogate innocent people." (Kassin and Gudjonsson, 2004: 36).

This police-generated mythology of the interrogator as human lie detector is not only wrong but also dangerous for the obvious reason that it can easily lead a detective to make an erroneous judgment about an innocent suspect's guilt based on little or nothing more than his body language and then mistakenly subject him to an accusatorial interrogation that can lead to a false confession. This occurred in both of the persuaded false confessions mentioned earlier. Escondido, California police decided that Michael Crowe was lying (and thus guilty of murdering his sister Stephanie) in large part because they believed he initially seemed "curiously unemotional" and thus, unlike other members of his family, wasn't grieving his sisters' death normally (White, 2001a: 172). And McHenry County Sheriff's deputies decided that Gary Gauger was lying to them and thus guilty of brutally slaying both of his parents because of what they perceived to be his unemotional response to the bloody murders (Lopez, 2002). The Crowe and Gauger cases are not exceptional: the social science research literature is replete with case examples of innocent suspects who were coercively interrogated (and ultimately confessed falsely) only after they were misclassified as guilty because detectives misinterpreted their body language and demeanor and thereafter erroneously presumed their guilt (Leo and Ofshe, 1998a; Drizin and Leo, 2004).

The human lie detector mythology is dangerous not only because it leads police to mistakenly classify the innocent as guilty on the flimsiest of criteria, but also because it significantly increases detectives' *confidence* in the accuracy of their erroneous judgments (Kassin and Fong, 1999; Meissner and Kassin, 2002, 2004). Misplaced confidence in one's erroneous judgments is never a good thing, but that is especially true in investigative police work because the stakes—an innocent person's freedom and reputation, the escape of the guilty and their ability to commit additional crimes—can be so high. Erroneous prejudgments of deception lead to what Meissner and Kassin (2002) have called the *investigator response bias* (i.e., the tendency to presume a suspect's guilt with near or complete certainty). The overconfident police detective who mistakenly decides an innocent person is a guilty suspect will be far less likely to investigate new or existing leads, evidence, or theories of the case that point to other possible suspects. As Kassin and colleagues have demonstrated, erroneous but confidently held prejudgments of deception also increase the likelihood that the investigators will subject the innocent suspect to an accusatorial interrogation in which they seek to elicit information and evidence that confirms their prejudgments of guilt and discount information and evidence that does not (Meissner and Kassin, 2002, 2004; Kassin, Goldstein, and Savitsky, 2003).

The findings of Kassin and his colleagues' are consistent with my own field observations. In the more than 2,000 interrogations I have studied, I have rarely encountered interrogators who remember most of the specifics from the laundry lists of supposed nonverbal and verbal indicators of deception taught by interrogation training firms such as Reid and Associates. Rather, detectives tend to confidently believe that they can reliably infer whether a subject is lying or telling the truth based on their own intuitive analysis of his body language and demeanor. They sometimes refer to their superior human lie detection skills as stemming from a "sixth sense" common to police detectives (Leo, 1996c). The unfortunate effect is that interrogators will sometimes treat their hunch (or "gut") as somehow constituting direct evidence of the suspect's guilt and then confidently move into an aggressive interrogation. In my analysis of disputed confession cases, I have found that interrogators are often more certain in their belief in a suspect's guilt than the objective evidence warrants and tenaciously unwilling to consider the possibility that their intuition or behavioral analysis is wrong. These tendencies may be reinforced by an occupational culture that teaches police to be suspicious generally and does not reward them for admitting mistakes or expressing doubts in their judgments (Skolnick, 1966; Simon, 1991).

Apart from their training, experience and job culture, police detectives are—just like everyone else—subject to normal human decision-making biases and errors that cause people to believe things that are not true (Gilovich, 1991). These decision-making biases include the tendency to attribute more meaning to random events than is warranted, to base conclusions on incomplete or unrepresentative information, to interpret ambiguous evidence to fit one's preconceptions, and to seek out information that confirms one's preexisting beliefs while discounting or disregarding information that does not. All of these normal human decision-making biases are not only amply present in police work, but also compounded by the adversarial nature of American criminal investigation (Findley and Scott, 2006).

The Second Mistake: The Coercion Error

COERCIVE INTERROGATION

Once detectives misclassify an innocent person as a guilty suspect, they will often subject him to an accusatorial interrogation. This is because getting a confession becomes particularly important when there is no other evidence against the suspect, and typically no credible evidence exists against an innocent but misclassified suspect. Thus detectives typically need a confession to successfully build a case. By contrast, when police correctly classify and investigate the guilty, there is often other case evidence and so getting a confession may be less important. Interrogation and confession-taking also become especially important forms of evidence-gathering in high-profile cases where there is great pressure on police detectives to solve the crime and no other source of potential evidence to be discovered (Gross, 1996). Hence, the vast majority of documented false confession cases occur in homicides and high-profile cases (Drizin and Leo, 2004).

Once interrogation commences, the primary cause of police-induced false confession is psychologically coercive police methods (Ofshe and Leo, 1997b). By psychological coercion, I mean either one of two things: police use of interrogation techniques that are regarded as inherently coercive in psychology and law; or police use of interrogation techniques that, cumulatively, cause a suspect to perceive that he has no choice but to comply with the interrogators' demands. Usually these amount to the same thing. Psychologically coercive interrogation techniques include some examples of the old third degree, such as deprivations (e.g., of food, sleep, water, or access to bathroom facilities), incommunicado interrogation, and inducing extreme exhaustion and fatigue. In the modern era, however, these techniques are rare. Instead, when today's police interrogators employ psychologically coercive techniques, it usually consists of (implicit or express) promises of leniency and threats of harsher treatment. As Ofshe and Leo (1997b: 1115) have written, "the modern equivalent to the rubber hose is the indirect threat communicated through pragmatic implication." As we saw in Chapter 4, threats and promises can take a variety of forms, and they are usually repeated, developed, and elaborated over the course of the interrogation. The vast majority of documented false confessions in the post-*Miranda* era either have been directly caused by or involved promises or threats (Leo and Ofshe, 1998a; Drizin and Leo, 2004).

The second form of psychological coercion—causing a suspect to perceive that he has no choice but to comply with the wishes of the interrogator—is not specific to any one technique but may be the cumulative result of the interrogation methods as a whole. If one understands the psychological structure and logic of contemporary interrogation, it is not difficult to see how it can produce this effect. As we have seen, the custodial environment and physical confinement are intended to isolate and disempower the suspect. Interrogation is designed to be stressful and unpleasant, and it becomes more stressful and unpleasant the more intensely it proceeds and the longer it lasts. Interrogation techniques are meant to cause him to perceive that his guilt has been established beyond any conceivable doubt, that no one will believe his claims to innocence, and that by continuing to deny the detectives' accusations he will only make his situation (and the ultimate outcome of the case against him) much worse. The suspect may perceive that he has no choice but to comply with the detectives' wishes because he is fatigued, worn down, or simply sees no other way to escape an intolerably stressful experience. Some suspects come to believe that the only way they will be able to leave is if they do what the detectives say. Others comply because they are led to believe that it is the only way to avoid a feared outcome (e.g., homosexual rape in prison). When a suspect perceives that he has no choice but to comply, his resulting compliance and confession are, by definition, involuntary and the product of coercion (Ofshe and Leo, 1997b).

VULNERABLE SUSPECTS

Even though psychological coercion is the primary cause of police-induced false confessions, individuals differ in their ability to withstand interrogation pressure and thus in their susceptibility to making false confessions (Gudjonsson, 2003). All other things being equal, those who are highly suggestible or compliant are more likely to falsely confess. Individuals who are highly suggestible tend to have poor memories, high levels of anxiety, low self-esteem, and low assertiveness—personality factors that also make them more vulnerable to the pressures of interrogation and thus likely to falsely confess (Kassin and Gudjonsson, 2004). Interrogative suggestibility tends to be heightened by sleep deprivation, fatigue, and drug or alcohol withdrawal (Blagrove, 1996; Harrison and Horne, 2000). Individuals who are highly compliant tend to be conflict avoidant, acquiescent, and eager to please others, especially authority figures (Gudjonsson, 2003).

But highly suggestible or compliant individuals are not the only ones who are unusually vulnerable to the pressures of police interrogation. So are the mentally retarded or cognitively impaired, juveniles, and the mentally ill. Mental retardation is, of course, a cognitive disability that limits a person's ability to learn, process, and understand information. Psychologists typically measure a person's cognitive disability through IQ or other intelligence tests. The standard for mental retardation is an IQ of 70 or below. There are four levels of mental retardation: mild, moderate, severe, and profound. The vast majority of the mentally retarded (close to 90 percent) fall into the mild range (Cloud, Shepherd, Barkhoff, and Shur, 2002). Because mental retardation may not always be obvious, it can be easy to overestimate a person's intellectual capacity.

Mentally retarded individuals are more likely to confess falsely for a variety of reasons (Perske, 1991; Conley, Luckasson, and Bouthilet, 1992; Cloud et al., 2002). First, because of their subnormal intellectual functioning—low intelligence, short attention span, poor memory, and poor conceptual and communication skills—they are simple-minded, slow-thinking, and easily confused. They do not always understand statements made to them or the implications of their answers. They often lack the ability to think in a causal way about the consequences of their actions. Their limited intellectual intelligence translates into a limited social intelligence as well: they do not always fully comprehend the context or complexity of certain social interactions or situations, particularly adversarial ones, including a police interrogation. They are not, for example, likely to understand that the police detective who appears to be friendly is really their adversary, or to grasp the long-term consequences of making an incriminating statement. They are thus highly suggestible and easy to manipulate. They also lack self-confidence, possess poor problem-solving abilities, and have tendencies to mask or disguise their cognitive deficits and to look to others—particularly authority figures—for the appropriate cues to behavior.

For all of these reasons, the mentally retarded are highly susceptible to leading, misleading, and erroneous information. It is therefore easy to get them to agree with and repeat back false or misleading statements, even incriminating ones.

Second, as many researchers have noted, the mentally retarded are eager to please. They tend to have a high need for approval and thus are prone to being acquiescent (Finlay and Lyons, 2002). They have adapted to their cognitive disability by learning to submit to and comply with the demands of others, especially authority figures (Ellis and Luckasson, 1985; Gudjonsson, Rutter, and Pearse, 1993). Because of their desire to please, they are easily influenced and led to comply in situations of conflict. Some observers refer to this as "biased responding": the mentally retarded answer affirmatively when they perceive a response to be desirable and negatively when they perceive it to be undesirable. They will literally tell the person who is questioning them what they believe he or she wants to hear. A related trait is the "cheating to lose" syndrome: the mentally retarded eagerly assume blame or knowingly provide incorrect answers in order to please, curry favor with, or seek the approval of an authority figure. It is not difficult to see how their compliance and submissiveness, especially with figures of authority, can lead the mentally retarded to make false confessions during police interrogations.

Third, because of their cognitive disabilities and learned coping behaviors, the mentally retarded are easily overwhelmed by stress. They simply lack the psychological resources to withstand the same level of pressure, distress, and anxiety as mentally normal individuals (Ellis and Luckasson, 1985; Gudjonsson et al., 1993). As a result, they tend to avoid conflict. They may experience even ordinary levels of stress—far below that felt in an accusatorial police interrogation—as overwhelming. They are therefore less likely to resist the pressures of confrontational police questioning and more likely to comply with the demands of their accusers, even if this means knowingly making a false confession. The point at which they are willing to falsely tell a detective what he wants to hear in order to escape an aversive interrogation is often far lower than for a mentally normal individual, especially if the interrogation is prolonged. There have been numerous documented cases of false confessions from the mentally retarded in recent years (see, e.g., Drizin and Leo, 2004).

Youth is also a significant risk factor for police-induced false confessions (Drizin and Colgan, 2004; Owen-Kostelnik, Reppucci, and Meyer, 2006). Many of the developmental traits that characterize the mentally retarded may also characterize young children and adolescents. Many juveniles too are highly compliant. They tend to be immature, naively trusting of authority, acquiescent, and eager to please adult figures. They are thus predisposed to be submissive when questioned by police. Juveniles also tend to be highly suggestible. Like the mentally retarded, they are easily pressured, manipulated, or persuaded to make false statements, including incriminating ones. Youth (especially young children) also lack the cognitive capacity and judgment to fully understand the nature or gravity of an interrogation or the long-term consequences of their responses to police questions. Like the mentally retarded, juveniles also have limited language skills, memory, attention span, and information-processing abilities compared to normal adults. Juveniles also are less capable of withstanding interpersonal stress and thus more likely to perceive aversive interrogation as intolerable. All of these traits explain why they are more vulnerable to coercive interrogation and more susceptible to making false confessions.

Finally, people with mental illness (e.g., psychosis) are also disproportionately likely to confess falsely (Redlich, 2004), especially in response to police pressure. The mentally ill possess any number of psychiatric symptoms that make them more likely to agree with, suggest, or confabulate false and misleading information to detectives during interrogations. These symptoms include faulty reality monitoring, distorted perceptions and beliefs, an inability to distinguish fact from fantasy, proneness to feelings of guilt, heightened anxiety, mood disturbances, and a lack of self control (Gudjonsson, 2003; Kassin and Gudjonsson, 2004). In addition, the mentally ill may suffer from deficits in executive functioning, attention, and memory; become easily confused; and lack social skills such as assertiveness (Redlich, 2004). These traits also increase the risk of falsely confessing. While the mentally ill are likely to make voluntary false confessions, they may also be easily coerced into making compliant ones. As Salas (2004: 264, 274) points out: "Mental illness makes people suggestible and susceptible to the slightest form of pressure; coercion can take place much more easily, and in situations that a 'normal' person might not find coercive." As a result, "the mentally ill are especially vulnerable either to giving false confessions or to misunderstanding the context of their confessions, thus making statements against their own best interests that an average criminal suspect would not make."

It is important to emphasize, however, that police induce most false confessions from mentally normal adults (and as the result of psychologically coercive interrogation methods).

The Third Mistake: The Contamination Error

As we saw in Chapter 5, a confession includes a postadmission narrative that police usually direct and sometimes even script. The detective's goal is to elicit a persuasive account that successfully incriminates the suspect. But by pressuring an innocent suspect who has already said "I did it" to accept a particular account and suggesting crime facts to him, detectives, in effect, contaminate the suspect's narrative and thus help create the false confession. A detailed postadmission narrative is what makes a confession—even ones later proven to be indisputably false—appear to be such an authentic and persuasive piece of evidence. This is because, as we saw in Chapter 5, the presence of detailed crime knowledge gives the suspect's narrative verisimilitude and the appearance of corroboration. Judges and juries thus find such confessions compelling (Leo et al., 2006), especially if the details are perceived as vivid, accurate, and unique (Kassin, 2006).

If the entire interrogation is audiotaped or videotaped, then it may be possible to trace how and when the interrogator implied or suggested the correct answers for the suspect to incorporate into his postadmission narrative. If, however, the entire interrogation is not recorded—and the vast majority of documented false confession cases are not—then there may be no way to prove that the interrogator contaminated the narrative. Instead, a "swearing contest" is likely to ensue, in which the interrogator claims the suspect provided details known only to the perpetrator and the suspect claims that the police fed him details that he regurgitated back to them. And, as noted earlier, police almost always win the swearing contest (Kamisar, 1980), often claiming that the interrogator simply asked the suspect to tell the truth and that he finally did. The contamination of the postadmission narrative is thus the third mistake in the trilogy of police errors that, cumulatively, lead to the elicitation and construction of a suspect's false confession.

Conclusion

In the last quarter of a century, an extensive and sophisticated research literature has emerged on the psychological processes of interrogation that lead to false confessions (see, e.g., Ofshe and Leo, 1997b; Leo, 2001b; Davis and O'Donahue, 2003; Kassin and Gudjonsson, 2004; Costanzo and Leo, 2007). Yet the *myth of psychological interrogation* persists. Most people continue to view false confessions as irrational and self-destructive, and thus cannot understand why an innocent person would make one, especially to a serious crime. Without an understanding of the coercive power of psychological interrogation methods, most people fall prey to what psychologists have called "fundamental attribution error" (Ross, 1977) or "correspondence bias" (Gilbert and Malone, 1995): the tendency to discount situational influences on behavior and assume that behavior is fundamentally voluntary, even in coercive environments. The proclivity to view false confessions as nonexistent and nonsensical prevents both criminal justice officials and lay people from seeing how interrogation methods can manipulate a suspect to view the act of confessing falsely as his best available option (Ofshe and Leo, 1997b).

Common to both compliant and persuaded false confessions are the interrogation techniques that induce them: isolation, accusation, confrontation, attacks on denials, false-evidence ploys, pressure, repetition, time-limited offers, lengthy questioning, and a range of inducements. These techniques and others cause the innocent suspect to become distressed, confused, fearful, distraught, and overwhelmed. They also cause him to lose confidence in his ability to resist the interrogators' accusations and sometimes even in the reliability of his memory. Whether compliant or persuaded, innocent people confess falsely when the interrogation process has reduced them to a state of desperation and they see the act of confessing as their only escape (Ofshe and Leo, 1997b).

Although isolation, accusation, and false-evidence ploys are the primary techniques through which investigators break down a suspect's resistance, they are rarely enough, by themselves, to elicit false confessions. Usually some form of psychological coercion—typically inducements that communicate a promise of benefit or a threat of harm—is necessary (Ofshe and Leo, 1997b). In compliant false confessions, the coercive inducement is usually what drives the interrogation forward to confession. In persuaded false confessions, it is the successful attack on the suspect's confidence in the reliability of his memory, a process that is accelerated when investigators also use coercive inducements. Individual vulnerabilities (e.g., suggestibility, compliance, youth, low IQ) also increase the risk of a false confession. But the fact that police have elicited a confession from an innocent person does not mean that he will always be prosecuted, convicted, or incarcerated. To fully understand the false confession problem in the American criminal justice system, we must also look at its institutional consequences. It is to that topic that we turn next.

CHAPTER 7

Miscarriages of Justice

Invariably, the confession—whether a signed document or an oral admission—has been displayed as the most useful single piece of evidence any prosecutor or judge could produce, a talisman capable of magically dispelling any public doubts about the guilt of the accused, and also of eradicating any private misgivings held by the authorities responsible for arrest and punishment.

—Selwyn Raab (1967)

Convicting the wrong person is one of the worst professional errors you can make—like a physician amputating the wrong arm.

—Richard Ofshe (1995)

Any plausible guess at the total number of miscarriages of justice in America in the last fifteen years must be in the thousands, perhaps tens of thousands.

—Gross, Jacoby, Matheson, Montgomery, and Patil (2005)

The study of wrongful convictions has a long history in America. For more than eight decades, writers—mostly lawyers, journalists, and activists—have documented numerous convictions of the innocent and described their causes and consequences (Borchard, 1932; Radin, 1964; Scheck, Neufeld, and Dwyer, 2000). Yet only recently, after many years of neglect, has a critical mass of social scientists emerged to research the problem (Westervelt and Humphrey, 2001; Forst, 2004; Leo, 2005). This heightened scholarly interest is undoubtedly related to technological and political developments. With the advent of DNA technology and its application to criminal cases, numerous prisoners have been exonerated in the past decade after many years of unjust incarceration, sometimes on death row

(Scheck et al., 2000). DNA testing has transformed our understanding and consciousness of the fallibility of human judgment in the criminal justice system by demonstrating with certainty that errors have been committed repeatedly. In the past decade, there have been more newspaper stories, magazine articles, and television documentaries on the plight of the wrong-fully convicted than ever before (Warden, 2003b). As a result, there is greater recognition across the political spectrum that the wrongful convic-tion of the innocent is a real and ongoing problem.

The study of miscarriages of justice in America began with Edwin Bor-chard's pioneering book, *Convicting the Innocent* (1932). Challenging the con-ventional wisdom that innocent people are never convicted in the United States, Borchard detailed sixty-five cases in which innocent individuals were wrongfully prosecuted, convicted, and incarcerated. Borchard shifted the research question from *whether* innocent individuals are wrongfully convicted to *why* and *what can be done* about it. Borchard identified a number of causes of wrongful conviction—for example, eyewitness misiden-tification, perjured testimony, and police and prosecutorial misconduct—as well as policy solutions to the problem. Subsequent empirical studies have elaborated on the multiple causes of wrongful conviction first identified by Borchard (Frank and Frank, 1957; Radin, 1964; Bedau and Radelet, 1987). In all of these studies, false confessions have featured prominently as one of the leading causes. To a large extent, Borchard's pioneering study set the template that empirical studies of miscarriages of justice would follow for many years to come. Borchard's book was primarily descriptive rather than analytical, however.

Until the late 1980s, there was no systematic, social-scientific study of the causes, patterns, and consequences of miscarriages of justice in America. This changed with Hugo Bedau and Michael Radelet's (1987) landmark study, "Miscarriage of Justice in Potentially Capital Cases," published in the *Stanford Law Review.* Identifying 350 wrongful convictions in potentially capital cases in America from 1900 to 1987, Bedau and Radelet analyzed the causes of these errors, the reasons they were discovered, and the number of innocents who had been executed. Significantly, Bedau and Radelet found that false confessions played a causal role in 49 of the 350 miscarriages of justice, or approximately 14 percent.

Bedau and Radelet's article contributed the largest and most compelling data set on wrongful convictions. That at least 350 people have been wrong-fully convicted of potentially capital crimes in the twentieth century is highly disturbing, if not downright horrifying. Approximately 90 percent of them were officially declared innocent after their convictions. Thus, even if one disputes Bedau and Radelet's conclusion in any particular case, it would be difficult to meaningfully dispute the larger pattern of their findings.

Following Bedau and Radelet's influential article, the 1990s were a period of renewed study of miscarriages of justice. Lawyers and scholars published a number of books (Yant, 1991; Connery, 1996; Walker and Starmer, 1999) and articles on the topic. While most were in the Borchard tradition of case description and policy prescription (Fisher, 1996; Parloff, 1996; Protess and Warden, 1998; Humes, 1999), they called attention to old issues in new ways (or at least with newer cases) and laid the groundwork for the biggest and potentially most important development yet in the study of miscarriages of justice—the advent of DNA testing and its application to criminal investigation.

DNA testing has been particularly important in postconviction cases in which a defendant had long claimed that his conviction was erroneous and when biological evidence remained that could be used to conclusively test his claim. DNA testing has proven wrongful convictions in scores of cases, including capital cases (Scheck et al., 2000). Edward Connors, Thomas Lundregan, Neil Miller, and Tom McEwen's (1996) study was the earliest statement of the ability of DNA testing to conclusively establish the fact of wrongful convictions. They examined twenty-eight wrongful convictions in which DNA testing subsequently established the prisoner's innocence; approximately 18 percent of the convictions were attributable to false confessions.

Since publication of the Connors study, DNA testing has become increasingly sophisticated, and many other wrongfully convicted individuals have been exonerated and released from prison (www.innocenceproject.org). Barry Scheck and Peter Neufeld, co-founders of the Innocence Project at Cardozo School of Law, and others have worked on cases in which DNA testing has led to the release of wrongfully convicted prisoners. As of 2000, 62 innocent people had been exonerated by DNA evidence (Scheck et al., 2000); 15 according to Garre of those cases (or 24 percent) involved false confessions. By May of 2007, 200 wrongly convicted prisoners had been exonerated and released according to Garret (2008); 31 of these wrongful convictions (16 percent) were caused by false confessions (http://www.innocence project.org).

The advent of DNA testing and the window it opened onto the errors of the legal system has permanently altered the nature and study of miscarriages of justice in America. Most importantly, DNA testing has established factual innocence with certainty in so many postconviction cases that it has become widely accepted, in just a few short years, that wrongful convictions occur with troubling regularity in the American criminal justice system, despite our high-minded ideals and the numerous constitutional rights that are meant to safeguard the innocent. It is one thing for Bedau and Radelet (1987) to argue, based on their judgment of the totality of facts and documentary record in individual cases, that hundreds of innocent individuals have been wrongfully convicted and incarcerated; it is quite another thing for DNA testing to establish prisoners' factual innocence in case after case. More than at any time since publication of Borchard's book in 1932, the problem has been defined as not whether or how frequently miscarriages of justice occur, but why they occur so frequently and what can be done to prevent and remedy them.

In recent years, studies by Leo and Ofshe (1998a, 2001), Scheck et al. (2000), Warden (2003a), Drizin and Leo (2004), and Gross et al. (2005), as well as the ongoing database of DNA exonerations catalogued by the Innocence Project, have systematically documented and analyzed numerous wrongful convictions and false confessions. In these studies, the percentage of miscarriages of justice involving false confessions range from 14 to 60 percent. These modern studies thus establish, once again, the problem of false confessions remains a leading cause of the wrongful conviction of the innocent. As Welsh White (2001a: 185) has pointed out, "as soon as a police-induced false confession is accepted as true by the police, the risk that the false confession will lead to a wrongful conviction is substantial."

Identifying and Documenting False Confessions

Proving Confessions False

As I use the term, a false confession is a confession (the "I did it" statement plus the narrative of how and why the crime occurred) that is factually false and given by a person who is entirely innocent of the crime he stands accused of. False confessions are difficult to discover because neither the state nor any organization keeps records of them. And even if they are discovered, false confessions are notoriously hard to establish because of the difficulty proving the confessor's absolute innocence. As a result, they are sometimes characterized with different degrees of certainty. Leo and Ofshe (1998a,

2001), for example, have classified false confessions into three categories: proven, highly probable, and probable false confessions. A *proven* false confession is one that is indisputably false because at least one piece of dispositive evidence objectively establishes, beyond any doubt, that the confessor could not possibly have been the perpetrator of the crime (Leo and Ofshe, 1998a). A *highly probable* false confession is one in which "the evidence overwhelmingly indicated that the defendant's confession was false . . . [and] led to the conclusion that [the confessor's] innocence was established beyond a reasonable doubt," and a *probable* false confession is one in which "a preponderance of the evidence indicated that the person who confessed was innocent" (Leo and Ofshe, 1998a: 437).

There are only four ways in which a disputed confession can be classified as "proven" beyond any doubt to be false (Leo and Ofshe, 1998a). The first occurs when it can be objectively established that the suspect confessed to a crime that did not even happen (Leo and Ofshe, 1998a). This is what occurred, for example, in the case of Dianne Tucker, Medell Banks, and Victoria Banks, three mentally retarded defendants who were convicted by an Alabama jury of killing Ms. Banks's newborn child. After the three had served several years in prison, scientific testing determined that Ms. Banks was incapable of giving birth to a child, as she had a tubal ligation operation which prevented her from getting pregnant (Drizin and Leo, 2004).

The second way a disputed confession can be classified as "proven" false is when it can be objectively established that it would have been physically impossible for the confessor to have committed the crime (Leo and Ofshe, 1998a). For example, in three different Chicago cases—those of Mario Hayes, Miguel Castillo, and Peter Williams—jail records proved that the defendants were in jail at the times the crimes were committed (Drizin and Leo, 2004).

The third way a disputed confession can be classified as "proven" false occurs when the true perpetrator is identified and his guilt is objectively established (Leo and Ofshe, 1998a). The case of Christopher Ochoa—which is discussed later in this chapter—is a prime example. Ochoa, a former high school honor student, confessed to the rape and murder of Nancy DePriest in an Austin, Texas, Pizza Hut in 1988. He was freed in 2001 when Achim Marino, a prisoner serving three life sentences for armed robbery, came forward and admitted that he killed DePriest. Marino led authorities to the murder weapon and the bag in which he placed the money, and DNA testing matched his semen to that found at the crime scene (Drizin and Leo, 2004).

The fourth way a disputed confession can be classified as a "proven" false confession occurs when scientific evidence—in recent years, most commonly DNA evidence—dispositively establishes the confessor's innocence (Leo and Ofshe, 1998a). Michael Crowe falls into this category. Crowe, along with Joshua Treadway and Aaron Hauser, were set to stand trial for the 1998 murder of Michael's twelve-year-old sister, Stephanie, when DNA testing proved that blood found on the sweatshirt of Richard Tuite was Stephanie's. Charges against the boys were dropped and Tuite was eventually convicted of the murder (Drizin and Leo, 2004).

Only a small number of cases involving a disputed confession come with independent evidence that allows the suspect to prove his or her innocence beyond dispute, however. Actual innocence, as commentators have repeatedly pointed out, is very difficult to verify (Givelber, 1997). It is the rare disputed confession that can be proven indisputably false because doing so is akin to proving a negative. In the typical case, a crime did, in fact, occur, and it was not physically impossible for the confessor to have committed it, even if the facts suggest that that is extremely unlikely. Moreover, it is rare to find scientific evidence (or any other evidence for that matter, especially with the passage of time) that proves the confessor's innocence absolutely, even if there is considerable scientific evidence tending to show that the suspect did not commit the crime and other substantial evidence that casts doubt on his confession. Specifically, in most disputed confession cases, there is no DNA evidence available to compare with the confessor's DNA, and in many disputed confession cases DNA that could have definitively resolved the reliability of the confession was not preserved. Finally, it is the rare perpetrator who comes forward to acknowledge his guilt in order to exonerate the wrongly convicted false confessor. And on the rare occasion when a true perpetrator does come forward, his claims are rarely believed by police and prosecutors (who have a vested interest in maintaining that they arrested, prosecuted, and convicted the right person the first time around). The true perpetrator's claims are typically credited only when an overwhelming amount of independent evidence makes acknowledging the false confessor's innocence unavoidable. This too is rare.

It is thus only in a small minority of cases that the innocent defendant even has the opportunity to prove that his confession was false. The circumstances that allow him to do so are fortuitous, since he has no control over them. In the vast majority of alleged false confession cases, it is therefore impossible to completely remove any possible doubt about the confessor's innocence, even if all the credible case evidence strongly suggests that the confession is false and none of it suggests that it is true. As a result, after reviewing available case evidence, researchers often classify confessions as false on the basis of probabilistic judgments (see, e.g., Pratkanis and Aronson, 1991; Wright, 1994; Leveritt, 2002). In the absence of absolute proof of innocence, there is no other choice (see, e.g., Radelet, Bedau, and Putnam, 1992; Acker et al., 2001; Lofquist and Harmon, 2005).

Drawing on the generally accepted principle in law enforcement (as well as among social scientists and legal scholars) that valid confessions are supported by logic and evidence whereas false ones are not (see, e.g., Langbein, 1978; Spence, 1982; Ayling, 1984), scholars have also evaluated the reliability of a suspect's confession by analyzing the fit (or lack thereof) between the descriptions in his postadmission narrative and the crime facts (Ofshe and Leo, 1997a; Leo and Ofshe, 1998b). In false-confession cases, the suspect typically does not have personal knowledge of the nonpublic crime facts (unless he has learned it from other sources); cannot lead police to new, missing, or derivative crime scene evidence; cannot provide them with missing information; cannot explain seemingly anomalous or otherwise inexplicable crime facts; and his confession is not corroborated by existing objective evidence (Leo and Ofshe, 1998a; Leo, Drizin, Neufeld, Hall, and Vatner, 2006). As a result, postadmission narratives of false confessors typically contain errors, and are inconsistent with or contradicted by objective case evidence. I discuss postadmission narrative analysis as a method of analyzing the reliability of a suspect's confession in greater detail in Chapter 8.

Documenting False Confessions

Despite the inherent difficulties of identifying false confessions, researchers have documented numerous false confessions through case studies (see, e.g., Ganey, 1989; Mones, 1995; Davis, 1996; Taylor, 2002) and archival/documentary studies (Bedau and Radelet, 1987; Leo and Ofshe, 1998a, 2001; Scheck et al., 2000; Warden, 2003a; Drizin and Leo, 2004; Gross et al., 2005). So many interrogation-induced false confessions have been documented in recent years that there is no longer any dispute about their occurrence.

Since the late 1980s, six studies alone have documented approximately 250 interrogation-induced false confessions.[1] Bedau and Radelet (1987), it will be recalled, found forty-nine miscarriages of justice in capital cases caused by false confessions. Leo and Ofshe (1998a, 2001) identified sixty cases of proven, highly probable, and probable police-induced false confession in the post-*Miranda* era (i.e., after 1966). Scheck et al. (2000) reported on the first sixty-two U.S. cases of wrongful conviction established through DNA exoneration beginning in 1989; by May, 2007, the number of DNA exonerations had grown to 200 (http://www.innocenceproject.org). At least sixteen percent (31/200) of these wrongful convictions were caused by false confession (Garrett, 2008). Warden (2003a) studied the role of false confession in miscarriages of justice in homicide prosecutions in Illinois since 1970, and found that 60 percent (25/42) of those wrongfully convicted had falsely confessed. Replicating and extending Leo and Ofshe's (1998a, 2001) study, Drizin and Leo (2004) collected and analyzed a cohort of 125 proven false-confession cases in the post-*Miranda* era. Most recently, Gross et al. (2005) identified 340 official exonerations of wrongly convicted individuals from 1989 to 2003; 15 percent of the convictions had resulted from false confessions. These six studies are listed in Table 7.1.

Taken together, these six studies reveal several important aspects of the problem of false confessions in America. First, they provide abundant evidence that police-induced false confessions continue to occur regularly and "are of sufficient magnitude to demand attention," as Welsh White has put it (2001a: 154). Collectively these studies alone document approximately 250 police-induced false confessions—the majority of which have occurred within the last two decades—and corroborate much of what we already know from dozens of case studies. The problem of false confession is not limited to a small number of cases. These studies reveal that false confessions are

Table 7.1. Studies of Documented False Confessions

Author(s)/year	No. in study	No. of false confessions	% Wrongful convictions due to false confessions
Bedau and Radelet (1987)	350	49	14
Leo and Ofshe (1998a, 2001)	60	60	N/A
Warden (2003a)	42	25	60
Drizin and Leo (2004)	125	125	N/A
Gross et al. (2005)	340	51	15
Innocence Project (2007); Garrett (2008)	200	31	16

therefore not an anomaly but a systemic feature of American criminal justice, despite procedural safeguards such as *Miranda* rights and a constitutional prohibition against legally coercive interrogation techniques. Moreover, as Gross et al. (2005: 545) have noted, "false confessions have more impact on false convictions than their numbers suggest, since quite often they implicate other innocent people in addition to the confessor." Each of these cases advertises the existence of many other false confessions that will never be discovered or come to the attention of researchers or policy makers. Unless police change their procedures for selecting suspects and their interrogation practices, false confessions will continue to occur regularly.

Second, these six studies demonstrate that false confessions continue to be a leading cause of miscarriages of justice in America. In Bedau and Radelet's (1987) study, false confessions were the third leading cause of wrongful conviction. In Warden's (2003a) study they were the single leading cause. That false confessions regularly lead to wrongful convictions of the innocent is not surprising because, as I discuss in the next section of this chapter, confessions are the most damning and compelling evidence the state can bring against the accused, and criminal justice officials and lay jurors regularly fail to discriminate between true and false confessions.

Third, these studies show that police-induced false confessions appear to occur primarily in the more serious cases, especially homicides and other high-profile felonies (Gross, 1996). More than 80 percent of the 125 false confessions documented by Drizin and Leo (2004), for example, occurred in homicide cases. Gross et al. (2005) found that 80 percent of the false confessions in their sample were to murder too. In fact, false confessions may be the *single leading cause* of wrongful convictions in homicide cases. More than two-thirds of the DNA-cleared homicide cases documented by the Innocence Project were caused by false confessions (Lassiter and Ratcliff, 2004: 3). This figure is consistent with Warden's (2003a) study, which found that false confessions were the leading cause of wrongful conviction in Illinois homicides since 1970. Police-induced false confessions dominated the problem of Illinois exonerations in capital cases (Turow, 2003). As Gross (1996: 486) has pointed out, "false confessions are three to four times more common as a cause of miscarriages of justice for homicide cases than for other crimes."

There are several reasons why false confessions are a far more common cause of wrongful convictions in both capital and noncapital homicide prosecutions. As Gross (1996, 1998) has observed, police investigate homicides and other serious felonies differently than less serious cases. Police are under greater institutional pressure to solve serious and high-profile cases and therefore put more time, effort, and pressure into interrogating suspects—conducting longer and more intense interrogations—and trying to elicit confessions. Investigators are thus more likely to use psychologically coercive techniques or simply wear down a suspect. In homicides, the fact that the victim is dead and police frequently lack any eyewitnesses makes getting a confession even more important. Many homicides would go unsolved without a confession. Just as robbery cases are typically resolved by eyewitness evidence, homicides are typically resolved by confessions (Gross, 1996).

The Frequency of False Confessions and Wrongful Convictions

Despite the hundreds of documented false confessions in recent decades, we do not know the frequency at which they occur or the rate at which they lead to the wrongful conviction of the innocent. No well-founded estimates have ever been published. Nor is it presently possible for social scientists to provide one (Leo and Ofshe, 1998b). To authoritatively estimate the incidence of police-induced false confessions among all interrogations, researchers would need to identify a representative universe of cases in which police interrogated suspects, randomly sample a subset in sufficient numbers to make meaningful statistical inferences, and then determine the truth or falsity of each confession. Further, because it is not possible to reach reliable estimates of the incidence of false confessions, it is also not possible to estimate how often false confessions lead to wrongful convictions.

There are at least three reasons why it is presently not possible to devise a quantitative empirical study that would accomplish these objectives (Leo and Ofshe, 1997). First, neither the government nor any private organizations keep records or collect statistics on the number or frequency of interrogations in America. As a result, there is no way to know how often police interrogate suspects or how frequently suspects confess, whether truthfully or falsely. Lacking an organized database, each researcher has to assemble his or her own database of selected (and thus statistically unrepresentative) cases. The only way to locate true and false confession cases, absent access to police and prosecutors' case files (which is difficult, sometimes impossible, to obtain), is through public information searches. Cases that have not been discussed in prior scholarship or by the media or published in court opinions will not be known to researchers unless they learn of them through chance or happen to know the false confessors' lawyers.

Second, even if one does identify a set of disputed interrogations or false confession cases, it may be difficult or simply impossible as a practical matter to locate or obtain primary case materials such as police reports, pretrial and trial transcripts, and other relevant documents. The custodians of such materials may not be willing to cooperate with researchers, the materials may no longer exist, or they may never have existed at all. One particular problem is that most police interrogations are not electronically recorded and it therefore may be impossible to reconstruct what occurred during the interrogation or to assess the reliability of a confession if the interrogator educated the suspect about the crime facts. Without access to these types of primary case materials, researchers will not be able to determine with a reasonable degree of certainty whether a particular confession is true or false.

Third, even if an electronic recording of an interrogation exists and even if the researcher is able to assemble primary or secondary source materials, it may not be possible to determine with a sufficient degree of certainty whether a disputed confession was false because of the inherent difficulty of proving that the accused did not commit the crime. In the vast majority of alleged false-confession cases, it is therefore impossible to completely remove any possible doubts about the confessor's innocence, even if all the credible case evidence strongly suggests that the suspect's confession is false and none of it suggests that the suspect's confession is true. In other words, even with the best available evidence, it may be difficult to unequivocally determine the ground truth (i.e., what really happened) in criminal cases. Because it is not possible to reach valid or reliable estimates of the incidence of false confessions, it is also not possible to estimate how often false confessions lead to wrongful convictions.

Nevertheless, there is good reason to believe that the documented cases of interrogation-induced false confessions understate the extent of the phenomenon.[2] False confessions are rarely publicized. They are likely to go unreported by the media, unacknowledged by police and prosecutors, and unnoticed by researchers. As many have pointed out, the documented cases of interrogation-induced false confessions are therefore likely to represent only the tip of a much larger problem (Gudjonsson, 2003; Leo and Ofshe, 1998a). Indeed, recent studies suggest that interrogation-induced false confessions may be a bigger problem for the American criminal justice system than ever before (Drizin and Leo, 2004). Researchers have documented far more false confessions in recent years than in any previous time period. If there is no worse error than the wrongful conviction and incarceration of the innocent, then police-induced false confessions—especially in capital cases (White, 2003)—are one of the most serious problems in the American criminal justice system today.

The Consequences of False Confessions

The Power of Confession Evidence and the Risk of Wrongful Conviction

Confessions are the most incriminating and persuasive evidence of guilt that the state can bring against a defendant. False confessions are therefore the most incriminating and persuasive *false* evidence of guilt that the state can bring against an *innocent* defendant. Former U.S. Supreme Court Justice William Brennan's observation that "no other class of evidence is so profoundly prejudicial" (*Colorado v. Connelly*, 1986: 182) is amply supported by social science research (Miller and Boster, 1977; Kassin and Neumann, 1997; Kassin and Sukel, 1997; Leo and Ofshe, 1998a; Drizin and Leo, 2004). Confessions strongly bias the perceptions and decision-making of criminal justice officials and jurors alike because most people assume that a confession—especially a detailed one—is, by its very nature, true. Confession evidence therefore tends to define the case against a defendant, usually overriding any contradictory information or evidence of innocence (Leo and Ofshe, 1998a). If introduced against a defendant at trial, false confessions are highly likely to lead to wrongful convictions—even when they are elicited by questionable interrogation methods and are not supported by other case evidence. As Leo and Ofshe (1998: 492) have pointed out, "with near certainty, false confessions lead to unjust deprivations of liberty. Often they also result in wrongful conviction and incarceration, sometimes even execution."

A confession sets in motion a seemingly irrefutable presumption of guilt among justice officials, the media, the public, and jurors (Leo and Ofshe, 1998a). This chain of events, in effect, leads each part of the system to be stacked against the confessor; he will be treated more harshly at every stage of the investigative and trial process (Leo, 1996a). He is significantly more likely to be incarcerated prior to trial, charged, pressured to plead guilty, and convicted. Moreover, the presence of a confession creates its own set of confirmatory and cross-contaminating biases (Findley and Scott, 2006), leading both officials and jurors to interpret all other case information in the worst possible light for the defendant. For example, a weak and ambiguous eyewitness identification that might have been quickly dismissed in the absence of a confession will instead be treated as corroboration of the confession's validity (Castelle and Loftus, 2001). As the case against a false confessor moves from one stage to the next in the criminal justice system, it gathers more force and the error becomes increasingly difficult to reverse.

It all starts with the police. Once they obtain a confession, they typically close their investigation, deem the case solved, and make no effort to pursue any exculpatory evidence or other possible leads—even if the confession is internally inconsistent, contradicted by external evidence, or the result of coercive interrogation (Leo, 1996a; Ofshe and Leo, 1997b). For once they elicit a confession it serves to confirm their presumption of guilt. Even if other case evidence emerges suggesting or even demonstrating that the confession is false, police almost always continue to believe in the suspect's guilt and the accuracy of the confession (Leo and Ofshe, 1998a; Drizin and Leo, 2004).

Another reason police typically close their investigation after obtaining a confession is their poor training about the risks of psychological interrogation and police-induced false confessions (Leo and Ofshe, 1998a; Davis and O'Donahue, 2003). From their inception in the early 1940s, interrogation training manuals and programs have virtually neglected the subject of police-induced false confessions, despite considerable published research documenting their existence and effects. The widely cited Inbau and Reid manual, for example, did not discuss the problem of false confessions until its fourth edition in 2001. And despite adding a chapter on the subject then, it—like every other American interrogation manual and training program—continues to insist that the methods it advocates are not "apt to lead an innocent person to confess" (2001: 212), an erroneous assertion that is contradicted by a sizable body of empirical research (Ofshe and Leo, 1997a, b; Leo and Ofshe, 1998a; Davis and O'Donahue, 2003; Gudjonsson, 2003; Drizin and Leo, 2004; Kassin and Gudjonsson, 2004). As a result, American police remain poorly trained about the psychology of false confessions, why their methods can cause the innocent to confess, the types of cases in which false confessions are most likely to occur, and how to recognize and prevent them.

The presumption of guilt and the tendency to treat more harshly those who confess extend to prosecutors. Like police, prosecutors rarely consider the possibility that an innocent suspect has falsely confessed. Some are so skeptical of the idea of police-induced false confessions that they stubbornly refuse to admit that one occurred even after DNA evidence has unequivocally established the defendant's innocence (Kassin and Gudjonsson, 2004). Once a suspect has confessed, prosecutors tend to charge him with the highest number and types of offenses, set his bail higher (especially in serious or high-profile cases), and are far less likely to initiate or accept a plea bargain to a reduced charge (Leo and Ofshe, 1998a). The confession becomes the centerpiece of the prosecution's case.

Even defense attorneys tend to presume confessors are guilty and treat them more harshly. They often pressure confessors to accept a guilty plea to a lesser charge in order to avoid the higher sentence that will inevitably follow from a jury conviction (Nardulli, Eisenstein, and Fleming, 1988). As the California Supreme Court has noted, "the confession operates as a kind of evidentiary bombshell which shatters the defense" (*State v. Cahill*, 1993: 497). American judges also tend to presume that confessors are guilty and treat them more punitively. Conditioned to disbelieve defendants' claims of innocence or police misconduct, judges rarely suppress confessions, even highly questionable ones (Givelber, 2000).

If the defendant's case goes to trial, the jury will treat the confession as more probative of his guilt than any other type of evidence (short of a videotape of him committing the crime), especially if, as in virtually all high-profile cases, the confession receives pretrial publicity (Kassin and Sukel, 1997; Miller and Boster, 1977; Leo and Ofshe, 1998a). False confessions are thus highly likely to lead to wrongful convictions. In their study of 60 false confessions, Leo and Ofshe (1998a, 2001) found that 73 percent of the false confessors whose cases went to trial were erroneously convicted; 81 percent were convicted in Drizin and Leo's (2004) study of 125 false confessions.

These figures are remarkable. If representative, they indicate that a false confessor whose case goes to trial stands a 73 to 81 percent chance of being convicted, even though there is no reliable evidence corroborating his confession. Taken together, these studies demonstrate that a false confession is a dangerous piece of evidence to put before a judge or jury because it profoundly biases their evaluations of the case in favor of conviction—so much so that they will allow it to outweigh even strong evidence of a suspect's innocence (Leo and Ofshe, 1998a). Jurors simply do not appropriately discount false-confession evidence, even when the defendant's confession was elicited by coercive methods and the other case evidence strongly supports his innocence. False-confession evidence is thus highly, if not inherently, prejudicial to the fate of any innocent defendant in the American criminal justice system. As Welsh White (2001a: 155) has noted, "the system does not have safeguards that will prevent the jury from giving disproportionate weight to such confessions."

The high conviction rates of false confessors are even greater when we consider the number of false confessors who plead guilty rather than take their cases to trial: 12 percent did in Leo and Ofshe's (1998a, 2001) sample of 60 cases, and 11 percent did in Drizin and Leo's (2004) sample of 125 cases. Counting the false confessors in both samples whose cases were not dismissed prior to trial, more than 78 percent in the first study and more than 85 percent in the second were wrongfully convicted, either by plea bargain or trial.

The findings from these studies of aggregated false confessions cases are consistent with those from experiments and public opinion surveys. They all point to the same conclusion: that a confession is "uniquely potent" (Kassin and Neumann, 1997: 469) in its ability to bias the trier of fact in favor of the prosecution and lead to a wrongful conviction (Leo and Ofshe, 1998a). Experimenters have demonstrated that mock jurors also find confession evidence more incriminating than any other type of evidence (Miller and Boster, 1977; Kassin and Neumann, 1997). Kassin and Sukel (1997) found that confessions greatly increased the conviction rate even when mock jurors viewed them as coerced, were instructed to disregard them as inadmissible, and reported afterward that they had no influence on their verdicts. Most Americans simply accept confession evidence at face value. When false confessors subsequently retract their confessions, they are often not believed, or their retractions are perceived as further evidence of their deceptiveness and thus guilt (Ofshe and Leo, 1997a).

If a false confessor is convicted, he will almost certainly be sentenced more harshly, and the likelihood of discovering his innocence will drop precipitously. At sentencing, trial judges are conditioned to punish defendants for claiming innocence (since it costs the state the expense of a jury trial) and for failing to express remorse or apologize. And once a defendant is convicted and imprisoned, it is exceedingly rare that criminal justice officials will take seriously his claim that he confessed falsely and was wrongfully convicted. As Gudjonsson (2003) has pointed out, the criminal justice system is poor at discovering, admitting, or remedying its errors, especially after an innocent suspect has been convicted. Indeed, the system *officially* presumes his guilt after he is convicted, treats the jury's verdict with deference, and interprets any new evidence in the light most favorable to the prosecution.

Until recently, with the advent of DNA testing, virtually no one in the criminal justice system took seriously any innocent prisoner's claim that he was wrongly convicted, especially if the conviction was based on a confession to police. And most people still tend to presume the validity of convictions. One reason is that the system does not provide any regular mechanisms for reviewing the substantive basis of convictions. It is simply the prisoner's officially discredited word against that of an entire system. Absent a remarkable stroke of luck or social intervention, the wrongfully convicted false confessor will never be able to officially prove his innocence. Police-induced false confessions are thus among the most fateful of all official errors (Leo and Ofshe, 1998a).

The Myriad Harms of False Confessions

As mentioned above, virtually all false confessions result in some deprivation of the innocent suspect's liberty. Some scholars have focused only on false-confession cases leading to wrongful convictions (Fisher, 2002), but this neglects the harm the system imposes on those who are not convicted. They may still lose their freedom for extended periods of time and suffer a number of other significant harms: the stigma of criminal accusation (particularly if the person has falsely confessed to serious crimes such as murder or rape); damage to their personal and professional reputations (even if charges are dropped or the innocent defendant is eventually acquitted); loss of income, savings, a job, or career (sometimes resulting in bankruptcy); and the emotional strain of being apart from one's friends and family (which sometimes results in marital separation or divorce).

As Leo and Ofshe (1998a) have pointed out, one metric for measuring the harm suffered by false confessors is the extent of the deprivation of their liberty. The length of deprivation may vary from a brief arrest to pretrial incarceration pending trial to imprisonment for years to lifelong incarceration (or even the death penalty). In some cases, suspects are arrested and detained but never charged because the police or prosecutors realize their errors before the charging decision. In other cases, the suspect is indicted but charges are dropped prior to trial because either prosecutors eventually realize the defendant's innocence or they are forced to drop charges when a trial judge suppresses the confession as involuntary, leaving them with no evidence with which to proceed (Leo and Ofshe, 1998a; Drizin and Leo, 2004). And then there are those false-confession cases that proceed to trial, most of which result in wrongful conviction, as discussed.

Innocent false confessors who are acquitted may still end up spending many years in pretrial detention (i.e., jail) because they were unable to make bail in light of the seriousness of the crime. Those who are wrongly convicted, whether by plea bargain or trial, often spend years, if not decades, in prison. A number of innocent false confessors have been sentenced to death (e.g., Earl Washington, Joseph Giarratano, Gary Gauger, John Knapp, Rolando Cruz, Hubert Geralds, Alejandro Hernandez, Ronald Jones, David Keaton, Robert Lee Miller, Johnny Ross, Frank Lee Smith), spending many years on death row before they were exonerated, if at all (Radelet et al., 1992; Leo and Ofshe, 1998a; Scheck et al., 2000; Drizin and Leo, 2004). As we have seen, a few have almost certainly been executed (Leo and Ofshe, 1998a; Lofquist and Harmon, 2005; Prejean, 2005).

Pathways to Wrongful Conviction

Introduction

The process through which a false confession results in a wrongful conviction is far more complicated and less well understood than the processes through which police elicit and construct false confessions. For it involves multiple actors—not just police and suspects, but prosecutors, defense attorneys, judges, and juries—and thus multiple (psychological, sociological, and institutional) causes and errors. For a wrongful conviction based on a false confession to occur, (1) the police must misclassify an innocent person as a guilty suspect; (2) they must subject that individual to an interrogation that results in a false confession; (3) the prosecution must decide to file charges against the false confessor, usually despite the lack of any other evidence against him; (4) the prosecution must convince a judge that probable cause exists to believe the innocent defendant committed the crime or crimes of which he stands accused; (5) the prosecution's case against the false confessor must survive any pretrial motions by the defense for exclusion of the confession evidence; and (6) assuming that the defense does not initiate or accept a plea bargain, a jury must unanimously agree that the innocent defendant is guilty beyond any reasonable doubt. And for the wrongfully convicted false confessor to remain incarcerated, appellate courts must reject his postconviction counsel's procedural challenges to the erroneous verdict.

With so many points in the criminal process at which the case against an innocent person may become derailed, and with the need for so many criminal justice professionals to be wrong in so many of their judgments, the process that produces a wrongful conviction is anything but simple. Though we are accustomed in the age of DNA testing and exoneration to witnessing wrongfully convicted individuals walk out of prison on a regular basis, the production of a miscarriage of justice is still stunning. Wrongful convictions represent a complete failure, if not breakdown, in the procedural safeguards and discretionary decision-making of the criminal justice system. There is no outcome that the system is, in theory, more structured to avoid. It can occur only if there are multiple and conjunctural errors by numerous criminal justice officials and triers of fact, who, at every stage of the criminal process, fail to identify, understand, and reverse the errors that occurred in the earlier stages. Although the many cognitive errors (in perception, reasoning, and decision-making) and erroneous actions that lead to wrongful convictions are beyond the scope of this chapter, I want to focus on two fundamental processes that help transform a false confession into a wrongful conviction. The first is the use of what Gisli Gudjonsson (2003) has called "misleading specialized knowledge" to create the appearance that a false confession is true. The second is the more well known and related problem of "tunnel vision" and "confirmation bias" that leads criminal justice officials and jurors to ignore the possibility that the confession is false.

Misleading Specialized Knowledge

The use of misleading specialized knowledge occurs when police investigators feed the suspect unique nonpublic crime facts—facts that are not likely guessed by chance—and then insist that these facts originated with the suspect. Awareness of the facts is sometimes referred to as "guilty" or "inside" knowledge. When included in the suspects' postadmission narrative, the facts are believed to reveal that he possesses information that only the true perpetrator would know and therefore he must be guilty.

Unlike truly guilty knowledge, however, misleading specialized knowledge is pernicious because it is used so effectively to convict an innocent person. When police interrogators feed nonpublic crime facts to a false confessor and then insist that these facts originated with him, they are, in effect, fabricating evidence against him (Garrett, 2005). Misleading specialized knowledge is powerful evidence because it appears to corroborate the defendant's confession. In many of the documented wrongful convictions involving false confessions, some or all of the following pattern emerges: When the reliability of the defendant's confession is called into question, police rely on misleading specialized knowledge to persuade prosecutors that the confession must be true; prosecutors rely on misleading specialized knowledge to persuade judges and juries that the confession must be true; defense attorneys rely on misleading specialized knowledge to persuade their clients to accept plea bargains; judges and juries rely on misleading specialized knowledge to convict false confessors; and appellate courts rely on misleading specialized knowledge to uphold their convictions.

Whether intentional or not, police use of misleading specialized knowledge poses a serious problem for the American criminal justice system because its presence in an unrecorded false confession virtually guarantees that the innocent defendant will be wrongfully convicted. Whether it is due to inadvertent influence, strong institutional pressure to solve cases (especially high-profile ones), or some other combination of factors, misleading specialized knowledge appears to be present in many of the documented wrongful convictions based on police-induced false confessions. It is especially troubling that in these cases police investigators never acknowledged that they fed the false confessor the nonpublic crime facts that were used to corroborate his false confession—even when he incorporated into his confession facts that police believed to be true at the time of his interrogation but later turned out to be false.

Below I discuss two cases that illustrate how police interrogators used misleading specialized knowledge to create the appearance that an innocent defendant's false confession was reliable and thus virtually assured his wrongful conviction.

Case Studies

Earl Washington, Jr.

On June 4, 1982, Rebecca Lynn Williams, a nineteen-year-old woman, was raped and murdered at her apartment in Culpeper, Virginia. Ms. Williams was stabbed thirty-eight times by her assailant but lived long enough to tell police that a lone black man, whom she did not know, had raped her. On May 21, 1983, Fauquier County Sheriff's Investigator Terry Schrum and Deputy Denny Zeets arrested Earl Washington, a twenty-three-year-old mentally retarded farmhand and day laborer, in a nearby town for the assault of one of his neighbors, Hazel Weeks, and the burglary of a pistol from her house. During their initial two-hour questioning of Washington, Zeets and Schrum elicited a confession to the assault of Mrs. Weeks and the theft of her pistol—and to everything else that they asked him about. After a break for lunch, Zeets and Schrum continued to interrogate Washington about other, unsolved crimes, and he confessed to several, including three rapes that police later determined he could not have committed. On a hunch, based on what he described as Washington's nervous body language, Schrum interrogated Washington about the Williams murder too. Washington confessed to it as well, though only to the murder since neither Schrum nor Washington knew that Williams had been raped.

Fauquier County authorities notified the Culpeper Police of Washington's confession to the murder of Williams, and the next day, May 22, Culpeper Officer Harlan Hart and Special Agent of the Virginia State Police Curtis Wilmore interrogated Washington further about the murder and sexual assault of Williams. As with the interrogations by Fauquier County police, these interrogations were not recorded. After approximately an hour of interrogation, Wilmore wrote a statement in longhand and typed it up for Washington (who could not read well) to sign. This statement, which was written in an open-ended question-and-answer format, purported to capture what occurred during the one hour that Wilmore and Hart said they interrogated Washington, and he confessed to Williams's rape and murder.

Washington's confession contained numerous errors that should have tipped off Wilmore and Hart that he was ignorant of the crime facts. For example, Washington said that he stabbed Williams two to three times, but she had been stabbed thirty-eight times. Washington said that Williams was black—she was white. Washington described her as short, though she was 5′ 8″ tall. Washington said that she was not fat—in fact, she weighed 180 pounds. Washington said that he gained entry to her apartment by kicking the door down, but the crime scene indicated no forced entry. Washington also stated that he saw no one else in the apartment, yet two of Williams's young children were present during the attack. And Washington could not lead the interrogators to any new, missing, or derivative crime scene evidence. Following his confession, Wilmore and Hart asked Washington to take them to the scene and lead them to the murder weapon, but he could do neither.

Despite the numerous errors in Washington's postadmission narrative, Officers Hart and Wilmore insisted that his confession must be true because he provided details that only the perpetrator would know. Relying almost exclusively on his confession, the prosecutor would make the same argument at his trial.

In January 1984, the jury convicted Earl Washington of the rape and murder of Rebecca Williams in less than an hour, then sentenced him to death. Washington would spend more than ten years on Virginia's death row; he once came within nine days of being executed (Edds, 2003). In 1993, however, a DNA test indicated that the seminal material found in Williams's vagina could not have come from Washington, Williams, or her husband, either individually or collectively, and that Washington could have contributed to it only if another person with the same genetic trait had also done so (White, 2003). However, since Williams had told police she was raped and stabbed by a single assailant, this was impossible. The DNA result therefore exonerated Washington entirely. Nevertheless, outgoing Virginia Governor Douglas Wilder refused to pardon him, but in 1994 Wilder commuted his capital sentence to life in prison.

In 2000, a more sophisticated round of DNA tests demonstrated that the semen found in Williams's vagina could not have come from Washington under any circumstances. After learning this, Virginia Governor James Gilmore granted Washington an absolute pardon on October 2 (though Washington would not be released from prison until the following February). Altogether, Washington spent more than seventeen years in prison for a rape-murder he did not commit. During this time, five different appellate courts (including the United States Supreme Court) upheld his conviction eight separate times (Edds, 2003).

The Washington case is a cautionary tale. Police use of misleading specialized knowledge contributed not only to his wrongful conviction and lengthy incarceration but also to his near execution, despite overwhelming evidence of innocence. Officers Wilmore and Hart essentially fabricated the details of his confession by feeding him facts that Washington then regurgitated back to them. Wilmore and Hart's notes indicate that they educated him about the manner in which Rebecca Williams was killed, where her body was found, that it was unclothed, that she had been raped, that she was white, where the rape had occurred in her apartment, and the location of the crime overall (her apartment). As Joseph Buckley (2003: 7) has argued: "By inappropriately revealing to Earl Washington the important details of the homicide of Rebecca Williams, and the subsequent failure of the officers to develop any independent corroborative details from Earl, the police officers *created* a false confession" (emphasis added).

Perhaps most significantly, Hart and Wilmore fed Washington eight non-public crime facts that he could not have guessed by chance:

That the bedroom where the rape occurred was located in the back of the apartment;

That a shirt believed to belong to the perpetrator was found in the apartment;

That this shirt was found in the back bedroom;

That this shirt was found in or on a dresser;

That this shirt had blood on it;

That blood believed to have come from the perpetrator was found in the back bedroom;

That a radio was on during the assault; and

That the victim wore a halter top.

Hart and Wilmore insisted that these facts—and all the others in his type-written statement—originated with Washington and therefore proved the reliability of his confession and his guilt.

Washington insisted all along, however, that these details came entirely from the interrogators. "I ain't know nothing about the crime," he said. "They told me about the crime, how they want me to say this and that . . . They kept telling me they know I commit the crime in Culpeper. . . . I told them I didn't commit no crime. Then they kept telling me how the crime went" (Cornwall, Hall, Glasberg, Weinstein, and Rosenfeld, 2006: 6). Once the DNA evidence established Washington's innocence and identified the true perpetrator as convicted felon Kenneth Tinsley, it became clear that Washington had been telling the truth all along. After feeding him the facts and pressuring him to incorporate them into his confession, Hart and Wilmore had drafted Washington's written confession to make it appear that he had offered the critical details himself, making the confession seem both voluntary and reliable. Two days after the interrogation, Wilmore de-scribed in his police report that Washington "gave pertinent information about the crime that no one knew with the exception of himself." (Virginia State Police Report, 1983: 1).

Hart and Wilmore's deception did not end there, however. They also mis-represented to the prosecutor and jury that the nonpublic facts in Wash-ington's confession originated with him, without prompting or suggestion, in response to their open-ended questions. The only evidence that the prosecutor presented against Washington at his trial was his confession and the shirt left at the crime scene by the perpetrator but falsely claimed by Washington. The prosecutor emphasized that the nonpublic details in Washington's statement showed its reliability, telling the jury that "you'll also hear the defendant told [police] a number of different things that could only have been known by someone who had actually committed the offense" (Edds, 2003: 50). Washington's false and fabricated confession statement, and the illusion of its reliability, led to his wrongful conviction and death sentence.

The confession statement was also responsible for the many years Washington subsequently spent in prison while legal authorities continued to affirm his conviction and their belief in his guilt. After Washington's conviction, Wilmore and Hart also told appellate prosecutors that they had not suggested or fed nonpublic crime facts to Washington, claiming that they had been careful to avoid it. In 1984 the Virginia Supreme Court denied Washington's appeal because it mistakenly believed that Washington had provided nonpublic details, as did the Fourth Circuit Court of Appeals (*Earl Washington, Jr. v. Edward W. Murray et al.*, 1993: 1285, 1290, 1292) almost a decade later:

> The strength of the prosecution's case . . . rests in the numerous details of the crime that Washington provided to the officers as they talked with him. Our review of this evidence, as heard by the jury, indicates that petitioner knew so much about this crime that the jury could afford his confessions substantial weight . . . Washington had supplied without prompting details of the crime that were corroborated by evidence taken from the scene by the observations of those investigating Williams' apartment.

Governor Wilder denied Washington an absolute pardon in 1993, commuting his death sentence to life in prison instead because he mistakenly believed the same thing—despite the DNA evidence of Washington's innocence: "A review of the trial evidence, including the confessions of Earl Washington, Jr. reveals that he had knowledge of evidence relating to the crime it can be argued only the perpetrator would have known" (Cornwall et al., 2006: 15–16). Although Washington was pardoned in 2000 and released from prison in 2001 as a result of the DNA testing in his case, the State of Virginia never apologized to Washington or acknowledged responsibility for his wrongful conviction, incarceration and near execution. But in 2006, a federal jury found that Agent Wilmore had fabricated the confession evidence against Washington and awarded Washington $2.25 million in damages.

Christopher Ochoa

On October 24, 1988, Nancy DePriest, a twenty-year-old mother, was tied up, raped, and murdered at the Pizza Hut where she worked in Austin, Texas. Two weeks later, twenty-two-year-old Christopher Ochoa, who worked at another Pizza Hut, and his friend, eighteen-year-old Richard Danziger, ordered a beer at the Pizza Hut where DePriest had been murdered. They spoke to the security guard about the killing, asked where De-Priest's body had been found, and said they had come to drink a beer in her memory. Suspicious employees then called the police. Two days later, police picked up Ochoa, a former high school honor student with no criminal record, and Danziger for questioning.

For over two days, Austin police detectives Hector Polanco, Bruce Boardman, and Ed Balagia interrogated Ochoa, mostly off-tape. In Ochoa's recounting, the detectives yelled at, harassed, and threatened him for hours; denied his requests for an attorney; told him that he failed three separate polygraph tests; claimed that Danziger was in the next room and about to implicate him; threatened to throw the book at him if he did not cooperate; threw a chair at him and threatened him with more violence if he continued to deny their accusations; threatened to put him in a jail cell where he would be "fresh meat" (implying that he would be homosexually raped by prison inmates); and said that they would make sure he would be sent to death row and "given the needle" if he did not confess.

Over the course of the two days, Ochoa agreed to make three different statements, each more incriminating than the last, and each falsely implicating Danziger. According to Ochoa, he and Danziger had raped DePriest, then Ochoa had shot her in the head. Ochoa's confessions contained details that had not been made public, including the kind of gun used (a .22 caliber pistol) and the fact that a blue Pizza Hut apron had been stuffed into the sink to flood the restaurant, apparently to destroy evidence. Consistent with the police's theory at the time, Ochoa also stated that he had repeatedly sodomized DePriest, though it was later learned that the minute rectal tears discovered postmortem had been caused by a thermometer inserted in De-Priest's anus during the autopsy, not by sodomy. According to Ochoa, he confessed because Detective Polanco had bullied and intimidated him, threatening him with violence and the death penalty if he did not admit killing DePriest. Detective Polanco also supplied Ochoa with the details of the rape and murder by asking him leading questions, explicitly directing him what to say, showing him pictures of the autopsy and the crime scene, and starting and stopping the tape until Ochoa guessed the right answers (Ochoa, 2005: 23):

> They start tape recording it, but the problem was that any time I came to a de-
> tail in the restaurant, it was wrong, and then they would get mad. They would
> say, "Well, was this item there?" I would say, "Yeah . . ." "Then what color was
> it?" They had me guessing for the right color. They would start the tape and
> then would have to stop it 'cause I got the detail wrong. So they would start it,
> stop it, till they got the details. It took a long time.

Eventually Ochoa signed a five-page, single-spaced confession that de-scribed in great detail how he and Danziger had robbed the Pizza Hut, and tied up, raped, and murdered DePriest.

Ochoa was indicted for capital murder and Danziger for aggravated sexual assault. To avoid the death penalty—and on the advice of his attorney—Ochoa eventually pled guilty to first-degree murder. As a condition of his plea bargain, he was forced to testify against Danziger at Danziger's trial. Al-though Danziger had adamantly maintained his innocence from the begin-ning and testified at his trial that Ochoa and the detectives were lying about his involvement, the jury convicted him after less than three hours of delib-eration. The judge sentenced both he and Ochoa to life in prison. One year later, in 1991, a fellow prison inmate, who mistook Danziger for someone else, repeatedly kicked Danziger in the head with steel-toed shoes, causing Danziger to suffer permanent brain damage and leaving him in need of life-long medical care.

In 1996, however, another prison inmate, Achim Joseph Marino, began writing letters to a number of people and organizations—including the Austin Police, the Austin District Attorney's Office, the *Austin-American Statesman,* the American Civil Liberties Union and then Texas Governor George W. Bush—saying that he was the one who had raped and murdered Nancy DePriest. Marino, who was serving three life sentences for aggravated robbery, had be-come a born-again Christian in prison and now wanted to confess to his ear-lier crimes and clear Ochoa and Danziger. Almost no one believed him, how-ever, until November 2000, when DNA testing matched semen found on DePriest to Marino and excluded both Ochoa and Danziger. (Before the testing, the Austin Police Department had tried, unsuccessfully, to establish a connection between Marino and Ochoa and Danziger.) Marino's letter to the Austin Police also contained a detailed description of the crime scene and instructed police where to locate the fruits of the crime (DePriest's keys, the currency bag from Pizza Hut that had contained the money, and the handcuffs Marino had used to bind DePriest's wrists). The police found them, just as Marino had said they would, in the attic of his mother's house in El Paso, Texas. Marino also told Austin Police that they would find the gun used to kill DePriest in the possession of the El Paso Police, who had confiscated it from him after a robbery arrest; ballistics tests subsequently verified that it was the murder weapon.

In 2001, Ochoa and Danziger were officially exonerated and released from prison, after serving twelve years for crimes they did not commit. Both Ochoa and Danziger subsequently filed civil lawsuits against Austin police officials: Ochoa settled his claims for $5.3 million; Danziger settled his for over $9 million (Weinstein, 2006).

Like Earl Washington's, Ochoa's remarkably detailed confession contained numerous nonpublic crime facts that the police and prosecutors had maintained originated with him and therefore verified its reliability. These details literally convinced everyone, including Ochoa's and Danziger's defense attorneys, of their guilt and thus contributed to their wrongful convictions. When Ochoa told his defense attorney that he was innocent, the attorney responded: "There's a detailed confession, you gotta be guilty" (Ochoa, 2005: 24), and angrily insisted that he plead guilty, which Ochoa did. Years later, before the DNA testing was done, Ochoa's defense attorney said that the testing was a waste of time because "there was not a chance that Ochoa was innocent" (Findley and Scott, 2006: 332). Danziger was subsequently convicted on the basis of Ochoa's detailed confession and trial testimony against him; without them there would not have been any significant evidence to link him to the crime. Danziger's attorney, Berkeley Bettis, later stated, "I left that trial feeling the state had proved beyond a reasonable doubt that my client was guilty" (*Texas Monthly*, 2001: 97). The trial judge echoed this sentiment, "Any jury hearing [Ochoa's] testimony would have found those two guys guilty," because, he said, Ochoa's confession and testimony "contained details police said only a witness to the crime could have known" (Berlow, 2000: 2).

Because we now know that Ochoa is innocent and had not been to the crime scene the day of the offense, we can say with certainty that his interrogators had supplied the nonpublic details that he incorporated into his confession. An Austin Police Department investigation into the wrongful convictions of Ochoa and Danziger arrived at the same conclusion, noting that Ochoa's confession contained details that only the police and perpetrator would know and that Ochoa had given some details that police knew to be inaccurate but that they had corrected in his typed confession (Osborne, 2001). As in the Earl Washington and Bruce Godschalk cases, the police concocted a confession against Ochoa by coercing him into falsely confessing and then fabricated the details of his confession to make it appear self-corroborating to prosecutors, the judge, the jury, and the media. The Austin detectives also coerced Ochoa into incorporating a story line into his confession, including an elaborate description of Ochoa and Danziger's plan for the robbery, how and where they planned to meet the morning of the murder, how they entered the crime scene, and their conversation with the victim prior to assaulting her—a story line that made it appear more compelling and authentic. This coerced and fabricated story line along with the misleading specialized knowledge supplied by the detectives ultimately led to Ochoa's and Danziger's wrongful convictions and twelve-year incarceration.

Tunnel Vision and Confirmation Bias

Police-induced false confession is one of the most prominent and enduring causes of wrongful conviction, but there are others: eyewitness misidentification, perjured jailhouse "snitch" testimony, forensic fraud and error, and police and prosecutorial suppression of exculpatory evidence, for example (Leo, 2005; Christianson, 2004). The big-picture studies of wrongful convictions in the modern era typically aggregate documented cases of miscarriages of justice and then count the number and percentage of wrongful convictions attributable to each of these legal causes of error (Bedau and Radelet, 1987; Scheck et al., 2000; Gross et al., 2005).

The phenomena of tunnel vision and confirmation bias, however, cut across (and are thus present in) all of these types of legal error. Tunnel vision is the psychological process that causes an individual to focus exclusively on one possibility or outcome to the exclusion of all others (see, generally, Tavris and Aronson, 2007). In the criminal justice system, it is the tendency to "focus on a suspect, select and filter the evidence that will 'build a case' for conviction, while ignoring or suppressing evidence that points away from guilt" (Martin, 2002: 848). Confirmation bias is the psychological tendency to seek out and interpret evidence in ways that support existing beliefs, perceptions, and expectations, and to avoid or reject evidence that does not (Gilovich, 1991). Tunnel vision and confirmation bias are pervasive in the criminal justice system and present in all wrongful convictions. From a behavioral perspective, rather than a legal one, they are thus the leading cause of wrongful convictions in America and elsewhere (Martin, 2002; Findley and Scott, 2006). A closer look at tunnel vision and confirmation bias in the criminal process sheds light both on why the police interrogation process produces false confessions and on why false confessions often lead to wrongful convictions.

Tunnel vision and confirmation bias are involved in each of the multiple pathways through which police elicit and shape false confessions. The first error in the sequence of steps that leads to a false confession, as we have seen, is the misclassification of an innocent person as guilty. Police typically make this error based on gut hunches, erroneous assumptions (Ofshe and Leo, 1997a), crime-related schemas or profiles (Davis and Follette, 2002), or their flawed training in behavioral analysis that encourages them to mistakenly believe that they can become highly accurate human lie detectors (Kassin and Fong, 1999; Meissner and Kassin, 2004). Tunnel vision may have already led investigators at this point to prematurely but confidently conclude that the innocent suspect is guilty. Confirmation bias then leads investigators to seek out information and evidence that affirms this belief and to reject or discount information and evidence that does not. The processes of tunnel vision and confirmation bias at this stage are compounded by the institutional pressures on police from multiple sources (their supervisors, prosecutors, victims, the community, politicians, officials, the media, as well as their high caseloads), especially in serious and high-profile cases, to solve crimes quickly (Findley and Scott, 2006).

The subsequent interrogation process involves tunnel vision and confirmation bias by definition: Interrogators assume guilt, seek only statements and information that confirm their assumption, and not only ignore but also discourage statements (such as denials, verbalizations of innocence, and explanations) that do not. As Findley and Scott (2006: 335) point out:

> The very notion of an "interrogation," therefore, expressly embraces the foundational problems with tunnel vision—a premature conclusion of guilt, and an unwillingness to consider alternatives. In this context, however, the tunnel vision is not inadvertent, but deliberate; police are taught that this

is the way to advance their investigation. Cognitive biases are openly encouraged.

That tunnel vision and confirmation bias can and do lead to false
confessions—as well as the process through which it does so—has been repeatedly documented in aggregated case studies (Leo and Ofshe, 1998a;
Drizin and Leo, 2004), experimental studies (Kassin and Fong, 1999;
Meissner and Kassin, 2002; Kassin, Goldstein, and Savitsky, 2003), and documentary studies (Ofshe and Leo, 1997a, b) of police interrogation and false
confession.

The problems of tunnel vision and confirmation bias can also taint the
postadmission process of interrogation. Indeed, police interrogation is just
as rife with tunnel vision and confirmation bias in the postadmission phase
as it is in the preadmission phase. Detectives rarely stop to consider the possibility that they are interrogating an innocent person and that the admissions they are eliciting may be false. Joseph Buckley's remarkable assertion
"we don't interrogate innocent people" (Kassin and Gudjonsson, 2004: 36)
captures the problem of confirmation bias and tunnel vision. Once interrogators obtain an admission, they treat it as confirmation of their belief in
the suspect's guilt rather than as a hypothesis to be tested against case evidence. As a result, they usually continue to interrogate in a manipulative,
suggestive, and leading manner, and shape the confession to successfully
build a case against the suspect.

The problems of tunnel vision and confirmation bias do not end with police investigators, though. Prosecutors, defense attorneys, judges, and jurors are also subject to tunnel vision and confirmation bias, especially once
they learn that someone has written or signed a confession statement that
contains a plausible narrative of how and why the crime occurred as well
as detailed knowledge of the crime facts. Once a suspect has confessed, the
formal presumption of innocence is quickly transformed into an informal
presumption of guilt that biases the subsequent decisions of fact-finders
and overrides their analysis of exculpatory evidence (Leo and Ofshe,
1998a). In many false-confession cases, prosecutors appear to seek out
only information that is consistent with their belief in the defendant's guilt,
often ignoring, dismissing, or even suppressing contradictory or exculpatory evidence. If the defendant is exonerated, they then frequently refuse
to acknowledge his innocence or admit that any mistakes were made, even
in the most egregious cases. As commentators have noted, the tunnel vision

and confirmation bias of prosecutors stem from many sources: the institutional and political culture of their offices (Medwed, 2004), role pressures and "conviction psychology" (Fisher, 1988; Findley and Scott, 2006), and the problems of receiving one-sided and incomplete evidence from police investigators and only feedback that is consistent with their assessments of guilt (Findley and Scott, 2006). Even defense attorneys sometimes succumb to tunnel vision and confirmation bias once they learn that their client has confessed, ruling out the possibility of innocence, as the Ochoa case illustrates. Juries too allow the power of confession evidence to bias their judgments, and they tend to selectively ignore and discount evidence of innocence in false confession cases (Kassin and Sukel, 1997; Leo and Ofshe, 1998a).

In short, even when they are false, confessions appear to be such powerful evidence of guilt that they almost automatically trigger tunnel vision and confirmation bias among the criminal justice officials and jurors who must evaluate confessions, blinding them to the possibility of error.

Conclusion

There is no piece of erroneous evidence that is more likely to lead to a wrongful conviction than a false confession (Kassin and Neumann, 1997; Leo and Ofshe, 1998a). Criminal justice officials and jurors treat confessions as "the crème de la crème of prosecutorial proof" (Davies, 2006). The consequences are predictable: false confessors whose cases are not dismissed pretrial will be convicted the vast majority of the time (Leo and Ofshe, 1998a; Drizin and Leo, 2004).

Every wrongful prosecution and conviction based on a police-induced false confession represents a systemic failure. This is not a problem of "bad apples." False confessions do not occur because individual police intentionally seek to incriminate or frame the innocent. Nor do wrongful convictions occur because individual prosecutors, judges, or jurors set out to convict and incarcerate the innocent. The series of perceptions and decisions that ultimately lead to miscarriages of justice are typically based on ignorance, bias, and negligence, not malice. They occur for a combination of reasons: poor training, shoddy police work, violation of rules, tunnel vision and confirmation bias, and suppression of exculpatory evidence, to name a few. False confessions lead to miscarriages of justice when the procedural safeguards and multiple points of official discretion built into the system fail.

As Gross et al. (2005: 542) have pointed out: "One way to think of false convictions is as a species of accidents. Like many accidents, they are caused by a mix of carelessness, misconduct, and bad luck." Like accidents, wrongful convictions based on false confessions can be minimized or even prevented—if we care to face up to the systemic sources of carelessness, misconduct, and bad luck.

Minimizing or preventing police-induced false confessions and the miscarriages of justice they spawn will require more than merely changing the rules of criminal procedure. It will require greater scrutiny of the police interrogation process by outsiders, for police often fail to acknowledge the problem, attempt to understand (let alone reform) it, or even admit to their role in causing it. It will thus require greater transparency in both the preadmission and postadmission phases of interrogation. It will also require that criminal justice officials, jurors, and the public become more skeptical about the probative value of confession evidence. Confessions are among the least reliable forms of evidence because they are based on the vagaries and fallibility of human testimony, perception, and belief, and are products of a guilt-assumptive influence process that relies on pressure, manipulation, deception, and sometimes even coercion. To be considered reliable, confession evidence must be corroborated by independently supplied details of the crime or other credible case evidence (Leo et al., 2006).

The consequences of false confessions are predictable: as my own research with Richard Ofshe and Steve Drizin has demonstrated, false confessors whose cases are not dismissed pretrial will be convicted (by plea bargain or jury trial) 78 to 85 percent of the time, even though they are completely innocent (Leo and Ofshe, 1998a; Drizin and Leo, 2004). Unless criminal justice officials and policymakers try to better understand why this occurs and change the system that regularly produces these outcomes, the status quo will persist. Poorly trained, but confident, police investigators will continue to misclassify innocent persons as guilty suspects; they will continue to interrogate innocent suspects deceptively, manipulatively, and/or coercively based on an unwavering (yet mistaken) presumption of guilt; and they will continue to construct persuasive, if false, narratives of innocent suspects' culpability that are laced with misleading specialized knowledge. District attorneys will continue to prosecute innocent false confessors, whom judges and juries will continue to wrongfully convict and incarcerate. Some—like Earl Washington and Christopher Ochoa—will eventually have their erroneous convictions discovered and overturned, will be released from prison, and will recover large civil judgments that end up costing city, county, and state municipalities millions of dollars. But many other factually innocent, yet wrongly incarcerated, false confessors will never have their erroneous convictions discovered or overturned and, instead, will remain in prison while the true perpetrators are presumably free to commit other violent crimes.

It behooves criminal justice officials not only to acknowledge and better understand the role that false confessions play in creating and perpetuating miscarriages of justice, but also to introduce meaningful policy reforms that will prevent false confessions from occurring and leading to the wrongful conviction and/or incarceration of the innocent.

CHAPTER 8

Policy Directions

The most unique feature of police station questioning is its characteristic secrecy. It is secrecy which creates the risk of abuses, which by keeping the record incomplete makes the rules about coercion vague and difficult to apply, which inhibits the development of clear rules to govern police interrogation and which contributes to public distrust of the police. Secrecy is not the same as the privacy which interrogation specialists insist is necessary for effective questioning.

—Bernard Weisberg (1961)

It is not because a police officer is more dishonest than the rest of us that we should demand an objective recordation of the critical events. Rather, it is because we are entitled to assume that he is no less human—no less inclined to reconstruct and interpret past events in a light most favorable to himself—that we should not permit him to be a "judge of his own cause."

—Yale Kamisar (1980)

A legal system will do almost anything, tolerate almost anything, before it will admit the need for reform in its system of proof and trial.

—John Langbein (1978)

In this book, I have examined the evolution, structure, and practice of police interrogation in the American criminal justice system. I have argued that police interrogators act like highly partisan adversaries in order to manage the contradictions underlying interrogation in America. The guiding principle of the American adversary system is that every actor should pursue his or her own self-interest. Yet it is almost never in a person's self-interest to participate in an activity that will lead to his incrimination, prosecution, or deprivation of liberty. To solve crimes at a socially acceptable rate, however, American police need to enlist the participation of criminal suspects in their own incrimination. This is the fundamental contradiction that lies at the heart of all police interrogation in America. In the era of the third degree, American police resolved this contradiction simply by forcing suspects—through violence, duress, or fear—to participate in their own incrimination and make confessions. When the third degree became socially controversial and then legally impermissible, American police turned to manipulation, deception, and more subtle forms of psychological coercion to enlist suspects in their own incrimination and conviction.

Police interrogation as it is practiced in the American adversary system raises at least two fundamental policy problems that are not easily resolved. The first is the problem of coerced (or otherwise unfairly obtained) self-incrimination and involuntary confession. Police must necessarily apply some amount of psychological pressure, fraud, and inducement to manipulate criminal suspects to make incriminating statements that they usually do not want to give and that rarely benefit them. As David Simon has noted (1991: 199), "a criminal confession can never truly be called voluntary. With rare exception, a confession is compelled, provoked and manipulated from a suspect by a detective who has been trained in a genuinely deceitful art."

The second is the problem of unreliable fact-finding and erroneous verdicts. As we have seen, police interrogators are not neutral or impartial investigators of case facts: their goal is not to get the literal truth so much as it is to build a case against the suspect by incriminating him and constructing a persuasive narrative of his guilt that will ensure his successful prosecution and conviction. As a result, American police interrogators' pre- and postadmission interrogation techniques and strategies sometimes result in unreliable and/or false confessions, as we saw in Chapters 6 and 7.

The first reform question raised by these two problems is whether the practice of interrogation should be kept or abolished. There is no constituency that advocates abolishing interrogation outright. However, some have argued that it should not be permitted without the presence of counsel (Ogletree, 1987), that the state should be prohibited from using confession evidence at trial (Rosenberg and Rosenberg, 1989), or that the state should be able to rely only on the fruits of confessions (i.e., physical evidence and third-party testimony that the confessions led to) rather than the defendant's statements themselves (Amar, 1997).

It is hard to imagine the outright abolition of interrogation. Every criminal justice system allows state authorities to question or pressure suspected offenders to elicit information. Interrogation is a necessary and valuable investigative activity because, even in this modern age of science and technology, oral information remains the most important resource in investigating and apprehending offenders. We still need confession evidence to solve some crimes, especially serious ones such as homicides (Gross, 1996).

If interrogation is necessary and thus here to stay, the next question is: Who should do it? Although police are entrusted with the interrogation function in America, in some countries (such as Japan) prosecutors also interrogate criminal defendants (Johnson, 2002), and in others (such as France and Italy) judges and magistrates do (Slobogin, 2003b). Some American scholars have argued that interrogation should be conducted or supervised by a judicial officer (Kauper, 1932; Amar, 1997) instead of police. Another possibility would be to create a separate nonpolice agency within the criminal justice system (such as an independent branch of the judiciary) to interrogate suspects. Lloyd Weinreb (1977: 42) has suggested that we "establish the office of a magisterial investigator, or investigating magistrate, whose responsibility for investigating and preparing a case for prosecution is distinct from the work of the police."

These are reasonable ideas in the abstract, but they would require changing the structure of the adversary system as we know it and likely undermine the effectiveness of interrogation procedures. To direct judges, judicial magistrates, or an independent branch of the judiciary to interrogate suspects would be to change the role of the judiciary from umpire to partisan inquisitor; it is thus inconsistent with the division of labor and oversight in a formally adversarial system. Because an adversary system demands the separation of investigative, prosecutorial, and judicial functions, the police remain the most appropriate institution to conduct investigations and interrogations in America.

With this understanding, I argue that we should focus on policy reforms that can best achieve the American adversary system's tripartite goals of protecting individual legal rights, checking unwarranted or overreaching state power, and promoting truth-finding. I argue that policy reforms must first address the fundamental problem of accurate and complete fact-finding in the interrogation process (without which individual rights cannot be meaningfully protected and state power cannot be adequately checked). The challenge for a democratic society with an adversarial criminal justice system is to structure the rules of procedure and the restraints on police behavior such that interrogation is conducted fairly and in a way that will produce the most reliable confession evidence possible. No legal policy reform by itself is sufficient to achieve these ends, but I believe that several are necessary.

Law and Legal Reform

Law remains the primary means through which police interrogation practices and confession evidence are regulated. The law of confession evidence in America dates back to the late nineteenth century, though it draws on principles from English common-law doctrines that date back even further. Although a recitation of the American law of criminal procedure is beyond the scope of this chapter, it is important to describe the basic legal structure for regulating confession evidence to put into context and assess various policy alternatives.

Three legal doctrines in particular govern the admissibility of confession evidence: the Fourteenth Amendment due process voluntariness test; the Sixth Amendment right to counsel; and, most centrally in the modern era, the Fifth Amendment *Miranda* doctrine. These legal doctrines specify (albeit, sometimes rather vaguely) the conditions under which improper police practices may lead courts to exclude confession evidence from the defendant's trial. All three advance, to various degrees, the adversary system's underlying goals.

The Fourteenth Amendment Voluntariness Test

HISTORY AND EVOLUTION

Before the late seventeenth century, out of court confessions—even if they were the involuntary product of coercion—were admissible into evidence. In the mid-1880s, however, the Supreme Court began to evaluate the admissibility of confessions. The Court initially relied on the common-law voluntariness test, which was intended to protect against the danger of unreliable or untrustworthy confessions and thus exclude them. The original common-law voluntariness test assumed that "a criminal suspect subjected to threats or other forms of intimidation might make a false confession to save himself from further coercion" (Stephens, 1973: 17). However, the early Supreme Court cases in the late nineteenth century also conceived of the voluntariness test as a rule to protect individual freedom or autonomous decision-making from improper influences that might render a confession involuntary, thus excluding confessions that were obtained by threat or promise (Penney, 1998). Confessions were to be admitted only if they were "uninfluenced by hopes of reward or free of punishment" (*Hopt v. Utah*, 1884: 584); they were to be excluded if police interrogation deprived a suspect of his freedom of will or choice such that his statement could not be considered voluntary.

The underlying purpose of the voluntariness test, though, was never entirely clear and would continue to evolve throughout the twentieth century (White, 2001a). Initially (and arguably through at least the 1950s), the dominant rationale of the due process voluntariness test was to promote reliability in the trial process by excluding confessions that were likely to be false or untrustworthy because they were products of police coercion or improper influence (Penney, 1998). However, the idea that courts should admit into evidence only confessions that were the product of a free and independent will also began to gain ascendance in 1930s and 1940s. A third but subordinate rationale underlying the voluntariness test was the idea that confessions elicited through fundamentally unfair police methods should be excluded so as to deter offensive police behavior, regardless of whether the suspect confessed involuntarily or his statements were likely to be trustworthy. The goals of reliability, protecting free wills, and fundamental fairness correspond roughly to the three goals of the adversary system: protecting individual rights, checking state power, and promoting truth-finding.

Although courts relied on the common-law voluntariness test to adjudicate confession cases in the late nineteenth and early twentieth centuries, it was not until 1936 that the United States Supreme Court first used the Due Process Clause of the Fourteenth Amendment to regulate confessions in state cases. In *Brown v. Mississippi*, three black tenant farmers accused of murdering a white farmer were whipped, pummeled, and tortured until they provided detailed confessions. Unanimously reversing the convictions of all three defendants, the Supreme Court established the Due Process Clause as the constitutional test for assessing the admissibility of confessions in state cases. In addition to state common-law standards, trial judges would now have to apply a new federal due process standard when evaluating the admissibility of confession evidence.

From 1936 to 1964, the Supreme Court reviewed thirty-five cases in which it relied on the due process voluntariness test to regulate police interrogation practices and set standards for the admissibility of confession evidence. In some cases, the Court appeared to invoke the voluntariness test primarily to prevent the admission of untrustworthy or unreliable confession evidence in order to guard against erroneous convictions. For example, the Court relied on this rationale in *Chambers v. Florida* (1940) to exclude the confessions of four African American men who had been interrogated for a week, threatened with mob violence, and denied food and sleep. In other cases, such as *Ashcraft v. Tennessee* (1944), in which a suspect was interrogated incommunicado continuously for thirty-six hours, the Court ruled the defendant's confession involuntary on the principle that the law must protect a suspect's ability to make free choices in the face of sustained police pressure. In yet other cases during this era, the Court seemed to exclude confessions as involuntary primarily to deter oppressive and unfair police interrogation methods, not simply to guard against erroneous convictions and overborne wills. For example, in *Malinski v. New York* (1945), the Court excluded the confession of a defendant who had been stripped and kept naked for three hours before being provided a blanket, and who confessed after seven hours of intermittent and mild questioning.

During this era it was not always clear which of these three rationales the Supreme Court would rely on when evaluating a confession's voluntariness under the Fourteenth Amendment's due process test. Nevertheless, the Court did appear to designate certain police interrogation methods— including physical force, threats of harm or punishment, lengthy or incommunicado questioning, solitary confinement, denial of food or sleep, and promises of leniency—as presumptively coercive and therefore constitutionally impermissible. The Court also considered the suspect's personal characteristics (age, intelligence, education, mental stability, prior contact with law enforcement, etc.) in determining whether his confession was voluntary. The due process voluntariness test assessed whether the pressures and techniques of the interrogation, as they interacted with the suspect's personal susceptibilities, were sufficient to render his confession involuntary. There is, however, no litmus test under the Fourteenth Amendment's Due Process Clause; courts must determine a confession's voluntariness on a case-by-case basis.

The due process voluntariness test continued to evolve in the 1950s and 1960s as the Supreme Court made clear that the reliability or trustworthiness of a suspect's confession—historically the common-law justification for excluding an involuntary or coerced confession—was no longer relevant to a determination of its voluntariness. An entirely false or unreliable confession could, logically, now be considered voluntary and thus admissible into evidence against a criminal defendant. In *Rogers v. Richmond* (1961), the Court held that the test for a confession's admissibility must be whether the police interrogation methods were such "as to overbear petitioner's will to resist and bring about confessions not freely self-determined—a question to be answered with complete disregard of whether or not petitioner in fact spoke the truth" (*Rogers v. Richmond*, 1961: 543–544). The Supreme Court's other confession cases during this era similarly focused on whether the interrogation exerted sufficient pressure on a suspect to overbear his independent free will or capacity for autonomous choice. While the Court's due process cases also displayed a concern for deterring abusive or improper police interrogation practices, the overbearing-of-the-will standard now became the primary consideration of the modern Fourteenth Amendment's due process voluntariness test.

If there was any doubt about the role of a confession's reliability in the determination of its admissibility under the due process voluntariness test, the Supreme Court appeared to put it to rest in *Colorado v. Connelly* in 1986. In this case, a mentally ill individual approached a police officer and gave an unsolicited confession to murder because he believed he was receiving "command hallucinations" from God. The Supreme Court held that the defendant's confession was voluntary under the Fourteenth Amendment's due process test because the police did not use any coercive or overreaching methods to elicit it. The Court said that the reliability of the defendant's statement should have no role in the determination of its voluntariness and thus admissibility. A confession's lack of trustworthiness, it argued, would not tend to establish that it is involuntary. Instead, the Court (*Colorado v. Connelly*, 1986: 167) declared that a statement given by someone in the suspect's condition "might be proved to be quite unreliable, but this is a matter to be governed by the evidentiary laws of the forum . . . not by the Due Process Clause of the Fourteenth Amendment."

In sum, the contemporary Fourteenth Amendment's due process voluntariness test is concerned almost exclusively with protecting a suspect's independent free will and capacity for autonomous decision-making from coercive or otherwise improper police influence during interrogation. Trial judges are to evaluate, in their totality, both the police interrogation methods and the suspect's vulnerabilities on a case-by-case basis. If the trial judge determines that the interrogation pressures overbore the defendant's free will, then the confession will be excluded as involuntary under the Fourteenth Amendment and cannot be used against the defendant in future trial proceedings. Otherwise, the Fourteenth Amendment does not prohibit the state from using confession evidence against the accused at trial.

IMPACT

The Fourteenth Amendment's due process test has never been studied empirically. Its precise impact on police interrogation practices or on confession and conviction rates is therefore unknown. However, there is a scholarly consensus that the historical impact of the due process cases during the early to middle twentieth century was, along with the Wickersham Commission report and the movement for police professionalization, to contribute significantly to the decline and disappearance of the third degree (Leo, 1992). Beginning with *Brown v. Mississippi* in 1936, the Supreme Court's Fourteenth Amendment due process cases appear to have exercised a civilizing effect on American police by setting standards for what constituted impermissibly coercive or offensive interrogation practices in both state and federal cases. To some extent, the Court's due process cases from 1936 to 1964 helped eliminate the third degree as a mainstream or acceptable interrogation method.

One reason the contemporary impact of the Fourteenth Amendment's due process test has not been studied empirically is that since 1966 the Supreme Court has addressed the question of whether a confession was voluntary in only a few cases. As we will see below, the due process test has largely been displaced by the Fifth Amendment's *Miranda* warning and waiver test. Although both doctrines in theory are supposed to be applied independently of one another, trial courts in practice tend to assume that confessions are voluntary under the Fourteenth Amendment's due process test if the police appear to have elicited a legally sufficient *Miranda* waiver (White, 2001a). The due process voluntariness test thus appears to be largely meaningless today except in extreme cases. Put differently, American trial courts rarely find that police interrogation methods were sufficient to overbear a suspect's free will and render a confession involuntary and thus inadmissible.

As many scholars have recognized, the Fourteenth Amendment's voluntariness test is both conceptually and practically flawed (Kamisar, 1963; Schulhofer, 1981; Penney, 1998). Perhaps the central problem is the insoluble ambiguity, if not indeterminacy, of the concept of voluntariness. The voluntariness test is ultimately a metaphysical inquiry with no clear resolution because there is no way to get inside the head of a suspect and objectively discern whether his will or capacity for free choice was overborne by police pressures. The voluntariness test therefore invites judges "to give weight to their subjective preferences when performing the elusive task of balancing" (Schulhofer, 1981: 870). Yale Kamisar (1963) made this point many years ago when he argued that voluntariness was a fiction that allows judges to vilify interrogation techniques they do not approve of and beautify those that they do. The voluntariness test thus provides little guidance to trial judges in individual cases. The problem is compounded by the case-by-case nature of the test, which invites inconsistent application. For the same reasons, the voluntariness test also provides little guidance to police detectives about the boundary between permissible and impermissible interrogation techniques. It remains an unsatisfactory method for resolving disputed confessions. Even the Supreme Court has acknowledged that voluntariness is conceptually confusing and practically unhelpful (see *Miller v. Fenton*, 1985). It is therefore not surprising that the Fourteenth Amendment's voluntariness test has largely been displaced by other legal standards.

The Sixth Amendment Right to Counsel

Americans have enjoyed a constitutional trial right to counsel in federal cases since the ratification of the Bill of Rights in 1791. This right was incorporated into state constitutions through the Fourteenth Amendment in capital offenses in 1932. It was subsequently modified in 1963 to include all felony offenses. The underlying rationale of the Sixth Amendment is to protect a suspect's right to a fair trial. In 1964, however, the Supreme Court in *Massiah v. United States* held that a suspect was entitled to the protections of the Sixth Amendment upon indictment. The Supreme Court subsequently held that a suspect has a right to legal representation as soon as judicial proceedings have been initiated against him, whether by formal charge, preliminary hearing, indictment, information, or arraignment. At that point, police thus cannot interrogate a suspect about matters relating to those proceedings absent an explicit relinquishment (i.e., a knowing and voluntary waiver) of the suspect's Sixth Amendment right to legal representation. Because virtually all police interrogation in America occurs prior to charges being filed or judicial proceedings commencing, however, the Sixth Amendment right to counsel is almost always irrelevant to the admissibility of confessions. In other words, there has been no discernible impact of the Sixth Amendment right to counsel on police interrogation.

The Fifth Amendment: Miranda v. Arizona

THE *MIRANDA* DOCTRINE

In 1966, the Supreme Court decided *Miranda v. Arizona,* ushering in a new era in the American law of confessions. In *Miranda,* the Supreme Court applied the Fifth Amendment privilege against self-incrimination—that "no person should be compelled in any criminal case to be a witness against himself"—to the pretrial interrogation process. According to the Supreme Court in *Miranda,* modern police interrogation was fundamentally at odds with the privilege against self-incrimination because it contained inherently compelling pressures that threatened to undermine a suspect's ability to freely decide whether to provide information to police during interrogation. Modern interrogation was inherently compelling from the Court's perspective because of the combination of (1) incommunicado custody in a police-dominated atmosphere and (2) psychological pressures and inducements to confess. After analyzing leading police training manuals, the Court argued that even the most "enlightened and effective" interrogation techniques relied on psychological manipulation, intimidation, and trickery for their efficacy, threatening to overbear a suspect's will and violate the dignity and liberty interests the constitutional privilege against self-incrimination was intended to protect. The Supreme Court in *Miranda* thus held that the Fifth Amendment privilege against self-incrimination required procedural safeguards prior to any custodial questioning in order to dispel the inherent compulsion of psychological interrogation, or else the state could not use a suspect's interrogation-induced statements against him at trial.

More specifically, the Supreme Court held that police must forewarn suspects of their rights to silence and appointed counsel before any custodial questioning can legally commence. The typical *Miranda* warning thus reads as follows:

You have the right to remain silent;

Anything you say can and will be used against you in a court of law;

You have the right to an attorney;

If you cannot afford an attorney, one will be appointed to you free of charge.

The Court required the fourfold *Miranda* warnings in all cases in which "questioning [was] initiated by law enforcement officers after a person has been taken into custody or otherwise deprived of his freedom of action in a significant way" (*Miranda v. Arizona*, 1966: 444). In addition, the Court held that the state must demonstrate that the suspect's waiver of these constitutional rights was made "voluntarily, knowingly and intelligently" (*Miranda v. Arizona*, 1966). As a result, police interrogators were directed to follow up the fourfold *Miranda* warnings with two further questions designed to elicit an explicit waiver:

Do you understand these rights?

Having these rights in mind, do you wish to speak to me?

On their face, the *Miranda* warning and waiver requirements seem relatively straightforward. In the last forty years, however, the Supreme Court has substantially weakened *Miranda*'s original vision and carved out significant exceptions to the *Miranda* rule (Weisselberg, 1998; Thomas and Leo, 2002). For example, in *Harris v. New York* (1971), the Court held that even if police interrogators violated suspects' *Miranda* rights, prosecutors could still use the defendant's illegally obtained statements to impeach him at trial if he chooses to testify in his defense. In *North Carolina v. Butler* (1979), the Court held that a waiver requires only that the suspect understands the warnings and is willing to talk, not that the police explicitly *ask* him whether he understands the warnings nor that they explicitly *ask* him whether he wishes to speak to them. In *New York v. Quarles* (1984), the Court held that police need not administer *Miranda* warnings before interrogating a suspect if their questioning arises from a reasonable concern for public safety. In *Missouri v. Seibert* (2004), Missouri policed interrogated a suspect without first issuing warnings, obtained a confession, and then issued warnings and obtained a waiver. The Court held that the statement resulting from this two-step procedure is admissible so long as curative measures—such as an additional warning that explains the inadmissibility of the prewarning statement or a break in time and circumstances between the prewarning statement and the

Miranda warning—are taken. And in *United States v. Patane* (2004), the Court reaffirmed that a violation of *Miranda* does not require the exclusion at trial of the physical evidence or "fruits" to which the suspect's statement leads. In addition to these exceptions, the Supreme Court has weakened or limited the *Miranda* ruling in other cases, sometimes even creating incentives for police to violate it (Clymer, 2002). Nevertheless, the Court has refused to overrule *Miranda*, holding in *Dickerson v. United States* (2000) that *Miranda* is based on the Constitution and thus cannot be legislatively overturned by statute.

THE IMPACT OF *MIRANDA*

Miranda has become one of the most well known and controversial Supreme Court decisions in American history, simultaneously celebrated and reviled (Leo and Thomas, 1998). Since the moment it was decided in 1966, the *Miranda* decision has spawned voluminous newspaper coverage, political and legal debate, and academic commentary. The *Miranda* warnings themselves have become so well known through television that most people recognize them immediately; indeed, they have become a part of American folklore, as the Supreme Court appeared to recognize when it declared that *"Miranda* has become embedded in routine police practice to the point where the warnings have become part of our national culture" (*Dickerson v. United States* (2000: 443). Yet *Miranda* has remained a source and symbol of controversy throughout its five-decade existence.

From all the attention it has received, one might reasonably infer that the impact of the *Miranda* decision—on police, criminal suspects, confession and conviction rates, and the American public—has been enormous. The empirical studies of *Miranda*'s effects, however, mostly tell a different story (see Leo, 2001a; Thomas, 2003). The scholarly consensus is that *Miranda*'s impact in the real world is, for the most part, negligible.[1]

Suspects

Miranda appears to have made little difference to most custodial suspects who are interrogated. The overwhelming majority (78 to 96 percent) waive their rights and appear to consent to interrogation, implicitly or explicitly (Leo, 1998). As Patrick Malone (1986: 368) has pointed out, *"Miranda* warnings have little or no effect on a suspect's propensity to talk . . . Next to the warning label on cigarette packs, *Miranda* is the most widely ignored piece of official advice in our society." Moreover, once a suspect has waived his rights, *Miranda* does not restrict deceptive, suggestive, or manipulative interrogation techniques; hostile or overbearing questioning styles; lengthy confinement; or any of the "inherently compelling" conditions of modern accusatorial interrogation that may lead a suspect to confess. Once interrogators recite the fourfold warning and obtain a waiver, *Miranda* is irrelevant to both the process and the outcome of the subsequent interrogation. And very few suspects later invoke their rights after first waiving them.

Police
Police have successfully adapted to *Miranda* in the last four decades. Following an initial adjustment period, they have learned how to comply with *Miranda*—or at least how to create the appearance of complying—and still elicit a high percentage of incriminating admissions and confessions. As discussed in Chapter 4, police have devised multiple strategies to avoid, circumvent, nullify, or simply violate *Miranda* and its invocation rules in their pursuit of confession evidence. Because police have learned how to "work *Miranda*" to their advantage—i.e., to issue *Miranda* (or avoid having to issue) warnings in ways that will result in legally accepted waivers—*Miranda* exerts minimal restraint on police interrogation, contrary to the intentions and beliefs of the Warren Court as well as its many contemporary liberal and progressive supporters. As one commentator has pointed out, *Miranda* has become a "manageable annoyance," the anti-climax of virtually all custodial police questioning (Hoffman, 1998). All of this is, arguably, exactly the opposite of the Warren Court's intentions when it created the *Miranda* rules. If the goal of *Miranda* was to reduce the kinds of interrogation techniques and custodial pressures that create stationhouse compulsion and coercion, then it appears to have failed miserably. The reading of rights and the taking of waivers has seemingly become an empty ritual.

Not only has *Miranda* largely failed to achieve its goals, but police have transformed it into a tool of law enforcement, a public relations coup that could not have been foreseen at the time it was decided. By largely controlling when and how the *Miranda* warnings are issued, as well as the construction of case facts surrounding *Miranda* disputes, American police have taken the advantage in *Miranda*. In other words, *Miranda* has mostly helped, not hurt, law enforcement. Besides displacing de facto the case-by-case voluntariness standard as the primary test of a confession's admissibility, it has shifted courts' analysis from the voluntariness of a confession to the voluntariness of a *Miranda* waiver. As Slobogin (2003b: 310) puts it, "*Miranda* has (inadvertently) sabotaged the voluntariness inquiry." *Miranda* has thus helped the police shield themselves from evidentiary challenges, rendering admissible otherwise questionable and/or involuntary confessions. *Miranda* not only fails to provide police with any guidelines about which police interrogation techniques are impermissible, but, because it is seen as a symbol of professionalism, *Miranda* also reduces the pressure on police to reform their practices on their own initiative.

Prosecutors

Prosecutors overwhelmingly support *Miranda* (Gruhl and Spohn, 1981). As George Thomas (2000) and others (American Bar Association, 1988; Garcia, 1998) have pointed out, *Miranda* facilitates the prosecutor's tasks of getting statements admitted, gaining leverage during plea bargaining, and ultimately winning convictions. Prosecutors also like *Miranda* because it makes law enforcement appear more professional, causes juries to attach greater weight to confession evidence, and allows prosecutors to argue that an involuntary confession was constitutionally obtained. Just as importantly, *Miranda* rarely imposes significant costs on prosecutors; it is rare that an admission or confession will be suppressed from evidence in trial proceedings because of a *Miranda* violation.

Trial Courts

Miranda has eased the lot of trial judges. By creating a seemingly objective, regular, and consistent rule, Miranda has made it far easier for trial courts to decide whether a confession should be admitted into evidence. As Malone (1986: 377) has pointed out, "staccato Miranda conversations, with their uniform statements and check the box answers, are easier for courts to evaluate than sprawling hours-long interrogations." The cost, however, appears to be borne by the accused. The Supreme Court observed that when the police "have adhered to the dictates of *Miranda*," a defendant will rarely be able to make even "a colorable argument that his self-incriminating statement was compelled" (*Dickerson v. United States*, 2000: 444). As White (2001b: 1220) has pointed out, "A finding that the police have properly informed the suspect of his *Miranda* rights thus often has the effect of minimizing the scrutiny afforded interrogation practices following the Miranda waiver." Others have gone further, suggesting that as long as Miranda warnings were given, courts have ignored interrogation misconduct, freeing the police to coerce suspects as long as they first Mirandized them.

There are data to support this view. A survey of recent decisions suggests that once police have complied with *Miranda* and received a waiver, it is, indeed, difficult to establish that the defendant's confession was coerced or involuntary (White, 2001b). Thus, while *Miranda* has done very little to change the psychological methods and process of interrogation, it has changed, de facto, the standard by which confessions are admissible into evidence, creating a bright line but diminishing the salience and effectiveness of the voluntariness test by lulling judges into admitting confessions with little inquiry into voluntariness. For if a "swearing contest" arises, judges, as we've seen, virtually always believe the police officer's testimony, especially if the suspect had signed a written waiver.

While it may have initially increased the professionalism of American police, *Miranda*'s contemporary impact thus appears rather limited. Once feared to be sand in the machinery of criminal justice, *Miranda* has now become part of the machine. Police, prosecutors, and courts have all adapted to and diluted *Miranda*, using it to advance their own objectives rather than to enforce the privilege against self-incrimination or the right to counsel (Kamisar, 1996). *Miranda* imposes few, if any, serious costs on them or the criminal justice system as a whole. It does not impede law enforcement. It also offers few benefits to its intended recipients. Rather than eliminating compulsion inside the interrogation room, it has motivated police to develop more subtle and sophisticated interrogation strategies. How police "work" *Miranda* makes a mockery of the notion that a suspect is effectively apprised of his rights and has a continuous opportunity to exercise them. *Miranda* not only offers no protection against coercive interrogation, but it may also have weakened legal safeguards by shifting the focus from whether the interrogation was coercive to whether the interrogator properly read the suspect the four-line, ten-second *Miranda* catechism. And *Miranda* offers suspects little, if any, protection against false confessions (Leo, 1998; Stuntz, 2001).

Moving Past Voluntariness and Miranda*: Bringing Reliability Back In*

Concerns that jurors place too much stock in confession evidence historically gave rise to a series of rules designed to exclude unreliable confessions at trial and prevent erroneous convictions. These doctrines, which developed both in the common law of evidence and under the Constitution, fell into two distinct categories: the voluntariness rule and the corroboration rule.

By barring interrogations that involved coercive tactics, courts under the Fourteenth Amendment's voluntariness test sought to reduce the possibility of wrongful convictions based on false confessions. In the past half-century, however, Supreme Court decisions have made clear that the Constitution is not concerned with unreliable confession evidence, and does not require state courts to undertake a reliability analysis prior to admitting a confession at trial. In contrast to the voluntariness doctrine, the corroboration rule requires that confessions be corroborated by independent evidence to be admissible. The rule was implemented to serve three primary purposes: to prevent false confessions, provide incentives to law enforcement to seek additional evidence, and protect against the tendency of jurors to view confession evidence uncritically (Leo et al., 2006).

The corroboration rule encompasses both the corpus delicti rule (requiring evidence only of the crime itself) and the trustworthiness standard (requiring independent evidence supporting the confession). The corpus delicti rule developed from the universally established common-law principle that an out-of-court statement, such as a confession, is not readily admissible. The orthodox version of the rule quite literally requires corroboration of the corpus delicti, or the body of the crime. Under the orthodox corpus delicti rule, to establish guilt in a criminal case the prosecution must show that a harm or injury occurred by a criminal act. The rule does not require corroboration that the defendant was the perpetrator of the act, nor does it demand support of any other element of the crime. The rule's original purpose was to protect individuals who falsely confessed to a crime that was never committed. Such false confessions, however, are rare (but see Warden, 2005). The far more frequent occurrence involves a person falsely confessing to a crime that did occur (Leo and Ofshe, 1998a; Drizin and Leo, 2004). Unfortunately, the rule seems unconcerned with this reality: "There seems to be little distinction between convicting a person for a crime that was never committed and convicting a person for a crime that was committed by someone else" (*State v. Mauchley*, 2003: 483).

By concentrating on whether a crime occurred rather than whether a confession is true or false, the corpus delicti rule subordinates the trustworthiness of a confession to proof of a crime. The rule assumes that "if the State can introduce independent evidence supporting the occurrence of the charged crime, a confession about the crime must be reliable" (Ayling, 1984: 1128). But this has been disproved by countless false confessions to very real crimes (Leo and Ofshe, 1998a; Drizin and Leo, 2004). Because the corpus delicti rule concerns itself with proof of the crime rather than the trustworthiness of the confession, it will fail to ferret out false and unreliable confessions. Moreover, in certain cases it will bar the admission of reliable confessions, which has caused some prosecutors to call for its abolition (Taylor, 2005). It is often difficult for prosecutors to satisfy the requirement that they prove that the harm or injury was the result of a criminal act when there is no tangible injury or the injury is difficult to prove (e.g., child molestation or child death by smothering) (Leo et al., 2006). In addition, as the definitions of crimes have grown increasingly more complicated and precise, "defining what the State must show to establish the charged crime was committed before a confession may be admitted has become more difficult and it has made the rule even more unworkable" (*State v. Mauchley*, 2003: 486).

Several state courts and the federal district courts have chosen to adopt a different rule of corroboration, most often termed the "trustworthiness standard" (Leo et al., 2006). In marked contrast to the corpus delicti rule, the trustworthiness standard requires corroboration of the confession itself rather than corroboration that a crime was committed. Under the trustworthiness standard, before the state may introduce a confession it "must introduce substantial independent evidence which would tend to establish the trustworthiness of the [confession]" (*Opper v. United States*, 1954: 93). In effect, the trial court judge acts as a gatekeeper and must determine, as a matter of law, that a confession is trustworthy before it can be admitted. In making the trustworthiness determination, the judge is to consider "the totality of the circumstances" (*State v. Mauchley*, 2003: 490). Only after a confession is deemed trustworthy by a preponderance of the evidence may it be admitted into evidence.

Determinations of trustworthiness hinge on whether there is independent evidence that a crime has occurred. When there is no such evidence, a court may rely on "other evidence typically used to bolster the credibility of an out-of-court statement" to establish the trustworthiness of the confession (*United States v. Singleterry*, 1994: 737). Factors used to substantiate the credibility and reliability of an out-of-court statement in other circumstances include "evidence as to the spontaneity of the statement; the absence of deception, trick, threats or promises to obtain the statement; the defendant's positive physical and mental condition, including age, education, and experience; and the presence of an attorney when the statement is given" (*State v. Mauchley*, 2003: 488). When no substantial independent evidence of a crime exists, the court may also look to the overall facts and circumstances to determine whether the confession is consistent (Leo et al., 2006). When there is substantial independent evidence, a confession may be deemed trustworthy if it "demonstrates the individual has specific knowledge about the crime" (*State v. Mauchley*, 2003: 488). Three factors that tend to demonstrate personal knowledge are (1) providing information that "leads to the discovery of evidence unknown to the police," (2) providing information about "highly unusual elements of the crime that have not been made public," and (3) providing "an accurate description of the mundane details of the crime scene which are not easily guessed and have not been reported publicly," because "mundane details [are] less likely to be the result of suggestion by police" (*State v. Mauchley*, 2003: 488). In this way, the judge measures the "degree of fit" between the confession and the facts of a crime when assessing trustworthiness (Leo and Ofshe, 1998a; *State v. Mauchley*, 2003).

Perhaps the most promising and obvious aspect of the trustworthiness standard in preventing the use of false confessions is its focus on the reliability of the confession itself rather than on evidence that a crime has been committed. By allowing the trial court judge to act as a gatekeeper, the trustworthiness standard can prevent false or unreliable confessions from being admitted into evidence (Leo et al., 2006).

REINVIGORATING RELIABILITY

The Ofshe–Leo Test
Ofshe and Leo (1997b; Leo and Ofshe, 1998a) have argued that the reliability of a suspect's confession can be evaluated by analyzing the fit (or lack thereof) between the descriptions in his postadmission narrative and the crime facts in order to determine whether the suspect's postadmission narrative reveals the presence (or absence) of guilty knowledge and whether it is corroborated (or disconfirmed) by objective evidence. A suspect who committed the crime will possess personal (that is, nonpublic) knowledge about both dramatic and mundane crime facts that are known only by the perpetrator, the police, or the victim (for example, the location of the weapon, items taken during the crime, and specific aspects of the crime scene such as the color of paint on the wall or the pattern in the carpet). A suspect who did not commit the crime will not possess personal knowledge of the crime details unless the suspect has preexisting knowledge, or the

police have contaminated the suspect by educating him about the crime scene facts during the interrogation process. Assuming that the suspect does not possess preexisting knowledge and has not been contaminated by police suggestion, the probative value of crime facts and details accurately provided in the suspect's postadmission narrative is inversely proportionate to the likelihood that such details could have been guessed by chance.

Absent preexisting knowledge or contamination, the postadmission narratives of the guilty true confessor and innocent false confessor will therefore look different. The guilty confessor's postadmission narrative will likely demonstrate personal knowledge of crime facts; will be able to lead police to new, missing, or derivative crime scene evidence; will be able to provide them with missing information; will be able to explain seemingly anomalous or otherwise inexplicable crime facts; and will likely be corroborated by existing objective evidence. By contrast, the innocent confessor will not be able to supply accurate crime details in a postadmission narrative unless the confessor guesses them by chance; will not be able to lead police to new, missing, or derivative evidence; will not be able to explain crime scene anomalies or other unique or unlikely aspects of the crime; and the postadmission narrative will not be corroborated by existing objective evidence. Instead, the innocent false confessor's postadmission narrative will likely be replete with guesses and errors, and will be either inconsistent with or contradicted by the objective case evidence. In short, the postadmission narrative of a suspect who is confessing truthfully will tend to fit with the crime facts and objective physical evidence, whereas the postadmission narrative of an innocent suspect who is confessing falsely will not.

In many cases, analyzing the fit between a suspect's postadmission narrative and the crime facts and existing objective case evidence provides a standard against which to evaluate the statement's likely reliability. As Leo and Ofshe (1998a: 438–439) have specifically pointed out:

> There are at least three indicia of reliability that can be evaluated to reach a conclusion about the trustworthiness of a confession. Does the statement (1) lead to the discovery of evidence unknown to the police? (e.g., location of a missing weapon that can be proven to have been used in the crime, location of missing loot that can be proven to have been taken from the crime scene, etc.); (2) include identification of highly unusual elements of the crime that have not been made public? (e.g., an unlikely

method of killing, mutilation of a certain type, use of a particular device to silence the victim, etc.); or (3) include an accurate description of the mundane details of the crime which are not easily guessed and have not been reported publicly? (e.g., how the victim was clothed, disarray of certain furniture pieces, presence or absence of particular objects at the crime scene, etc.).

Ofshe and Leo (1997b; Leo, 1998) have argued that courts should insist on a minimum standard of reliability, and thus independent corroboration, before admitting a confession into evidence. Otherwise, its prejudicial impact will outweigh its probative value. Ofshe and Leo (1997b) have further argued that the fit analysis necessary to determine a confession's likely reliability can be properly conducted only if police have electronically recorded the interrogation in its entirety. Without this, there is no way to objectively resolve the "swearing contest" between police and the suspect over who said what during the interrogation.

Developing a New Reliability Test Based on the Ofshe–Leo Fit Standard

There is little dispute that the factors identified by Ofshe and Leo should contribute to an assessment of confession evidence reliability. They are routinely relied upon by all parties in the criminal justice system to assess reliability. For example, defense attorneys, prosecutors, and police all agree that a suspect who knows nonpublic information that only the true perpetrator would know and which can be independently verified is probably telling the truth (Leo et al., 2006). For this very reason, police officers are trained to hold back information from the press and suspects during questioning (Inbau, Reid, Buckley, and Jayne, 2001). When police announce an arrest, and prosecutors file charges or argue to juries that a confession is reliable, the fact that suspects were able to recount such nonpublic details is trumpeted as evidence that the right man is in custody.

Law enforcement officers also agree that a confession is reliable if it leads them to information that they did not already know. Investigators are trained that a confession is only as good as the evidence corroborating it, and nothing corroborates a confession better than a suspect who leads them to a murder weapon, bloody clothes, proceeds of a robbery, or the like (Inbau et al., 2001). The absence of such corroboration, however, does not necessarily mean that a confession is unreliable. Such evidence may not exist in every case—bloody clothes may be burned, weapons may be disposed of, and money can be spent, for example (Inbau et al., 2001).

The third Ofshe–Leo factor relating to the reliability of a confession is the extent to which the suspect's account of the crime fits with the objectively knowable facts of the crime. Are there errors in the fit? If so, do these errors concern matters the suspect is not likely to lie about (for example, mundane as opposed to dramatic crime scene details)? Similarly, if the suspect gets some general facts correct, but misses on many specifics, are the matters that the suspect gets right not likely to be guessed by chance? Absent police contamination or preexisting knowledge, an innocent suspect should get a crime scene fact correct only when making a lucky guess, and the likelihood of making lucky guesses decreases with the number of possible answers to the question.

In many of the false confession cases I have studied, there were significant errors in the suspect's account that should have pointed the police officers to the probability that the suspect was guessing and was not involved in the crime (Leo and Ofshe, 1998a; Drizin and Leo, 2004). Innocent false confessors are often most ignorant of many of the crime scene details, making their postadmission narratives replete with errors. These errors cast doubt on the reliability of the suspect's confession and suggest that it is "of little or no value as evidence of guilt" (Ofshe and Leo, 1997b: 997).

A New Reliability Test

Judges evaluating the reliability of confessions that are products of recorded interrogations should weigh three factors: (1) whether the confession contains nonpublic information that can be independently verified, would be known only by the true perpetrator or an accomplice, and cannot likely be guessed by chance; (2) whether the confession led the police to new evidence about the crime; and (3) whether the suspect's postadmission narrative fits the crime facts and other objective evidence.

As in the case of voluntariness hearings, challenges to the reliability of confession evidence should commence upon filing a motion to exclude the confession by the defense. The motion can be styled as a motion in limine under local rules of evidence that track Federal Rule of Evidence 403.[2] Although confession evidence failing to satisfy one or more of the indicia of reliability in our test is clearly relevant under the Federal Rules of Evidence, it may not be particularly probative of a suspect's guilt. Because juries often see confession evidence as dispositive of guilt even when it is false, its prejudicial effect can be devastating to an innocent defendant (Leo and Ofshe, 1998a). This is why Rule 402 allows judges to exclude unreliable evidence on the ground that its probative value is outweighed by its prejudicial effect.

Defendants will bear the burden of demonstrating unreliability but need only marshal some evidence that the confession is unreliable based upon the tripartite "totality of the circumstances" test outlined above. The ultimate burden of persuasion, however, falls on the prosecution. Because the jury is the ultimate fact-finder with respect to the truth or falsity of a confession, the standard for admissibility should be less than "beyond a reasonable doubt." Steve Drizin, Peter Neufeld, Bradley Hall, Amy Vatner, and I have proposed a "preponderance of the evidence" standard (Leo et al., 2006).

A hearing on the issue of confession reliability should proceed only after any attempt to exclude a confession on grounds of involuntariness. The reason for this is simple: the truth or falsity of the confession is not relevant to a determination of its voluntariness. If judges were to conduct reliability assessments first, their comparison of the contents of the confession with the corroborating evidence could color their assessments of voluntariness (Ayling, 1984).

Pretrial assessments of the reliability of confession evidence need not lead to the kind of lengthy, contested motions often seen in voluntariness hearings. In most cases, witnesses would not need to be called, the defense could submit its reasons why the confession is not reliable in its pleadings, the state could reply, and the judge could view and analyze the recorded confession and rule on the pleadings after argument. To the extent that prosecutors must demonstrate evidence of a fit, the nonpublic facts known by the defendant and the evidence recovered as a result of the defendant's statements would allow them to do so in most cases by proffer or affidavit.

More generally, the kind of evidentiary evaluation my colleagues and I have proposed (Leo et al., 2006) is one that trial courts do all the time to prevent unreliable or nonprobative evidence from biasing, confusing, or misleading juries. Judges are routinely called upon to decide whether to admit reliable evidence. The requirement in a criminal case that the evidence presented to the jury have sufficient indicia of reliability is neither new or novel. For example, the rules of evidence prohibiting the admissibility of hearsay testimony are rooted in concerns about unreliability. Similarly, the numerous exceptions to the hearsay rule are grounded in the idea that some forms of hearsay are so trustworthy as to be admissible whether or not the declarant is available (Federal Rules of Evidence, 803, 804). Judges may also admit hearsay statements not specifically covered by a hearsay exception if the statement has "equivalent circumstantial guarantees of trustworthiness" (Federal Rules of Evidence, 807).

The Movement for Electronic Recording of Interrogations

History

Constitutional law has largely failed to effectively regulate American police interrogation. The Fourteenth Amendment's due process voluntariness test and the Fifth Amendment's *Miranda* warnings offer, in practice, little protection against psychological coercion or offensive police methods. These doctrines also fail to prevent the elicitation of false or unreliable confessions, their admission into evidence, and the wrongful prosecutions and convictions they spawn.

There is in addition a far more basic problem: police in America usually fail to create a record of the interrogation. Without a record, there is simply no way of objectively knowing what actually occurred: at best, human memory is incomplete, selective, and prone to bias; at worst, litigants may intentionally distort, understate, exaggerate, or misrepresent what transpired. Not surprisingly, in the absence of an interrogation record, the parties will often dispute what occurred. The only way to resolve such disputes is to deem one of the versions of the facts more credible than the other—that is, to guess which side is more likely telling the truth. As we have seen, courts invariably credit the police version of events (Kamisar, 1980; White, 2001a; Slobogin, 2003b) and thus almost always admit disputed confessions into evidence. This means that the police have largely been able to determine the factual record that judges and juries rely on to determine whether a defendant's confession was voluntary or reliable.

The most fundamental policy problem with American police interrogation practices therefore is not the failure of the mostly symbolic and largely ineffectual constitutional laws that set out to regulate it, but inadequate record-keeping and thus unreliable fact-finding. Without a factual record of the entire interrogation, there often can be no adequate review of whether police used coercive or improper methods or whether the suspect gave unreliable or false statements. More broadly, without a factual record of the entire interrogation, there is no way to ensure that the three goals of the adversary system (protecting legal rights, checking state power, and promoting truth-finding) are achieved in the interrogation process. This is a rather curious state of affairs, since the easiest and most neutral of all possible reforms would simply be to require that police electronically record interrogations from start to finish. It is all the more curious when we consider how inexpensive, ubiquitous, and readily available high-quality recording technology has become in recent years.

The movement for electronic recording of interrogations, however, has been picking up momentum, and a few states already require it by law in some or all cases. In 1985, the Alaska Supreme Court required, as a matter of due process under their state constitution, that police electronically record all custodial interrogations when feasible, or else any statements would be inadmissible at trial (*Stephan v. State*, 1985). In 1994, the Minnesota Supreme Court used its supervisory powers over the administration of justice to require that state police record the entirety of interrogations in all criminal cases (*State v. Scales*, 1994). In 2003, the Illinois state legislature passed a statute requiring police to electronically record custodial interrogations in homicide investigations starting in 2005. In 2003, the District of Columbia adopted a statute requiring the police chief to establish procedures for the electronic recording of interrogations by the Metropolitan Police Department; in 2005 the chief issued a policy requiring electronic recording to the greatest extent feasible in dangerous or violent crimes. In 2004, Maine adopted a statute requiring that state law enforcement agencies electronically record interrogations in many felony crimes. In 2005, New Mexico also passed legislation requiring police to record interrogations when reasonably possible in all felony cases starting in 2006. In 2005, the New Jersey Supreme Court implemented a statewide mandatory recording requirement, after considering the recommendations of a special committee they appointed to study the issue following their ruling in *State v. Cook* (2004). In 2005, the Wisconsin Supreme Court ruled that its state police must record custodial interrogations of juveniles *(In re: Jerrell*, 2005); in 2006, the Wisconsin legislature passed a bill requiring police to electronically record all adult interrogations as well. In 2007, North Carolina passed legislation that their state police start recording all custodial interrogations in homocide cases starting in March, 2008. In addition, other state supreme courts have recommended that police record interrogations, ever year recording bills now come before state legislatures, and many police departments on their own have begun to voluntarily record interrogations (Geller, 1992; Sullivan, 2004, 2006).

Although recording has been gaining traction in recent years, "calls to electronically record interrogations are almost as old as the technology itself," as

Steve Drizin and Marissa Reich (2004: 620) have pointed out. For more than seventy years, progressives—not only legal advocates and law professors but also police leaders—have been calling for more accurate record-keeping during interrogations. In the early 1930s, before the advent of tape-recording technology, a number of reformers made this suggestion in response to the public revelations of third-degree interrogation methods and the problem of wrongful convictions. In 1931 the Wickersham Commission concluded its *Report on Lawlessness in Law Enforcement* by proposing that interrogations be a matter of public record in order to "furnish a foundation of dependable information" (1931: 192) that would serve as a check against the third degree. One year later in 1932, Edwin Borchard, in his pioneering book *Convicting the Innocent,* advocated that interrogation should be "carried on . . . in the presence of phonographic records, which shall alone be introduced as evidence of the prisoner's statements" (Borchard, 1932: 371). Similarly, the American Civil Liberties Union (1933: 3) proposed that "when prisoners are subjected to examination by police officers an official stenographer should be present." These reformers sought to eliminate the secrecy of the interrogation process, because they believed it would not only help eliminate third-degree methods but also enable fact-finders to make more accurate assessments of the voluntariness and trustworthiness of confession evidence and improve the relationship between the police and the public (Drizin and Reich, 2004).

The first explicit call for tape-recording interrogations came not from legal reformers, however, but from police themselves. In the first American interrogation manual ever published, W. R. Kidd (1940) called for the verbatim recording of interrogations, either through a sound recording if one was available or a stenographer if one was not. Kidd was also the first person to explicitly call for *video*-recording of interrogations. Although the technology was not fully established at the time, Kidd recommended that police use "sound movies" because they had "all the advantages of sound recordings with the additional value of actually showing what the defendant and interrogator were doing at the time" (Kidd, 1940: 65). Dedicating an entire chapter in his manual to this subject, Kidd argued that recording interrogations would "trap the suspect in lies" and assist police during and after the interrogation. Kidd (1940: 64) added:

Sound recordings . . . cannot successfully be challenged in court. By their very nature they refute any implications that the third degree has been used. Sound-recording systems are somewhat expensive to install but, properly handled, can easily pay for their installation because . . . long and expensive jury trials can often be avoided by playing the record for the benefit of the defense attorney, who in turn recognizes the inadvisability of attempting to defend the case, and pleads his client guilty.

Although several subsequent police training manuals would echo Kidd's endorsement of recording (see, e.g., O'Hara, 1956; Arther and Caputo, 1959), the law enforcement community was divided on the issue (see, e.g., Inbau, 1961). Throughout the 1960s, 1970s, 1980s, and 1990s, police trainers and leaders would almost universally oppose any taping requirements, however (Inbau, Reid, and Buckley, 1986).

The first modern legal reformer to call for electronic recording was Bernard Weisberg (1961). He was skeptical of the ability of police to regulate themselves or of courts to effectively regulate police in the absence of a factual record. Weisberg (1961) argued that electronic recording would end the swearing contest, eliminate police abuses, and help clarify legal rules about coercion and voluntariness, allowing courts to provide greater guidance to police about the line between permissible and impermissible interrogation methods. Weisberg viewed electronic recording as a particularly apt solution to the problem of regulating interrogation because it would eliminate the secrecy of custodial questioning (which he believed was the root cause of police abuses, public distrust, and ineffective legal regulation) while preserving its privacy (which law enforcement insisted was necessary for effective interrogation). Other legal reformers such as University of Michigan Law Professor Yale Kamisar (1965) and Stanford Psychology Professor Philip Zimbardo (1967) echoed Weisberg's call for electronic recording, and in 1975 the American Law Institute's *Official Draft of a Model Code of Pre-Arraignment Procedure* called for the use of sound recording during interrogations "to aid the resolution of factual disputes" and "to provide clear and enforceable rules governing the period between arrest and judicial appearance" (American Law Institute, 1975: 39). But these calls also went unheeded (Drizin and Reich, 2004).

The electronic recording of interrogations was all but dead until 1985, when the Alaska Supreme Court held, as a due process requirement under its state constitution, that police must electronically record custodial interrogations from start to finish for a defendant's confession to be admissible at trial (*Stephan v. State,* 1985). Although this ruling was and remains exceptional, American police in the late 1980s increasingly began to experiment with voluntarily recording interrogations and confessions. In 1990, William Geller undertook a detailed and systematic nationwide survey of police recording practices, finding that one-sixth of all police and sheriff departments at the time (approximately 2,400 law enforcement agencies) videotaped at least some of their interrogations and confessions (Geller, 1992). Geller's 1990 survey revealed that most of the departments using videotaping had been doing so for at least five years.

Although recording remained unpopular with most of law enforcement in the 1990s, an increasing number of police departments began to use it, as Geller had predicted. The issue was increasingly litigated in the appellate courts in the 1990s, though all but one court (*State v. Scales*, 1994) rejected imposing such a requirement on police (Donovan and Rhodes, 2000). By the mid-1990s, however, the idea that all police interrogations should be recorded was rapidly gaining currency as a feasible policy reform, as numerous authors from across the political spectrum began to advocate it (see, e.g., Cassell, 1996; Leo, 1996b; Alschuler, 1997). As Sullivan (2004: 2) has pointed out, "The literature on this subject has an invariable theme: recording custodial questioning is necessary to prevent police from using coercive tactics during unrecorded interrogations and misstating what the suspect said."

The most important impetus for the movement to record interrogations has been the changing public perception of the likelihood of error in the criminal justice system as a result of media coverage of false confessions and wrongful convictions. Many of these cases involved DNA exonerations of innocent individuals who had been imprisoned for years. The "innocence revolution" ultimately led numerous reformers and professional organizations to call for mandatory electronic recording of all custodial interrogations. In 2002, Illinois Governor George Ryan's Capital Case Commission recommended that police be required to record all homicide interrogations; capital case and innocence commissions in other states have similarly endorsed recording requirements. In 2004, the American Bar Association passed a resolution urging police across the country to videotape their interrogations.

At the time of this writing, eight states (Alaska, Minnesota, Illinois, Maine, New Mexico, Wisconsin, New Jersey, and North Carolina) and the District of Columbia have laws requiring police to record interrogations in their entirety in some or all criminal cases. Recently the supreme court of one more state, Massachusetts, sought to promote recording of interrogations, but stopped short of a mandatory videotaping requirement (*Commonwealth v. Di-Giambattista,* 2004); instead, it authorized the use of cautionary instructions in the absence of electronic recording, a move that the State of New Jersey adopted as well (*State v. Cook,* 2004) before mandating electronic recording. Legislative bills requiring electronic recording are currently pending in a number of other states and cities across the country.

There is even a growing movement among law enforcement agencies to record interrogations. In 2004, Thomas Sullivan (co-chair of Governor George Ryan's Commission on Capital Punishment) published a survey of 260 law enforcement agencies in 41 states that currently record custodial interrogations from start to finish in felony cases (Sullivan, 2004).[3] Significantly, Sullivan found that recording was "an efficient and powerful law enforcement tool" that enjoyed strong support among the police surveyed: "virtually every officer with whom we spoke, having given custodial recordings a try, was in favor of the practice . . . Many experienced officers said they would not consider returning to non-recorded sessions, and expressed surprise when told that most police in the United States do not record in serious felony investigations" (Sullivan, 2004: 6, 15). Even the training firm Reid and Associates, which opposed recording interrogations for many years (Inbau et al., 1986), now favors the practice (Buckley and Jayne, 2005). Jayne (2004: 11) concluded that "the requirement of electronic recording in custodial cases is not only feasible, but may have an overall benefit to the criminal justice system."

Nevertheless, most police departments still do not record interrogations, and many of those who do tape selectively or only tape the admission (Slobogin, 2003a). A majority of law enforcement agencies continue to oppose the practice of recording altogether. The Federal Bureau of Investigation, regarded by some as an exemplar of police professionalism, still refuses to record interrogations as a matter of policy (Sullivan, 2007). Several major urban police departments, including those in New York City, Philadelphia, and Baltimore, have also resisted recording requirements (Drizin and Reich, 2004). Other law enforcement agencies have expressed hostility to the suggestion that they voluntarily record their interrogations.

The Benefits of Electronic Recording

Electronic recording is the most important and compelling policy reform available for the problems of American police interrogation (Leo and

Richman, 2007). Recording offers numerous benefits—to police, prosecutors, judges, juries, and society in general—and few costs. Unlike some potential reforms, the recording of police interrogations is not a zero-sum solution: it benefits all parties who value accurate fact-finding and more informed decision making. Moreover, electronic recording is uniquely situated to advance the three underlying goals of the adversary system.

RECORDING PROMOTES TRUTH-FINDING

Taping creates an objective, comprehensive, and reviewable record of an interrogation, making it unnecessary to rely on the incomplete, selective, and potentially biased accounts of the disputants about what occurred. The indisputable record it provides is "law enforcement's version of instant replay" (Sullivan, 2004: 6). Taping prevents untruthful allegations and faulty recollections from being treated as fact. For example, it prevents suspects from falsely accusing police of failing to give them *Miranda* warnings or using coercive interrogation methods. Taping also prevents police from making false claims about the suspect's behavior or statements. Recording removes secrecy from the interrogation process and eliminates the gap in our knowledge that the Supreme Court complained of more than four decades ago in the *Miranda* decision.

Electronic recording also promotes truth-finding by preventing false confessions and erroneous convictions. By removing the secrecy of interrogation, electronic recording opens up police practices to the possibility of external scrutiny, and thus interrogators are less likely to use impermissible or questionable techniques, including the psychologically coercive and improper ones that are the primary cause of false confessions. As electronic recording becomes increasingly institutionalized, it may even change the culture of interrogation such that police learn to rely less on the kinds of methods that lead to false and unreliable statements.

Even if police continue to elicit some false confessions, electronic recording will help prevent them from being introduced into the stream of evidence that can lead to wrongful convictions. For recording also creates a permanent and objective record for judges and juries to review. It thus provides a means by which third parties such as courts can monitor police practices and enforce other safeguards (White, 1997). If there is a question about the propriety of police techniques or the reliability of the suspect's statements, police managers can review the taped interrogation and transcript to decide whether to present the case to the prosecutor. Recording will thus allow police to monitor and regulate better their interrogation practices and determine the reliability of the statements they elicit. Even if detectives and police managers fail to recognize a confession as false, the prosecutor is in a better position to assess its reliability when there is an electronic recording of the entire interrogation. A recording allows the prosecution to evaluate the police methods, how the suspect responds to questions, and whether the suspect independently provides nonpublic details about the offense.

Still, false confessions sometimes slip through police and prosecutorial filters; even the most well-meaning police and prosecutors make erroneous judgments. In many false confession cases, trial judges have ruled that the confession was voluntary, and in all of the cases in which false confessions have led to wrongful convictions, judges and juries—when asked to evaluate the interrogation—have found the confessions to be reliable evidence of guilt (Drizin and Leo, 2004). A recording of the entire interrogation helps prevent these types of errors and contributes to reliable fact-finding by allowing judges and jurors to make more factually informed decisions about whether to admit confessions into evidence and what weight to put on them when determining guilt or innocence. An electronic recording also provides judges with more reliable information to determine whether police used coercive or improper methods and thus elicited an involuntary or unreliable confession. And a recording helps juries make more informed evaluations of whether interrogations were coercive and confessions reliable. For example, it allows judges and juries to better assess a defendant's state of mind and the sincerity of any remorse he expresses.

By preserving a complete record for all to review, electronic recording makes more meaningful the multiple safeguards in the criminal justice system that are designed to filter out erroneous and unreliable evidence more meaningful, improving the reliability of evidence used in criminal trials. To the extent that electronic recording of interrogations prevents criminal justice officials from wrongfully pursuing the innocent, it will also help them rightfully pursue the guilty.

RECORDING PROVIDES A CHECK AGAINST UNWARRANTED STATE POWER

Checking unwarranted state power has always been one of the most fundamental goals of the adversary system. The electronic recording of interrogations is a brilliant solution to the problem of unchecked police power in the interrogation room and the potential for abuses because it eliminates secrecy. By unmasking the adversarial nature of the interrogation process and opening it up to outside scrutiny, recording allows for more effective monitoring by prosecutors, judges, and juries. Recording also creates the basis for more systemic oversight of police practices by appellate courts and legislatures. As Drizin and Reich (2004: 628) have argued, the knowledge it yields "would empower these bodies to become more informed about current problematic tactics, and then to clarify and develop more specific rules regarding proper police behavior, in turn giving police clearer guidance on where the line for acceptable behavior is drawn."

RECORDING PROTECTS LEGAL RIGHTS

The electronic recording of interrogations also promotes the adversary system's goal of protecting individual legal rights. In particular, it gives meaning to the Fourteenth Amendment's right to due process and the Fifth Amendment's privilege against self-incrimination that, as we have seen, are the means through which courts regulate police interrogations and confession evidence. Although the right to record a police–suspect encounter is not guaranteed by the Constitution, electronic recording is, in many ways, a precondition for the meaningful exercise, protection, and enforcement of a suspect's Fourteenth and Fifth Amendment constitutional rights in the interrogation room.

Substantive due process requires that we legally mandate the electronic recording of custodial interrogations (Leo, 1996b). This is true for two reasons. First, recording a suspect's interrogation is the only way to provide trial courts with the factual evidence necessary to determine whether his statements were voluntary or products of coercion. A complete verbatim record of the interrogation is necessary for courts to render accurate and fair voluntariness judgments. As Christopher Slobogin (2003a: 316–317) has argued, "When an interrogation is not taped . . . objective analysis of voluntariness can never occur."

Second, the government is required to preserve exculpatory evidence (*Brady v. Maryland*, 1963), and recording is the only way to preserve interrogation and confession evidence. Absent a recording, trial courts and juries are left to speculate about whether anything that was done or said during the interrogation by either party tends to prove the innocence of the suspect.

In some cases, the failure to record an interrogation will be tantamount to failure to preserve the most important evidence necessary to achieve a fair and accurate trial outcome. Hence it is difficult to imagine how the Fourteenth Amendment's Due Process Clause could do anything other than require verbatim preservation of interrogations and confession evidence. Other than having a stenographer present (which is highly impractical), electronic recording is literally the only way for the government to meet its obligation to preserve exculpatory evidence and thus preserve the underlying constitutional right.

The same is true for the Fifth Amendment privilege against self-incrimination. As Yale Kamisar (1965) pointed out many years ago, electronic recording of the *Miranda* warning and waiver requirements is the only way to ensure that the suspect's underlying constitutional rights are protected. According to the *Miranda* decision, the state bears the burden of demonstrating that the police properly gave the fourfold warnings and that the suspect knowingly and voluntarily waived them. It is incumbent on the prosecution to provide evidence of this, yet absent a recording there is simply no way to adequately determine whether the police complied with the *Miranda* requirements or whether the suspect provided a knowing and voluntary waiver.

Additional Benefits

ELECTRONIC RECORDING IS A LAW ENFORCEMENT TOOL

Since the early 1980s, the use of video technology has become increasingly common in American law enforcement. Today's police routinely employ video recording in a variety of contexts, including documenting crime scenes, recording sobriety tests, and conducting surveillance and undercover operations. Police use video and recording technology in these investigative activities because it allows them to collect, document, and process evidence more efficiently and effectively. The same is true for the recording of custodial interrogations.

Electronic recording of interrogations is an effective investigative tool for a number of reasons. First, it allows police to investigate suspects more thoroughly. By creating a record of the entire interrogation, it improves the ability of police to assess whether a suspect was involved in the crime. Detectives can review the interrogation as a case unfolds and in light of subsequent evidence. Recording preserves the details of a suspect's statement that may have initially been overlooked but subsequently became important. It also permits other officers to evaluate the accuracy of the statement.

Second, electronic recording allows police to interrogate suspects and elicit admissions and confessions more effectively. By recording rather than taking notes, detectives are better able to focus on their interrogation strategy and getting information from suspects, who appear to be less defensive when police are not taking notes (Sullivan, 2004). And in multiperpetrator cases, detectives will be able to use videotaped statements against co-conspirators more effectively than written statements (which some suspects might think are fabricated). Recordings will help detectives better prepare for the interrogation of subsequent suspects too. Some police believe that recording interrogations actually increases the rate at which they obtain confessions (Sullivan, 2004).

Third, recording allows police to present the results of their interrogations in court more effectively. As the Alaska Supreme Court noted many years ago (*Stephan v. State*, 1985: 1161), "A recording, in many cases, will aid law enforcement efforts by confirming the content and the voluntariness of a confession, when a defendant changes his testimony or claims falsely that his constitutional rights were violated."

Fourth, recording assists in police interrogation training by allowing detectives and their superiors to analyze what worked and what did not in previous cases.

Finally, electronic recording of interrogations also helps prosecutors secure convictions. Prosecutors report that recording not only allows them to evaluate and prepare their cases more thoroughly but also enhances their bargaining power during plea negotiations, leading to more guilty pleas (Geller, 1992; Sullivan, 2004). Recording also reduces the number of pretrial motions to suppress statements and confessions. If police interrogate suspects lawfully, there is no basis for defense attorneys to successfully challenge the interrogators' behavior or the admissibility of the defendant's statements. And with a recording, if a case goes to trial, judges and juries are more likely to convict, because a recorded confession is more credible and convincing evidence of guilt than a police officer's summary of the interrogation. As one Oklahoma detective told Sullivan (2004: 9–10), "There is nothing better than a video and audio tape of a confession obtained by a skillful detective whose questions, demeanor, and methods are as important as the confession."

ELECTRONIC RECORDING SAVES TIME AND MONEY

Electronic recording also conserves scarce resources in an overburdened criminal justice system. It saves money by reducing the time that police, prosecutors, judges, and juries must spend reconstructing, testifying about, or evaluating interrogations and confessions. True, police departments must expend funds for purchasing and installing recording equipment, and for the tapes themselves (unless the recording is digital) and their mainte-nance and storage. But these front-end costs—which legislatures should al-locate funds for—will be repaid many times over by the savings in the time and resources of police, prosecutors, judges, and jurors. If police electroni-cally record the entire interrogation, their departments no longer need to have a second interrogator present for the sole purpose of taking notes on the suspect's statements. Instead, recording permits police departments to free up personnel for other projects and investigations, a potentially signif-icant savings considering the length of interrogations. Officers also no longer need to prepare reports on their interrogations from handwritten notes, freeing up more time. In addition, recording saves police time and resources in court by preventing unnecessary litigation of false claims of police improprieties, particularly about alleged *Miranda* violations (Geller, 1992). When police record, there will be fewer pretrial motions to suppress and fewer trials. Even if there are motions and trials, the court can view the interrogations directly and therefore call fewer witnesses to testify. Thus, recording also saves the time of prosecutors, defense attorneys, judges, and juries in court.

ELECTRONIC RECORDING PROFESSIONALIZES
THE INTERROGATION PROCESS

Electronic recording professionalizes the interrogation function by opening it up to greater external review. That improves the quality of interrogation and lends greater credibility to detective work—especially in urban communities where police may be distrusted by large segments of the populations—by demonstrating to prosecutors, judges, and juries the lawfulness of police methods and the confessions they obtain. Detectives who know they will be videotaped are more likely to prepare their strategies beforehand and to be more self-conscious about their conduct during questioning. They are thus less likely to violate constitutional standards or engage in unprofessional or illegal interrogation practices. Electronic recording should improve relations between police and the public when an interrogation is controversial in a high-profile case. As Drizin and Reich (2004: 628) have argued, "Public trust of the police would also increase because the public would know that police are no longer scared to expose their actions." And by removing secrecy from interrogations, recording should increase public perceptions of the legitimacy of the criminal justice system more generally.

Potential Objections to Electronic Recording

Although electronic recording of interrogations has become increasingly common in American law enforcement, many police departments continue to resist it. Their arguments against recording essentially fall into three categories: that it inhibits suspects from talking and thus lowers the confession rate; that it is too costly; and that it is not feasible. None of these arguments are persuasive, however.

The notion that recording prevents suspects from making incriminating statements has never been empirically supported. On the contrary, a number of studies—including one by the International Association of Chiefs of Police (1998)—have concluded that electronic recording does not cause suspects to refuse to talk, fall silent, or stop making admissions (Geller, 1992; Sullivan, 2004). This is true for two reasons. In most states, police are not required to notify suspects that they are recording and thus can do so surreptitiously. And even in those states where permission is required, most suspects consent and quickly forget about the recording (which need not be visible) (Slobogin, 2003a). Of course, even if the suspect does not consent to electronic recording, detectives can still take notes. The irony of the criticism that electronic recording has a chilling effect on suspects is that exactly the opposite appears to be true. As Sullivan (2004: 22) has noted, "the majority of agencies that videotape found that they were able to get more incriminating information from suspects on tape than they were in traditional interrogations." In a recent survey of police interrogators in Alaska and Minnesota, more police reported that electronic recording benefits the prosecution (48 percent) than that it benefits the prosecution and defense equally (45 percent) or that it mostly benefits the defense (7 percent) (Buckley and Jayne, 2005).

The argument that electronic recording is too costly is both misconceived and wrong. Any cost–benefit analysis of recording must take into account the costs and benefits to the entire criminal justice system, not just to police. They include the savings in salary and court time by police, prosecutors, and judges in reconstructing and resolving disputed interrogations and confessions. The cost–benefit analysis must also take into account the costs and benefits to the criminal justice system that cannot be reduced to a monetary value, such as the greater accuracy of prosecutorial charging decisions, judicial rulings, and jury verdicts. Moreover, the benefits of electronic recording vastly outweigh the front-end costs of installing and maintaining it. As Slobogin (2003a: 315) has written, "In a day when municipalities are spending thousands of dollars on scores of closed circuit TVs for the purpose of monitoring the public streets, paying for a camera in the interrogation room is unlikely to break the budget." State legislatures should allocate additional funds for electronic recording, though, because it is unfair to expect police departments to bear all the costs.

As for the argument that it is not feasible for police to record interrogations under all circumstances, recording laws and proposals tend to pertain only to custodial interrogations. And while police are concerned that good-faith operator mistakes or equipment failures will automatically result in the exclusion of confession evidence, that need not be the case. In states where electronic recording is required by law, there are always "safety valves" or exceptions to prevent police from being punished for nonwillful failures to record. Perhaps the best way to handle questions of feasibility, as several states have done, is to require the prosecution to persuade the trial court, by a preponderance of the evidence, that recording was not feasible under the circumstances in order for any unrecorded confession to be admissible.

Apart from these three objections, much law enforcement opposition to electronic recording appears to be born of police inexperience or ignorance about what it actually entails. As Sullivan (2004: 18) has observed: "The law enforcement personnel who oppose recording custodial interviews are almost invariably those who have never attempted to do so. They speculate about potential, hypothetical problems, whereas those who have recorded for years do not express similar misgivings."

The Logistics of Recording

The logistics of electronic recording should be relatively straightforward. As a first step, interrogation rooms must be fitted for electronic recording equipment, and detectives must be trained on how to use and maintain the equipment. Many police departments have relied on videotapes, but others are increasingly using digital technology, which improves picture resolution, allows for easier reproduction, and conserves storage space. Whether video or digital, the mechanism of recording should bear an internal date/time stamp or digital clock. And, as the research by Dan Lassiter and his colleagues (Lassiter, Greers, Munhall, Handley, and Beers, 2001; Lassiter and Greers, 2004) has shown, the recording technology should not be focused exclusively on the suspect, but should have multiple cameras focusing equally on the detectives and the suspect to capture the totality of the encounter and minimize biased interpretations of the interrogation.

Piecemeal Policy Reforms

Introduction

There is no single law, policy reform, or panacea that will solve all the problems associated with police interrogation and confession evidence in America; a multiprong approach is necessary. Although mandatory electronic recording is the most promising and comprehensive solution, other reforms deserve our consideration as well. The earlier these reforms occur in the criminal process, the more effective they will be. The reforms discussed below are not zero-sum solutions but benefit all parties, and they operate systemically rather than case-by-case. They also promote the adversary system's tripartite objectives of truth-finding, checking state power, and protecting individual rights.

Improve Police Interrogation Training

In the aftermath of the third-degree scandals in the 1920s and 1930s, American police began to receive professional training on how to interrogate criminal suspects and elicit admissions and confessions. Some of the police interrogation manuals that codify this training are well known and influential in police circles, while others are obscure. Much interrogation training material is unpublished but circulated in-house. Today's police typically receive some but not much training in the academy prior to becoming police officers, but receive more sustained instruction once they are promoted to detective. Most American detectives have thus taken elementary, intermediate, or advanced interrogation training. This training typically involves instruction on the interpretation of a suspect's body language, demeanor, and nonverbal behavior for truth-telling and deception; the various psychological techniques and strategies of interrogation; and the law of interrogation and confession. Police interrogation training may also involve role-playing exercises, test-taking, and certification.

As we have seen, police training has professionalized the interrogation function and contributed to the decline of police brutality in the interrogation room, especially during the middle third of the twentieth century. It has also educated police about the law of interrogation and how to elicit statements that will not be excluded by trial courts. But interrogation training has contributed to some of the failures of interrogation too—in particular, police-induced false confessions. American police are poorly trained to understand the psychology of interrogation, suspects' decision-making, and confessions. They are also poorly trained to evaluate the reliability of confessions and to recognize false ones. Most interrogators thus do not realize how the methods of psychological interrogation can cause an innocent person to confess falsely.

To reduce the number of false and unreliable confessions, police interrogation training needs to be significantly improved in at least three ways. First, interrogators need to be taught that they cannot reliably intuit whether a suspect is innocent or guilty based on their perceptions of his demeanor, body language, and nonverbal behavior. As we have seen, scientific research has repeatedly demonstrated that the deception-detection training materials of police are flawed, that their judgments of deception are highly prone to error, and—perhaps not surprisingly—that interrogators cannot accurately assess their own lie-detection skills (Vrij, 2000; Granhag and Strömwall, 2004; Memon, Vrij, and Bull, 2003;). Their pseudo-scientific training in "behavior analysis" falsely increases their confidence in their lie-detection skills, rendering them even more certain in their erroneous judgements (Ekman and O'Sullivan, 1991; Kassin and Fong, 1999;Vrij, Mann, and Fisher, 2006).

All too often, especially in high-profile cases, interrogators wrongly presume a suspect must be guilty merely because of his nonverbal behavior during their initial interaction with him. As a result, they subject him to the manipulative methods of accusatorial interrogation. And once they elicit a confession, they treat it as confirmation of their initial presumption of guilt, even if it does not fit the facts of the crime. The innocent suspect now may well be on his way to a wrongful conviction.

Because the psychological methods of modern interrogation are sufficiently powerful to induce false confessions, no one should ever be interrogated unless there is a reasonable basis for believing in his guilt. Police interrogators need to be properly trained that they are not human lie detectors and that they endanger the innocent when they subject someone to high-pressure interrogation based merely on their hunches about the meaning of his demeanor.

Detectives also need to receive better training about the variety and causes of police-induced false confessions. Interrogation trainers and manuals must stop perpetuating the *myth of psychological interrogation*. Interrogators need to be taught that their techniques can cause normal people to confess falsely, and, more importantly, why. If interrogators are taught the logic, principles, and effects of their psychological interrogation methods, they will not only be more knowledgeable about the causes of false confessions but also more effective at eliciting truthful ones. Detectives also need to be taught about the distinguishing characteristics of different types of false confessions and how to prevent them.

In addition, interrogators must receive better training about the indicia of reliable statements and how to properly distinguish between them. Detectives virtually always treat a suspect's "I did it" statement as if it is self-validating—even if it is not supported by logic or evidence—merely because it supports their presumption of guilt. Yet as Ofshe and Leo (1997b) have pointed out, a suspect's "I did it" statement may turn out to be either evidence of innocence or evidence of guilt. It should be treated as neutral initially and then tested against the case facts.

Detectives need to be taught that the proper way to assess the reliability of a suspect's confession is by analyzing the fit between his postadmission narrative and the crime facts to determine whether it reveals guilty knowledge and is corroborated by existing evidence (Ofshe and Leo, 1997b). As one police manual states, "an uncorroborated confession is not worth the paper it is written on" (Oakland Police Department, 1998: 72). Interrogators thus should not ask any leading or suggestive questions in the post-admission portion of the interrogation, and should obtain as complete and detailed a postadmission narrative as possible. They also need to be trained to recognize their confirmation biases, to initially treat admission statements as neutral hypotheses to be tested against case facts, and to systematically analyze the probative value of a suspect's postadmission narrative.

Require Probable Cause to Interrogate

As research shows, police sometimes misclassify an innocent person as guilty based on flimsy evidence (Ofshe and Leo, 1997b)—for example, that he did not behave the "right way" when first approached, that he is related to or knew the victim, or that he fit a general profile (Davis and Leo, 2006). Once police classify person as guilty, their goal is no longer to investigate his possible involvement in the crime but to get him to make incriminating statements. Therefore, one of the best ways to prevent police from eliciting false confessions is to only interrogate suspects for whom there exists probable cause of guilt (Davis and Leo, 2006; see also Covey, 2005). By subjecting the basis for the decision to interrogate to an independent review by a third party, a probable cause requirement could prevent fishing expeditions and ill-conceived interrogations, thus screening out the kinds of cases that tend to lead to false confessions.

To be effective, a preinterrogation probable cause requirement must be formal, and there must be consequences for its violation. Police could be required to present the evidence establishing probable cause to a judge or magistrate *before* being allowed to interrogate. Although many suspects are now interrogated after they have been arrested, this does not necessarily mean that probable cause of their guilt was established prior to their arrest. Moreover, detectives should not be permitted to circumvent a probable cause requirement merely by telling a suspect before questioning that he is free to leave at any time, thereby recasting the custodial interrogation as a noncustodial interview. This is, of course, how American police presently circumvent the need to give *Miranda* warnings in many cases, and there is every reason to believe they would use the same ruse to circumvent a probable cause requirement they did not like. All interrogation could require a probable cause determination to go forward, whether or not the interrogation is custodial. The only way a formal probable cause requirement would be effective is if police are required to seek probable cause *whenever* they interrogate a suspect, if they are required to record the interrogation in its entirety (to avoid a dispute about the purpose of the questioning), and if the penalty for violation of the requirement is exclusion of any admissions or confessions at trial.

Regulate Interrogation Techniques

PROHIBIT IMPLICIT AND EXPLICIT PROMISES AND THREATS

Another way to prevent false confessions is to regulate more effectively the interrogation techniques that produce them. As we have seen, modern interrogation methods are sophisticated and powerful; designed for the guilty, they invariably lead to some false confessions and wrongful convictions when misapplied to the innocent. The external regulation of interrogation methods has been left to trial and appellate courts. In theory, the courts are supposed to deter improper interrogation by excluding confessions that are involuntary products of coercive or otherwise impermissible methods. This, of course, includes deprivations (e.g., of food or sleep), unreasonably lengthy interrogation, inducing extreme exhaustion and fatigue, or explicit threats of physical violence. In the modern era, however, promises of leniency and threats of punishment, whether implicit or explicit, are the primary cause of police-induced false confessions (Ofshe and Leo, 1997b). It is these techniques—particularly the minimization and maximization strategies discussed in Chapter 4—that trial courts must make greater efforts to regulate to reduce the number of police-induced false confessions.

In 1897 in *Bram v. United States*, the Supreme Court constitutionalized the common-law rule against the use of threats and promises, holding that any confession induced by "a direct or implied promise, however slight," violated the Fifth Amendment. This ruling held for almost 100 years, until 1991 when in *Arizona v. Fulminante* the Supreme Court in dicta disclaimed *Bram*'s rule prohibiting the admission of confession elicited by any promises. As a result, trial courts must decide whether a confession induced by a promise is involuntary by looking at the totality of the circumstances. At the present time, promises and threats appear to usually render a confession involuntary and thus inadmissible (absent a showing that the promise failed to induce the confession). Trial courts vary across states, however, over what constitutes an impermissible promise that will overbear the will of a suspect. As Welsh White (2003: 1013) has observed:

> The majority of states hold that, in determining whether a confession is involuntary under the totality of circumstances test, the fact that interrogators made a promise of leniency is one factor to be considered . . . A few states, however, hold that a confession induced by any promise of leniency is inadmissible; and several others hold that confessions induced by promises that would be likely to cause an innocent person to confess are inadmissible.

Appellate courts need to create an unambiguous, bright line rule prohibiting, under all circumstances, any implicit or explicit promises, offers, or suggestions of leniency in exchange for an admission. This would include any inducement that reasonably communicates a promise, suggestion, or offer of reduced charging, sentencing, or punishment; freedom; immunity; or police, prosecutorial, judicial, or juror leniency in exchange for an admission or confession. Appellate courts also need to create an unambiguous rule prohibiting, under all circumstances, any implicit or explicit threat or suggestion of harm in the absence of an admission. This would include any inducement that reasonably communicates higher charging, a longer prison sentence, or other harsher punishment in the absence of an admission or confession. It is important to have a broad-based rule because, as research has demonstrated, the use of minimization techniques (such as the Reid-based accident, provocation, and self-defense scenarios) communicate implied promises and threats (Kassin and McNall, 1991; Ofshe and Leo, 1997b; Russano, Meissner, Narchet, and Kassin, 2005). Appellate courts must exclude all promises of leniency (or their functional equivalents) because they create an unacceptable risk that police will elicit false, unreliable, or untrustworthy confessions. The Due Process Clause of the Fourteenth Amendment is intended to maintain accurate procedures, and it must continue to be interpreted to require the state to use procedures that do not wrongfully convict the innocent (White, 1998).

LIMITING OTHER INTERROGATION TECHNIQUES

Appellate courts and legislatures may also wish to revisit the issue of whether (or to what extent) deceptive, false, dishonest, and misleading interrogation techniques should be legally impermissible. Many scholars have argued that false-evidence ploys may heighten the risk of eliciting false or unreliable confessions (White, 1997, 2001a,b; Kassin and Gudjonsson, 2004; McMullen, 2005; Gohara, 2006). As an empirical matter, police lying about evidence is almost always necessary for eliciting false confessions: except in rare circumstances, you just do not get false confessions without police deception. One reason is that false-evidence ploys, if believed, promote the perception of suspects that the evidence will establish their guilt in the eyes of third parties and thus that they are powerless to change their fate unless they confess. Another reason is that false-evidence ploys may cause some suspects to doubt their memory. Yet such ploys usually will not result in false confessions unless they are accompanied by coercive interrogation techniques, such as (implicit or explicit) promises or threats.

Courts and legislatures may also wish to consider prohibiting or limiting the types of deception that interrogators use because they violate existing professional and ethical standards. As social policy we may wish to prevent or reduce police lying during custodial questioning because the ends of interrogation do not always justify deceptive means, especially since interrogation fraud may not be necessary to elicit truthful confessions from the guilty (no one has yet empirically demonstrated that it is). Although most appellate courts have upheld the use of false-evidence ploys and the other kinds of interrogation deception, trickery, and fraud discussed in this book, numerous scholars have argued that these kinds of techniques are so offensive that the statements they elicit should be excluded as involuntary *per se* (White, 1979; Roppe, 1994; Young, 1996). Whether false-evidence ploys and other deceptive interrogation techniques should remain permissible or are so offensive that they should be prohibited or more severely limited is a complex issue (Skolnick and Leo, 1992) that both courts and legislatures should explore if they wish to improve the quality of American justice. It is striking that the most fundamental policy solution of all—the reform of interrogation techniques and strategies—is currently so low on just about everyone's list of proposed solutions.

Finally, courts and legislatures may wish to specify time limits for interrogations. Lengthy incommunicado interrogation is not only inherently unfair, but, as recent research has documented, far more common in false confession cases than other ones. Routine interrogations last less than two hours on average (Leo, 1996a), but interrogations leading to false confessions often last longer than six hours (Drizin and Leo, 2004). In my recent study with Steve Drizin of 125 proven false confessions, we found that the average length of interrogation was 16.3 hours (Drizin and Leo, 2004). Longer interrogations appear to increase the risk of false confessions by fatiguing suspects and thus impairing their ability and motivation to resist police pressures. Exhaustion, as Davis and O'Donahue (2003: 957) have pointed out, "may lead to greater interrogative suggestibility via deficits in speed of thinking, concentration, motivation, confidence, ability to control attention, and ability to ignore irrelevant or misleading information." Specifying a time limit on interrogations of no more than four hours should diminish the risk of eliciting false confessions while maintaining the ability of police to elicit true confessions from the guilty (Costanzo and Leo, 2007). For as Inbau et al. (2001: 597) pointed out, "rarely will a competent interrogator require more than approximately four hours to obtain a confession from an offender, even in cases of a very serious nature . . . Most cases require considerably fewer than four hours."

Additional Safeguards for Vulnerable Populations

As we have seen, some types of individuals—the mentally handicapped, the mentally ill, and juveniles in particular—are especially vulnerable to the pressures of accusatorial interrogation. They tend to be more easily led into giving involuntary or unreliable statements and are thus disproportionately represented in the documented false confession cases (Drizin and Leo, 2004). One way to compensate for their vulnerabilities would be to simply prohibit police from interrogating them. Most people, however, would probably regard such a proposal as not worth the cost (i.e., lost confessions and convictions); to my knowledge, no commentator currently advocates this position. Another solution would be to continue to allow police to interrogate individuals from these vulnerable populations but to create additional safeguards and limits to minimize the risk of eliciting untruthful and untrustworthy confessions from them.

ADDITIONAL PROTECTIONS FOR THE MENTALLY HANDICAPPED AND THE MENTALLY ILL

Since the outward characteristics of the mentally handicapped and mentally ill are not always obvious to the untrained eye, police should receive additional training on how to recognize such persons as well as how to most effectively elicit information from them. There are a number of policies that law enforcement can enact to increase their knowledge about vulnerable individuals and decrease the risks of eliciting unreliable statements from them.

The Broward County Sheriff's Office in Florida—whose investigators had earlier elicited false confessions from developmentally disabled suspects in several high-profile cases (Drizin and Leo, 2004)—has adopted model policies for interrogating mentally vulnerable suspects. Each Broward County detective must annually receive specialized training in recognizing the characteristics of a developmentally disabled suspect and in how to properly question one to minimize the risk of prompting false confessions. Before questioning such a suspect, detectives are to immediately notify their supervisors and make a reasonable effort to afford an appropriate adult the opportunity to be present during all questioning. Interrogators are also instructed to take special care in advising developmentally disabled suspects of their constitutional rights, requiring them to "speak slowly and clearly and ask subjects to explain their response rather than simply answer yes or no." Because the developmentally disabled are "easily persuaded" and "eager to please authority figures," detectives are trained to avoid leading or suggestive questions and ones that "tell the suspect the answer the detectives expect" (Drizin and Leo, 2004).

As a final check against false confessions, before a developmentally disabled suspect can be charged with a crime, any confession taken from him must undergo a thorough "Post Confession Analysis" by a unit supervisor, or, if there is no evidence corroborating the confession, by a team consisting of a psychologist, an assistant state's attorney, and a criminal investigation commander. This evaluation involves weighing numerous factors, including whether the suspect was able to provide an accurate description of the major and minor details of the crime and crime scene, whether he was able to identify unusual or unique elements of the crime or scene that were not publicly known, and whether he provided information to the police that led to the discovery of previously unknown evidence.

ADDITIONAL PROTECTIONS FOR YOUNG CHILDREN AND JUVENILES

Because they share many of the same characteristics as the developmentally disabled—such as eagerness to comply with adult authority figures, impulsivity, immature judgment, and inability to recognize and weigh risks when making decisions—juvenile suspects should be afforded the same protections. Detectives should receive specialized training on the psychological vulnerabilities of juveniles that predispose them to comply more readily with demands to confess. Prior to any questioning, detectives should notify a supervisor so that the interrogation can be monitored. During questioning, detectives should use simple language; speak slowly and clearly; avoid leading, suggestive, and forced-choice questions; and take regular breaks. Once detectives have elicited a statement or admission from a juvenile suspect, they should subject it to the same postconfession analysis described earlier to more fully analyze its reliability and protect against false confessions.

In addition, juveniles should also be provided with an appropriate adult during questioning, such as a lawyer or other person who is specially trained to fill this role (see Owen-Kostelnik, Reppucci, and Meyer, 2006). In the wake of the Ryan Harris case discussed in Chapter 6 as well as several other false confession cases involving children and teenagers in Chicago, the state of Illinois enacted a law requiring that all children younger than thirteen years of age be provided access to attorneys before being interrogated in murder and sex-offense cases. Moreover, the Cook County State's Attorney's Office convened the Juvenile Court Competency Commission, a panel of experts from many disciplines, to study the ability of young people to understand and meaningfully participate in the interrogation process and court proceedings. The Commission recommended barring the state from using any uncounseled statements against children under seventeen in proceedings in which they face potential adult punishments, requiring that the entire custodial interrogation of juveniles charged with felonies be videotaped, and developing more effective procedures to ensure that a minor's parent or guardian is present during questioning (Drizin and Leo, 2004).

Expert Witness Testimony

The use of social science expert testimony in cases involving a disputed interrogation or confession has become increasingly common (Leo, 2001b; White, 2003; Kassin and Gudjonsson, 2004; Soree, 2005). There is now a substantial and widely accepted body of scientific research on this topic, and the vast majority of American case law supports the admissibility of such expert testimony (Costanzo and Leo, 2007). Although there have been a few cases in which courts have not permitted expert testimony, they are exceptional; social psychologists have testified in hundreds of criminal and civil trials that have generated no written opinions (Kassin and Gudjonsson, 2004). As Kassin and Gudjonsson (2004: 59) noted, "In this new era of DNA exonerations, however, it is now clear that such testimony is amply supported not only by anecdotes and case studies of wrongful convictions, but also by a long history of basic psychology and an extensive forensic science literature."

Expert witness testimony in disputed cases may be necessary because the traditional procedures of the adversarial system (such as opening and closing arguments, cross-examination of witnesses, and cautionary instructions to juries) are not sufficient to safeguard innocent individuals against the likelihood of wrongful convictions based on unreliable confession evidence. The purpose of expert witness testimony is to educate triers of fact about the general findings from social scientific research on interrogation and confession so that they can better understand the psychological principles, practices, and processes of modern interrogation and thereby more accurately discriminate between reliable and unreliable confessions.

Expert witness testimony may reduce the number of police-induced false confessions that lead to wrongful convictions through its effect on the judge at pretrial suppression hearings, its effect on jurors at trial, and its effect on police and prosecutors. The purpose of expert witness testimony at suppression hearings is to assist the judge in analyzing whether the interrogation was coercive and thus whether the defendant's confession should be admissible at trial. Interrogation experts may usefully testify at pretrial suppression hearings about the nature of interrogation training and practices, the social scientific literature on interrogation and confessions, and why certain interrogation methods are regarded as coercive and therefore likely to overcome an individual's will. With such testimony, judges are more likely to exclude from evidence coerced confessions. As a result, expert witness testimony at suppression hearings may result in the admission of fewer police-induced false confessions at trial, which may result in fewer wrongful convictions.

If a disputed confession is introduced at trial, the jury will want to know how an innocent person could have been made to confess falsely, especially to a heinous crime (Leo, 2004b). The purpose of social science expert witness testimony at trial is to provide a general overview of the research on interrogation and confession in order to assist the jury in making a fully informed decision about what weight to place on the defendant's confession. More specifically, social science expert witnesses can aid the jury by (1) discussing the scientific literature documenting police-induced false confessions; (2) explaining how and why particular interrogation methods and strategies can cause the innocent to confess; (3) identifying the conditions that increase the risk of false confession; and (4) explaining the principles of postadmission narrative analysis. By educating the jury about the psychology, causes, and indicia of false confessions, expert witness testimony at trial should reduce the number of confession-based wrongful convictions.

Finally, the use of social science expert witness testimony in suppression hearings and trials may also influence the future behavior of police and prosecutors. When interrogation experts testify, police and prosecutors take notice—especially in high-profile cases that rest entirely on disputed confession evidence (like the Central Park jogger case, for example). Police do not like to have their poor training, technical flaws, or courtroom lies exposed; to be criticized for using inappropriate or coercive methods; or to be shown to have elicited demonstrably unreliable or false confessions. Prosecutors do not like to be criticized for indicting defendants based solely on coerced or false confessions, to be forced to dismiss charges after a judge suppresses the defendant's confession, or to have defendants acquitted. By exposing flaws in a detective's interrogation methods or in the prosecution's case against a defendant, social science expert witness testimony in disputed confession cases may deter police misbehavior in the long run and improve police and prosecutorial screening practices. It may lead to a decline in the use of psychologically coercive interrogation methods, the number of false confessions that police elicit and prosecutors introduce into evidence at trial, and thus the number of innocent men and women who are wrongfully convicted.

Jury Instructions

A final potential reform is the use of cautionary instructions to juries. In theory, such instructions should increase jury sensitivity about the confession evidence they are being asked to evaluate and thus lead to more accurate verdicts and fewer wrongful convictions based on unreliable confessions. Although jury instructions are rare in confession cases, recently two state supreme courts have focused on them as a way to reform interrogation practices and guarantee the use of more reliable confession evidence and accurate jury verdicts. In *Commonwealth v. DiGiambattista* (2004), the Supreme Judicial Court of Massachusetts ruled that any confession resulting from an unrecorded interrogation will entitle the defendant to a jury instruction urging caution in the use of that confession (533–534):

> When the prosecution introduces evidence of a defendant's confession or statement that is the product of a custodial interrogation or an interrogation conducted at a place of detention (e.g., a police station) and there is not at least an audiotape recording of the complete interrogation, the defendant is entitled (on request) to a jury instruction advising that the State's highest court has expressed a preference that such interrogations be recorded whenever practicable, and cautioning the jury that, because of the absence of any recording in the case before them, they should weigh evidence of the defendant's alleged statement with great caution and care.

More recently, the New Jersey Supreme Court, in the aftermath of *State v. Cook* (2004), appointed a special committee to evaluate the issue of electronic recording of police interrogations. The committee recommended that defendants in New Jersey be entitled to a cautionary instruction, similar to the one spelled out by the Supreme Judicial Court of Massachusetts in *Commonwealth v. DiGiambattista*, in the event that New Jersey police fail to electronically record custodial interrogations in their entirety (Report of the Special Committee on Recordation of Custodial Interrogations, 2005). Based on these recommendations, the New Jersey Supreme Court subsequently adopted a rule mandating recordings statewide and cautionary jury instructions for nonrecorded statements (Sullivan, 2006).

Jury instructions are traditionally a reform of last resort because they affect only the small percentage of cases that actually go to trial. Because they occur at the end of a case, they are also the least forward looking or systemic of all proposed policy reforms. Interestingly, the Supreme Courts of Massachusetts and New Jersey have both recommended jury instructions not so much for their traditional function of helping the jury evaluate specific evidence but as a way to motivate police and prosecutors to introduce only the most reliable form of evidence (i.e., electronically recorded interrogations and confessions) by punishing them with a cautionary instruction if they fail to do so. By contrast, traditional jury instructions are given regardless of the form of evidence the state introduces and specify what factors the jury should give weight to.

Jury instructions offer several advantages. Because they are given by the judge, they are typically viewed as more independent and carry more weight than if they had been given by either of the parties. They are also able to go beyond the scope of the evidence and arguments introduced by the parties, and they should simplify the jury's decision-making and thus lead to fewer erroneous verdicts. With respect to interrogations and confession evidence, the cautionary instructions recommended by the Supreme Courts of Massachusetts and New Jersey are actually quite forward looking and systemic by, in effect, seeking to motivate police and prosecutors to electronically record all interrogations and confessions. One can, however, imagine more traditional jury instructions that might educate a jury about the risks of particular interrogation techniques, the principles of postadmission narrative analysis, or the importance of external corroboration. Jury instructions are thus one way for courts to reform the investigation process and enhance jury sensitivity in order to guarantee the admissibility of more reliable confession evidence and more accurate verdicts.

Conclusion

No amount of attention to the means will resolve the debate about
the ends of criminal justice . . . We can be certain, however, that if
we do not attend closely to the means, the most nobly conceived
ends will be futile.

    —Lloyd Weinreb (1977)

The history of confession law proves that neither the use of police
nor the use of lying was an integral component of obtaining confessions originally; thus, it was not a historical necessity. Once police
assumed the role of interrogator, however, they quickly adopted
lying as a technique to obtain confessions.

    —Deborah Young (1996)

A system of law enforcement which comes to depend on the "confession" will, in the long run, be less reliable and more subject to
abuses than a system which depends on extrinsic evidence independently secured through skillful investigation.

    —United States Supreme Court in *Escobedo v. Illinois* (1964)

There have been three distinct, if overlapping, eras in the history of American police interrogation. Each has been characterized by
different assumptions about the practice and problems of interrogation and
confession-taking, as well as the best regulatory solutions. The first was the
era of the third degree. As we have seen, this era was characterized by the
widespread and systematic use of physical coercion and psychological duress
to elicit confessions and punish suspects. The symbol that best captures the
era of the third degree is the rubber hose or perhaps the blackjack. This era
was characterized not only by routine police violence and lawlessness, however, but also by progressive opposition to the third degree, muckraking

318

journalism about police abuses, and many attempts (from within law enforcement as well as from outside it) to reform interrogation. The influential Wickersham Commission Report in 1931 both responded and contributed to a crisis of confidence in the American criminal justice system, after which the third degree began to decline. Perhaps the high water mark of this era was the Supreme Court's decision in *Brown v. Mississippi* (1936), which unanimously prohibited police use of physical violence to elicit confessions.

Brown v. Mississippi arguably ushered in the next era, which we might call the era of professional reform or the era of psychological interrogation. Police now focused on developing a psychology of manipulation, deception, and persuasion. As we saw in Chapter 3, they responded to the scandals of the 1920s and 1930s by turning interrogators into human lie detectors and psychological manipulators. The twin symbols of this era are the polygraph and the interrogation training manual: both were conceived as substitutes for the third degree and teach police how to overcome a suspect's resistance to making incriminating statements. In this era, the courts have largely regulated interrogation practices and confession evidence by emphasizing issues of procedure and the abstract psychology of volition. Appellate courts have expanded and contracted the meaning of the Fourteenth Amendment's due process voluntariness test, but it is ultimately vague, subjective, and inherently contradictory (Schulhofer, 1981). Perhaps the high water mark of the era of psychological interrogation—at least from the perspective of professional reform—was the Supreme Court's decision in *Miranda v. Arizona* in 1966.

To some extent we remain in this second era: Today police continue to develop and receive training in seemingly more sophisticated, if equally pseudo-scientific, lie-detection technologies and manipulative interrogation approaches; detectives continue to use a psychology of omniscience and persuasion to elicit incriminating statements; and courts continue to look to the ritualistic *Miranda* procedures and the indeterminate due process voluntariness test when deciding whether to admit or suppress confession evidence. To be sure, there have been a number of third-degree scandals in the last seventy years—in the Philadelphia police department in the 1970s, the Nassau County, New York police department in the 1980s, and the Los Angeles police department in the 1990s, for example. But with the exception of the scandal over the use of interrogation torture in Area 2 of the Chicago police department in the 1980s and 1990s (see Conroy, 2000), these scandals have been isolated, short-lived, and, perhaps more importantly, universally condemned by the police establishment and other criminal justice leaders.

The project of the police reformers in the 1930s and 1940s has succeeded, at least on its own terms: American police interrogation has been both professionalized and psychologized in the last seventy-five years.

Despite these successes, I believe that we quietly entered a third era sometime in the 1990s. This might be called the era of innocence. Its leading symbol is the DNA test that leads to the release of an innocent prisoner. In the last decade, hundreds of wrongfully prosecuted and wrongfully convicted men and women have been exonerated through pre- and postconviction DNA testing, although far more have proven their innocence through other means (Drizin and Leo, 2004; Gross et al., 2005). "The release of an innocent person from prison," Erik Luna (2005: 1201) has observed, "has become a recurring public event, varying only by the facts of the case and the apparent cause of wrongful conviction." As we've seen, police-induced false confession is the cause about 15–20 percent of the time. The "innocence revolution" has shaken public confidence in the American criminal justice system and led to a renewed focus on the problem of reliable evidence and reliable verdicts.

The renewed focus on actual innocence has led to greater scrutiny of police interrogation practices and confessions. It has also prompted increasing calls for mandatory electronic recording of interrogations so that criminal justice officials and triers of fact will be better able to evaluate the reliability of police-induced confessions. In 2002, when I began writing this book, only two states—Alaska and Minnesota—required electronic recording of felony interrogations. In both cases, the state supreme courts had imposed the requirement (*Stephan v. State of Alaska*, 1985; *Minnesota v. Scales*, 1994). At the time of this writing, six more states (Illinois, Maine, New Mexico, Wisconsin, New Jersey, and North Carolina) and the District of Columbia have required electronic recording in some or all felony cases. Most of these new laws have been promulgated by state legislatures, not appellate courts. Moreover, the ruling of the state supreme court of Massachusetts that juries are entitled to cautionary instructions if police fail to electronically record interrogations has prompted law enforcement in this state to join the many other police departments across the country that voluntarily record their interrogations.

The push for electronic recording has become something of a national movement, with mandatory recording bills before many state legislatures year in and year out. A sea change has taken place in the practice, regulation, and public consciousness of police interrogation that was almost unthinkable only fifteen years ago. It is only a matter of time, I believe—maybe a decade, maybe longer—before the electronic recording of interrogations in their entirety will be either legally required or voluntarily adopted by virtually all medium-sized and large police departments in America. As Buckley and Jayne (2005: 5) have surmised, "in the not too distant future, electronic recording of interviews and interrogations will be as accepted a practice by law enforcement as the investigator's use of computer technology is today."

Despite the changes in practice and regulation, though, the adversarial structure of American police interrogation has remained constant across the three eras. Interrogators continue to assume a partisan role that is often more about case-building and impression management than impartial investigation. They still seek to elicit incriminating statements from a presumed guilty suspect that will help the state prosecute him, weaken his position in plea negotiations, and minimize the possibility of an acquittal. Interrogators still try to "win" cases by successfully outsmarting the suspect, breaking down his resistance, and eliciting an admission—that can be directed or shaped into a persuasive confession—to secure a conviction. In the American adversary system, police interrogation continues often to be more of a prosecutorial function than an investigative one.

The strategic orientation of interrogators stems largely from what I have called the fundamental contradiction of American police interrogation: although it is almost never in a person's self-interest to incriminate himself, police are under tremendous pressure to solve crimes by obtaining admissions that will survive external scrutiny, particularly from courts. As a result, American detectives believe it is necessary to engage in fraud, psychological manipulation, and impression management to effectively elicit and manage confession evidence that will lead to convictions. Obscuring the true nature and purpose of interrogation, they work to create the illusion that they share a common, rather than adverse, interest with the suspect; that their objective is to help, not hurt, him; and that he is better off by confessing than by denying culpability or remaining silent.

The fundamental contradiction of American police interrogation is not likely to go away unless we change the structure of our adversary system or devise alternative means of solving crime that lessen our need for confession evidence. Short of this, the many contradictions, tensions, and paradoxes of police interrogation cannot be fully resolved so much as managed, more or less effectively, depending on our values and commitments.

Contemporary American interrogation fails, to varying degrees, to fulfill the three goals of the adversary system: protecting individual rights, checking unwarranted or overreaching state power, and promoting truth-finding. In-dividual rights in the interrogation room are defined largely by Fifth Amend-ment *Miranda* warnings that are quickly read, minimized, and forgotten, and by an overly abstract and elusive Fourteenth Amendment due process volun-tariness test that requires judges and juries to do the impossible—get inside the defendant's head and make existential judgments about whether his will was overborne. Defense attorneys rarely bring suppression motions, and trial courts—the guarantors of individual rights—rarely find that police interroga-tors acted improperly and suppress confessions. Detectives almost always win disputes with defendants because they control the means of knowledge pro-duction about what occurred in the interrogation room and why the suspect confessed. Once detectives have elicited and shaped the suspect's confession in this early stage of the criminal process, the suspect's fate in the later stages is usually determined. Because confession evidence is so damning, it almost always leads to plea bargains by defendants, who thereby forgo their Fifth and Fourteenth Amendment trial rights.

As it is currently structured, American police interrogation also runs counter to the second goal of the adversary system. While American police no longer rely on the third degree to elicit confessions, they continue to enjoy a virtual monopoly of unchecked power in the interrogation room. Their powers are virtually unparalleled by any other actor in the criminal justice system. They have the legal ability to isolate, deceive, trick, and manipulate—activities that in some other contexts would be regarded as criminal fraud. They have the power to use inducements that imply material benefits, some-times even prosecutorial or judicial leniency, to obtain from suspects the most incriminating evidence of guilt possible. They engage in a kind of negotiation and deal-making with suspects that is, in effect, the functional equivalent of plea bargaining, but without defense attorneys. Perhaps their most significant power, though, is their ability to influence and shape the narrative of the sus-pect's culpability. Because these practices occur out of view of judges and juries—absent an electronic recording—they mostly escape the adversary system's set of checks and balances.

The third goal of the adversary system is promoting truth-finding. Here too American police interrogation, as it is currently structured and practiced, falls short. The interrogation process remains fraught with the potential for unreliability and error. Perhaps the root cause of this problem is that Amer-ican interrogators are, in the words of police trainers Brian Jayne and Joseph Buckley (1993: 31), "adversaries [who] use persuasion and propaganda to

further their cause." Their "cause" is, of course, eliciting incriminating statements, ideally a full confession, from a suspect whose guilt they presume.
As a result of their adversarial orientation, American police interrogators
subordinate the investigative goal of truth-finding to the prosecutorial goal
of case building and conviction. Police induce false confessions that appear
true when they make three sequential errors: the misclassification error,
the coercion error, and the contamination error. These mistakes are typically products of poor interrogation training, poor interrogation practices,
tunnel vision, and confirmation bias.

The problem of eliciting unreliable confessions is not limited to the interrogation of the innocent, however. The structure and practice of American
police interrogation creates the risk that detectives will elicit partially or entirely unreliable confessions from the guilty as well. The classification, coercion, and contamination errors also occur in interrogations of guilty suspects. For example, interrogators' theory of a suspect's role in a crime may
be erroneous: the suspect may have been the driver rather than the shooter
in a gang killing; or the suspect may have sexually touched but not pene-
trated the victim; or the suspect may have committed only one, not three,
robberies. When detectives rely on pseudo-scientific lie-detection technologies like the polygraph or folkloric belief systems such as behavioral analysis
rather than on hard investigative work and real case evidence to form their
theories, they are going to be wrong, in whole or in part, a substantial percentage of the time.

The initial error has important consequences for the reliability of confessions even from suspects who may have committed a crime. Because interrogation is guilt presumptive, detectives often do not seek out or respond to
the corrective feedback necessary to adjust their erroneous theories but instead simply launch into accusatorial interrogation. Their preadmission interrogation techniques—especially lies about nonexistent evidence and the
use of scenarios that communicate promises and threats over the course of
a lengthy interrogation—may easily lead the partially guilty suspect to perceive that he has no meaningful choice but to agree with the detectives'
false theory. The detectives' postadmission interrogation techniques may
then cause him to agree to a narrative of his culpability that is also partially
false. This outcome should not surprise us in a system that allows detectives
to use fraud and impression management to elicit and shape confession evidence and yet provides few external checks on the process through which
this occurs. Although no organization or agency has compiled any statistical

data on the problem of over-confessing, the number of partially false confessions from the guilty may exceed the number of wholly false confessions from the innocent.

I believe that the practice and regulation of police interrogation will become more consistent with the ideals of American justice once electronic recording becomes standard across the country. As I argued in Chapter 8, recording creates the conditions necessary to better ensure reliable outcomes, check overreaching police power, and protect legal rights. The eventual widespread adoption of electronic recording may even usher in a fourth era in American history. I believe that this will be an era in which police, policymakers, and the public reevaluate the morality, legality, and effects of deceptive interrogation techniques, and courts rely on more substantive criteria to regulate the admissibility of confession evidence.

But electronic recording will not be a panacea. The two central moral questions for the practice and regulation of American police interrogation that I posed in Chapter 1 remain: What value should we place on confession evidence? And what means should we permit police to use to elicit it?

My own belief is that we may be more reliant on the word of the accused than we need to be. In the American criminal justice system, interrogation is the primary means through which police investigate and solve crimes, just as plea bargaining is the primary means through which prosecutors secure convictions. Because of the fallibility of human perception and the potentially corrupting effect of social influence—especially when police are legally permitted to lie about evidence, manipulate perceptions of consequences, and create alternative realities—testimonial evidence may be the weakest and potentially most unreliable type of evidence. It is among the easiest to coerce and fabricate, yet among the most difficult to independently corroborate. Paradoxically, however, judges, juries, and the American public tend to treat statements and confessions as the most persuasive type of evidence, especially when they are detailed. If this book counsels anything, it is that we should be more skeptical about the probative value of confession evidence in the American criminal justice system because of the interrogation process through which it is presently elicited and constructed.

Police interrogation is a legitimate form of criminal investigation in a democratic society so long as it is conducted properly. And confession evidence is valuable in many cases so long as it is reliable. But American police need to improve the quality of the confession evidence they elicit to achieve their own goals of apprehending offenders and solving crimes.

More generally, the criminal justice system needs to do a better job of sepa-rating the innocent from the guilty in cases that rely entirely, or even par-tially, on confession evidence. As Russano, Meissner, Narchet, and Kassin (2005: 481) have argued, "the goal of the criminal justice system should be to implement procedures that are diagnostic, meaning those that increase the rate of true confessions while minimizing the rate of false confessions." Though police will inevitably elicit some false confessions, the system needs to develop better means of filtering out this type of unreliable evidence so that it does not enter them into the stream of evidence used to prosecute and convict innocent people (Leo et al., 2006).

Apart from the probative value of confession evidence, there remains a normative question about the means with which we allow detectives to elicit it. As electronic recording becomes increasingly commonplace in the coming years, police interrogation practices will become more visible and thus more open to scrutiny. As the veil of secrecy is lifted, criminal justice officials, policymakers, and the public may begin to question the necessity, morality, and effects of deceptive interrogation practices. Some scholars presently oppose the use of deception during interrogation. Their objec-tions, as we have seen, are multiple: that it corrupts the integrity of the fact-finding process, undermines public trust in the criminal justice system, elicits untrustworthy confession evidence, and encourages police to lie in other contexts (Skolnick, 1982; Young, 1996; McMullen, 2005).

But there is only one reason to support the use of deceptive interrogation techniques: a belief that the ends justify the means. At least since the 1969 U.S. Supreme Court decision *Frazier v. Cupp*, this has become an article of faith among police, prosecutors, trial courts, and appellate courts. But, to repeat: no one has yet empirically demonstrated that police deception during inter-rogation is necessary to elicit true confessions from guilty suspects who oth-erwise would not confess and who otherwise would not be convicted but for their confessions (Young, 1996). There is some empirical evidence, however, that confronting a suspect with fabricated evidence he believes to be false re-duces the likelihood of confessing (Kebbell, Hurren, and Roberts, 2006).

But as I have shown in this book, police deception during interrogation is not simply a matter of lying about this or that piece of alleged evidence to create a "ruse" or momentarily bluff an otherwise reluctant suspect into confessing. Rather, American police interrogation is defined by its multiple and systemic deceptions, and is thus more accurately described as fraudu-lent. Police lie not only about the specific facts of a case or evidence they pretend to possess, but, more fundamentally, about the nature of their role in the interrogation process and the consequences of confessing to them. They pretend to be the suspect's institutional agent and induce him to comply with their wishes by offering to help him, when, in fact, they are really the exact opposite—the agents of his adversary (the prosecutor) who wish to take away his liberty. Police deception extends beyond preadmission techniques to the postadmission interrogation process, as detectives seek to shape the narrative of the suspect's guilt so that others will find it compelling. They also seek to manage the narrative of what occurred during the interrogation and why the suspect confessed to divert criticism from their practices. To return to the words of police trainers Buckley and Jayne, interrogators use "propaganda to further their cause"—but the propaganda, or what I have called impression management, is used both inside and outside the interrogation room. American police interrogators deceive not only suspects; they also deceive us. Any normative analysis of the propriety of police deception during interrogation must take into account the full depth and scope of this phenomenon.

If I am right that police use of deception during interrogation will become increasingly controversial as electronic recording becomes standard across the United States, then courts, legislatures and executive branch policy-makers may start to look for new ways of regulating police questioning of suspects. Some scholars have suggested that Britain offers one model for possible interrogation reform (Sear and Williamson, 1999). In 1984, England and Wales enacted the Police and Criminal Evidence Act (PACE) in response to several high-profile wrongful convictions based on false confessions. PACE made it illegal for British police interrogators to lie about evidence to induce confessions. PACE also required them to record or otherwise memorialize the entirety of their interrogations. PACE and other English police reforms have changed the culture of British police interrogation. Prior to PACE, British interrogation—like American interrogation today—was confrontational, and its purpose was to elicit incriminating statements and confessions. After PACE, British interrogation moved to a model of investigative interviewing that is more conversational and designed to obtain information, not confessions (Sears and Williamson, 1999; but see also Bryan, 1997). Despite the change, the confession rate in Britain has not gone down, and it remains higher than the American rate (Gudjonsson, 2003).

With all its cultural, historical, and legal differences, Britain ultimately may not offer a feasible alternative or model of reform for American police interrogation. It, nevertheless, offers an important object lesson. The normative upshot of my empirical analysis in this book is that we must take the adversary system out of the interrogation room—as the English have done—to improve the quality of our interrogation practices and the quality of confession evidence police obtain. We must always remember that American interrogation is supposed to occur at the preadversary stage of the legal process, before any charges have been filed or formal adversary proceedings have commenced. Police interrogation should be an investigative function, not a prosecutorial one. It should therefore not be guilt presumptive, and its purpose should not be to incriminate the suspect in order to build a successful case against him. Instead, the goal of American police interrogation should always be to get the truth—even if the truth proves the detectives' theories wrong, demonstrates the suspect's innocence, or elicits information that favors the defense over the prosecution—not to get a conviction. Only by deadversarializing the police interrogation process will we be able to achieve the ideals of American justice.

NOTES

REFERENCES

INDEX

Notes

1. Police Interrogation and the American Adversary System

1. There are two exceptions to this rule. In Louisiana, the state can obtain a conviction if ten of twelve jurors vote in favor of guilt, and in Oregon the state can obtain a conviction if eleven of twelve jurors vote for guilt.
2. The Sixth Amendment applies to all postindictment interrogation, but most interrogation occurs before indictment, so the Sixth Amendment is almost always not applicable to interrogation.

2. The Third Degree

1. Shortly before his case was to go to trial, Tony Colletti was found in his cell hanging by a thirty-two-inch belt attached to a three-inch pipe above his head. Colletti's two cellmates said that he had committed suicide and that they had not interfered, which the police regarded as the truth. However, Colletti's defense attorney, William Marsteller, believed that Colletti could not have killed himself because the belt was too short to allow the body to drop and the overhead pipe too big for Colletti to have adjusted the belt. Rather, Marsteller believed that Colletti was intentionally killed by his two Italian cellmates (who had been released before Cleveland police allegedly found the body) because the murder of Colletti's wife had the earmarks of an Italian gang killing. According to Marsteller, Colletti knew the gangsters who killed her, and they feared this information would be made public at Colletti's trial. In addition, Marsteller believed that Colletti's death had prevented a police scandal because Marsteller had made public his intention at Colletti's trial of publicly exposing the Cleveland Police Department's use of the third degree, which flourished in Cleveland, but, according to the Wickersham Commission, in "an exceptionally undercover way" (Wickersham Commission Files). Colletti's injuries from the interrogation—marks, bruises, and swellings around his hips and waist—had been documented in his police medical records, and Marsteller had planned to call five witnesses (a police physician, a police nurse, two deputy sheriffs, and a former prosecuting attorney) who all witnessed Colletti's injuries shortly after his interrogation. Even the victim's family believed

in Colletti's innocence and assisted his defense attorney in preparing his case. Because the charges against Colletti rested entirely on his recanted confession—all the physical evidence, including ballistics, failed to match Colletti—and because Colletti had ample documentation that the Cleveland police detectives had used third-degree methods in eliciting it, Marsteller and Colletti had been confident of a full acquittal (Wickersham Commission Files). "Ending in death though it did," as Ernest Jerome Hopkins (1931: 265) noted, "the affair was successfully hushed up; three months after its occurrence the chief of police . . . blandly assured me that he had no recollection of the case."

2. On May 20, 1929 President Herbert Hoover appointed the eleven-member Commission on Law Observance and Enforcement to comprehensively examine the shortcomings of the American criminal justice system, and to make "such recommendations for reorganization of the administration of federal laws and court procedure as may be found desirable" (Congressional Record, 71 Cong., 1 Pt. 1, p. 5). Its members included some of the most prominent individuals in American law and public life, such as Harvard Law School Dean Roscoe Pound, former Secretary of War (under President Woodrow Wilson) Newton Baker and Chicago attorney Frank Loesch, President of the Chicago Crime Commission. Hoover was concerned about abuses in law enforcement, the growth of organized crime, disobedience of the law, a perceived crime wave, and, of course, the problem of Prohibition. In July 1931, the Commission issued fourteen reports, which covered such wide-ranging topics as the causes of crime; Prohibition and the enforcement of the Prohibition laws; criminal procedure; and penal institutions, probation and parole, among others. The reports had little immediate impact, except for *Lawlessness in Law Enforcement* (Volume 11), which documented the widespread practice of the third degree in police work (see Calder, 1993; Walker, 1998).

3. In police circles at the time, the term "goldfish" referred to a length of cable or rubber hose used to strike a suspect without leaving marks (Wickersham Commission Files).

3. Professionalizing Police Interrogation

1. Virtually all contemporary interrogation training involves behavior analysis of one form or another, whether it is called the Behavioral Analysis Interview (Inbau et al., 2001), kinesics (Walters, 2003), the analysis of physical symptoms (Rabon, 1992), verbal and nonverbal clues (Hess, 1997), body language (Holmes, 2003), the Credibility Assessment Interview (Behavioral Analysis Training Institute, 2001), or anything else (e.g., "psycho-physiological basis of the forensic assessment," Gordon and Fleisher, 2006).

2. Some interrogation training firms go further. The Behavioral Analysis Training Institute, for example, advised police "When in doubt—interrogate" (2001: 43).

5. Constructing Culpability

1. The Pennsylvania Superior Court that affirmed Godschalk's conviction on appeal specifically cited the nonpublic facts contained in his confession as evidence of its reliability (451 Pa.Super. 425 (1996): "He confessed to raping both of the women and also admitted that he had moved the tampon of the second victim, a detail of the rape which had not been released to the public. Appellant also described the position of the victims during the rapes, another detail which had not been released to the public."

6. False Confessions

1. In addition, McConville et al. (1991: 68) proposed a separate category called *coercive passive* confession, which they have argued occurs "when the process of questioning induces suspects to adopt the confession form without necessarily adopting or even understanding the substance of what has been accepted or adopted." McCann (1998: 449) has suggested broadening Kassin and Wrightsman's typology to include confessions coerced by someone other than police. He proposes another category called *coercive reactive* false confessions, which occur "when an individual (who may or may not be a criminal suspect) confesses in order to avoid or escape some coercive action that arises out of a relationship with one or more individuals other than police." And Costanzo and Leo (2007) have distinguished between instrumental and authentic confessions.
2. Another possible exception may be Kenzi Snyder. In the month following her interrogation, Snyder reported having "two competing set of memories" (Ryan, 2006: 204). Like Ingram's interrogations, however, hers too contained recovered memory techniques not common in American police interrogation. However, unlike Ingram, Snyder "never fully accepted the idea that she committed the crime" (Ryan, 2006: 213, quoting Richard Ofshe).
3. The interrogators in Kenzi Snyder's case also induced trance (See Ryan, 2006; Newsome, 2006), and, like Ingram's, her interrogation contained hypnotic, relaxation, mind-emptying, and visualization techniques that are common in recovered memory therapy but extremely rare in American police interrogation. Snyder's confession is thus also unique and not borne of ordinary police interrogation.

7. Miscarriages of Justice

1. Although the total number of false confessions documented in all six studies is 340, some of the same false confessions are included in more than one study. These six studies thus identify approximately 250 interrogation-induced false confessions.
2. Almost a decade ago, Paul Cassell (1999) argued that false confessions are not a serious problem in the American criminal justice system. For a detailed response to his claims, see Leo and Ofshe (2001) and White (2001a).

8. Policy Directions

1. Paul Cassell (1996; Cassell and Fowles, 1998) has argued that *Miranda* has harmed law enforcement by leading to many lost confessions and lost convictions. For a detailed response to his arguments, see Schulhofer (1996a, b), Donahue (1998), and Feeney (2000).
2. Rule 403 states: "Although relevant, evidence may be excluded if its probative value is substantially outweighed by the danger of unfair prejudice, confusion of the issues, or misleading the jury, or by considerations of undue delay, waste of time, or needless presentation of cumulative evidence" (Federal Rules of Evidence, 403).
3. Sullivan's data set now includes "over 450 police and sheriff's departments in small, medium and large communities from almost every state . . . that customarily record a majority of their custodial interrogations—by audio, video or both—in a defined class of felony investigations" (Sullivan, 2006: 178).

References

Published Works

Acker, James, Brewer, Thomas, Cunningham, Eamonn, Fitzgerald, Allison, Flexon, Jamie, Lombard, Julie, Ryn, Barbara, and Stodghill, Bivette (2001). No appeal from the grave: Innocence, capital punishment and the lessons of history. In S. D. Westervelt and J. A. Humphrey, Eds., *Wrongly convicted: Perspectives on failed justice* (pp. 154–173). Newark, NJ: Rutgers University Press.

Adams, Susan (1996, October). Statement analysis: What do suspects' words really reveal? *FBI Law Enforcement Bulletin, 65,* 12–20.

Ageloff, Hilda (1928, November 28). The third degree. *New Republic,* p. 28.

Alder, Ken (2007). *The lie detectors: The history of an American obsession.* New York: The Free Press.

Alschuler, Albert (1997). Constraint and confession. *Denver University Law Review, 74,* 957–988.

Amar, Akhil (1997). *The constitution and criminal procedure.* New Haven: Yale University Press.

American Bar Association (1988). *Criminal justice in crisis.* Washington, DC: American Bar Association.

American Law Institute (1975). *Official draft of a model code of pre-arraignment procedure.* Philadelphia: The American Law Institute.

Amsterdam, Anthony, and Bruner, Jerome (2000). *Minding the law.* Cambridge, MA: Harvard University Press.

Arther, Richard, and Rudolph Caputo (1959). *Interrogation for investigators.* New York: William C. Copp.

Ayling, Corey (1984). Corroborating confessions: An empirical analysis of legal safeguards against false confessions. *Wisconsin Law Review, 1984,* 1121–1204.

Bandes, Susan (2001). Policing the criminal justice system: Tracing the pattern of no pattern: Stories of police brutality. *Loyola of Los Angeles Law Review, 34,* 665–680.

Bartlett, Robert (1986). *Trial by fire and water: The medieval judicial ordeal.* Oxford: Clarendon Press.

Becker, Robert, and Martin, Andrew (1995, April 18). Vicious killer or gentle farmer? Two portraits emerge of Gary Gauger. *Chicago Tribune*, A1.

Bedau, Hugo Adam, and Radelet, Michael L. (1987). Miscarriages of justice in potentially capital cases. *Stanford Law Review, 40*, 21–179.

Bedau, Hugo, Radelet, Michael, and Putnam, Constance (2004). Convicting the innocent in capital cases: criteria, evidence, and inference. *Drake University Law Review, 52*, 587–603.

Begg, Moazzam (2006). *Enemy combatant: My imprisonment at Guantanamo, Bagram and Kandahar*. New York: The New Press.

Berlow, Alan (2000, October 31). *Texas Justice*. Salon.com.

Blagrove, Mark (1996). Effects of length of sleep deprivation on interrogative suggestibility. *Journal of Experimental Psychology: Applied, 2*, 48–59.

Bond, C. F., and DePaulo, B. M. (2006). Accuracy of deception judgments. *Personality & Social Psychology Review, 10*, 214–234.

Booth, Bates (1930). Confessions and methods employed in procuring them. *Southern California Law Review, 4*, 83–102.

Borchard, Edward M. (1932). *Convicting the innocent: Errors of criminal justice*. New Haven: Yale University Press.

Bowden, Mark (2003, October). The dark art of interrogation. *Atlantic Monthly*, 51–76.

——— (2007, May). The ploy. *Atlantic Monthly*, 54–68.

Brooks, Peter (2000). *Troubling confessions: Speaking guilt in law and literature*. Chicago: University of Chicago Press.

Bryan, Ian (1997). *Interrogation and confession: A study of progress, process and practice*. Brookfield: Ashgate.

Buckley, David, and Jayne, Brian (2005). *Electronic recording of interrogations*. Chicago: John E. Reid and Associates.

Calder, James (1993). *The origins and development of federal crime control police: Herbert Hoover's initiatives*. Westport, CT: Praeger.

Carlson, Peter (1998, September 13). You have the right to remain silent. . . . ; But in the post-*Miranda* age, the police have found new and creative ways to make you talk. *Washington Post Magazine*, 6–11, 19–24.

Carte, Gene, and Carte, Elaine (1975). *Police reform in the United States: The era of August Vollmer, 1905–1932*. Berkeley: University of California Press.

Cassell, Paul (1996). *Miranda's* social costs: An empirical reassessment. *Northwestern University Law Review, 90*, 387–499.

——— (1999). The guilty and the innocent: An examination of alleged cases of wrongful conviction from false confessions. *The Harvard Journal of Law and Public Policy, 22*, 523–597.

Cassell, Paul, and Fowles, Richard (1998). Handcuffing the cops? A thirty-year perspective on *Miranda's* harmful effects on law enforcement. *Stanford Law Review, 50*, 1055–1145.

Castelle, George, and Loftus, Elizabeth (2001) Misinformation and wrongful convictions. In S. D. Westervelt and J. A. Humphrey (Eds.), *Wrongly convicted: Perspectives on failed justice* (pp. 17–35). Newark, NJ: Rutgers University Press.

Chafee, Zechariah (1931, November). Remedies for the third degree. *Atlantic Monthly*, 621–630.

Chisolm, B. O., and Hart, H. H. (1922). Methods of obtaining confessions and information from persons accused of crime. *The Fifty-First Congress of the American Prison Association* (pp. 3–19). New York: Russell Sage Foundation.

Christianson, Scott (2004). *Innocent: Inside wrongful conviction cases.* New York: New York University Press.

Clark, C. L., and Eubank E. (1927). *Lockstep and corridor: Thirty-five years of prison life.* Cincinnati: University of Cincinnati Press.

Cloud, Morgan, Shepherd, George, Barkoff, Alison, and Shur, Justin (2002). Words without meaning: The constitution, confessions and mentally retarded suspects. *University of Chicago Law Review, 69,* 495–624.

Clymer, Steven (2002). Are police free to disregard *Miranda? Yale Law Journal, 112,* 447–552.

Cohen, Stanley (2003). *The wrong men: America's epidemic of wrongful death row convictions.* New York: Carroll & Graf Publishers.

Conley, Ronald, Luckasson, Ruth, and Bouthilet, George, Eds. (1992). *The criminal justice system and mental retardation: Defendants and victims.* Baltimore: Paul H. Brookes.

Connery, Donald, ed. (1996). *Convicting the innocent: The story of a murder, a false confession and the struggle to free a wrong man.* Cambridge, MA: Brookline Books.

Connors, Edward, Lundregan, Thomas, Miller, Neil, and McEwen, Tom (1996). *Convicted by juries, exonerated by science: Case studies in the use of DNA evidence to establish innocence after trial.* Washington, DC: Department of Justice.

Conroy, John (2000). *Unspeakable acts, ordinary people: The dynamics of torture.* Berkeley: University of California Press.

Corwin, Miles (1996, March 25). False confessions and tips still flow in Simpson case, crime: Such calls have been common since Lindbergh kidnapping. About 500 confessed to Black Dahlia killing. *Los Angeles Times,* A1.

Costanzo, Mark, and Leo, Richard (2007). Research findings and expert testimony on police interrogations and confessions to crimes. In Mark Costanzo, Daniel Krauss, and Kathy Pezdek (Eds.), *Expert psychological testimony for the courts.* Mahwah, NJ: Lawrence Erlbaum.

Covey, Russell (2005). Interrogation warrants. *Cardozo Law Review, 26,* 1867–1946.

Davies, Sharon (2006). The reality of false confessions—lessons of the Central Park Jogger case. *New York University Review of Law and Social Change, 30,* 209–253.

Davis, Deborah, and Follette, William (2002). Rethinking probative value of evidence: Base rates, intuitive profiling and the postdiction of behavior. *Law and Human Behavior, 26,* 133–158.

Davis, Deborah, and Leo, Richard A. (2006). Strategies for preventing false confessions and their consequences. In Mark Kebbell and Graham Davies (Eds.), *Practical psychology for forensic investigations and prosecutions* (pp. 121–149). New York: John Wiley & Sons.

Davis, Deborah, and O'Donahue, William (2003). The road to perdition: Extreme influence tactics in the interrogation room. In William O'Donahue and Erick Levinsky (Eds.), *Handbook of forensic psychology* (pp. 897–996). San Diego: Academic Press.

Davis, Kenneth (1996). *The wrong man: A true story.* New York: Avon Books.

Davison, S. E., and Forshaw, D. M. (1993). Retracted Confessions: Through opiate withdrawal to a new conceptual framework. *Medicine, Science and the Law, 33,* 285–290.

Deakin, Thomas (1988). *Police professionalism: The renaissance of American law enforcement.* Springfield, IL: Charles C Thomas.

DePaulo, B. (1994). Spotting lies: Can humans learn to do better? *Current Directions in Psychological Science, 3,* 83–86.

DePaulo, B., Lindsay, J, Malone, B., Muhlenbruck, L., Charlton, K., and Cooper, H. (2003). Cues to deception. *Psychological Bulletin, 129,* 74–112.

Dershowitz, Alan (1982). *The best defense.* New York: Vintage.

———— (1996). *Reasonable doubts: The criminal justice system and the O.J. Simpson case.* New York: Simon & Schuster.

———— (2002). *Why terrorism works: Understanding the threat, responding to the challenge.* New Haven: Yale University Press.

Dilworth, Donald (1976). *The blue and the brass: American policing, 1890–1910.* Gaithersburg, MD: International Association of Chiefs of Police.

Donahue, John (1998). Did *Miranda* diminish police effectiveness? *Stanford Law Review, 50,* 1147–1180.

Donovan, Daniel, and Rhodes, John (2000). Comes a time: The case for recording interrogations. *Montana Law Review, 61,* 223–249.

Douglas, John (1995). *Mind hunter: Inside the FBI's elite serial unit.* New York: Scribner (with Mark Olshaker).

Douthit, Nathan (1975). Police professionalism and the war against crime. In George L. Mosse (Ed.), *Police forces in history* (pp. 317–333). London: Sage Publications.

Doyle, James (2005). *True witness: cops, courts, science, and the battle against misidentification.* New York: Palgrave Macmillan.

Drizin, Steven, and Colgan, Beth (2004). Tales from the juvenile confession front: A guide to how standard police interrogation tactics can produce coerced and false confessions from juvenile suspects. In G. Daniel Lassiter (Ed.), *Interrogations, confessions, and entrapment* (pp. 127–162). New York: Kluwer Academic.

Drizin, Steven, and Leo, Richard A. (2004). The problem of false confessions in the post-DNA world. *North Carolina Law Review, 82,* 891–1007.

Drizin, Steven, and Reich, Marissa (2004). Heeding the lessons of history: The need for mandatory recording of police interrogations to accurately assess the reliability and voluntariness of confessions. *Drake Law Review, 52,* 619–646.

Drogin, Bob, and Miller, Greg (2004, February 6). CIA chief saw no imminent threat in Iraq; Tenet says his agency overestimated Hussein's illicit weapons and relied upon "fabricated" information from an "unreliable" source. *Los Angeles Times,* A1.

Edds, Margaret (2003). *An expendable man: the near-execution of Earl Washington, Jr.* New York: New York University Press.

Ekman, Paul (1992). *Telling lies: clues to deceit in the marketplace, politics and marriage.* New York: W.W. Norton.

Ekman, Paul, and O'Sullivan, Maureen (1991). Who can catch a liar? *American Psychologist, 46,* 913–920.

Ekman, Paul, O'Sullivan, Maureen, and Frank, Mark (1999). A few can catch a liar. *Psychological Science, 10,* 263–266.

Ellis, James, and Luckasson, Ruth (1985). Mentally retarded defendants. *The George Washington Law Review, 53,* 414–493

Ericson, Richard (1981). *Making crime: A study of detective work.* Canada: Butterworth & Co.

Faigman, David (1999). *Legal alchemy: The use and misuse of science in law.* New York: W. H. Freeman.

Federal Rules of Evidence (2006). Washington, DC: U.S. Government Printing Office.

Feeney, Floyd (2000). Police clearances: A poor way to measure the impact of *Miranda* on the police. *Rutgers Law Review, 32,* 1–114.

Feld, Barry (2006a). Juveniles competence to exercise Miranda rights: An empirical examination. *Minnesota Law Review, 91,* 26–100.

——— (2006b). Police interrogation of juveniles: A study of policy and practice. *Journal of Criminology and Criminal Law, 97,* 219–316.

Fiaschetti, Michael (1930a). The third degree as a cop sees it. *New York World,* 7

——— (March 8, 1930b). Forced convictions. Editorial. *New York Telegram,* 1.

Findley, Keith, and Scott, Michael (2006). The multiple dimensions of tunnel vision in criminal cases. *Wisconsin Law Review,* 291–398.

Finlay, W.M.L., and Lyons, E. (2002). Acquiescence in interviews with people who have mental retardation. *Mental Retardation, 20,* 14–29.

Fisher, Jim (1996). *Fall guys: False confessions and the politics of murder.* Carbondale: Southern Illinois University Press.

Fisher, Stanley (1988). In search of the virtuous prosecutor: A conceptual framework. *American Journal of Criminal Law, 15,* 197–261.

——— (2002). Convictions of innocent persons in Massachusetts: An overview. *Boston University Public Interest Law Journal, 12,* 1–72.

Fogelson, Robert (1977). *Big-city police.* Cambridge, MA: Harvard University Press.

Forest, Krista, Wadkins, T., and Miller, R. (2002). The role of pre-existing stress on false confessions: An empirical study. *Journal of Credibility Assessment and Witness Psychology, 3,* 23–45.

Forst, Brian (2004). *Errors of justice: Nature, sources and remedies.* New York: Cambridge University Press.

Frank, Jerome (1949). *Courts on trial: Myth and reality in American justice.* Princeton: Princeton University Press.

Frank, Jerome, and Frank, Barbara (1957). *Not guilty.* New York: Doubleday.

Franklin, Charles (1970). *The third degree.* London: Robert Hale.

Friedman, Lawrence (1993). *Crime and punishment in American history*. New York: Basic Books.

Ganey, Terry (1989). *St. Joseph's children: A true story of terror and justice*. New York: Carol Publishing Group.

Garcia, Alfredo (1998). Is Miranda dead, was it overruled, or it is irrelevant? *St. Thomas Law Review, 10*, 461–498.

Gardner, Earle Stanley (1952). *Court of last resort*. New York: Pocket Books.

Garrett, Brendan (2005). Innocence, harmless error, and federal wrongful conviction law. *Wisconsin Law Review, 2005*, 35–114.

Garrett, Brandan (2008). Judging innocence. *Columbia Law Review*, Forthcoming.

Gauger, Gary (2005). I stepped into a dream. In Lola Vollen and Dave Eggers (Eds.), *Surviving justice: America's wrongfully convicted and exonerated* (pp. 81–113). San Francisco: McSweeney's Books.

Geis, Gilbert (1959). In scopolamine veritas: The early history of drug-Induced statements. *Journal of Criminal Law, Criminology, and Police Science, 50*, 347–357.

Geller, William (1992). *Police videotaping of suspect interrogations and confessions: A preliminary examination of issues and practices. A report to the National Institute of Justice*. Washington, DC: U.S. Department of Justice.

Gilbert, D. T., and Malone, P. S. (1995). The correspondence bias. *Psychological Bulletin, 117*, 21–38.

Gilovich, Thomas (1991). *How we know what isn't so: The fallibility of human reason in everyday life*. New York: The Free Press.

Givelber, Daniel (1997). Meaningless acquittals, meaningful convictions: Do we reliably acquit the innocent? *Rutgers Law Review, 49*, 1317–1396.

———— (2000). Punishing protestations of innocence: Denying responsibility and its consequences. *American Criminal Law Review, 37*, 1363–1408.

———— (2001). The adversary system and historical accuracy: Can we do better? In S. D. Westervelt and J. A. Humphrey (Eds.), *Wrongly convicted: perspectives on failed justice* (pp. 253–268). Newark, NJ: Rutgers University Press.

Gohara, Miriam (2006). A lie for a lie: False confessions and the case for reconsidering the legality of deceptive interrogation techniques. *Fordham Urban Law Journal, 33*, 791–842.

Gordon, Nathan, and Fleisher, William (2006). *Effective interviewing and interrogation techniques* (2nd ed.). San Diego: Academic Press.

Gottschalk, Louis (1961). The use of drugs in interrogation. In Albert Biderman and Herbert Zimmer (Eds.), *The manipulation of human behavior* (pp. 96–141). New York: John Wiley & Sons.

Granhag, P. A., and Stromwall, L. A. (Eds.) (2004). *The detection of deception in forensic contexts*. Cambridge, UK: Cambridge University Press.

Grano, Joseph (1993). *Confessions, truth, and the law*. Ann Arbor: University of Michigan Press.

Greenwood, Peter, and Petersilia, Joan (1975). *The criminal investigation process: Summary and policy implications*. Washington, DC: U.S. Government Printing Office.

Gross, Samuel (1996). The risks of death: Why erroneous convictions are common in capital cases. *Buffalo Law Review, 44,* 469–500.

——— (1998). Lost lives: miscarriages of justice in capital cases. *Law and Contemporary Problems, 61,* 125–152.

Gross, Samuel, Jacoby, Kristen, Matheson, Daniel, Montgomery, Nicholas, and Patel, Sujata (2005). Exonerations in the United States, 1989 through 2003. *Journal of Criminal Law and Criminology, 95,* 523–553.

Gruhl, John, and Spohn, Cassia (1981). The supreme court's post-*Miranda* rulings: Impact on local prosecutors. *Law and Policy Quarterly, 3,* 29–54.

Gudjonsson, G. H. (2003). *The psychology of interrogations and confessions: A handbook.* New York: John Wiley & Sons.

Gudjonsson, Gisli, Clare, I., Rutter, S., and Pearse, J. (1993). Persons at risk during interviews in police custody: The identification of vulnerabilities (Royal Commission on Criminal Justice Research Study No. 12). London: Her Majesty's Stationery Office.

Haller, Mark (1976). Historical roots of police behavior: Chicago, 1890–1925. *Law & Society Review, 10,* 303–323.

Hanson, F. Allan (1993). *Testing testing: Social consequences of the examined life.* Berkeley: University of California Press.

Harbury, Jennifer (2006). *Truth, torture and the American way.* Boston: Beacon Press.

Harrison, Y., and Horne, J. (2000). The impact of sleep deprivation on decision making: A review. *Journal of Experimental Psychology: Applied, 6,* 236–249.

Hart, William (1981, March). The subtle art of persuasion. *Police Magazine,* 7–17.

Hartwig, Maria, Granhag, Par Anders, Stromwall, Leif, and Vrig, Aldert (2004). Police officers' lie detection accuracy: Interrogating freely vs. observing video. *Police Quarterly, 7,* 429–456.

Harvard Law Review (1930). The third degree, *43,* 617–623.

Henderson, George C. (1924). *Keys to crookdom.* New York: D. Appleton.

Henkel, Linda, and Coffman, Kimberly (2004). Memory distortions in coerced false confessions: A source monitoring framework analysis. *Applied Cognitive Psychology, 18,* 567–588.

Hepworth, Mike, and Turner, Bryan, S. (1982). *Confession: Studies and deviance and religion.* London: Routledge & Kegan Paul.

Hersh, Seymour M. (2004). *Chain of command: The road from 9/11 to Abu Ghraib.* New York: HarperCollins.

Hess, John (1997). *Interviewing and interrogation for law enforcement.* Cincinatti: Anderson.

Hilgendorf, Lindon, and Irving, Barrie (1981). A decision-making model of confessions. In M. Lloyd-Bostock (Ed.), *Psychology in legal contexts: Applications and limitations* (pp. 67–84). London: MacMillan.

Hoffman, Jan (1998, March 28). Some officers are skirting Miranda restraints to get confessions. *New York Times,* A1.

Holmes, Warren (2003). *Criminal interrogation: A modern format for interrogating criminal suspects based on the intellectual approach.* Springfield, IL: Charles C. Thomas.

Hopkins, Ernest Jerome (1931). *Our lawless police: A study of the unlawful enforcement of the law*. New York: Viking Press.

Horselenberg, R., Merckelbach, H., and Josephs, S. (2003). Individual differences and false confessions. *Psychology, Crime & Law, 9,* 1–8.

Huggins, Martha, Haritos-Fatouros, Mika, and Zimbardo, Philip (2002). *Violence workers: Police torturers and murderers reconstruct Brazilian atrocities*. Berkeley: University of California Press.

Humes, Edward (1999). *Mean justice: A town's terror, a prosecutor's power, a betrayal of innocence*. New York: Simon & Schuster.

Hyman, I., Husband T., and Billings, F. (1995). False memories of childhood experiences. *Applied Cognitive Psychology, 9,* 181–197.

Inbau, Fred (1942). *Lie detection and criminal interrogation*. Baltimore: Williams & Wilkins.

——— (1948). *Lie detection and criminal interrogation*. (2nd ed.). Baltimore: William & Wilkins.

——— (1961). Police interrogation—A practical necessity. *Journal of Criminal Law, Criminology, and Police Science, 52,* 16–20.

Inbau, Fred, and Reid, John (1953). *Lie detection and criminal interrogation* (3rd ed.). Baltimore: Williams & Wilkins.

——— (1962). *Criminal interrogation and confessions*. Baltimore: Williams & Wilkins.

——— (1967). *Criminal interrogation and confessions* (2nd ed.). Baltimore: William & Wilkins.

Inbau, Fred, Reid, John, and Buckley, Joseph (1986). *Criminal interrogation and confessions* (3rd ed.). Baltimore: Williams & Wilkins.

Inbau, Fred, Reid, John, Buckley, Joseph, and Jayne, Brian (2001). *Criminal interrogation and confessions* (4th ed.). Gaithersburg, MD: Aspen.

Indiana Law Journal (1953). Voluntary false confessions: A neglected area in criminal administration, *28,* 374–392.

Innes, Martin (2003). *Investigating murder: Detective work and the police response to homicide*. Oxford: Oxford University Press.

Innocence Project (2006). www.innocenceproject.org.

International Association of Chiefs of Police (1998, Fall). Videotaping interrogations and confessions. *Policy Review, 10,* 1–4.

International Police Magazine (1911, August). Police methods and their critics, p. 9.

Irving, Barrie, and Hilgendorf, Linden (1980). Police interrogation: The psychological approach. *Royal Commission on Criminal Procedure Research Study No. 1*. London: HMSO.

Jackall, Robert (2005). *Street stories: The world of police detectives*. Cambridge, MA: Harvard University Press.

Jayne, Brian (1986). The psychological principles of criminal interrogation. In Fred Inbau, John Reid, and Joseph Buckley (Eds.), *Criminal interrogation and confessions* (pp. 327–347). Baltimore: Williams & Wilkins.

——— (2004). Empirical experiences of required electronic recording of interviews and interrogations on investigators' practices and case outcomes. *Law Enforcement Executive Forum, 4,* 103–112.

Jayne, Brian, and Buckley, Joseph (1993, August). Misleading interrogation definitions studied. *PORAC Law Enforcement News, 25,* 31.

———— (1999). *The investigator anthology: A compilation of articles and essays about the Reid technique of interviewing and interrogation.* Chicago: John E. Reid and Associates, Inc.

Jerome, Richard (1995, August 13). Suspect confessions. *New York Times Magazine,* 28–31.

Johnson, David (2002). *The Japanese way of justice: Prosecuting crime in Japan.* Oxford: Oxford University Press.

Johnson, Gail (1997). False confessions and fundamental fairness: The need for electronic recording of custodial interrogations. *Boston University Public Interest Law Journal, 6,* 719–751.

Johnson, Marilynn (2003). *Street justice: A history of police violence in New York City.* Boston: Beacon Press Books.

Joseph, Albert (1995). *We get confessions.* Rochester: Printing Methods, Inc.

Journal of American Institute of Criminal Law and Criminology, 1912.

Kagan, Robert (2001). *Adversarial legalism: The American way of life.* Cambridge, MA: Harvard University Press.

Kamisar, Yale (1965). Equal justice in the gatehouses and mansions of American criminal procedure: From *Powell* to *Gideon,* From *Escobedo* to. . . . In A. E. Dick Howard (Ed.), *Criminal justice in our time.* Charlottesville, VA: University Press of Virginia.

———— (1980). *Police interrogation and confessions: Essays in law and policy.* Ann Arbor: University of Michigan Press.

———— (1996, June 10). *Miranda* does not look so awesome now. *Legal Times,* A22.

Kassin, Saul (1997a). The psychology of confession evidence. *American Psychologist, 52,* 221–233.

———— (1997b). False memories against the self. *Psychological Inquiry, 8,* 300–302.

———— (2005). On the psychology of confessions: Does *innocence* put *innocents* at risk? *American Psychologist, 60,* 215–228.

———— (2006). A critical appraisal of modern police interrogations. In Tom Williamson (Ed.), *Investigative interviewing: Rights, research, regulation.* Portland: Willan Publishing.

Kassin, Saul, and Fong, C. T. (1999). "I'm innocent!" Effects of training on judgments of truth and deception in the interrogation room. *Law and Human Behavior, 23,* 499–516.

Kassin, Saul, Goldstein, C. J., and Savitsky, K. (2003). Behavioral confirmation in the interrogation room: On the dangers of presuming guilt. *Law and Human Behavior, 27,* 187–203.

Kassin, Saul, and Gudjonsson, Gisli (2004). The psychology of confessions: A review of the literature and issues. *Psychological Science in the Public Interest, 5,* 35–67.

Kassin, Saul, and Kiechel, Katherine (1996). The social psychology of false confessions: Compliance, internalization, and confabulation. *Psychological Science, 7,* 125–128.

Kassin, Saul, and McNall, Karlyn (1991). Police interrogation and confessions: Communicating promises and threats by pragmatic implication. *Law and Human Behavior, 15,* 233–251.

Kassin, Saul, and Neumann, Katherine (1997). On the power of confession evidence: an experimental test of the fundamental difference hypothesis. *Law and Human Behavior, 21,* 460–484.

Kassin, Saul, and Sukel, Holly (1997). Coerced confessions and the jury. *Law and Human Behavior, 21,* 27–46.

Kassin, Saul, and Wrightsman, Lawrence (1985). Confession evidence. In Saul Kassin and Lawrence Wrightsman (Eds.), *The psychology of evidence and trial procedure* (pp. 67–94). Beverly Hills: Sage Publications.

Katz, Jack (1999). *How emotions work.* Chicago: University of Chicago Press.

Kauper, Paul (1932). Judicial examination of the accused—A remedy fore the third degree. *Michigan Law Review, 30,* 1224–1255.

Kebbell, Mark, and Hurren, Emily (2006). Improving the interviewing of suspected offenders. In Mark Kebbell and Graham Davies (Eds.), *Practical psychology for forensic investigations and prosecutions* (pp. 103–119). New York: John Wiley & Sons.

Kebbell, Mark, Hurren, Emily, and Roberts, S. (2006). Mock suspects' decisions to confess: Accuracy of eyewitness evidence is crucial. *Applied Cognitive Psychology, 20,* 477–486.

Keedy, Edwin (1937). The third degree and legal interrogation of suspects. *University of Pennsylvania Law Review, 85,* 761–777.

Kelman, Herbert (1958). Compliance, identification and internalization: Three processes of attitude Change. *Journal of Conflict Resolution, 2,* 51–60.

——— (1974). Further thoughts on processes of compliance, identification and internalization. In James Tedeschi (Ed.), *Perspectives on social power* (pp. 125–171). Chicago: University of Chicago Press.

Kidd, W. R. (1940). *Police interrogation.* New York: Police Journal.

Kleinmuntz, Benjamin, and Julian Szucko (1984). Lie-detection in ancient and modern times: A call for contemporary scientific study. *American Psychologist, 39,* 766–776.

Klockars, Carl (1980). The Dirty Harry problem. *The Annals, 452,* 33–47.

Langbein, John (1978). Torture and plea bargaining. *University of Chicago Law Review 46,* 1–21.

——— (2003). *The origins of the adversary trial.* Oxford: Oxford University Press.

Lardner, James, and Repetto, Thomas (2000). *NYPD: A city and its police.* New York: Henry Holt.

Larson, John A. (1932). *Lying and its detection: A study of deception and deception tests.* Chicago: University of Chicago Press.

Lassiter, G. Daniel (Ed.) (2004). *Interrogations, confessions, and entrapment.* New York: Kluwer Academic.

Lassiter, G. Daniel, Greers, Andrew, Munhall, Patrick, Handley, Ian and Beers, Melissa (2001). Videotaped confessions: Is guilt in the eye of the camera? In M. P. Zanna (Ed.), *Advances in experimental social psychology* (Vol. 33, pp. 189–254). San Diego: Academic Press.

Lassiter, G. Daniel, and Ratcliff, Jennifer (2004). Exposing coercive influences in the criminal justice system: An agenda for legal psychology in the twenty-first century. In G. Daniel Lassiter (Ed.), *Interrogations, confessions, and entrapment* (pp. 1–8). New York: Kluwer/Plenum.

Lassiter, G. Daniel, and Greers, Andrew (2004). Bias and accuracy in the evaluation of confession evidence. In G. Daniel Lassiter (Ed.), *Interrogations, confessions, and entrapment* (pp. 197–214). New York: Kluwer/Plenum.

Lavine, Emanuel (1930). *The third degree: A detailed and appalling expose of police brutality.* New York: Garden City Publishing.

——— (1936). *Secrets of the metropolitan police.* Garden City, NY: Garden City Publishing.

Lee, Wen Ho (2001). *My country versus me: The first-hand account by the Los Alamos scientist who was falsely accused of being a spy.* New York: Hyperion.

Leo, Richard A. (1992). From coercion to deception: The changing nature of police interrogation in America. *Crime, Law, and Social Change: An International Journal, 18,* 35–59.

——— (1994). Police interrogation and social control. *Social & Legal Studies, 3,* 93–120.

——— (1996a). Inside the interrogation room. *Journal of Criminal Law and Criminology, 86,* 266–303.

——— (1996b). The impact of *Miranda* revisited. *Journal of Criminal Law And Criminology, 86,* 621–692.

——— (1996c). *Miranda's* revenge: Police interrogation as a confidence game. *Law and Society Review, 30,* 259–288.

——— (1998). *Miranda* and the problem of false confessions. In Richard A. Leo and George C. Thomas III (Eds.), *The* Miranda *debate: Law, justice and policing* (pp. 271–282). Boston: Northeastern University Press.

——— (2001a). Questioning the relevance of *Miranda* in the twenty-first century. *University of Michigan Law Review, 99,* 1000–1029.

——— (2001b). False confessions: Causes, consequences, and solutions. In S. D. Westervelt and J. A. Humphrey (Eds.), *Wrongly convicted: perspectives on failed justice* (pp. 36–54). Newark, NJ: Rutgers University Press.

——— (2004a). The third degree and the origins of psychological police interrogation in the United States. In G. Daniel Lassiter (Ed.), *Interrogations, confessions, and entrapment* (pp. 37–84). New York: Kluwer Academic.

——— (2004b). Beating a bum rap. *Contexts, 3,* 68–69.

——— (2005). Re-thinking the study of miscarriages of justice: Developing a criminology of wrongful conviction. *Journal of Contemporary Criminal Justice, 21,* 201–223.

Leo, Richard A., Costanzo, Mark, and Shaked, Netta (2007). Psychological and cultural aspects of interrogations and false confessions: Using research to inform legal decision-making. Forthcoming in Joel Lieberman and Daniel Krauss (Eds.), *Psychology in the courtroom*. London: Ashgate.

Leo, Richard A., Drizin, Steven, Neufeld, Peter, Hall, Brad, and Vatner, Amy (2006). Bringing reliability back in: False confessions and legal safeguards in the twenty-first century. *Wisconsin Law Review, 2*, 479–539.

Leo, Richard A., and Ofshe, Richard (1997). Missing the forest for the trees: A response to Paul Cassell's 'balanced approach' to the false confession problem. *Denver University Law Review, 74*, 1135–1144.

——— (1998a). The consequences of false confessions: Deprivations of liberty and miscarriages of justice in the age of psychological interrogation. *Journal of Criminal Law and Criminology, 88*, 429–296.

——— (1998b). Using the innocent to scapegoat *Miranda:* Another reply to Paul Cassell. *The Journal of Criminal Law and Criminology, 88*, 557–577.

——— (2001). The truth about false confessions and advocacy scholarship. *The Criminal Law Bulletin, 37*, 293–370.

Leo, Richard A., and Richman, Kimberly D. (2007). Mandate the electronic recording of police interrogation. Forthcoming in *Crime and Public Policy*.

Leo, Richard A., and Thomas, George C. III (Eds.) (1998). *The Miranda debate: Law, justice, and policing*. Boston: Northeastern University Press.

Leo, Richard A., and White, Welsh S. (1999). Adapting to *Miranda:* Modern interrogators' strategies for dealing with the obstacles posed by *Miranda. Minnesota Law Review, 84*, 397–472.

Lesce, Tony (1990, August). SCAN: Detection deception by scientific content analysis, *Law and Order, 38*, 1–4.

Leveritt, Mara (2002). *Devil's knot: The true story of the West Memphis three*. New York: Atria Books.

Limpus, Lowell W. (1939). *Honest cop: Lewis J. Valentine*. New York: E. P. Dutton.

Loftus, Elizabeth (1979). *Eyewitness testimony*. Cambridge, MA: Harvard University Press.

——— (2004). The devil in confessions. *Psychological Science in the Public Interest, 5*, i–ii.

Loftus, Elizabeth, and Pickrell, Jacqueline (1995). The formation of false memories. *Psychiatric Annals, 25*, 720–725.

Lopez, Alberto (2002). $10 and a denim jacket? A model statute for compensating the wrongly convicted. *University of Georgia Law Review, 36*, 665–722.

Luban, David (1988). *Lawyers and justice: An ethical study*. Princeton: Princeton University Press.

Lubet, Steven (2002). *Nothing but the truth: Why trial lawyers don't, can't, and shouldn't have to tell the whole truth*. New York: New York University Press.

Luna, Erik (2005). System failure. *American Criminal Law Review, 42*, 1201–1218.

Lykken, David (1998). *Tremor in the blood: Uses and abuses of the lie detector*. New York: Plenum.

Magid, Laurie (2001). Deceptive police interrogation practices: How far is too far?, *Michigan Law Review, 99*, 1168–1210.

Maier, Thomas, and Smith, Rex (1986, December 5). Confessions: Reliance on getting confessions tied to abuses, weakened cases, *Newsday*, 5.

Malone, Patrick (1986). You have the right to remain silent: *Miranda* after twenty years. *American Scholar, 55,* 367–380.

Maple, Jack (1999). *The crime fighter: How you can make your community crime-free.* (With Chris Mitchell). New York: Broadway Books.

Marguilies, Joseph (2006). *Guantanamo and the abuse of presidential power.* New York: Simon & Schuster.

Martin, Diane (2002). Lessons about justice from the laboratory of wrongful convictions: Tunnel vision, the construction of guilt, and informer evidence. *UMKC Law Review, 70,* 847–864.

Marx, Gary T. (1988). *Undercover: Police surveillance in America.* Berkeley: University of California Press.

——— (1992). Commentary. *Crime, Law, and Social Change: An International Journal, 18,* 3–34.

Mathewson, Duncan (1929). The technique of the American detective. *The Annals of the American Academy, 146,* 214–218.

Mazzoni, Giuliana, Loftus, Elizabeth, and Kirsch, Irving (2001). Changing beliefs about implausible autobiographical events: A little plausibility goes a long way. *Journal of Experimental Psychology: Applied, 7,* 51–59.

McBarnet, Doreen (1981). *Conviction: Law, the state, and the construction of justice.* London: Macmillan.

McCann, Joseph (1998). A conceptual framework for identifying various types of confessions, *Behavioral Sciences and the Law, 16,* 441–453.

McConville, Mike, Sanders, Andrew, and Leng, Roger (1991). *The case for the prosecution: Police, suspects and the construction of criminality.* London: Routledge.

McCormick, Charles (1972). *Handbook of the law of evidence* (2nd ed.). St. Paul: West.

McCoy, Alfred W. (2006). *A question of torture: CIA interrogation, from the cold war to the war on terror.* New York: Metropolitan Books.

McCoy, Candace (1996). Police, prosecutors and discretion in investigation. In John Kleinig (Ed.), *Handled with discretion: Ethical issues in police decision-making* (pp. 159–177). Lanham: Rowman & Littlefield.

McMullen, Patrick (2005). Questioning the questions: The impermissibility of police deception in interrogations of juveniles. *Northwestern University Law Review, 99,* 971–1006.

McNally, Richard (2003). *Remembering trauma.* Cambridge, MA: Harvard University Press.

Medwed, Daniel (2004). The zeal deal: Prosecutorial resistance to post-conviction claims of innocence. *Boston University Law Review, 84,* 125–183.

Meissner, Christian, and Kassin, Saul (2002). "He's guilty!" Investigator bias in judgments of truth and deception. *Law and Human Behavior, 26,* 469–480.

——— (2004). "You're guilty, so just confess!" Cognitive and confirmational biases in the interrogation room. In G. D. Lassiter (Ed.), *Interrogations, confessions, and entrapment* (pp. 85–106). New York: Kluwer Academic.

Memon, Amina, Vrij, Aldert, and Bull, Ray (2003). *Psychology and law: Truthfulness, accuracy and credibility.* London: Jossey-Bass.

Miller, Gerald R., and Boster, F. Joseph (1977). Three images of the trial: Their implications for psychological research. In Bruce Sales (Ed.), *Psychology in the legal process* (pp. 19–38). New York: Pocket Books.

Miller, Gerald, and Stiff, James (1993). *Deceptive communication.* Thousand Oaks: Sage Publications.

Moley, Raymond (1932). *Tribunes of the people: The past and future of the New York magistrates' courts.* New Haven: Yale University Press.

Mollen, Milton (1994, July 7). *Commission report.* The City of New York commission to investigate allegations of police corruption and the anti-corruption procedures of the police department.

Mones, Paul (1995). *Stalking justice.* New York: Pocket Books.

Morris, William, and Morris, Mary (1988). *The morris dictionary of word and phrase origins* (2nd ed.). New York: Harper & Row.

Moston, Stephen, Stephenson, Geoffrey M., and Williamson, Thomas M. (1992). The effects of case characteristics on suspect behavior during police questioning. *British Journal of Criminology, 32,* 23–40.

Muehlberger, C. W. (1951). Interrogation under drug influence: The so-called "truth serum" technique. *Journal of Criminal Law, Criminology, and Police Science, 42,* 513–528.

Mulbar, Harold (1951). *Interrogation.* Springfield, IL: Charles C. Thomas.

Munsterberg, Hugo (1908). *On the witness stand.* New York: Doubleday.

Murphy, Charles J. (1929). Third degree: Another side of our crime problem. *Outlook, 151,* 522–526.

Napier, Michael, and Adams, Susan (2002, November). Criminal confessions; Applying interview and interrogation techniques can help law enforcement identify suspects and obtain and safeguard confessions. *FBI Law Enforcement Bulletin, 71,* 9–15.

Nardulli, Peter (1987). The societal costs of the exclusionary rule revisited. *University of Illinois Law Review, 1987,* 223–239.

Nardulli, Peter, Eisenstein, James, and Fleming, Roy (1988). *The tenor of justice: Criminal courts and the guilty plea process.* Urbana: University of Illinois Press.

National Institute for Truth Verification (2003). *Computer voice stress analyzer.* Training manual.

National Research Council (2003). *The polygraph and lie detection.* Washington, DC: The National Academies Press.

NBC Dateline (December 23, 1997). I confess; Man convinced by police interrogators that he killed his daughter confesses, but is later found innocent due to lack of evidence.

Newsome, Melba (2006, April). True crimes, false confessions. *O Magazine,* 235–236, 244–246, 249, 310.

Ochoa, Christopher (2005). My life is a broken puzzle. In Lola Vollen and Dave Eggers (Eds.), *Surviving justice: America's wrongfully convicted and exonerated* (pp. 13–46). San Francisco: McSweeney's Books.

O'Dwyer, William (1987). *Beyond the golden door.* Jamaica, NY: St. John's University Press.

Ofshe, Richard (1992). Inadvertent hypnosis during interrogation: False confessions due to dissociative state: misidentified multiple personality disorder and the satanic cult hypothesis. *Journal of Clinical and Experimental Hypnosis, 40,* 125–156.

Ofshe, Richard, and Leo, Richard A. (1997a). The social psychology of police interrogation: The theory and classification of true and false confessions. *Studies in Law, Politics and Society, 16,* 189–251.

——— (1997b). The decision to confess falsely: Rational choice and irrational action. *Denver University Law Review, 74,* 979–1122.

Ofshe, Richard, and Watters, Ethan (1994). *Making monsters: False memories, psychotherapy and sexual hysteria.* New York: Charles Scribner's Sons.

Ogletree, Charles (1987). Are confessions really good for the soul? A proposal to mirandize *Miranda. Harvard Law Review, 100,* 1826–1845.

O'Hara, Charles (1956). *Fundamentals of criminal investigation.* Springfield, IL: Charles C. Thomas.

Osborne, Jonathan (2001, February 8). Officers faulted in slaying inquiry; Many mistakes were made. *Austin-American Stateman,* A1.

Ost, James, Costall, A., and Bull, Ray (2001). False confessions and false memories: A model for understanding retractors' experiences. *Journal of Forensic Psychiatry, 12,* 549–579.

O'Sullivan, F. Dalton (1928). *Crime detection.* Chicago: O'Sullivan Publishing.

Owen-Kostelnik, Jessica, Reppucci, N. Dickson, and Meyer, Jessica (2006). Testimony and interrogation of minors: Assumptions about maturity and morality. *American Psychologist, 4,* 286–304.

Packer, Herbert (1968). *The limits of the criminal sanction.* Stanford, CA: Stanford University Press.

Paris, Margaret (1995). Trust, lies and interrogation. *Virginia Journal of Social Policy and Law, 3,* 3–66.

Parloff, Roger (1996). *Triple jeopardy.* Boston: Little, Brown.

Penney, Steven (1998). Theories of confession admissibility: A historical view. *American Journal of Criminal Law, 25,* 309–383.

Perske, Robert (1991). *Unequal justice: What can happen when persons with retardation or other developmental disabilities encounter the criminal justice system.* Nashville: Abingdon Press.

Piper, August (1994). "Truth serum" and "recovered memories" of sexual abuse: A review of the evidence. *The Journal of Psychiatry and Law, 21,* 447–471.

Pizzi, William (1999). *Trials without truth: Why our system of criminal trials has become an expensive failure and what we need to do to rebuild It.* New York: New York University Press.

Porter, Stephen, and Yuille, John (1996). The language of deceit: An investigation of the verbal clues to deception in the interrogation context. *Law and Human Behavior, 20,* 443–458.

Porter, Stephen, Yuille, John, and Lehman, Darrin (1999). The nature of real, implanted and fabricated memories for emotional childhood events: Implications for the recovered memory debate. *Law and Human Behavior, 23,* 517–537.

Pound, Roscoe (1909). The causes of popular dissatisfaction with the administration of justice. *American Bar Association Reporter, 29,* 395–417.

Pratkanis, Anthony, and Aronson, Elliott (1991). *Age of propaganda: The everyday use and abuse of persuasion.* New York: W. H. Freeman.

Prejean, Helen (2005). *The death of innocents: An eyewitness account of wrongful executions.* New York: Random House.

Protess, David, and Warden, Rob (1998). *A promise of justice.* New York: Hyperion.

Purvis, Melvin (1936). *American agent.* New York: Garden City Publishing.

Raab, Selwyn (1967). *Justice in the backroom.* Cleveland: World Publishing.

Rabon, Don (1992). *Interviewing and interrogation.* Durham, NC: Carolina Academic Press.

——— (1994). *Investigative discourse analysis.* Durham, NC: Carolina Academic Press.

Radelet, Michael, and Bedau, Hugo (1998). The execution of the innocent. *Law and Contemporary Problems, 61,* 105–124.

Radelet, Michael, Bedau, Hugo, and Putnam, Constance (1992). *In spite of Innocence: Erroneous convictions in capital cases.* Boston: Northeastern University Press.

Radin, Edwin (1964). *The innocents.* New York: William Morrow.

Redlich, Allison (2004). Mental illness, police interrogations, and the potential for false confession. *Law and Psychiatry, 55,* 19–21.

Redlich, Allison, and Goodman, Gail (2003). Taking responsibility for an act not committed: The influence of age and suggestibility. *Law and Human Behavior, 27,* 141–156.

Reid, John, and Inbau, Fred (1977). *Truth and deception: The polygraph ("lie-detector") technique* (2nd ed.). Baltimore: Williams & Wilkins.

Reppetto, Thomas A. (1978). *The blue parade.* New York: Free Press.

Roediger, H. L., and McDermott, K. B. (1995). Creating false memories: Remembering words not presented in lists. *Journal of Experimental Psychology: Learning, Memory, and Cognition, 21,* 803–814.

Roppe, Laura (1994). True blue? Whether police should be allowed to use trickery and deception to extract confessions. *San Diego Law Review, 31,* 729–773.

Rose, David (2004). *Guantanamo: The war on human rights.* New York: The New Press.

Rosenberg, Irene, and Rosenberg, Yale (1989). A modest proposal for the abolition of custodial confessions. *North Carolina Law Review, 68,* 69–115.

Rosett, Arthur, and Cressey, Donald (1976). *Justice by consent: Plea bargains in the American courthouse.* Philadelphia: J. B. Lippincott.

Ross, Lee (1977). The intuitive psychologist and his shortcomings: Distortions in the attribution process. *Advances in Experimental Social Psychology, 10,* 174–221.

Ross, Lee, and Nisbett, Robert (1991). *The person and the situation.* New York: McGraw-Hill.

Rumney, Philip (2005). The effectiveness of coercive interrogation: scholarly and judicial responses. *Crime, Law & Social Change, 44,* 465–489.

Russano, Melissa, Meissner, Christian, Narchet, Fadia, and Kassin, Saul (2005). Investigating true and false confessions within a novel experimental paradigm. *Psychological Science, 16,* 481–486.

Ryan, Harriet (2006). *Murder in room 103*. New York: Harper-Collins.

Salas, Claudio (2004). The case for excluding confessions of the mentally ill. *Yale Journal of the Law and Humanities*, 243–275.

Sanders, William (1977). *Detective work: A study of criminal investigations*. New York: The Free Press.

Sauer, Mark, and John Wilkens (1999, May 16). The bombshell, A1.

Scheck, Barry, Neufeld, Peter, and Dwyer, Jim (2000). *Actual innocence: Five days to execution and other dispatches from the wrongly convicted*. New York: Random House.

Scheppele, Kim (2006). Hypothetical torture in the "war on terrorism." *Journal of National Security Law and Policy, 1*, 285–340.

Schulhofer, Stephen (1981). Confessions and the court, *Michigan Law Review, 79*, 865–893.

——— (1996a). *Miranda's* practical effect: Substantial benefits and vanishingly small social costs. *Northwestern University Law Review, 90*, 500–563.

——— (1996b). *Miranda* and clearance rates. *Northwestern University Law Review, 91*, 278–294.

——— (2006). *Miranda v. Arizona:* A modest but important legacy. In Carol Steiker (Ed.), *Criminal procedure stories* (pp. 155–180). New York: Foundation Press.

Scientific content analysis handbook (1990). Laboratory for Scientific Interrogation.

Scorboria, Alan, Mazzoni, Guiliana, Kirsch, Irving, and Relyea, Mark (2004). Plausibility and belief in autobiographical memory. *Applied Cognitive Psychology, 18*, 791–807.

Sear, Lydia, and Williamson, Tom (1999). British and American interrogation strategies. In David Canter and Laurence Alison (Eds.), *Interviewing and deception* (pp. 67–84). Brookfield, VT: Ashgate Publishing.

Sears, Don (1948). Legal consequences of the third degree. *Ohio State Law Journal, 9*, 514–524.

Sedgwick, A. C. (1927. The third degree and crime. *The Nation, 124*, 666–667.

Segrave, Kerry (2004). *Lie detectors: A social history*. North Carolina: McFarland.

Senese, Louis (2005). *Anatomy of interrogation themes: The Reid technique of interviewing and interrogation*. Chicago: John E. Reid and Associates, Inc.

Shearer, Robert (1999, May–June). Statement analysis: SCAN or scam? *The Skeptical Inquirer, 23*, 40–43.

Sherman, Lawrence (1978). *Scandal and reform: Controlling police corruption*. Berkeley: University of California Press.

Shuy, Roger (1993). *Language crimes: The use and abuse of language evidence in the Courtroom*. Cambridge, MA: Blackwell.

——— (1998). *The language of confession, interrogation and deception*. Thousand Oaks: Sage Publications.

Simon, David (1991). *Homicide: A year on the killing streets*. Boston: Houghton Mifflin.

Skolnick, Jerome H. (1961). Scientific theory and scientific evidence: An analysis of lie detection. *Yale Law Journal, 70*, 694–728.

——— (1966). *Justice without trial: Law enforcement in a democratic society*. New York: John Wiley & Sons.

———— (1982) Deception by police. *Criminal Justice Ethics, 1,* 40–54.

Skolnick, Jerome H., and Fyfe, James J. (1993). *Above the law: Police and the excessive use of force.* New York: The Free Press.

Skolnick, Jerome H., and Leo, Richard A. (1992). The ethics of deceptive interrogation. *Criminal Justice Ethics, 11,* 3–12.

Slobogin, Christopher (2003a). Towards taping. *Ohio State Journal of Criminal Law, 1,* 309–322.

———— (2003b). An empirically based comparison of American and European regulatory approaches to police investigation. In Peter van Koppen and Steven Penrod (Eds.), *Adversarial versus inquisitorial justice: Psychological perspectives on criminal justice systems* (pp. 27–54). New York: Kluwer Academic.

Smith, Donald L. (1986). *Zechariah Chafee, Jr.: Defender of liberty and law.* Cambridge, MA: Harvard University Press.

Solan, Lawrence, and Tiersma, Peter (2005). *Speaking of crime: The language of criminal justice.* Chicago: University of Chicago Press.

Soree, Nadia (2005). When the innocent speak: False confessions, constitutional safeguards, and the role of expert testimony. *American Journal of Criminal Law, 32,* 191–263.

Spence, Donald P. (1982). *Narrative truth and historical truth: Meaning and interpretation in psychoanalysis.* New York: W. W. Norton.

Stephens, Otis (1973). *The supreme court and confessions of guilt.* Knoxville: University of Tennessee Press.

Strier, Franklin (1996). *Reconstructing justice: An agenda for trial reform.* Chicago: University of Chicago Press.

Stuntz, William (2001). *Miranda's* mistake. *Michigan Law Review, 99,* 975–999.

Sullivan, Thomas (2004). *Police experiences with recording custodial interrogations.* Chicago: Northwestern University School of Law, Center on Wrongful Convictions.

———— (2006). The time has come for law enforcement recordings of custodial interviews, start to finish. *Golden Gate University Law Review, 37,* 175–190.

———— (2007, April). Federal law enforcement agencies should record custodial interrogations. *The Champion,* 8–12.

Sutton, Willie (1976). *Where the money was.* New York: Viking Press.

Sylvester, R. (1910, May 10–13). A history of the "sweat box" and "third degree." Proceedings of the international Association of Chiefs of Police, 17th Annual Convention. Reprinted in J. H. Wigmore (1913), *The principles of judicial proof* (pp. 550–551). Boston: Little, Brown.

Tavris, Carol, and Aronson, Elliot (2007). *Mistakes were made (but not by me): Why we justify foolish beliefs, bad decisions and hurtful acts.* New York: Harcourt.

Taylor, Don (2005). Evidence beyond confession: Abolish Arizona's corpus delicti rule. *Arizona Attorney, 41,* 22–28.

Taylor, John (2002). *The count and the confession.* New York: Random House.

Texas Monthly (2001, January). Untrue confessions, *Texas Monthly,* 97.

Thomas, George C. III. (1996). Plain talk about the *Miranda* empirical debate: A "steady-state" theory of confessions. *U.C.L.A. Law Review, 43,* 933–959.

——— (2000). The end of the road for *Miranda v. Arizona?* On the history and future of rules for police interrogation. *American Criminal Law Review, 37,* 1–39.

——— (2004). Stories about *Miranda. Michigan Law Review, 102,* 1959–2000.

Thomas, George C. III, and Leo, Richard A. (2002). The effects of *Miranda v. Arizona:* "Embedded" in our national culture? *Crime and Justice: A Review of Research, 29,* 203–271.

Trovillo, Paul (1938a). A history of lie-detection. *American Journal of Police Science, 29,* 848–881.

——— (1938b). A history of lie-detection. *American Journal of Police Science, 30,* 104–119.

Tucker, John (1997). *May god have mercy: a true story of crime and punishment.* New York: W. W. Norton.

Turow, Scott (2003). *Ultimate punishment: A lawyer's reflections on dealing with the death penalty.* New York: Farrar, Straus and Giroux.

Van Wagner, E. (1938). *New York detective.* New York: Dodd, Mead.

Villard, O. G. (1927, October). Official lawlessness: The third degree and the crime wave. *Harpers Magazine, 155,* 605–624.

Volokh, Alexander (1997). *N* guilty men. *University of Pennsylvania Law Review, 146,* 173–216.

Vrij, Aldert (1994). The impact of information and setting on detection of deception by police detectives. *Journal of Nonverbal Behavior, 18,* 117–132.

——— (2000). *Detecting lies and deceit: The psychology of lying and the implications for professional practice.* London: John Wiley & Sons.

——— (2004). Why professionals fail to catch liars and how they can improve. *Legal & Criminological Psychology, 9,* 159–181.

Vrij, Aldert, and Mann, Samantha (2001). Who killed my relative?: Police officers' ability to detect real-life high stakes lies. *Psychology, Crime and Law, 7,* 119–132.

Vrij, Aldert, Mann, Samantha and Fischer, Ronald P. (2006). An empirical test of the Behavioral Analysis Interview. *Law and Human Behavior, 30,* 329–345.

Wagenaar, W., van Koppen, P., and Crombag, H. (1993). *Anchored narratives: The psychology of criminal evidence.* Harvester: St. Martin's Press.

Wald, Michael, Ayres, R., Hess, D. W., Schantz, M., and Whitebread, C. H. (1967). Interrogations in New Haven: The impact of *Miranda. The Yale Law Journal, 76,* 1519–1648.

Walker, Clive, and Starmer, Keir, Eds. (1999). *Miscarriages of justice: A review of justice in error.* London: Blackstone.

Walker, Samuel (1977). *A critical history of police reform: The emergence of professionalism.* Kentucky: Lexington.

——— (1980). *Popular justice: A history of American criminal justice.* Oxford: Oxford University Press.

——— (1993). *Taming the system: The control of discretion in criminal justice, 1950–1990.* Oxford: Oxford University Press.

——— (1998). *Popular justice: A history of American criminal justice* (2nd ed.). Oxford: Oxford University Press.

Walling, George (1887). *Recollections of a New York chief of police.* New York: Caxton Books.

Walters, Stan (2003). *Principles of kinesic interview and interrogation* (2nd ed.). Boca Raton: CRC Press.

Warden, Rob (2003a). The role of false confessions in Illinois wrongful murder convictions since 1970. Center on Wrongful Convictions Research Report. www.law.northwestern.edu/depts/clinic/wrongful/FalseConfessions.htm.

——— (2003b). The revolutionary role of journalism in identifying and rectifying wrongful convictions. *UMKC Law Review, 70,* 803–846.

——— (2005). *Wilkie Collins's the dead alive: The novel, the case, and wrongful convictions.* Evanston: Northwestern University Press.

Weinreb, Lloyd (1977). *Denial of justice: Criminal process in the United States.* New York: Free Press.

Weinstein, Henry (2006, July 21). Freed man gives lesson on false confessions. *Los Angeles Times,* B1, 10.

Weisberg, Bernard (1961). Police interrogation of arrested persons: A skeptical view. In Claude R. Sowle (Ed.), *Police power and individual freedom* (pp. 153–181). Chicago: Aldine.

Weisselberg, Charles (1998). Saving *Miranda. Cornell Law Review, 84,* 109–192.

Westervelt, Saundra, and Humphrey, John, Eds. (2001). *Wrongly convicted: Perspectives on failed justice.* Newark, NJ: Rutgers University Press.

White, Welsh S. (1979). Police trickery in inducing confessions. *University of Pennsylvania Law Review, 127,* 581–629.

——— (1997). False confessions and the constitution: Safeguards against untrustworthy evidence. *Harvard Civil Rights-Civil Liberties Law Review, 32,* 105–157.

——— (1998). What is an involuntary confession now? *Rutgers Law Review,* 2001–2057.

——— (2001a). *Miranda's waning protections: Police interrogation practices after Dickerson.* Ann Arbor: University of Michigan Press.

——— (2001b). Miranda's failure to restrain pernicious interrogation practices. *Michigan Law Review, 99,* 1211–1247.

——— (2003). Confessions in capital cases. *University of Illinois Law Review, 2003,* 979–1036.

Wickersham Commission Report (1931). National Commission on Law Observance and Law Enforcement (1931). *Report on lawlessness in law enforcement.* Washington, DC: U.S. Government Printing Office.

Wicklander, Douglas (1979). Behavioral interviews to a confession. *Police Chief, 10,* 40–42.

——— (1980). Behavioral analysis. *Security World, 13,* 141–161.

Wigmore, John (1970). *Evidence in trials at common law* (3rd ed.). Boston: Little, Brown.

Wilkens, John (1998, December 1). Speaking of truth: Investigators speak highly of voice stress machines, but tests can't prove that they "detect" lies. *San Diego Union-Tribune,* E1.

Williams, James (2000). Interrogating justice: A critical analysis of the police interrogation and its role in the criminal justice process. *Canadian Journal of Criminology, 42*, 209–240.

Willemse, Cornelius (1931). *Behind the green lights.* New York: Alfred A. Knopf.

Wilson, James Q. (1968). *Varieties of police behavior: The management of law and order in
eight communities.* Cambridge, MA: Harvard University Press.

Winters, Alison (2005). The making of the "truth serum." *Bulletin of Historical Medicine, 79*, 500–533.

Witt, April (2001, June 4). In Prince George's homicides, no rest for the suspects.
The Washington Post, 1.

Wright, Lawrence (1994). *Remembering Satan: A case of recovered memory and the shat-
tering of an American family.* New York: Alfred A. Knopf.

Yant, Martin (1991). *Presumed guilty: When innocent people are wrongly convicted.* Buffalo: Prometheus Books.

Young, Deborah (1996). Unnecessary evil: Police lying in interrogations. *Connecticut
Law Review, 28*, 425–478.

Zimbardo, Philip (1967). The psychology of police confessions. *Psychology Today, 1*,
17–20, 25–27.

———— (1971). Coercion and compliance: The psychology of police confessions. In
C. Perruci and M. Pilisuk (Eds.), *The triple revolution* (pp. 492–508). Boston:
Little, Brown.

Zimring, Frank, and Frase, Richard (1979). *The criminal justice system: Legal materials.*
Boston: Little, Brown.

Zulawski, David, and Wicklander, Douglas (2002). *Practical aspects of interview and interrogation* (2nd ed.). Boca Raton: CRC Press.

Cases

Arizona v. Fulminante, 499 U.S. 279 (1991)

Ashcraft v. Tennessee, 322 U.S. 143 (1944)

Berkemer v. McCarty, 468 U.S. 420 (1984)

Brady v. Maryland, 373 U.S. 83 (1963)

Bram v. United States, 168 U.S. 532 (1897)

Brown v. Mississippi, 297 U.S. 278 (1936)

California v. Beheler, 463 U.S. 1121 (1983)

Chambers v. Florida, 309 U.S. 227 (1940)

Colorado v. Connelly, 479 U.S. 157 (1986)

Commonwealth v. DiGiambattista, 813 N.E.2d 516 (Mass. 2004)

Commonwealth of Pennsylvania v. Bruce Godschalk, 451 Pa. Super. 425 (1996)

Dickerson v. United States, 530 U.S. 428 (2000)

Earl Washington, Jr. v. Edward W. Murray et al., 4 F.3d 1285 (1993)

Escobedo v. Illinois, 378 U.S. 478 (1964)

Florida v. Cayward, 552 So.2d 971 (1989)

Frazier v. Cupp, 394 U.S. 731 (1969)

Gideon v. Wainwright, 372 U.S. 335 (1963)

Harris v. New York, 401 U.S. 222 (1971)

Hopt v. Utah, 110 U.S. 574 (1884)

In re Jerrell, 699 N.W.2d 110 (Wis. 2005)

Malinski v. New York, 324 U.S. 401 (1945)

Massiah v. United States, 377 U.S. 201 (1964)

Miller v. Fenton, 474 U.S. 104 (1985)

Miranda v. Arizona, 384 U.S. 436 (1966)

Missouri v. Seibert, 124 S. Ct. 2601 (2004).

New York v. Quarles, 467 U.S. 649 (1984)

North Carolina v. Butler, 441 U.S. 369 (1979)

Opper v. United States, 348 U.S. 84 (1954)

Oregon v. Elstad, 470 U.S. 298 (1985)

Rogers v. Richmond, 365 U.S. 534 (1961)

State v. Cahill, 5 Cal.4th (1993)

State v. Cook, 847 A.2d 530 (N.J. 2004)

State v. Kelekolio, 74 Haw. 479 (1993)

State v. Parker, 337 S.E.2d, 487 (N.C. 1985)

State v. Mauchley, 67 P.3d 477 (Utah 2003)

State v. Scales, 518 N.W.2d 587 (Minn. 1994)

Stephan v. State, 711 P.2d 1156 (Alaska 1985)

Townsend v. Sain, 372 U.S. 293 (1963)

United States v. Patane, 542 U.S. 630 (2004)

United States v. Singleterry, 29 F.3d 733 (1st Cir. 1994)

Unpublished Materials

Affadivit of Raymond Lundin, Special Agent, Kansas Bureau of Investigation. November 23, 1999.

American Civil Liberties Union (1933). Methods of combating the third degree. Unpublished manuscript. Behavioral Analysis Training Institute (2001). *Interview and interrogation trechinques: A behavioral approach to investigative interviewing.* Training materials.

Buckley, Joseph. Report in the case of *Earl Washington, Jr. v. Kenneth Buraker, et al.* Case No. 3:02-CV-00106. December 8, 2003.

Cornwall, Deboarh, Hall, Robert, Glasberg, Victor, Weinstein, Barry, and Rosenfeld, Steve. January 17, 2006. Plaintiff Earl Washignton, Jr.'s Brief in Opposition to Defendand Curtis Reese Wilmore's Summary Judgemnt Motion. *Earl Washington, Jr. v. Kenneth H. Buraker, et al.* Civil Action No. 3:02CV106.

Declaration of Derek Niegemann. December 14, 1999. *United States v. Derek Niegemann.* No. CR 99-20155-JF. United States District Court for the Northern District of California.

Deposition of Corethian Bell. May 27, 2005. *Corethian Bell vs. Chicago Police Detective M. Cummings et al.* Chicago, Illinois. Case No. 02L08857.

Deposition of Corey Beale. May 3, 2005. Upper Marlboro, Maryland. *Corey Beale v. Prince George's County et al.* Case No: DKC-012389.

Deposition of Michael Crowe. December 18, 2002. *Stephen Crowe et al. v. City of Escondido et al.* Case No: 99-0241-R.

Interrogation transcript of Howard Allen. July 14, 1987. Indianapolis, Indiana Police Department.

Interrogation transcript of Brandon Blackmon. May 23, 1996. Wichita, Kansas Police Department.

Interrogation transcript of Daniel Blank. November 13, 1997. St. John Sheriff's Police Department. Shreveport, Louisiana.

Interrogation transcript of Jackson Burch. April 10, 1973. Palm Beach County, Florida.

Interrogation transcript of Anthony Cain. March 24, 2004. Los Angeles Police Department.

Interrogation transcript of Michael Crowe (1998a). January 22, 1998. Escondido, California Police Department.

Interrogation transcript of Michael Crowe (1998b). January 23, 1998, Volume 1. Escondido, California Police Department.

Interrogation transcript of Michael Crowe (1998c). January 22, 1998. Volume 2. Escondido, California Police Department.

Interrogation transcript of Michelle Davis. September 21, 1999. Cayuga County Sheriff's Department. Cayuga County, New York.

Interrogation transcript of Jerome Denny. Sacramento County. January 26, 2005.

Interrogation transcript of Juan Diaz. September 29, 1998. Oceanside, California Police Department.

Interrogation transcript of Deron Ford. February 22, 2005. San Diego Police Department.

Interrogation transcript of Ricky Ford. August 16, 2000. Solano County, California Sheriff's Office.

Interrogation transcript of Alex Garcia. October 26, 1991. Maricopa County, Arizona Sheriff's Office.

Interrogation transcript of Peter Gonazalez. November 11, 1996. Anaheim, California Police Department.

Interrogation transcript of Sean Harrill. April 4, 1999. Los Angeles Police Department.

Interrogation transcript of William Ethridge Hill, Jr. October 29, 1997. Austin, Texas Police Department.

Interrogation transcript of Jose Jacobo. May 6, 1999. Los Angeles Police Department.

Interrogation transcript of Duane Johnson. January 8, 1998. Los Angeles Police Department.

Interrogation transcript of Harold Kramer. May 18, 1999. Minnesota Bureau of Criminal Apprehension and Federal Bureau of Investigation.

Interrogation transcript of William Laughlin. July 6, 2000. Anaheim, California Police Department.

Interrogation transcript of Victor Lee. June 9, 1995. Fullerton, California Police Department.

Interrogation transcript of John Lopez. March 14, 1993. Commerce City, California Police Department.

Interrogation transcript of Jose Luna. January 19, 2000. Humboldt County, California Sheriff's Department.

Interrogation transcript of Oscar Macias. October 6, 1999. Santa Cruz County, California Sheriff's Department.

Interrogation transcript of Paul Miller. June 17, 1999. Hamilton County, Indiana Sheriff's Department.

Interrogation transcript of Donald Perry. October 4, 1999. Stockton, California Police Department.

Interrogation transcript of Marcos Ranjel. March 20, 1997. San Francisco Police Department.

Interrogation transcript of Henry Rodriguez. July 27, 1998. Fullerton, California Police Department.

Interrogation transcript of Prudencio Sanchez. October 17, 1997. Monterey County, California Sheriff's Office.

Interrogation transcript of Jimmy Thomas. April 21, 1998. Jerome County, Idaho Sheriff's Office.

Interrogation transcript of Stanley Vaughn. September 28, 1998. San Diego Police Department.

Interrogation transcript of Dontay Weatherspoon. April 14, 1998. Los Angeles Police Department.

Interrogation transcript of Farrell Wildcat. January 25, 1999. Fort Hall, Idaho Police Department.

Interrogation transcript of Erwin Young. June 21, 1997. San Pablo/Richmond, California Police Department.

Interview of Walter Casper by Richard Leo. March 28, 2000.

Interview of Sergeant Charlie D. by Richard Leo. June 21, 1993.

Interview of Detective Frank D. by Richard Leo. September 19, 1993.

Interview of Emile DeWeaver by Richard Leo. June 27, 1998.

Interview of Beverly Edwards by Richard Leo. April 3, 1998.

Interview of Paul Ingram by Richard Leo. January 4, 2005.

Interview of John Irvin by Richard Leo. January 14, 2000.

Interview of Sergeant Michael O. by Richard Leo. June 22, 1993.

Interview of David Saraceno by Richard Leo. April 11, 1998.

Interview of Stephanie Traum by Richard Leo. July 24, 1999.

King of Prussia, Pennsylvania. January 14, 1987. *Commonwealth v. Bruce Godschalk.*

Lofquist, William, and Harmon, Talia (2005). Fatal errors: Compelling claims of executions of the innocent in the post-Furman era. Unpublished manuscript.

Marshall, Lawrence (1994). Brief of Appellant. *State of Illinois v. Gary A. Gauger.* In the Appellate Court of Illinois, Second District. Circuit Court No. 93 CF 322. Filed October 18, 1994.

Memorandum from Detective Bruce Saville to District Attorney Bruce Castor. June 15, 2001. Upper Merion Township Police Department. King of Prussia, Pennsylvania. *Commonwealth v. Bruce Godschalk.*

Oakland, California Police Department (1998). *Analytic interviewing.* Unpublished interrogation training manual.

Papke, Rick (1995). The Confrontation Interrogation Technique. Number 9A. Los Angeles Police Department Interrogation Training Materials. December, 1995.

Police Report of R. F. Armstrong (1998). Colorado Springs Police Department. March 11, 1998. *State of Colorado v. Robert Edwards.*

Police Report of Dale Fox (1998). Colorado Springs Police Department, Police Report. February 4, 1999. *State of Colorado v. Rhonda Pitts.*

Police Report of Bruce Saville (1987). Upper Merion Township Police Department.

Reid, John E. Reid and Associates, Inc. (1991a). *The Reid technique: Interviewing and interrogation.* Unpublished course booklet.

——— (1991b). *The Reid technique of specialized interrogation Strategies.* Unpublished course booklet.

——— (2000). *The Reid technique of interviewing and interrogation.* Chicago, IL: Reid. Unpublished course booklet.

Report of the Special Committee on Recordation of Custodial Interrogations (2005). Special Committee Appointed by the New Jersey Supreme Court. Unpublished Report.

Shertz, Laurie (2004). Personal e-mail correspondence. May 13, 2004.

Stanley, Christine (2005). Respondent's Reply Brief After Evidentiary Hearing Re Habeas Petition. In re *Joel Alcox v. People of the State of California.* Case No. SM0502131118281.

Statement of Bobby Gene Benton. March 29, 2000. Medford, Oregon. Case No: 99-0637-FE.

Statement of Bruce Godschalk. November 29, 1999. Upper Merion Township Police Department. King of Prussia, Pennsylvania. *Commonwealth v. Bruce Godschalk.*

Statement of Kevin Mohr. July 10, 1999. *United States v. Kevin Mohr.* United States Marine Corps. Marine Corps Base. Pearl Harbor, Hawaii. Island Judicial Circuit.

Statement of Tony Ringer. March 28, 2001. Hamilton County, Ohio.

Statement of William Schofield. July 14, 1997. *State of Washington v. William Schofield.* Case No 97-1-00287-7. Clark County, WA.

Statement of Ronald Suzukawa. November, 1999. Alexandria Police Department. Commonwealth v. Ronald Suzukawa. General District Court of City of Alexandria.

Taped Confession of Bruce Godschalk to the Upper Merion Township Police Department. King of Prussia, Pennsylvania. January 13, 1987.

Testimony at trial of Thomas Battle. *The People of the State of California v. Thomas Lee Battle.* Case No: FVI-012605. February 27, 2003. Victorville, CA. San Bernardino County Superior Court.

Testimony of Anthony Belovich (1987). Suppression Motion. *State of Tennessee v. Sedley Alley.* Nos: 85–05085, 85–05086, 85–05087. In the Criminal Court of Tennessee at Memphis. Thirtieth Judicial District. March 5, 1987.

Testimony of Detective Martin Devlin. September 7, 1993. *Commonwealth v. Walter Ogrod.* In the Court of Common Pleas, First Judicial District of Pennsylvania. Case No. 3278. p.52.

Testimony of Douglas Johnson. Trial. November 20, 1981. *State of Kansas v. Eddie James Lowery.* Case No: 81CR575.

Testimony of Terry King. December 11, 1995. *Terry King v. State of Tennessee.* Case No. 33878 & 37810. Knox County Criminal Court. Knox County Tennessee.

Testimony of Eddie Lowery (1981a). Suppression Motion Hearing. November 12, 1981. *State of Kansas v. Eddie James Lowery.* Case No: 81CR575

Testimony of Eddie Lowery (1981b). Trial. November 19–20, 1981. *State of Kansas v. Eddie James Lowery.* Case No: 81CR575.

Testimony of Eddie Lowery (1982). Trial. January 6, 1982. *State of Kansas v. Eddie James Lowery.* Case No: 81CR575.

Testimony of Harry Malugani Trial Testimony (1981). Trial. November 19–20, 1981. *State of Kansas v. Eddie James Lowery.* Case No: 81CR575.

Testimony of Detective Bruce Saville. May 28–29, 1987. Suppression Hearing. *State of Pennsylvania v. Bruce Godschalk.* Commonwealth of Pennsylvania, County of Montgomery, Court of Common Pleas. Case No: 00934-87.

Testimony of L. Bradlee Sheafe, Special Agent, Federal Bureau of Investigation. November 16, 1999. *United States v. Willis Mark Haynes.* Case No: PJM-98-0520. United States District Court for the District of Maryland. Southern Division.

Virginia State Police Report (1983). Special Agent Curtis Wilmore. Case No: 82-2-0263.

Wickersham Commission Files. National Archives, Suiteland, MD, and Washington, DC.

Index

Harvard University Press is a member of Green Press Initiative (greenpressinitiative.org), a nonprofit organization working to help publishers and printers increase their use of recycled paper and decrease their use of fiber derived from endangered forests. This book was printed on 100% recycled paper containing 50% post-consumer waste and processed chlorine free.